GW01367051

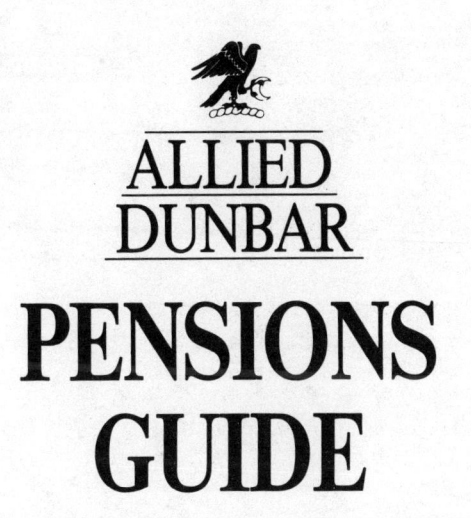

ALLIED DUNBAR

PENSIONS GUIDE

ALLIED DUNBAR

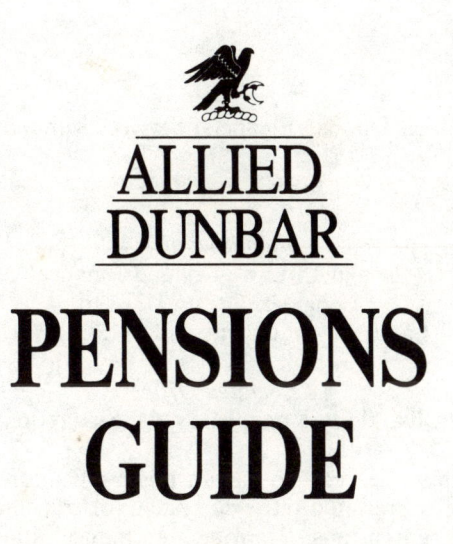

PENSIONS GUIDE

by
Anthony M Reardon, ACII

LONGMAN

© Allied Dunbar Financial Services Limited 1992

ISBN 0 85121 8830

Published by
Longman Law, Tax and Finance
Longman Group UK Ltd
21–27 Lamb's Conduit Street, London WC1N 3NJ

Associated Offices
Australia, Hong Kong, Malaysia, Singapore, USA

All rights reserved. No part of this publication may be reproduced, stored in a retrieval system, or transmitted, in any form or by any means, electronic, mechanical, photocopying, recording, or otherwise, without either the prior written permission of the publishers, or a licence permitting restricted copying issued by the Copyright Licensing Agency Ltd, 90 Tottenham Court Road, London W1P 9HE.

No responsibility for loss occasioned to any person acting or refraining from action as a result of the material in this publication can be accepted by the author or publishers.

The views and opinions of Allied Dunbar may not necessarily coincide with some of the views and opinions expressed in this book which are solely those of the author and no endorsement of them by Allied Dunbar should be inferred.

A CIP catalogue record for this book is available from the British Library.

Printed in Great Britain by Mackays of Chatham, Kent

Preface

Since the publication of the third edition of the *Pensions Guide* in the autumn of 1990 there has been continued change in pensions law and practice.

Although the Finance and Social Security Acts in 1991 and 1992 did not contain any major changes to pensions, the fall-out from previous changes began to have an effect: the Inland Revenue published new Practice Notes relating to approved pension schemes in October 1991, the first codification of their practice since 1979. Between October 1990 and August 1992 16 Memoranda have been published either by the Occupational Pensions Board or by the Pension Schemes Office (PSO), previously called the Superannuation Funds Office. These new Practice Notes and Memoranda have had a considerable impact on the running of approved pension schemes.

Draft regulations on the investment of pension scheme assets, which had generated much discussion in the pensions industry, were finally enacted in March 1992 in the wake of the Maxwell scandal. The return of the Conservative government after the General Election in April 1992 meant that the major pension changes promised by the Labour Party did not take place; these may have involved changes to the State Earnings Related Pension Scheme and contracting-out of SERPS.

The European Court of Justice has also made its mark: following its decision in *Barber* v *GRE*, agreement was reached in the Maastricht Summit to limit the retrospective effects of the *Barber* decision. This was a welcome decision for employers who were concerned at the likely high costs of equalising pension benefits which had accrued before the judgment. However, the Maastricht Treaty itself is now under threat as it is unlikely to be ratified by the EC Member States and so the whole question of the retrospective nature of the *Barber* decision has now been opened up again.

Like the previous editions of this book, the fourth edition is mainly directed toward private business owners, both directors and self-employed, who have control or influence over their own pension arrangements, and to professional pensions practitioners. It may also be of interest to the larger employer who is considering setting up a pension plan for the first time or altering his existing pension scheme arrangements

This book reflects current legislation and existing Inland Revenue practice as at August 1992: the relevant statutory extracts are contained in the Appendices. There is also a glossary of terms used by pensions practitioners.

I acknowledge with thanks the valuable assistance given to me by my colleagues: Stuart Reynolds LLB, Ray Dean BSc, Mike Rawle, Anne Taylor and Nicola Peers.

August 1992.

Contents

		Page
Preface		v
1	**Employed v self-employed**	1
1.1	Forthcoming changes	3
2	**Historical notes**	7
2.1	Early schemes and legislation	7
2.2	Old and new codes	8
2.3	Top hat schemes	9
2.4	Lifetime service agreements	10
2.5	Growth of executive pension plans	11
2.6	Small self-administered pension schemes	12
2.7	Development of state benefits	12
2.8	More recent changes	13
3	**Inland Revenue approval**	15
3.1	Pension Schemes Office	15
3.1.1	The purpose of approval	15
3.1.2	Conditions for approval	16
3.2	Other legislation and case law	19
3.2.1	Social Security Act 1973	19
3.2.2	Social Security Pensions Act 1975	19
3.2.3	Employment Protection (Consolidation) Act 1978	19
3.2.4	Social Security Act 1985	20
3.2.5	Social Security Act 1986	20
3.2.6	Sex Discrimination Act 1986	20
3.2.7	Finance (No 2) Act 1987	21
3.2.8	Finance Act 1989	21
3.2.9	Social Security Act 1989	21
3.2.10	Social Security Act 1990	21

Contents

3.3	Trusts	22
3.3.1	Setting up the trust	22
3.4	How to obtain Revenue approval	23
3.5	PSO approval	25
3.6	Simplified schemes	26
3.7	Unapproved schemes	26

4 Maximum permitted benefits   **27**

4.1	Who can qualify?	27
4.2	Who cannot qualify?	27
4.3	Recent changes	28
4.3.1	Pre-1987 members	29
4.3.2	1987–1989 members	29
4.3.3	Post-1989 members	29
4.4	Retirement ages	29
4.5	Maximum benefits	30
4.6	Maximum pension	30
4.6.1	60ths scale	30
4.6.2	Uplifted 60th scale (pre-1987 members)	31
4.6.3	Accelerated scale (1987–1989 members and post-1989 members)	32
4.7	Definitions of 'final salary'	33
4.8	Dynamised or indexed final remuneration	35
4.9	Retained pension benefits	37
4.10	Pension increases (escalation)	39
4.11	Cash lump sums	39
4.11.1	80ths scale	39
4.11.2	Uplifted 80ths scale (for pre-1987 members)	40
4.11.3	Accelerated scale (1987–1989 members)	41
4.11.4	Scale for post-1989 members	43
4.12	Retained lump sum benefits	44
4.13	Pension values of lump sums	45
4.14	Death benefits	46
4.14.1	Benefits on death after retirement	46
4.14.2	Benefits on death in service	48
4.15	Retirement	50
4.15.1	Retirement before normal retirement date	50
4.15.2	Early retirement (not through ill health)	51
4.15.3	Early retirement through ill health	52
4.15.4	Benefits on late retirement	52
4.15.5	Options on retirement	53
4.16	Trivial benefits	54
4.17	Combinations of schemes	54
4.18	Finance (No 2) Act 1987	54

Contents ix

4.19	Finance Act 1989	56
4.20	Opting for post-1989 benefits	57
4.21	Associated employments	57
4.21.1	Connected schemes	58
4.21.2	Permanent community of interests	58
4.22	Multiple employments	59

5 Unapproved pension schemes   61

5.1	Introduction	61
5.2	Summary of effects of changes	61
5.3	Retirement benefits scheme	62
5.3.1	Relevant benefits	63
5.4	Taxation of contributions — position of the employer	65
5.5	Obtaining tax relief	65
5.6	Taxation of contributions — position of the employee	66
5.7	Taxation of the fund	68
5.8	Taxation of lump sum benefits	68
5.9	Taxation of pensions	69
5.10	Inheritance tax	69
5.11	National Insurance contributions	70
5.12	Social security legislation	71
5.13	Uses of unapproved schemes	71
5.14	Death in service benefits	72
5.15	Accounting for costs	73
5.16	Future trends	73

6 Company directors   77

6.1	Controlling director — definition	78
6.2	Retained benefits	80
6.3	Pensionable service	80
6.4	Serious ill-health	80
6.5	Continuous service/continued rights	81

7 Funding methods   83

7.1	Funding of group schemes	83
7.2	Funding individual arrangements	84
7.2.1	Funding for capital	85
7.2.2	Annuity rates	85
7.2.3	Salary increases	86
7.3	Yield assumption	87

x Contents

7.3.1	Maximum permissible contributions—Inland Revenue changes		87
7.3.2	New schemes		88
7.3.3	Existing schemes		89
7.4	Annual and special/single contributions—tax relief		89
7.4.1	The employer — regular contributions		89
7.4.2	The employer — single contributions		90
7.5	Dependant's death in retirement benefits		92
7.6	Personal contributions		92
7.7	Over-funding		92
7.8	Death in service benefits		93
7.9	Annual and single premiums		94
7.10	Decreasing term assurance		94

8 Insured pension arrangements   95

8.1	With-profits policies	95
8.2	Unit-linked policies	97
8.3	Charging structures	97
8.3.1	Allocation to units	97
8.3.2	Type of units	98
8.3.3	Management charges	99
8.3.4	Bid/offer prices	99
8.3.5	Policy charges	99
8.4	Types of investment funds	100
8.5	Deposit administration	100
8.6	Unitised with-profits policies	101
8.7	Comparisons of unit-linked funds	101

9 Small self-administered schemes and insurance company hybrid schemes   105

9.1	Self investment	106
9.2	Restrictions on self-investment	106
9.2.1	Investment of scheme funds	107
9.2.2	Investment in property	107
9.2.3	Notification of transactions	108
9.2.4	Pensioneer trustee	108
9.2.5	Shares in the employer's company	108
9.2.6	Investments in works of art, valuable chattels, etc	109
9.2.7	Borrowings	109
9.2.8	Provision of information	109
9.2.9	Company loans	109

Contents xi

9.2.10	Commercial property		110
9.3	Company shares		111
9.4	Other Inland Revenue requirements		112
9.4.1	Pensioneer trustee		112
9.4.2	Investment strategy		113
9.4.3	Inland Revenue scrutiny		113
9.4.4	Death in service benefits		113
9.4.5	Purchase of pensions		113
9.4.6	Provision of information to Inland Revenue		113
9.5	Cost of setting up a small self-administered scheme		114
9.6	Key advantages and disadvantages of small self-administered schemes		115
9.7	Property purchase		116
9.7.1	Property purchase — summary		120
9.8	Insurance-based hybrid schemes		121

10 Topping up group schemes — 125

10.1	Group schemes	125
10.2	Additional voluntary contributions	126
10.3	Augmentation under the group scheme	127
10.4	Topping-up through executive pension plans	128
10.5	Salary sacrifice	130
10.6	Dividend waiver	131
10.7	Bonus sacrifice	132
10.8	Effect of income sacrifice on National Insurance contributions	132
10.9	Free-standing AVCs	133
10.9.1	Over-provision	134
10.9.2	Estimating benefits	135
10.9.3	Transitional arrangements	136

11 State benefits — 137

11.1	Objective of the earnings related state pension	137
11.2	State scheme contributions	138
11.3	Upper and lower earnings limit	141
11.4	Qualifying conditions	142
11.5	Employment beyond pensionable age	142
11.6	Amount of pension	143
11.7	Annual rate of SERPS	143
11.7.1	Pre-April 1988 calculation	143
11.7.2	Post-April 1988 calculation	144
11.7.3	Major differences	144
11.8	Increases during payment	145

xii Contents

11.9	Deferred pension	145
11.10	Widows' benefits	146
11.11	Husband dies leaving children	147
11.12	Husband dies leaving no children	147
11.13	Widowers' benefits	148
11.13.1	Original basis	148
11.13.2	Modified basis	148
11.14	Summary of state pensions	149
11.15	Adequacy of state pensions	151
11.16	DSS leaflets	152
11.17	Contracting-out	152

12 Contracting-out of the State Earnings Related Scheme   153

12.1	Abolition of requisite benefit test	154
12.2	Guaranteed minimum pensions	155
12.2.1	Original basis	155
12.2.2	Revised basis	155
12.2.3	Major difference	155
12.3	Deferred GMP	156
12.4	Widow's GMP	156
12.5	Increases during payment	157
12.6	Contracting-out after 1988	157
12.7	Contracting-out through personal pensions	158
12.8	Mechanics of contracting-out through personal pension schemes	158
12.9	The 2% incentive	160
12.10	Who should contract-out?	161
12.11	Contracting-out through money purchase schemes	162
12.12	The effects of contracting-out on employers' schemes	163
12.13	Contracting back into SERPS	165

13 Executive pensions and inheritance tax planning   167

13.1	Deferring retirement	168
13.2	Personal contributions	169
13.3	Restrictions on 20% directors	170
13.4	Options at retirement	170
13.5	Continuation facilities	171
13.6	Summary	172

14 Personal pension schemes and retirement annuities 173

14.1	Background	173
14.1.1	How personal pension schemes and retirement annuities work	174
14.1.2	Comparison of personal pension schemes and retirement annuities	174
14.1.3	Benefits	176
14.1.4	Open market option	178
14.1.5	Types of pension available	179
14.1.6	Death before taking benefits	180
14.1.7	Life cover	180
14.2	Personal pension schemes in more detail	181
14.2.1	Existing retirement annuities	182
14.2.2	Earnings and eligibility	182
14.2.3	Net relevant earnings	185
14.2.4	Allowable maximum	185
14.2.5	Associated employments	186
14.2.6	Summary of calculation	187
14.2.7	Capital allowances and Business Expansion Schemes	188
14.2.8	Interest	188
14.2.9	Maximum contributions (as a percentage of net relevant earnings)	189
14.2.10	Interaction of contributions to personal pension schemes and retirement annuities	190
14.2.11	Overfunding	192
14.2.12	Tax relief	192
14.2.13	Pension relief at source	194
14.2.14	Carry forward/carry back facilities	194
14.2.15	Carry forward of unused relief	194
14.2.16	Carry back provisions	195
14.2.17	Mechanics of carry back	196
14.2.18	Carry back — effect of status	196
14.2.19	Administrative requirements	196
14.2.20	Late assessments	198
14.2.21	Investigation settlements	198
14.3	Specific benefits under personal pension schemes and retirement annuity contracts	199
14.3.1	Death benefits	199
14.3.2	Flexible trusts	199
14.3.3	Inheritance tax implications	200
14.3.4	Putting existing policies in trust	202
14.3.5	Disability benefits	203

xiv   Contents

14.3.6	Tax treatment of pensions	205
14.3.7	Overseas aspects	206
14.4	Specialised occupations	208
14.4.1	Lloyd's underwriters	211
14.4.2	Doctors and dentists	211
14.5	Benefit levels	216
14.6	Other schemes for partners	218
14.6.1	Retired partner's annuities	218
14.7	Self-managed schemes for partners	219
14.7.1	Friendly societies	224

15 Tax planning hints through pensions — 225

15.1	Executive pension plans: planning hints	225
15.2	Personal pension schemes and retirement annuity contracts: planning hints	231

16 Leaving service benefits — 235

16.1	Preservation of benefits	235
16.2	Deferred pensions	236
16.3	Problems of the early leaver	238
16.3.1	Frozen pensions	238
16.4	Section 32 annuity	239
16.5	Personal pension plans	240
16.5.1	Assignment of an individual policy under an executive pension plan	242
16.5.2	Transfer values	242
16.5.3	Right to a transfer value	242
16.5.4	Calculation of transfer values	242
16.6	Refunds of members' contributions	244
16.7	Which schemes may permit a transfer value?	245
16.8	Effects of Social Security Act 1990	245
16.8.1	Defined benefit schemes	246
16.8.2	Money purchase schemes	246
16.8.3	Deferred pensions	246
16.9	Golden handshakes	247
16.9.1	Application of the 'golden handshake' legislation	247
16.9.2	Close companies	248
16.9.3	Pensioning 'golden handshakes'	249
16.10	'Hancocks'	249

17 Pension loans — 251

17.1	Comparing costs	252
17.2	Recent developments	254
17.3	Loan purposes	254
17.3.1	Unsecured loans	255
17.3.2	Interest rates	255
17.4	Personal loans — differences under executive pension plans for directors	256

18 Various aspects of executive pension plans — 257

18.1	Investment companies	257
18.2	Service companies	258
18.3	Special occupations — retirement dates	259
18.4	Retirement dates below age 50	259
18.5	International aspects of executive pension plans	260
18.5.1	Definitions	260
18.5.2	Overseas employer with UK resident employees	261
18.5.3	Offshore plans	262
18.5.4	Corresponding approval	262
18.5.5	Section 614 plans (known previously as section 218 plans)	263
18.5.6	UK resident employer with overseas resident employees	263
18.6	Pensioners resident abroad	263
18.7	Overseas transfers	264

19 Retirement options — investment considerations — 265

19.1	Types of pension available	265
19.2	Purchased life annuities	266
19.3	Investing the cash lump sum	268
19.4	Increasing current income	268
19.5	Producing income in the future	270

20 Pensions — the future — 271

20.1	Equal treatment for men and women in pension schemes	271
20.1.1	The EC	271
20.1.2	Equalisation of state pension ages	272
20.2	Investor protection	272

20.3	Insured pension schemes	273
20.4	Personal pension schemes	274
20.5	Divorce	274

Appendices 275

1	Glossary of terms	275
2	Memorandum No 109 (August 1991)	287
3	1991 Inland Revenue Practice Notes Part 20	303
4	ICTA 1988, ss 590–612, 618–655 and Schedule 23 (as updated by FA 1991)	319

Index 401

Other titles

1 Employed v self-employed

Pensions for these two categories differ considerably: if you are employed, you may join a pension plan where the only limits on the benefits relate to your salary: if you are self-employed, the limits are related not to your salary, but to the contributions that you may pay. The potential for pension provision is far greater if you are employed although the scope for this has been reduced following changes introduced in the Finance Act 1989 (see Chapter 4).

Pension arrangements available to the employed, including directors, are usually known as executive pension plans, occupational pension schemes, company pension schemes, superannuation funds or variations on that theme. Such schemes can be introduced for the benefit of employees of not only companies, but also sole traders, partnerships, charities and other bodies.

If you are self-employed or if you are employed but not a member of a company scheme, you are eligible for a personal pension scheme. The forerunner of the personal pension scheme was the retirement annuity contract also commonly known as the self-employed retirement annuity: it is still possible to contribute to these contracts although new ones are no longer permitted by law.

Pension arrangements for the employed and the self-employed enjoy considerable tax concessions which are broadly similar. The surrounding legislation, however, is separate and differs in many ways.

Provided a company pension plan or personal pension scheme is approved by the Inland Revenue, contributions paid by the employer and the employee will be tax deductible. The fund will be exempt from income tax on investments and deposits and capital gains tax on the disposal of investments. The benefits may be taken in the form of a tax-free lump sum and a pension which will be treated as earned income.

The gulf which previously existed between the pension arrangements for the employed and the self-employed prior to Finance Act 1989 has narrowed considerably. Benefits under new occupational pension schemes are restricted for high earners through the application of an earnings limit which stands at £75,000 for the tax year 1992/93. Under personal pension schemes higher contributions, as a percentage of earnings, can now be paid, compared with contributions to retirement annuities, although contributions are also restricted to earnings of £75,000.

A comparison of the contributions that may be invested at intervals throughout the term to retirement, if salary increases at 8.5% per annum compound, is set out below:

Table 1.1

Male aged 30, initial salary £20,000, retirement at 60.

Future Age	Salary progression	*Personal Pension Scheme* % Salary	Amount	*Executive Pension Plan* % Initial salary	Amount
30	£ 20,000	17.5%	£ 3,500	88%	£17,600
40	£ 45,220	20.0%	£ 9,044	88%	£17,600
50	£102,242	25.0%	£25,560	88%	£17,600
55	£153,736	30.0%	£46,120	88%	£17,600

Table 1.2

Male aged 40, initial salary £30,000, retirement at 60.

		Personal Pension Scheme		Executive Pension Plan	
Future Age	Salary progression	% Salary	Amount	% Initial salary	Amount
40	£ 30,000	20.0%	£ 6,000	102%	£30,600
50	£ 67,830	25.0%	£16,957	102%	£30,600
55	£101,992	30.0%	£30,598	102%	£30,600

Notes:

(1) Under the Executive Pension Plan, allowance is made at the outset for future salary increases, assumed to be 8.5% pa compound and fund growth assumed to be 9% pa. If, in practice, salary and fund growth rises at this rate the contributions will continue at a level amount. If salary increases at a greater level, and or fund growth is lower, higher contributions will be permitted.

(2) Under the Personal Pension Scheme, the amount that can be paid is based on the actual salary and the percentage contribution which applies at that age.

(3) The Executive Pension Plan contributions which assume completion of at least 20 years' service with the employer by age 60, may vary slightly from insurer to insurer, and exclude the cost of providing dependants' pensions and life assurance benefits. The contributions for the Personal Pension Scheme are fixed by law.

1.1 Forthcoming changes

In April 1992 the Inland Revenue proposed changes to the maximum contributions that could be paid into 'earmarked' pension schemes, ie: typically schemes for a few members, usually directors or key executives of an employer where benefits are specifically identifiable. In the past, the assumptions used in calculating maximum contributions to the schemes created a bias in favour of pension arrangements for the employer. The changes proposed by the Inland Revenue, which were intended to take effect towards the end of 1992 but which may be delayed will redress the balance significantly, as the following tables show:

Table 1.3

Male aged 30, initial salary £20,000, retirement at 60.

		Personal Pension Scheme		Executive Pension Plan	
Future Age	Salary progression	% Salary	Amount	% Initial salary	Amount
30	£ 20,000	17.5%	£ 3,500	25%	£ 5,000
40	£ 38,976	20.0%	£ 7,795	25%	£ 9,744
50	£ 75,960	25.0%	£18,990	25%	£18,990
55	£106,040	30.0%	£31,812	25%	£26,510

Table 1.4

Male aged 40, initial salary £30,000, retirement at 60.

		Personal Pension Scheme		Executive Pension Plan	
Future Age	Salary progression	% Salary	Amount	% Initial salary	Amount
40	£30,000	20.0%	£ 6,000	40%	£12,000
50	£58,465	25.0%	£14,616	40%	£23,386
55	£81,618	30.0%	£24,485	40%	£32,647

Notes
(1) Under the Executive Pension Plan, allowance is made at outset for future salary increases, assumed to be 6.9% per annum compound, and fund growth, assumed to be 8.5% per annum. If the salary increases at a greater level and/or fund growth is lower, higher contributions may be paid in future. The cost of providing dependants' pensions and life assurance benefits has been excluded.
(2) Under the Personal Pension Scheme, the amount that can be paid is based on the actual salary and the percentage contribution which applies at that age.

The revised basis clearly has the effect of significantly reducing the gap between maximum contributions that may be paid under arrangements of the self-employed as compared to employees.

However the differences in the underlying systems remain unchanged:

(1) For the self-employed there are no specific limits on benefits. The restrictions on contribution input, however, make it imperative that contributions are started as early as possible.
(2) For employees, whilst contributions are now restricted, the underlying limits are still on benefits. If as a result of the new contribution basis, and, for example, substantial salary increases close to retirement, the fund is in practice insufficient to provide maximum benefits, then a further single contribution may be made just prior to retirement to bridge the shortfall.

2 Historical notes

2.1 Early schemes and legislation

One early example of a scheme is seen in the famous case of *Hancock v General Reversionary and Investment Company Ltd* [1919] 1 KB 25, which established the important principle that a company which purchases an annuity for a retiring employee may set the cost against its profits for tax purposes as a business expense. It is still quite common for 'Hancock annuities' to be set up for retiring employees (see Chapter 16).

The 1918 Income Tax Act gave life assurance tax relief to employees contributing to a retirement benefit scheme using insurance policies. The Finance Acts of 1921 and 1930 provided, amongst other things, for the approval of superannuation funds set up under irrevocable trust and for the Commissioners of Inland Revenue to regulate such schemes.

New pensions legislation was introduced by the 1952 Income Tax Act and re-enacted in the consolidating Income and Corporation Taxes Act 1970. By 1970, however, the conditions for approval of pension schemes derived from a combination of legislation, case law and Inland Revenue practice. The Civil Service Superannuation Scheme was the model by which all private schemes were judged. The tax treatment of pension fund investments varied from total freedom to partial exemption from capital gains tax but no exemption from income tax, depending entirely on the type of benefit being provided, for example, cash, pension or death benefit. It was common for trustees of these old pension schemes to seek approval of 3/4 of the benefits under s 208 (giving complete tax-free treatment but requiring all benefits to be taken in pension form) and 1/4 of the benefits under s 222 of the Income and Corporation Taxes Act 1970 (allowing benefits to be taken in cash but giving limited relief) — giving rise to the expression '3/4, 1/4 Schemes'.

2.2 Old and new codes

The case for simplification, if not outright reform, was recognised in the late 1960s resulting in a 'New Code' of approval introduced by FA 1970, Part II, Chapter II. The New Code introduced a concept of one single fund with total freedom from tax on both contributions and investment income.

From 1970 to 1973 it was possible to seek approval under either Old or New Code, but from 1973 only New Code Schemes were approvable. By April 1980 even existing Old Code Schemes had to be re-approved by the Inland Revenue under the New Code.

The differences between the Old and New Codes which have had the most dramatic effect on the subsequent growth in pension schemes were probably as follows:

(1) The ability to fund for maximum pensions over ten rather than 20 years.
(2) Full tax relief on contributions paid by an employee and employer irrespective of the type of benefit being provided.
(3) The ability to set up a pension scheme which would provide a tax free cash sum in isolation. Under the Old Code it was necessary to restrict the amount of the tax free lump sum to 1/4 of the pension being provided, so that it was impossible to fund solely for a tax-free cash sum.
(4) Freedom from tax on all investments irrespective of the benefits being provided except for a period when development land tax was charged on real and deemed realisations of development value.
(5) The concept of approvable death in service benefits.

FA 1973, s 15 extended FA 1970 by allowing 'controlling directors' to be included in New Code pension schemes.

F(No 2)A 1987 brought in a number of significant changes to pension scheme practice. In some ways the changes meant a reversion to the Old Code regime in that:

(1) Maximum pensions for persons joining pension schemes on or after 17 March 1987 could be provided only if 20 years service with the employer could be completed by retirement, rather than ten.
(2) Pension schemes set up to provide only tax-free cash sums on retirement are restricted. Generally, if the *maximum* tax-

free cash sum is required the *maximum* pension benefit has to be provided under the scheme.
(3) Measures have been introduced to restrict the benefits which may be enjoyed by high earners, including 'controlling directors'.

FA 1989, Sched 6 introduced further limitations to all members of new occupational pension schemes set up from 14 March 1989 and, in respect of new members joining from 1 June 1989, schemes set up before that date. Details are given in later chapters but the principal change was the maximum level of earnings on which retirement benefits could be based. This was set at £60,000 in 1989/90 and is increased each year in line with increases in the Retail Prices Index, and stands at £75,000 in 1992/93.

2.3 Top hat schemes

The top hat scheme first gained prominence after the war as a simple, but effective means of reducing the burden of income tax; in those days the top rate was 97.5%. The proceeds of endowment schemes could be taken completely tax-free at the end of a period of employment. The 1947 Finance Act was an attempt to make top hats less attractive by restricting the amount of pension which could be commuted for a tax free lump sum to 25% but in fact it only succeeded in boosting their popularity by giving them respectability.

The early top hat schemes were straightforward endowment assurance policies set up by a director giving up part of his income or an increment, a device known as 'salary sacrifice'. Top hat schemes were approved retirement benefit schemes offering the following advantages:

- The director paid no tax on his 'contribution' (because it had been sacrificed).
- On death the proceeds of the endowment assurance policy were free of estate duty.
- On retirement, up to 1/4 of the policy was available as a tax-free capital sum.

However, there were some disadvantages which gained greater significance as time passed:

- Insurance companies could not invest contributions from top hat schemes into their tax-exempt pension funds but only

their life and annuity funds which did not offer such good returns.
- Direct personal contributions paid by the director were given only life assurance tax relief.
- Controlling directors, ie those owning more than 5% of the equity in a company which the directors between them controlled, were ineligible and could only take advantage of retirement annuities where the scope for contributions was very limited.

Following the passing of the 1973 Finance Act which allowed controlling directors to join New Code schemes, top hat schemes found a new lease of life.

Because of the changes which were brought about by the New Code, the modern top hat policy became a much more sophisticated vehicle than its predecessor, offering maximum flexibility in terms of benefits and investment options. Indeed, executive pension plans as they are now called, have become essential tools of tax planners with their ability to avoid income tax, capital gains tax, inheritance tax and corporation tax.

2.4 Lifetime service agreements

The 1973 Finance Act allowing controlling directors to join New Code schemes was passed in July 1973. In April of the same year, many controlling directors had completed special whole of life death in service arrangements to beat the Old Code time limit. Because it had not been necessary to obtain approval to death benefits under the Old Code, it was realised that unlimited sums assured through insurance policies written under trust could be established for controlling directors by their companies and, provided the company did not claim corporation tax relief on the premiums, the proceeds would be payable to beneficiaries free of estate duty.

These old death in service arrangements were unapproved and were designed to be self-funding (by surrendering bonuses which had been allotted to the policy to pay future premiums) after April 1980, by which date all continuing schemes required re-approval under the New Code.

The director for whose benefit the policy was set up had to have a lifetime service agreement and could not, in respect of the same employment, enjoy the benefits of a self-employed retirement annuity policy. It is unlikely that many of these lifetime service agreements would have been completed had it been known that shortly afterwards, controlling directors could set up New Code pension schemes for the first time. The Inland Revenue agreed to approve whole of life assurance policies issued by insurance companies as vehicles for retirement benefit schemes under New Code, provided that there was genuine evidence of a lifetime service agreement and the amount of benefit fell within normal New Code limits — essentially that the lump sum payable on death would be within four times salary at the date of death.

It was even possible to adapt the pre-1973 death in service arrangements to make them approvable under the New Code. If this were done, the company could offset its premium payments against profits for corporation tax purposes and the insurance company could put the premiums into its tax exempt fund instead of its tax-bearing life fund. In short, the premiums could be reduced.

Once again, many insurance companies marketed 'whole of life death in service' packages and controlling directors with serious capital transfer tax (the forerunner of inheritance tax) problems took advantage of these schemes. The Inland Revenue effectively put a stop to the practice by issuing their Memorandum No 41 which imposed a restriction on the discretionary distribution of death benefits on or after the age of 75. This Memorandum was followed by Memorandum No 59 which further tightened the rules. These rulings were not retrospective, however, so that some controlling directors still have advantageous arrangements which they are unable to change materially without causing the Memorandum No 59 restrictions to apply automatically.

2.5 Growth of executive pension plans

The creation and growth of the executive pension plan for the controlling director coincided with the development of unit-linked life assurance policies, pioneered by such companies as Hambro Life Assurance (now Allied Dunbar Assurance plc). By the end of the 1970s these companies had been joined by many other new companies and also very old established life assurance companies, all offering unit-linked as well as traditional with-profits policies.

The essential attraction of the unit-linked policy is the option given to the policyholder to decide his own investment strategy. He may choose to invest his contributions in a variety of sectors ranging from properties, equities, cash, gilts and overseas funds. Alternatively, the policy holder may leave the investment strategy to the insurance company under what is known as a 'managed fund'.

2.6 Small self-administered pension schemes

The late 1970s saw the development of small self-administered pension schemes, sometimes known as 'captives' where the employer sets up a pension scheme himself, with the assistance of various experts, rather than using an insurance company. The trustees have wider powers of investment compared with those allowed under a straightforward insured arrangement, in particular the ability to lend part of the pension fund back to the employer to assist the expansion of the business, to purchase shares in the employer's business and to purchase property which is leased to the employer. However, the Social Security Act 1990 has limited such 'self-investment' to 5% of the value of the pension fund unless the scheme membership is limited to '20% directors' of the company, and provided other conditions are met (see Chapter 9).

Insurance companies offer small self-administered schemes, usually providing all the necessary services and investment management if required but normally on the basis that a portion of the pension fund is invested in an insurance policy.

2.7 Development of state benefits

The 1960s and 1970s were notorious for the frequency with which governments invented new state schemes. Some never reached the statute book while others were overturned by an incoming administration. All tended to bear the name of their creators — the Boyd-Carpenter Graduated Pension Scheme, the Crossman Plan, the Keith Joseph Funded Pension Scheme and the Barbara Castle Earnings Related Scheme.

Although there was all-party consensus on the Castle Scheme, Norman Fowler, as Secretary of State for Health and Social Security, introduced measures in the Social Security Act 1986, which reduced benefits under the earnings related part of the state scheme (see Chapter 11).

As far as the director and senior executive of a company is concerned, however, it is only the earnings related part of the state scheme which has ever been of any influence in the provision of benefits.

2.8 More recent changes

The 1970s saw the start of legislative changes to improve the benefits of early leavers and provide for greater transferability between schemes. This continued into 1990 which saw further legislation to improve early leavers' benefits. The late 1980s saw significant changes to both occupational and personal pension schemes (covered in later chapters), increased the awareness of 'unapproved pension schemes' (see Chapter 5) and saw the beginning of anti-sex discrimination law in the field of pensions. Under the Sex Discrimination Act 1986, it is unlawful for employers to require female employees to retire at an earlier age than male colleagues. In its judgment on the *Barber* v *Guardian Royal Exchange* case the European Court ruled that redundancy pay and membership of a contracted-out pension scheme are 'pay' for the purposes of equal treatment directives of the European Community Council and the Treaty of Rome and that Mr Barber had been discriminated against by his employer even though the reason for the different treatment between him and his female colleagues was the different state retirement ages for men and women.

Chapter 20 looks at the effect of future legislation which is likely to proliferate following the *Barber* case, and others of a similar nature which are awaiting judgment by the European Court.

3 Inland Revenue approval

3.1 Pension Schemes Office

All pension schemes, to be tax effective, must be approved by the Pension Schemes Office (PSO) which is a branch of the Inland Revenue. Schemes which are used for contracting-out purposes also have to be approved by the Occupational Pensions Board (OPB). The OPB was set up in 1975 and has two main functions:

(1) to issue contracting-out certificates to occupational pension schemes and personal pension schemes which are to be contracted-out of the earnings related part of the state scheme (see Chapter 12) and,
(2) to examine and report on issues of public interest connected with pensions and referred to it from time to time by the Secretary of State for Social Security.

The PSO has built up a unique relationship with the pensions industry over many years and gives guidance and will offer comment on proposals put to it by interested organisations.

Thus the conduct of pension schemes is regulated by a largely voluntary code of practice based on undertakings given by the trustees of pension schemes to the PSO to conform with their requirements as stipulated from time to time.

3.1.1 The purpose of approval

It is often forgotten by directors when drawing up their service agreements or contracts of employment that the mere promise of a pension will constitute a 'retirement benefit scheme' in the eyes of the Inland Revenue who will tax it as a benefit in kind in the hands of the director.

There are many directors who have service agreements which promise pension benefits but which have never been seen by the

Inland Revenue and are potential tax traps: such agreements normally only come to light following a take-over or the merger of companies. These agreements will almost certainly be unapproved pension schemes requiring careful examination following FA 1989 (see Chapter 5).

One of the purposes of seeking approval from the PSO is to remove the liability for income tax from the employee. If the scheme is approved by the PSO as an exempt approved scheme, further advantages flow from this. If the promise to provide retirement benefits is funded by means of an exempt approved pension scheme the employer will be able to claim tax relief on the payment as a business expense. Exempt approval will also enable the trustees of funded schemes to invest fund monies without liability to income tax or capital gains tax.

Following a change of practice in October 1991, the Inland Revenue now maintain that an *ex gratia* payment can also constitute a retirement benefit scheme where the payment is made on retirement. Although many genuine redundancy payments will be free from tax as 'golden handshakes' (if they are up to £30,000 in value), other *ex gratia* benefits will need to be restricted to the normal limits and formal approval obtained.

3.1.2 Conditions for approval

The basic conditions which must be met before the PSO will approve a scheme as an exempt approved scheme are:

(1) That the scheme is established under irrevocable trusts for the sole purpose of providing relevant benefits in respect of service as an employee: 'relevant benefits' is defined in ICTA 1988, s 612(1) in very wide terms, and covers any type of financial benefit given in connection with the termination of an employee's service with a particular employer, including termination by reason of death, with the sole exception of benefits receivable only in the event of death by accident or disablement by accident during (though not necessarily arising out of) service.

(2) That the scheme is recognised by the employer and employees to whom it relates and that every employee who is or who has a right to be a member of the scheme has been given written particulars of all essential features of the scheme which concern him (sometimes known as an 'announcement letter').

(3) That there is a person resident in the UK who will be

responsible for the discharge of all duties imposed on the administrator of the scheme.
(4) That the employer is a contributor to the scheme. (Generally, the level of contribution must be at least 10% of the total contribution to the scheme.)
(5) That the scheme is established in connection with some trade or undertaking carried on in the UK by a person resident in the UK.
(6) That in no circumstances, whether during the subsistence of the scheme or later, can any amount be paid by way of repayment of an employee's contributions under the scheme (although this condition may be overridden by preservation provisions).
(7) That any benefit for an employee is a pension on retirement at a specified age not earlier than 60 and not later than 75, which does not exceed 1/60th of the employee's final remuneration for each year of service up to a maximum of 40 years.
(8) That any benefit for any widow of an employee is a pension payable on his death after retirement such that the amount payable to the widow by way of pension does not exceed 2/3rds of any pension or pensions payable to the employee.
(9) That no other benefits are payable under the scheme.
(10) That no pension is capable in whole or in part of surrender, commutation or assignment except so far as the scheme allows an employee on retirement to obtain by commutation of this pension, a lump sum or sums not exceeding in all 3/80ths of his final remuneration for each year of service up to a maximum of 40 years.

These are the primary conditions which, if met, entitle the scheme to all the tax advantages which approval can confer as of right and are contained in ICTA 1988, s 590. Very few schemes, however, exist which do not infringe one or more of these primary conditions, and approval under s 590 is normally only sought in very limited circumstances such as where a scheme is to be set up for directors of investment companies (of which more will be said in Chapter 18).

To cope with the vast majority of occupational pension schemes, the PSO relies on its discretionary powers which are extremely wide ranging and are set out in the PSO's practice notes, *Occupational Pension Schemes, Notes on approval under the Finance Act 1970 as amended by the Finance Act 1971* (IR 12 (1991)), published in October 1991. These new Practice Notes apply to new schemes not approved by 29 November 1991. The previous Practice Notes,

IR 12 (1979), with the additional requirements and classifications contained in subsequent memoranda, may continue to apply to schemes approved before 29 November 1991, although these may not necessarily be more advantageous.

The Practice Notes have to be interpreted alongside separate Joint Office Memoranda published by the Pension Schemes Office of the Inland Revenue and the Occupational Pensions Board.

In practice approval can be given to a scheme:

(1) which exceeds the limits imposed by the primary conditions as respects benefits for less than 40 years' service;
(2) which provides pensions for the widows or widowers of employees on death in service or for children or dependants of such employees;
(3) which provides, on death in service, a lump sum of up to four times the employee's final remuneration (exclusive of any refund of contributions);
(4) which allows benefits to be payable on retirement within ten years of the specified age, or on earlier incapacity;
(5) which provides for the return in certain contingencies of the employee's contributions;
(6) which relates to a trade or undertaking carried on only partly in the UK and by a person resident in the UK;
(7) which provides in certain contingencies for securing relevant benefits (but no other benefits) by means of an annuity contract approved by the Board and made with an insurance company of the employee's choice (ie a 'Section 32 annuity'); or
(8) to which the employer is not a contributor and which provides benefits additional to those provided by a scheme to which he is a contributor (ie a 'freestanding AVC').

The much wider benefits set out above are contained in ICTA 1988, s 591.

The PSO relies on written undertakings given to it by the trustees and administrators of pension schemes. It does have the power to withdraw approval at any time should it feel that the scheme is no longer meeting its requirements. The consequences of withdrawal of approval are penal since the contributions paid by the employers would be regarded as income in the hands of the members, tax relief on employees' contributions would be withdrawn and the fund itself would lose its tax exempt status.

A scheme which meets all the other conditions of approval set out above but which is not established under irrevocable trust may be approved by the PSO, but not exempt approved. The effect of this is to avoid a charge to income tax on the employee or director, but none of the other tax advantages apply.

3.2 Other legislation and case law

Although Chapter XIV of ICTA 1988 is the legislative base for approval of all pension schemes other legislation can have an influence on the scheme.

The most important pieces of legislation are:

3.2.1 Social Security Act 1973

This Act which became effective from April 1975 contained the original preservation requirements giving vested rights to members who left service having attained age 26 and having completed five years qualifying service from April 1975. The Act also prevented a refund of contributions on leaving service except in circumstances where vested rights would not apply. Subsequent Social Security Acts improved further the benefits of early leavers: in particular, the age 26 requirement was dropped and the qualifying service period was reduced to two years.

3.2.2 Social Security Pensions Act 1975

This Act established the current state scheme which started in April 1978. Many employers 'contract out' of the earnings related part of this scheme by providing guaranteed minimum requirements within an occupational scheme (see Chapter 12).

3.2.3 Employment Protection (Consolidation) Act 1978

Under this Act, an employer must give to new employees within 13 weeks of starting their employment, a statement of the main terms of their contract of employment, including reference to any pension scheme and where to find information on the scheme. If the scheme is used for contracting out of the State Earnings Related scheme, this must also be made known to the employee. There is also provision in this Act for pension schemes which are owed money by an employer which has gone into liquidation to make a claim on the Redundancy Fund.

3.2.4 Social Security Act 1985

This Act provided for improvements in the benefits of early leavers from pension schemes. With effect from 1 January 1986 employers were required to revalue the pension provided on leaving service at the lesser of the increase in the rate of the Retail Prices Index or 5% compound for each year between the date of leaving and the date of retirement. Revaluation applies only in respect of service with the employer from 1 January 1985 which means that the Act is not retrospective and therefore does not increase an employer's liability in respect of members who left the schemes formerly nor does it apply in respect of service with an employer up to January 1985 (but see reference below to Social Security Act 1990). This Act also provides for pension scheme trustees to disclose information to prospective members, current members and early leavers. The information to be provided relates to the member's own benefits under the scheme and also information relating to the scheme as a whole including its investment policy and finances. Provisions of the Act also compel scheme trustees to facilitate the payment of transfer values to another suitable scheme at the member's request.

3.2.5 Social Security Act 1986

This Act relaxed significantly the contracting-out requirements of occupational schemes. Since 6 April 1988 it has been possible for employers to set up occupational schemes which may be contracted-out on a money-purchase (sometimes known as 'defined contribution') basis. Up to that time contracting-out by occupational schemes was permitted only on a final-salary (or defined benefit) basis. This Act also provides for individuals to contract-out personally through a personal pension scheme. Measures relating to new pension providers, ie banks, building societies and unit trusts are contained in this Act.

3.2.6 Sex Discrimination Act 1986

This Act made it unlawful to require that a woman retires from work at an earlier age than a man in the same job. It also makes it illegal for an employer to refuse her training or to refuse to promote her because she is nearing retirement provided that these opportunities would have been offered to a man of the same age.

Strictly, this Act does not require the pension age under an occupational scheme to be the same for men and women nor require an equality of benefits under occupational schemes.

However, recent case law, in particular *Barber* v *GRE*, is likely to result in common pension ages under employer sponsored pension schemes (see Chapter 20).

3.2.7 Finance (No 2) Act 1987

This Act contained the tax framework of personal pension schemes introduced in the Social Security Act 1986. It amends those provisions now contained in ICTA 1988 relating to pension schemes for the self-employed and those who are in non-pensionable employment as well as to occupational schemes. This Act also brought in restrictions on the benefits permitted under occupational pension schemes.

3.2.8 Finance Act 1989

This Act contained further limitations on benefits which may be provided by occupational pension schemes, by reference to an earnings ceiling, £75,000 in 1992/93, and changes to contribution levels to personal pension schemes.

3.2.9 Social Security Act 1989

This Act contained important requirements for employers to ensure 'equal treatment' in relation to any employment-related benefit schemes'. 'Equal treatment' means that persons of one sex may not, on the basis of their sex, be treated less favourably than persons of the other sex. 'Employment-related benefit schemes' includes executive pension schemes which, typically, are set up for directors and key executives, and 'group personal pension plans'.

3.2.10 Social Security Act 1990

This Act strengthened the protection for early leavers from occupational schemes. Furthermore, all occupational schemes will soon have to pay annual increases (in line with increases in the Retail Prices Index up to 5%) to members for their pension rights which they build up after an 'appointed day' (expected to be before the end of 1991 but deferred pending the outcome of the debate on sex discrimination in relation to pension schemes).

If there is a surplus under the pension scheme the first call on the surplus will be to pay increases in pension to members for rights which they have built up before the 'appointed day'. When a scheme winds up, employers will have to ensure that any surplus is used to provide members with increases, in line with increases in the Retail Prices Index up to 5%, to all pension rights. Increases for pension rights before the 'appointed day' depend on increases already guaranteed and any surplus on winding up. These changes do not apply to money purchase schemes or to personal pension schemes. Regulations introduced on 1 July 1992 will make any deficiency of pension funds that are wound up a debt due from the employer to the trustees of the scheme.

This Act also established a Pensions Ombudsman (a complaints service) and the Pensions Tracing Registry to which persons may apply to obtain details of pension benefits to which they may have entitlement under previous employers' schemes.

3.3 Trusts

In order to obtain exempt approval, the scheme must be established under trust so that the assets of the pension scheme are legally separated from those of the employer.

The employer establishes the trust, appoints the first trustees and lays down the conditions under which employees and their dependants will benefit.

3.3.1 Setting up the trust

For the purposes of approval a trust can be created in a number of ways, all of which are acceptable to the Inland Revenue:

Formal deed
This method is generally used for large group pension schemes and consists of a formal deed under which the employer creates a trust and appoints trustees giving them various powers of investment, and also adopts formal rules. Often the trust is established by an interim deed and is followed by a definitive deed at a later stage.

Declaration of trust
This is similar to, though much shorter than a formal deed, and is normally used in connection with discretionary individual pension arrangements, for example, executive pension plans, where benefits are to be provided by an insurance company. This is a simple document whereby the employer normally appoints itself as one of the trustees or more commonly as the sole trustee.

Board resolution
Providing a company's memorandum and articles of association permit it, the Board of Directors may pass a board resolution which has the effect of creating a trust.

Employer trust
Sometimes a trust is created by an exchange of letters between the employer and the employee who is to benefit from the pension scheme. This is only used for individual pension arrangements where the scheme is being established for one employee or director.

The legislation requires the appointment of a UK resident person as scheme administrator, who will be liable for tax matters relating to the scheme. It is usual to appoint the scheme trustee(s) as administrator. The actual day to day administration of the scheme will normally be carried on by either an in-house office with the assistance of external advisors, or, where the scheme is insured, by the insurance company.

3.4 How to obtain Revenue approval

Applications for approval to schemes must be sent in writing to the PSO within at least six months from the establishment of the scheme, possibly longer, depending on the date of establishment, as follows:

Date scheme established	Date by which application must be received by PSO
In the 6 months ending 5 October	By the following 5 April
In the month ending 5 November	By the following 5 May
" 5 December	" 5 June
" 5 January	" 5 July
" 5 February	" 5 August
" 5 March	" 5 September
" 5 April	" 5 October

Subject to provisions for spreading tax relief forward (see Chapter 7) employer's contributions are relieved for tax purposes in the accounting year in which they are paid.

The application for approval must be accompanied by the appropriate return. There are three types of return, in a form and colour prescribed and supplied by the PSO: one for schemes open to more than one employee, one for individual arrangements and one for 'Hancock annuities'.

It is important that the standard returns are completed fully and accurately otherwise they will not be treated as valid applications for approval. The following information is included in the returns, but is not exhaustive.

(1) The full name, address and registered office of the employer.
(2) The status of the employer, for example, limited company, partnership, sole trader.
(3) The nature of the employer's business.
(4) The name of the scheme.
(5) The tax districts dealing with the employer's PAYE and corporation tax and the employer's reference numbers in those districts.
(6) A copy of the document establishing the scheme, for example, the trust deed, exchange of letters or declaration of trust if not already agreed as standard.
(7) A copy of the letter to employees describing the main features of the scheme.
(8) The commencement date of the scheme.
(9) Where appropriate (for example in the case of small self-administered schemes) actuarial reports concerning the funding of the scheme.
(10) Details of any existing schemes and their interaction with the new scheme which has been set up.
(11) The name and address of the administrator and trustee.
(12) Details of the person or persons who will be responsible for paying pensions. This is normally the trustees but in insured schemes the insurance company often pays pensions as agent for the administrator.
(13) The employer's financial year end.
(14) The number of members.
(15) The amount of ordinary annual contributions and date of first payment.
(16) The amount of any special contributions.
(17) The method of funding, for example, insured or self-administered together with full details of the employer's ordinary annual contributions and any special contributions to any other schemes.
(18) The names of any directors joining the scheme who:

(a) either on his/her own or with one or more associates beneficially owns or is able to control directly or indirectly

or through other companies 20% or more of the ordinary share capital of the company;
(b) at any time before 6 April 1973 was a controlling director, ie one who owned more than 5% of the shares in a company in which the directors collectively owned more than 50% of the shares.
(19) A list of all retained benefits — those earned from earlier membership of approved pension schemes or through self-employed retirement annuities, benefits under approved occupational pension schemes relating to earlier employments and under retirement annuity contracts and personal pension schemes relating to this or earlier employments. If the scheme is insured the insurance company will automatically obtain the above information through its application forms and will in turn pass them on to the PSO.

3.5 PSO approval

The PSO will not authorise provisional income tax relief on members' personal contributions until they have received the above items, and trustees' undertakings. Most insurance companies have agreed standard documents with the PSO so that final approval is normally a matter of waiting for the PSO to rubber stamp the documents.

Since 1 December 1987 the PSO have not notified the employer's Schedule D tax district that a scheme has been approved. Instead, the letter signifying approval lists the participating employers, and the date of approval, and it is the responsibility of the employer(s) or their agents to forward a copy to the appropriate tax district to support the initial claim for relief in respect of an employer's pension scheme contribution. This procedure ensures that tax inspectors have evidence of the entitlement to relief before them at a time a participating employer's accounts are examined for Sched D or corporation tax liability.

If employees are contributing towards the cost of the pension scheme, they will receive tax relief under PAYE: this means for example, that if an employee's salary amounts to £800 per month and is proposing to pay £50 per month to the pension scheme the employer will calculate tax by applying the employee's PAYE code to £750. This is known as the 'net pay arrangement' but an employer should not operate this until the local inspector has been notified that provisional tax relief has been allowed.

3.6 Simplified schemes

A simplified procedure for tax approval is available to schemes providing a package of benefits which need to satisfy only the minimal basic Revenue requirements. The procedure is available to a simplified defined contribution scheme, which offers only money purchase benefits and to which no limits on benefits will apply, although there is an overall limit on contributions. It will not be possible for such schemes to be self-administered, unless they are contracted-out on a money purchase basis.

3.7 Unapproved schemes

Since the introduction of the limit on the benefits which can emerge from new occupational pension schemes there has been increasing interest in unapproved schemes. These are not subject to Inland Revenue limits; for example, an employer could provide a pension equal to an employer's retiring salary.

Under the current legislation however, the major drawback is the choice forced on the employee between an immediate Schedule E charge on employer contributions (treated as a taxable benefit in kind) and an unsecured benefit (if the arrangement is unfunded). (Full details are contained in Chapter 5.)

4 Maximum permitted benefits

The purpose of this chapter is to look at the maximum levels of benefits which the PSO will approve for an employee including the considerable changes brought about by the Finance (No 2) Act 1987 and Finance Act 1989. The restrictions which apply to company directors are contained in the next chapter.

4.1 Who can qualify?

Any person who is an employee of an employer and therefore liable to pay tax under Schedule E may be provided with retirement and death benefits under an approved retirement benefit scheme.

The term 'employee' includes:

(1) Directors, whether controlling or not whose income is assessable under Schedule E;
(2) Part-time or temporary employees;
(3) Genuinely employed spouses of professional persons such as accountants, solicitors, doctors and dentists;
(4) Genuinely employed spouses of the self-employed;
(5) Salaried, not equity, partners in a partnership;
(6) UK resident employees of overseas employers;
(7) Domestic servants.

4.2 Who cannot qualify?

It is not possible to provide benefits under an approved retirement benefit scheme for anyone whose income is assessable under Schedule D, for example:

(1) Self-employed persons, whether sole proprietors or equity partners;

28 Allied Dunbar Pensions Guide

(2) Consultants whose only source of income is assessable under Schedule D;
(3) Directors of an investment company, although they are often entitled to receive low levels of Schedule E income from the company (see Chapter 18).

The first two categories listed above may, however, pay contributions to personal pension schemes and/or to retirement annuity contracts (see Chapter 14).

4.3 Recent changes

Occupational pension schemes have been subject to many changes in recent years. The principal changes were brought about by Finance (No 2) Act 1987 and Finance Act 1989. The relevant provisions are now consolidated in Part XIV of ICTA 1988. In broad terms, there are three categories of benefit structure depending upon the date of membership of the scheme, as set out below.

While the legislation sets out basic conditions which entitle a scheme to mandatory approval, it also confers wide discretionary powers on the PSO to approve schemes which do not fully comply. Most schemes seek discretionary approval, to which end the PSO has issued its own guidance as to (among other requirements) calculation of maximum benefits. That guidance is set out in what are commonly referred to as the 'Practice Notes' of which there are two current versions. The 1979 Practice Notes apply, generally speaking, to all schemes approved before 29 November 1991 and the 1991 Practice Notes to schemes approved on or after that date.

Simplifications to the calculation of maximum benefits were also introduced by Inland Revenue Memorandum 108, effective from 31 August 1991 and affecting all members of all schemes who retire on or after that date.

Membership categories

In broad terms the maximum benefits that may be provided depend on the date of joining the scheme, which categorises membership as follows:

4.3.1 Pre-1987 members

Pre-1987 benefits may be provided under schemes which were established before 17 March 1987 for members who joined before that date.

4.3.2 1987-1989 members

1987-1989 benefits may be provided under schemes which were established before 14 March 1989 for members who joined on or after 17 March 1987 and before 1 June 1989.

4.3.3 Post-1989 members

Post-1989 benefits may be provided for members joining schemes from 1 June 1989, regardless of when the scheme was established and also for members who joined, before 1 June 1989, schemes established on or after 14 March 1989.

In general terms each category is subject to more restrictions on the benefits which may be provided than its predecessor: pre-1987 pension benefits are better than 1987-1989 pension benefits which in turn are better than post-1989 pension benefits. However, it is possible to opt for post-1989 benefits where the result would be beneficial in certain circumstances, eg where enhanced early retirement benefits are required.

The benefits relating to the three categories are described later in this chapter.

4.4 Retirement ages

To obtain PSO approval of scheme membership it is necessary to stipulate a normal retirement age, which should be the best estimate of an employee's retiring age.

Under schemes approved on or after 29 November 1991, the permitted age range for both men and women is normally 60 to 75, although an earlier or later normal retirement age is possible in individual cases at the discretion of the PSO, eg in the case of a member who joins the scheme as a post-1989 member with the right to benefits on a pre-1987 basis.

Under schemes approved before 29 November 1991, post-1989 members of either sex are restricted to the age range 60 to 75.

However, the permitted ranges for pre-1987 and 1987–1989 members are 60 to 70 for men and 55 to 70 for women (subject to the special restrictions for controlling directors — see Chapter 6). Where it can be demonstrated that such a member is likely to continue working beyond age 70 it is possible to obtain approval of a later normal retirement age.

4.5 Maximum benefits

The maximum benefits available to an employee or director from a pension scheme normally depend on his years of service with the employer and his salary at or around retirement. Generally, the maximum pension which an employee can receive at his normal retirement date under Inland Revenue rules is 2/3rds of his final salary ('final salary' is explained below), of which he may be able to commute up to a maximum of 1.5 times final salary for a lump sum.

There is however, a distinction between what the Inland Revenue permits and what a particular pension scheme might provide: even if the pension fund has accumulated substantial amounts it is not possible to provide retirement benefits in excess of Inland Revenue limits. Conversely a pension scheme may provide benefits well below the maximum permitted by the Inland Revenue.

In the case of a post-1989 member who is a controlling director (see Chapter 6) and who retired on or after 31 August 1991, the Inland Revenue also requires that the limits described below apply to the *aggregate* of the member's occupational scheme benefits and those derived from retirement annuity contract/personal pension schemes relating to earnings with the same employer.

4.6 Maximum pension

4.6.1 60ths scale

The Inland Revenue will always permit a pension benefit of up to 1/60th of final salary for each year of service (this is known as the '60ths scale' or 'straight 60ths') so that a maximum pension of 2/3rds of final salary is obtained only after completing 40 years' service with the employer — an unlikely event for most people. If the period of service is less than 40 years the pension on retirement is calculated by multiplying the number of years of service with the employer by 1/60th of final salary.

Example 4.1

An employee retires after 27 years' service with his employer: his final salary is £20,000: the rules of the group pension scheme provide for a pension of 1/60th of final salary for each year of service: his retirement pension from the scheme will therefore be £9,000:

$$27/60\text{ths} \times £20{,}000 = £9{,}000 \text{ pa}$$

Very few employees and directors will complete 40 years' service with the same employer. It is still possible, however, for them to receive the maximum pension of 2/3rds of final salary under an enhanced accrual rate (if permitted by the rules of the scheme) depending on their category of membership.

4.6.2 Uplifted 60ths scale (pre-1987 members)

Under this scale the 2/3rds maximum is permitted if at least ten years' service has been completed with the employer at normal retirement date. Provided at least five years' service can be completed with an employer, higher benefits can be provided than under the straight 60ths scale.

The following table shows how pension entitlement can be accelerated.

Table 4.1

Years of service normal retirement age	Maximum pension as a fraction of final salary
1–5	1/60th for each year
6	8/60
7	16/60
8	24/60
9	32/60
10 or more	40/60

Example 4.2

An employee retires after eight years' service with his company. His final salary is £28,000. The rules of the pension scheme provide for a pension calculated on the uplifted 60ths scale.

His retirement pension from the scheme will therefore be £11,200, calculated as follows:

$$24/60 \times £28,000 = £11,200 \text{ pa}$$

If, as is usually the case, the period of service includes a part of a year, the uplifted 60ths scale is increased proportionately to reflect the service in the last year.

Example 4.3

The employee in the previous example retires after seven years and six months. His retirement pension from the scheme will be calculated as follows:

Number of 60ths after eight years	24
Number of 60ths after seven years	16
Increase obtained during twelve months	8
Increase obtained during six months	4
Number of 60ths after seven years and six months	16 + 4 = 20
Pension 20/60 × £28,000 = £9,333 pa.	

In arriving at the maximum pension obtainable on the 'uplifted 60ths scale', it is necessary to include a restriction to take account of additional pensions arising from any voluntary contributions and any 'retained benefits' (see below).

4.6.3 Accelerated scale (1987–1989 members and post-1989 members)

In respect of members joining schemes on or after 17 March 1987 or where a new scheme was established on or after that date, the maximum pension is 1/30th of final salary for each year of service. The 2/3rds maximum is therefore permitted only on completion of at least 20 years' service with the employer at normal retirement date (compared with ten under the uplifted 60ths scale).

Thus, the pension on the new accelerated scale is better than the maximum pension set out in Table 4.1 where the years of service to normal retirement age are seven or less. Where the years of service to normal retirement age are greater than seven the old uplifted 60ths scale is significantly better.

The following is a comparison of the two scales:

Table 4.2

	Pre-1987 members		1987–1989 members and post-1989 members	
Years of service	Fraction of final salary	Percentage of final salary	Fraction of final salary	Percentage of final salary
1	1/60	1.66%	2/60	3.33%
2	2/60	3.33%	4/60	6.66%
3	3/60	5.00%	6/60	10.00%
4	4/60	6.66%	8/60	13.33%
5	5/60	8.33%	10/60	16.66%
6	8/60	13.33%	12/60	20.00%
7	16/60	26.66%	14/60	23.33%
8	24/60	40.00%	16/60	26.66%
9	32/60	53.33%	18/60	30.00%
10	40/60	66.66%	20/60	33.30%
11	40/60	66.66%	22/60	36.60%
12	40/60	66.66%	24/60	40.00%
13	40/60	66.66%	26/60	43.33%
14	40/60	66.66%	28/60	46.66%
15	40/60	66.66%	30/60	50.00%
16	40/60	66.66%	32/60	53.33%
17	40/60	66.66%	34/60	56.66%
18	40/60	66.66%	36/60	60.00%
19	40/60	66.66%	38/60	63.30%
20	40/60	66.66%	40/60	66.66%

4.7 Definitions of 'final salary'

The bases for calculating final salary permitted by the PSO are as follows:

(a) Remuneration (on which Schedule E income tax liability has been assessed as final and conclusive) for any one of the five years preceding the normal retirement date: remuneration includes basic salary for the year in question together with the average of fluctuating emoluments, such as bonus or

commission, earned over a period of at least three consecutive years ending in the year in question.
(b) The annual average of total earnings (on which Schedule E income tax liability has been assessed as final and conclusive) over a period of at least three consecutive years ending not earlier than ten years before normal retirement date.

In the case of a controlling director, however, only definition (b) is acceptable.

'Fluctuating emoluments' means any earnings not paid on a fixed basis which are additional to basic wage or salary and, depending on the rules of the scheme, can include:

(1) Profit related pay (whether or not taxable).
(2) Overtime, commission, bonuses assessable to income tax under Schedule E.
(3) Benefits in kind which are assessable to income tax under Schedule E such as company car, company paid petrol, rent free accommodation.

Where fluctuating emoluments have been paid for less than three years they should (when calculating final salary in accordance with definition (a) above) be averaged over the period starting with the date they commenced or, if later, the beginning of the three-year period and ending on the last day of the basic salary year in question. PSO permission must however be sought if it is intended to include a fluctuating emolument paid only once.

Finance (No 2) Act 1987 and Finance Act 1989 brought about changes to the definition of 'final salary'. The changes apply to all members of occupational schemes, as follows:

(1) Income or gains from the acquisition or disposal of shares or interests in shares or options over shares acquired through share option, share incentive and profit sharing schemes, or from shares which give rise to a Schedule E tax liability, are excluded from the calculation of 'final salary'. However this exclusion does not apply:
 (i) where the shares or the option or other interest in shares which give rise, on or after 17 March 1987, to a Schedule E tax liability, were acquired or granted before that date; or
 (ii) where 'final salary' is determined for calculating maximum benefits on death in service (see below).

(2) Also excluded from 'final salary' is anything in respect of which tax is chargeable by virtue of ICTA 1988, s 148 (payments on termination of employment, eg golden handshakes) except where final salary is being used to calculate maximum benefits on death in service.
(3) In the case of a pre-1987 or 1987–1989 member, if the 'final salary' calculated in accordance with definition (a) exceeds £100,000 (or such other figure as may be prescribed by the Treasury) in any year from 6 April 1987 onwards, actual 'final salary' must be restricted to the amount calculated in accordance with definition (b) or, if greater, £100,000.
(4) In the case of a post-1989 member, 'final salary' under either definition is restricted to a maximum of £75,000 (for the 1992/93 tax year). This maximum will be adjusted annually in line with increases in the Retail Prices Index (measured from December to December) and rounded up to the next highest multiple of £600. A member who is subject to this upper limit may therefore be provided with a maximum pension of £50,000 pa on normal retirement in the 1992/93 tax year.
(5) Final remuneration may now also include:
   (a) remuneration received after termination of employment or retirement but on which the tax liability has been determined, provided that it was earned prior to termination and is treated as a fluctuating emolument;
   (b) remuneration assessable to tax under Schedule E but on which the tax liability has not yet been determined, provided that final remuneration is recalculated once the tax liability has been determined, but only for calculating immediate benefits.

4.8 Dynamised or indexed final remuneration

Final salary may be re-calculated as a notional figure known as dynamised final remuneration or indexed final remuneration by increasing the actual salary earned in a particular year by the increase in the Retail Prices Index (RPI) between the end of the year in question and normal retirement date. The result is to produce a pension which is related to the salary which an employee would have received if his previous years' salaries had kept pace with the cost of living.

Example 4.4

An employee who retired in January 1989 was in the fortunate position of being a member of a pension scheme which allowed final salary to be calculated as the average of the best three consecutive years' salary dynamised up to the date of retirement. The salary and RPI figures for the relevant years were:

Year	Salary	RPI
1981	£23,000	78.3
1982	£25,300	82.5
1983	£27,100	86.9
1984	£29,300	90.9
1985	£31,600	96.0
1986	£34,000	99.6
1987	£36,600	103.3
1988	£40,000	110.3
1989		

The dynamised final salaries will be:

1981	£23,000 × 110.3/78.3	= £32,400
1982	£25,300 × 110.3/82.5	= £33,825
1983	£27,100 × 110.3/86.9	= £34,397
1984	£29,300 × 110.3/90.9	= £35,553
1985	£31,600 × 110.3/96.0	= £36,307
1986	£34,000 × 110.3/99.6	= £37,652
1987	£36,000 × 110.3/103.3	= £39,080
1988		

Without dynamisation, the actual final remuneration for pension purposes would be the average of the best three consecutive years, 1986–1988, ie £36,866. With dynamisation it is possible for a final notional salary of £38,910 to be used, being the average of the dynamised salaries in 1986 and 1987 plus the salary in 1988.

Dynamisation however:

(1) May not be used to increase the tax free lump sum (see below) payable to a pre-1987 member unless the pension is increased to the same proportionate extent; that is dynamisation must be justified by the increase to the overall entitlement to benefits.

(2) May not cause the final salary of a 1987–1989 member used to calculate the tax free lump sum to exceed £100,000 (or such other figure as may be prescribed by the Treasury).

(3) May not be used to increase the final salary of a post-1989 member beyond the value of the 'earnings cap' as at the date of retirement.

4.9 Retained pension benefits

Depending on the context in which maximum permitted benefits under the current employer's scheme are being calculated, retained benefits can include:

(1) Deferred pensions and pensions in payment, in respect of previous employment, from:
  (a) any UK scheme which is approved or seeking approval, including any free standing additional voluntary scheme;
  (b) any statutory scheme (eg the Teacher's Superannuation Scheme);
  (c) any overseas scheme which the Inland Revenue regards as approved for UK tax relief purposes.
(2) The annuity equivalent of lump sums received or receivable from previous pension schemes defined under (1) above.
(3) Pensions and/or the annuity equivalent of lump sums arising from personal pension schemes or retirement annuity contracts relating to service with the same or a former employer, or to previous self-employment.
(4) Benefits relating to transfer payments from overseas schemes made to any of the arrangements defined in (1), (2) or (3) above.
(5) Funds to which s 608 of ICTA 1988 applies (ie 'Old Code' funds).
(6) Benefits arising from transfer payments received by the current employer's scheme.

and if the member retired before 31 August 1991

(7) Partnership retirement annuities.
(8) The annuity equivalent of any refunds of contributions (plus interest, if applicable) from previous schemes which exceed £2,000 and were received after the age of 45.

Benefits which would otherwise have to be taken into account may however be disregarded as retained benefits in the following circumstances

(1) If the member retires on or after 31 August 1991 and
  (a) his earnings in the first year of membership of the scheme do not exceed 1/4 of the earnings cap in force at the date of entry (for the 1992/93 tax year 1/4 × £75,000 = £18,750), and
  (b) he is not, and has not been in the ten years prior to joining the scheme, a controlling director in respect of the employment being pensioned,

although if the member is or was a member of more than one scheme of the employer it is the date of entry to the first of those schemes which determines if the exemption applies, so that there is no exemption if the member joined the first scheme before 31 August 1991.
(2) Where the benefits in question relate to a wholly concurrent employment/occupation.
(3) If the total retained benefits are equivalent to or less than a pension of £260 pa.
(4) Where the benefits relate to a transfer value received from an occupational pension scheme of the same employer.

Effect of retained pension benefits on maximum benefits

If a member's benefits are calculated on the 'straight' 60ths scale it is not in any event necessary to take retained benefits into account, *unless* that member is a controlling director in which case

(1) If the controlling director is:
 (a) a pre-1987 member; or
 (b) a 1987–1989 member; or
 (c) a post-1989 member who retired before 31 August 1991; the value of all personal pension scheme/retirement annuity contract benefits has to be deducted from the straight 60ths scale benefits in order to arrive at the occupational scheme maximum.
(2) If the controlling director is a post-1989 member who retires on or after 31 August 1991, the value of personal pension scheme/retirement annuity contract benefits are required to be taken into account by treating such benefits which relate to earnings from the same employer as if they were benefits which had been provided by the occupational scheme (other retained personal pension scheme/retirement annuity contract benefits relating to previous employment can be ignored).

Whenever pension benefits are to be provided on the pre-1987 member 'uplifted 60ths' scale or 1987–1989/post 1989 member accelerated scale, the sum of the member's retained benefits and pension benefits from his current employment must not exceed 2/3rds of his final salary. In this context the pension benefit of a post-1989 controlling director member, who retires on or after 31 August 1991, from his current employment is the aggregate of that payable from the occupational scheme and from personal pension schemes/retirement annuity contracts relating to earnings from the same employer.

4.10 Pension increases (escalation)

Pensions which have been paid to a retired employee or to his dependants may be increased to reflect increases in the RPI since retirement or up to the level of the maximum approvable pension payable on retirement and then subsequently increased in line with the RPI.

Example 4.5

An employee retires from the company on a final salary of £15,000 but receives only £4,000 from his pension scheme. It would be possible for his employer subsequently to increase his pension up to £10,000, ie, 2/3rds of his final salary (assuming that he had completed at least twenty years' service with the employer) with subsequent RPI increases on the pension of £10,000.

For members who retired before 31 August 1991, the maximum approvable pension at retirement includes any amount commuted for a lump sum. On retirement on or after 31 August 1991, however, the pension cannot be increased beyond the maximum residual pension as at the date of retirement, ie after deducting the annuity equivalent of any lump sum and any spouse's/dependant's pension provided by surrender of the member's pension from the maximum approvable before either or both of those events. The maximum residual may be subsequently increased in line with the RPI.

Many schemes limit the escalation of pensions in payment to a fixed percentage, say 3% pa or 5% pa compound, while other schemes provide increases on a discretionary basis from time to time. However, the Social Security Act 1990 requires improved benefits for some early leavers, and has encouraged the trend to provide escalation of pensions in payment at 5% pa (or RPI if less).

4.11 Cash lump sums

4.11.1 80ths scale

Most pension schemes allow an employee to give up part of his pension on retirement for a tax-free cash lump sum. Even if income is of paramount importance the tax-free lump sum should still be taken and then if necessary, converted into an income which would be taxed more favourably (see Chapter 18).

The maximum tax-free lump sum that can be provided for an

employee is 1½ times his final salary after completing 40 years' service at normal retirement date: this represents 3/80ths of his final salary for each year of service.

Example 4.6

If an employee retires after 27 years' service with his employer on a salary of £20,000, and his pension scheme provides that part of his pension may be given up for a tax-free cash sum of 3/80ths of his final salary for each year of service, his lump sum will therefore be £20,250.

4.11.2 Uplifted 80ths scale for pre-1987 members

Under Inland Revenue limits pre-1987 members can obtain the maximum lump sum after 20 years' service with the same employer if the pension scheme provides lump sum benefits at an enhanced accrual rate known as the 'uplifted 80ths' scale. There is no advantage in using this scale unless the employee has achieved eight years' service before normal retirement age because the accrual rate is the same as the '80ths' scale, ie, 3/80ths of final salary per year of service. Thereafter the lump sum accrual rate increases progressively until a lump sum of 120/80ths of final salary is obtained after 20 or more years' service.

Table 4.3

Years of service to normal retirement age	Maximum lump sum as a fraction of final salary
1–8	3/80ths for each year
9	30/80
10	36/80
11	42/80
12	48/80
13	54/80
14	63/80
15	72/80
16	81/80
17	90/80
18	99/80
19	108/80
20 or more	120/80

Example 4.7

An employee retires after fifteen years' service with his employer. His final salary is £18,000. The rules of the pension scheme provide for a tax free lump sum calculated on the uplifted 80ths scale.

His tax free lump sum from the scheme will therefore be £16,200, calculated as follows: 72/80 × £18,000 = £16,200.

If, as is usually the case, the period of service includes a part of a year, the uplifted 80ths scale is interpolated to reflect the service in the last year but the result must be a whole eightieth.

4.11.3 Accelerated scale (1987-1989 members)

It is not possible for a 1987-1989 member to be provided with a tax free lump sum on the uplifted 80ths scale in isolation, although a lump sum on the 80ths scale is always permitted (ie 3/80ths of final salary for each year of service) regardless of the amount, if any, of pension benefit.

Even where the occupational scheme provides for both pension and tax-free lump sum it is only possible to provide the maximum lump sum cash on the uplifted 80ths scale if the scheme provides the maximum approvable pension benefits on the accelerated scale for pensions, ie 1/30th of final salary for each year of service. However, where the pension provided is between 1/60th and 1/30th of final salary for each year of service an enhanced cash lump sum may be payable. The formula and examples are shown below.

In calculating the maximum tax-free lump sum, final salary is still capped at a figure of £100,000 (although this may be increased by Treasury Order). For an individual who could complete 20 years' service by retirement and whose scheme provides him with a maximum approvable pension, his tax-free lump sum will be limited to £150,000 even though his final salary might be, say, £200,000.

The formula for calculating the amounts of tax-free cash on the new accelerated scale is as follows:

Formula

Step 1 $$\frac{\text{Actual pension} - \text{basic pension (on 60ths scale)}}{\text{maximum pension (30ths scale)} - \text{basic pension (60ths scale)}} = \%$$

Step 2 Maximum Tax-Free Cash − basic Tax-Free Cash × % in Step 1 above

Step 3 Add result of Step 2 to basic Tax-Free Cash = Total Tax-Free Cash permitted

Example 4.8

Service 20 years
Final Salary £30,000
Actual Pension Provided £19,000 pa

Actual pension			=	£19,000
Basic pension (1/60 scale)	=	20/60th × FS	=	£10,000
Maximum pension	=	40/60th × FS	=	£20,000
Basic cash (3/80 scale)	=	60/80th × FS	=	£22,500
Maximum cash	=	1½ × FS	=	£45,000

(a) $\dfrac{19,000 - 10,000}{20,000 - 10,000}$ = $\dfrac{9,000}{10,000}$ = 90%

(b) 45,000 − 22,500 = 22,500 × 90% = £20,250

(c) 22,500 + 20,250 = £42,750 = Tax-Free Cash permitted

Example 4.9

Service 15 years
Final Salary £30,000
Actual Pension Provided £10,000 pa

Actual pension			=	£10,000
Basic pension (1/60)	=	15/60th × FS	=	£ 7,500
Maximum pension	=	30/60th × FS	=	£15,000
Basic cash (3/80)	=	45/80th × FS	=	£16,875
Maximum cash	=	90% × FS	=	£27,000

(a) $\dfrac{10,000 - 7,500}{15,000 - 7,500}$ = $\dfrac{2,500}{7,500}$ = 33⅓%

(b) 27,000 − 16,875 = 10,125 × 33⅓% = £3,375

(c) 16,875 + 3,375 = £20,250 = Tax-Free Cash permitted

Example 4.10

Service 18 years
Final Salary £75,000
Actual Pension Provided £40,000 pa

Actual pension			=	£40,000
Basic pension	=	18/60th × FS	=	£22,500
Maximum pension	=	36/60th × FS	=	£45,000
Basic cash	=	54/80th × FS	=	£50,625
Maximum cash	=	123.75% × FS	=	£92,812

(a) $\dfrac{40,000 - 22,500}{45,000 - 22,500}$ = $\dfrac{17,500}{22,500}$ = 77.77%

(b) 92,812 − 50,625 = 42,187 × 77.77% = £32,808

(c) 50,625 + 32,808 = £83,433 = Tax-Free Cash permitted

Example 4.11

Service 15 years
Final Salary £200,000
Actual Pension Provided £90,000 pa

Actual pension			=	£ 90,000
Basic pension	=	15/60th × FS	=	£ 50,000
Maximum pension	=	30/60th × FS	=	£100,000
Basic cash	=	45/80th × £100,000	=	£ 56,250
Maximum cash	=	90% × £100,000	=	£ 90,000

(a) $\dfrac{90,000 - 50,000}{100,000 - 50,000}$ = $\dfrac{40,000}{50,000}$ = 80%

(b) 90,000 − 56,250 = 33,750 × 80% = £27,000

(c) 56,250 + 27,000 = £83,250 = Tax-Free Cash permitted

4.11.4 Scale for post-1989 members

The maximum lump sum is the greater of 3/80ths of final salary (capped at £75,000 in 1992/93) for each year of service and the pension multiplied by 2.25: 'Pension' is the amount before commutation or any reduction in favour of widows/dependants and is calculated on the basis on which it will actually be paid, eg in monthly instalments, increasing in payment at 5% pa compound.

In the case of a controlling director who retires on or after 31 August 1991 it is also required that the 3/80ths limit applies to the aggregate benefit payable from the occupational scheme and any personal pension scheme/retirement annuity contract relating to earnings from the same employer. Similarly such benefits are aggregated for the purposes of the '2.25 ×' calculation.

4.12 Retained lump sum benefits

The retained lump sum benefits which it might be necessary to take into account are those arising from the arrangements described under retained pension benefits above, as are the circumstances in which retained lump sums may be disregarded.

If a member's benefits are calculated on the 3/80ths scale it is not necessary to take retained benefits into account, unless that member is a controlling director in which case:

(1) If the controlling director is:
    (a) a pre-1987 member; or
    (b) a 1987–1989 member; or
    (c) a post-1989 member who retired before 31 August 1991; the 3/80ths scale benefits cannot exceed a maximum of 1.5 × final salary minus the value of all personal pension scheme/retirement annuity contract retained benefits.
(2) If the controlling director is a post-1989 member who retires on or after 31 August 1991, the value of personal pension scheme/retirement annuity contract benefits are required to be taken into account by treating such benefits which relate to earnings from the same employer as if they were benefits provided by the occupational scheme (other retained personal pension scheme/retirement annuity contract benefits relating to previous employment can be ignored).

Where the date of retirement is before 31 August 1991 and lump sum benefit is to be provided for a pre-1987 or 1987–1989 member on the 'uplifted 80ths' scale or is to be enhanced in the case of a post-1989 member, the sum of the member's retained benefits and lump sum benefits from his current employment must not exceed 1.5 × final salary. On retirement on or after 31 August 1991, however:

(1) Retained benefits of any 1987–1989 non-controlling director can be disregarded in calculating benefit on the 'uplifted 80ths' scale.
(2) The 'uplifted 80ths' scale benefit for a 1987–1989 controlling director is subject to a maximum of 1.5 × final salary minus retained benefits from personal pension schemes/retirement annuity contracts *only*.
(3) All retained benefits of any post-1989 member can be disregarded.

The lump sum benefit of a post-1989 controlling director, who retires on or after 31 August 1991, from his current employment is in any event the aggregate of that payable from the occupational scheme and from personal pension schemes/retirement annuity contracts relating to earnings from the same employer.

4.13 Pension values of lump sums

If a lump sum is taken under a pension scheme, any pension benefit to which the employee would be otherwise entitled, is reduced. For pre-1987 and 1987–1989 members and post-1989 members retiring before 31 August 1991, the amount by which the member's pension is reduced depends on the member's age at retirement; the following table of factors was agreed between the PSO, the Association of British Insurers and the Association of Consulting Actuaries.

Table 4.4

	Age	Factor
Men	60	10.2
	65	9.0
	70	7.8
Women	55	12.2
	60	11.0
	65	9.8

Factors for intermediate ages are calculated by an increase or decrease of 0.02 per month of age difference.

The amount by which a pension reduces is obtained by dividing the factor into the cash available. For example, a male employee retiring at age 65 and accepting a tax-free lump sum of £18,000 will have his pension reduced by £2,000 pa.

Where pensions increase at a greater rate than 5% pa compound, the PSO insist that different factors are used to reflect this. Thus, if a pension increases at say, $8\frac{1}{2}\%$ pa compound automatically, the factor used for commutation purposes must incorporate an interest yield assumption of at least $11\frac{1}{2}\%$. In other words, the difference between the rate of increase in the pension and the yield assumed on investments must be 3% at least.

Trustees of pension schemes are not bound by any of these factors and may use less generous ones reflecting economic conditions from time to time. Insurance companies may agree tables of commutation factors with the PSO.

However for post-1989 members retiring on or after 31 August 1991 the commutation factor which must be used in calculating Inland Revenue limits is a unisex 12:1 regardless of escalation.

It is sometimes difficult for a retiring employee to decide whether he should take a tax-free lump sum or opt for a pension which will increase in payment. Chapter 18 deals with some of the considerations which should influence his decision.

4.14 Death benefits

4.14.1 Benefits on death after retirement

A pension can be provided for the widow or dependants of a former employee who dies in retirement. The maximum amount is 2/3rds of the maximum approvable pension which could have been provided for the employee himself ignoring his retained benefits from earlier occupations. As the maximum will normally be 2/3rds of the employee's final salary, the widow or dependant's maximum pension is 2/3rds of 2/3rds of the employee's final salary (4/9ths).

If the member retired before 31 August 1991 then any widow's/dependant's pension payable from the arrangements described under retained pension benefits above must be deducted from the 4/9ths maximum.

Whether or not retained benefits have to be taken into account,

Maximum permitted benefits 47

the widow's/dependant's maximum may be increased in line with the increase in the RPI since the date of the member's retirement.

The reduction in the maximum approvable member's pension for short-serving employees, which applies to 1987–1989 members and post-1989 members, also has the effect of reducing dependants' pensions.

Where pensions are paid to a widow and one or more dependants (or if there is no widow, to more than one dependant) no individual pension can exceed the above maximum, nor can the aggregate of all the pensions exceed the maximum pension which could have been provided for the employee.

It is possible for these pensions to increase in line with the RPI calculated from the date at which the employee would have retired (rather than from the time the widow's or dependant's pension commences).

A widow's or dependant's pension can start at the date of the employee's death (unless the employee's pension was guaranteed to be paid for a period exceeding five years, when the pension cannot start until the end of the guarantee period). The widow's pension and dependant's pension can continue for life or can cease or reduce on remarriage. Any pension received by a child must cease when the child ceases to be a dependant. A dependant is someone who is financially dependent on the employee. A widow's or dependant's pension must cease on death: no guaranteed period may apply as in the case of an employee's own pension, unless the pension has been provided by surrender.

An employee may surrender part of his own pension to provide one for his widow or dependant on his death in retirement, either because the widow/dependant has no pension entitlement in his or her own right or because the employee wishes to enhance an own right pension. The maximum pension which is allocated in this way must not exceed the amount of the reduced pension (either before commutation, or including the annuity equivalent of any separate lump sum) which is payable to the employee and if more than one allocated pension is provided, the limit applies to their aggregate value. A widow's or dependant's pension provided by this method can start at the date of the employee's death, even if his residual pension continues to be paid under a guarantee not exceeding five years.

The employee's pension can be guaranteed for a period of up to ten years, even though he dies during that period. If the guaranteed period is five years or less the balance of the pension payable following the death of the retired employee in that period can be paid as a lump sum. For example, if the employee's pension amounted to £1,000 pa, commencing at age 65 and the employee died at age 67, having received two instalments of pension a lump sum could be paid to his dependants amounting to £3,000. The destination of these payments can be at the discretion of the scheme trustees to a wide range of beneficiaries and are normally exempt from income tax and inheritance tax.

Widowers' pensions can be provided on a similar basis to widows' pensions as set out above.

4.14.2 Benefits on death in service

If death occurs in service the following maximum benefits may be provided.

Lump sums

A lump sum may be provided not exceeding the greater of £5,000, and four times the final remuneration of the employee at the date of death (minus any retained benefits), together with a refund of any personal contributions paid by the employee with or without interest: the interest may represent the actual rate of growth on those contributions. For post-1989 members, final remuneration is subject to the earnings limit of £75,000 (in 1992/93). Thus the maximum lump sum is £300,000 (plus a refund of personal contributions with growth, as before).

The retained benefits are those payable on death in service from the arrangements described under retained pension benefits above, but lump sum death benefits may be disregarded under the following conditions:

(1) Where the member satisfied the 1/4 earnings cap exemption.
(2) If the benefits total £2,500 or less.
(3) Where they represent a return of fund under a personal pension scheme or retirement annuity contract.
(4) When payable from a personal pension scheme providing contracted-out benefits only.
(5) When they are a refund of member contributions under an occupational scheme (other than a free standing AVC scheme).

(6) Where the benefits in question relate to a wholly concurrent employment/occupation.

The destination of lump sum death in service payments can be at the discretion of the trustees of the scheme in which case they are normally free of inheritance tax. The rules of the pension scheme will specify the classes of individual to whom such payments may be made. Normally the employee will have notified the trustees of his wishes regarding the person or persons to whom he would like the monies to be paid although the trustees are not bound by this nomination.

Spouses' and dependants' pensions

A pension for a spouse or dependant may be provided equal to 2/3rds of the maximum pension that could have been approved for the employee assuming he or she had not died but had continued in employment to normal retirement age with the same final salary as he or she was earning at the time of death. The maximum pension, therefore, is 4/9ths of the employee's salary at the date of death (subject to the earnings limit in the case of a post-1989 member).

Where the deceased member was a 1987–1989 member the maximum pension for a spouse or dependant may again be lower, as a result of the reduction in the maximum approvable member's pension for short-serving employees.

In the same way as on death in retirement, pensions can also be provided for other dependants, including children, providing the total income payable to spouses and dependants does not exceed the maximum level of pension which could have been provided for the deceased, had he or she remained in service to normal retirement age. A widow's or widower's pension is normally payable for life but could cease or reduce on remarriage. Pensions for children must cease at the age of 18 or completion of full time education or training, if later.

Escalation of death in service benefits

Spouse's and dependant's pensions may automatically increase in payment in a similar manner to that described above for members' pensions.

Dynamised final remuneration

In calculating maximum benefits on death in service, use may be made of dynamised final remuneration, as explained in 4.8.

50 Allied Dunbar Pensions Guide

Final remuneration need not be defined in the same terms as for the calculation of other benefits. It may be defined in the following ways:

(1) where basic salary only is involved, the annual rate of salary being received immediately before death;
(2) basic salary as above, plus the average of fluctuating emoluments during the three years (or the whole period of the employment if less) up to the date of death;
(3) the total earnings (fixed plus fluctuating) paid during a selected period of 12 months prior to death (the selected period may end either at the date of death, or on some convenient date, such as 5 April, or the end of the pension scheme year, falling not earlier than 36 months prior to the date of death).

Death in service after normal retirement date

Where an employee has deferred his retirement and dies during his extended service, benefits may be paid on either of the following bases:

(1) that he died before normal retirement date and therefore normal death in service benefits may be provided; or
(2) that he retired the day before he died and is, therefore, entitled to death in retirement benefits.

If an employee has taken any benefit at normal retirement date, for example, the tax-free cash sum and subsequently dies in service, any death benefits are limited to those payable on death after retirement.

The rules of the scheme will specify which method is to be used in the event of death during deferred retirement.

4.15 Retirement

4.15.1 Retirement before normal retirement date

An employee can take an immediate pension and lump sum if his employment is terminated or if he retires early, from age 50. Female employees who joined schemes approved before November 1991 can take immediate benefits at age 45, provided they are within ten years of their normal retirement date.

4.15.2 Early retirement (not through ill-health)

Pre-1987 members and 1987-1989 members

As an alternative to using the straight 60ths and 3/80ths scales, maximum benefits can be calculated in accordance with the formulae:

$$\frac{N}{NS} \times P \text{ or } \frac{N}{NS} \times LS$$

'N' is the number of years which have been completed in service to the point of early retirement (maximum 40).

'NS' is the number of years which could have been completed from the date of joining service to normal retirement date.

'P' and 'LS' are, respectively, the maximum pension and tax free lump sum which could have been approved had the employee retired at his normal retirement date but based on his final remuneration at the date of his early retirement.

For example, a pre-1987 member who joined the scheme at the age of 25, expecting to retire at age 60 but who retires early at the age of 50, on a salary of £9,000 per annum may be provided with a maximum early retirement pension of £4,285, calculated as follows:

£9,000 × 2/3rds × 25/35 = £4,285 pa

He could exchange part of the above early retirement pension for a lump sum calculated on a similar basis as follows:

£9,000 × 1½ × 25/35 = £9,642

These are the overall limits and include the value of any retained benefits (see above) which must be deducted from the value of 'P' and 'LS' before applying N/NS. Any dependants' benefits are then directly related to the reduced pension.

Post-1989 members

The method of calculating the pension is much simpler. The alternative to the straight 60ths benefit is normally a maximum of 1/30th of final remuneration for each year of service completed up to the date of early retirement. Thus, if an employee has completed twenty years service a maximum pension of 2/3rds of final remuneration may be provided from age 50 onwards.

Money purchase schemes

Under money purchase schemes approved before 29 November 1991 whose rules have been suitably drafted and under all money purchase schemes approved on or after 29 November 1991, the 'normal' early retirement pension maxima described above do not apply. The permitted maximum (as an alternative to straight 60ths) is the same as that on early retirement through ill health (incapacity), ie based on potential service to normal retirement age and final salary at the date of early retirement.

4.15.3 Early retirement through ill health

If the reason for early retirement is ill health, the maximum benefits payable are those which could have been payable at normal retirement date but based on the level of final remuneration at the date of early retirement.

Thus, a person with potentially at least twenty years' service to normal retirement date may receive a maximum early retirement pension of 2/3rds of his final salary in the event of early retirement through ill health. The same principle applies to his tax-free lump sum.

'Ill health' means incapacity (physical or mental) which prevents the employee from following his normal employment or seriously impairs his earning capacity.

Where an employee is in exceptional circumstances of ill health such that his life expectancy is undoubtedly very short by comparison with the norm for his age and sex (ie measured in months rather than years), he may be able to exchange the whole of his early retirement pension for an immediate cash sum although this will not be totally free of tax. The value of the pension which, but for the seriousness of the ill health, would not have been commutable, will be subject to tax at 20%.

4.15.4 Benefits on late retirement

An employee who remains in service after normal retirement date can be provided with such additional pension benefits up to the normal maximum as would be available assuming that his actual retirement date is his normal retirement date.

1987-1989 members
If his total service exceeds 40 years, he will be entitled to an additional pension of 1/60th of his final salary in respect of each year in excess of 40 which occurs after reaching normal retirement date: there is an overall maximum of 45/60ths of final salary at the date of retirement.

As an alternative to accruing additional 60ths, the maximum benefits available at normal retirement date may be increased by the greater of the actuarial increase reflecting the period of deferment and the growth in the underlying fund, or the increase in the RPI during the period of deferment.

A similar basis is used for calculating the increased tax free lump sum on late retirement. Where total service exceeds 40 years, each year over 40 occurring after normal retirement date can generate an additional lump sum of 3/80ths of final salary at the date of actual retirement, subject to a maximum lump sum of 135/80ths of final salary. Alternatively the lump sum available at normal retirement date can be increased on a reasonable basis — in line with the increase in the underlying pension funds investments.

Post-1989 membership
No additional benefits may be provided in respect of service completed beyond normal retirement date above the maximum approvable pension at normal retirement date.

14.15.5 Options on retirement

On reaching normal retirement date, it is normally possible (depending on the rules of the scheme) to:

(1) take all the benefits — cash and pension (it is likely in these circumstances that the employee will be retiring from the company);
(2) to defer all the benefits (consistent with continuing to work with the employer or joining a new employer);
(3) take the tax free lump sum and defer the pension or vice versa (while continuing in service).

Special rules apply to 20% directors, and are explained in Chapter 6.

In respect of post-1989 members option (2) is of limited value because the maximum approvable pension is not increased beyond normal retirement date and option (3) is not permitted.

Greater flexibility may be achieved by transferring the fund into a personal pension plan (see Chapter 14).

4.16 Trivial benefits

Where the total annual value of all pensions to an employee from the same employer do not exceed £260 pa it is possible for the whole of the pension to be commuted for a lump sum. This does not apply where the member who is entitled to a pension which exceeds £260 pa, commutes part of it for a lump sum and has a residual pension of £260 pa or less.

4.17 Combinations of schemes

The changes introduced by Finance (No 2) Act 1987 and Finance Act 1989 have given rise to questions about the levels of benefits which may be provided for members who move to new or reconstructed schemes or join schemes to provide additional benefits. It is the broad intention that members of a scheme who remain with the same employer or who effectively remain members of the same scheme should not be adversely affected by any subsequent changes.

4.18 Finance (No 2) Act 1987

Inland Revenue Memorandum No 87, issued in August 1987, describes those situations in which pre-1987 members will not normally be regarded as caught by the changes — which apply to 1987–1989 members — introduced by the Finance (No 2) Act 1987 as follows:

(1) Restructuring of a business (or re-organisation of pension arrangements) resulting in employees moving from one employer's scheme to another's, provided that both employers are within the same group and that such changes do not give accelerated rates of accrual under the pre-17 March rules where these were not previously available.
(2) A move (eg on promotion) from one scheme of an employer to another scheme of that same employer, or of another employer in the same group.
(3) The joining (eg on promotion) of a separate top-up scheme

which provides additional benefits to those under the main scheme in respect of which the individual remains a member.
(4) A move to a new or existing scheme of a new employer who has taken over the old employer (or all or part of his business), provided that the individual was a member of the old employer's scheme.
(5) Changes in the benefits structure of an existing scheme, provided that such changes do not give accelerated rates of accrual under the pre-17 March rules where these were not previously available.
(6) The exercise of a power of augmentation under the rules of an existing scheme to improve the benefits available to a member who joined before 17 March 1987, provided that the rules contained such a power before that date.
(7) Schemes or arrangements established before 17 March 1987, even if by then all the relevant documentation had not been finalised or no application for tax approval had been made. This will usually depend on the facts of a particular case but, as a general rule, a scheme will be in this category if, before 17 March 1987, the employer had entered into a contractual obligation to provide benefits.
(8) Changes to an existing scheme to permit it to contract out of SERPS or the establishment of a new scheme to enable existing members to contract out.
(9) Employees who leave their employer's scheme as a result of a temporary posting or secondment to another employer (whether in the United Kingdom or abroad), provided that at the time of leaving the scheme there was a definite intention to return and that on return they rejoin a scheme of the original employer, or of another employer in the same group.
(10) Individuals not covered by (9) above who cease to be members of their employer's scheme (whether or not they leave the employer's service), provided that they rejoin the scheme within one month. Where absence is due to maternity leave, temporary lay-off or redundancy a longer period may be appropriate.
(11) Employees serving a waiting period before becoming full members of the employer's scheme, provided that they were regarded as members before 17 March 1987, for preservation purposes.

The Finance (No 2) Act 1987 restrictions applying to 1987–1989 members, who, *after* 17 March 1987, joined schemes which were approved *before* the Act received Royal Assent on 23 July 1987, are set out in Schedule 23 to the Income and Corporation Taxes

Act 1988. However that Schedule permits the Inland Revenue to waive the 1987–1989 restrictions in relation to an employee:

(1) In circumstances prescribed by The Occupational Pension Schemes (Transitional Provisions) Regulations 1988;
(2) By the exercise of Inland Revenue discretion.

4.19 Finance Act 1989

The Inland Revenue published Memorandum 100 in October 1989 in which they reiterated their intention that, broadly speaking, scheme members whose benefit entitlement is on a pre-1987 or 1987–1989 basis should not be adversely affected, if, because of corporate changes, pension scheme reconstructions etc, they join new schemes to which the post-1989 restrictions apply. Regulations have now been made, the Retirement Benefits Schemes (Continuation of Rights of Members of Approved Schemes) Regulations 1990, which achieve this in relation to schemes approved before 27 July 1989.

In the 1991 Practice Notes the Inland Revenue has repeated that it may grant continued rights to pre-1987 and 1987–1989 members who would otherwise be joining schemes as post-1989 members in the following circumstances:

(1) Benefits on the old basis cease to accrue under a scheme for a member who:
    (a) changes schemes within an association of employers to which the new earnings restriction applies in aggregate; or
    (b) joins a scheme of an employer who has acquired, been acquired by, merged with or taken over the whole or part of the business of his employer; or
    (c) returns to the scheme (or joins an associated scheme as in (a) and (b) above) after a temporary secondment or posting, or within one month of returning to work after maternity leave, or
    (d) returns to the scheme (or joins an associated scheme as in (a) or (b) above within one month of any unpaid absence, or
    (e) in any other circumstance provided that the member rejoins the scheme within one month of ceasing to accrue benefits.

(2) Before 1 June 1989 the member joined a scheme established before 14 March 1989, and on or after 1 June 1989 joins a supplementary scheme.
(3) An employee who served a waiting period for a scheme established before 14 March 1989, provided he was regarded as a member before that date for preservation purposes.
(4) An employee who while not a member had a contractual right to benefits before 1 June 1989 in a scheme established before 14 March 1989.

The Finance Act 1989 restrictions applying to post-1989 members who *after* 14 March 1989 join schemes approved *before* the Act received Royal Assent on 27 July 1987 are set out in Sched 6 to that Act. However, that Schedule permits the Inland Revenue to waive the post-1989 restrictions:

(1) In the circumstances prescribed by The Retirement Benefit Schemes (Continuation of Rights of Members of Approved Schemes) Regulations 1990.
(2) By the exercise of Inland Revenue discretion.

4.20 Opting for post-1989 benefits

A pre-1987 member may opt to receive the benefits applicable to a post-1989 member if the trustees of the scheme are prepared to allow his benefits to be augmented and if the scheme rules are amended. For example, a pre-1987 member may wish to retire at age 50 on a pension of two-thirds of his final remuneration: this would not be permissible under pre-1987 rules although under post-1989 rules this would be permissible subject to the earnings cap.

A 1987-1989 member may opt to be classed as a post-1989 member should the result be beneficial. Once again the member has to accept the earnings cap but in these circumstances there is no requirement for the trustees of the scheme to permit the election because the right to make that election is conferred by statute.

4.21 Associated employments

It is not uncommon for an individual to draw earnings from two or more employments which are associated and for these employments to provide pension benefits for the individual.

The Finance Act 1989 provides that employers are associated if one is controlled by the other (eg parent and wholly owned subsidiary) or both are controlled by the same third party (eg wholly owned subsidiaries of the same parent).

4.21.1 Connected schemes

For post-1989 members this means that:

(1) Two or more schemes of such associated employers are *connected schemes* if:
    (a) there is a period during which the member is an employee of the associated employers;
    (b) that period is one for which benefits are payable under the scheme of each associated employer;
    (c) under each scheme that period counts as service with the relevant associated employer.

(2) Under any occupational scheme the Inland Revenue limits apply to the total benefits payable:
    (a) in respect of all associated employers participating in the scheme; and
    (b) from all connected schemes; and
    (c) if the member is a controlling director who retires on or after 31 August 1991, from personal pension schemes/ retirement annuity contracts relating to earnings from associated employers participating in the scheme.

(3) The earnings cap applies to aggregate pensionable remuneration payable from associated employers providing benefits under the scheme and/or under any connected scheme.

For all members moves between such associated employers can (and for post-1989 members must) be regarded as constituting a single unbroken employment. Pre-1987 or 1987–1989 members who make that move therefore have, usually, a continued right to benefits calculated on pre-1987 or 1987–1989 limits, whether they remain in the same scheme or join another of the associated employers.

4.21.2 Permanent community of interests

The Inland Revenue will also approve the inclusion in a scheme which although not an associated employer in terms of the statutory definition, is associated with the employer who established the scheme through a permanent community of interests, such as common management or shareholders, interchangeable or jointly employed staff or interdependent operations, eg one selling the bulk of the other's products.

Where employers are associated through a permanent community of interests

(1) Moves between them by pre-1987 and 1987–1989 members who are not controlling directors can be regarded as constituting a single unbroken employment with continued benefit rights (ie they are treated the same as those who move between employers who are associated in terms of the statutory definition).
(2) The benefits of pre-1987 and 1987–1989 and post-1989 controlling directors must be calculated separately for each employment and the limits applying to each will depend, generally speaking, on the date of joining the relevant employer.

If however the scheme was approved before 27 July 1989 any member will, where appropriate, have continued rights to pre-1989 limits if he joins an employer which participated in the scheme before 14 March 1989, irrespective of the nature of the association between the employers.

4.22 Multiple employments

It is not uncommon for people to have two or more completely separate employments, one assessable under Schedule D and the other or others assessable under Schedule E. Examples might be a teacher working for a local authority who also does private tuition work, or an accountant in practice who is also a director in his family firm. In these cases retirement and death benefits may be provided through an approved retirement benefit scheme in respect of the service and income from the Schedule E employment while completely separate pension provision may be made through retirement annuity contracts and personal pension schemes in respect of the Schedule D income.

If the earnings from the multiple employments are classified under Schedule E then retirement benefit schemes may be set up in respect of each separate employment, although complications arise if the employments are neither associated (see above) nor wholly concurrent.

Where the concurrent employment extends to only part of the member's overall service with the employers, the benefits from one scheme relating to a period when the employments are not concurrent must be taken into account under the other as retained benefits, ie as if they were benefits of a previous employer, unless:

(1) In relation to a pre-1987 or 1987–1989 member the employers are associated through control (see above) and:
   (a) each participates in the other's scheme; or
   (b) only one employer participates in both schemes, in which case the scheme with the single employer will have to take only the non-concurrent benefits relating to service with the associated employer under the other scheme into account as retained benefits.
(2) In relation to a post-1989 member, the schemes are connected schemes (see above).

5 Unapproved pension schemes

5.1 Introduction

Finance Act 1989 allowed employers to establish unapproved pension schemes providing benefits in excess of those permitted under approved schemes (see Chapter 4). This change in legislation was partly cosmetic in that it disguised the restrictions placed on new approved occupational schemes by Finance Act 1989. The change also provides opportunities for employers to provide more flexible remuneration packages for high earners who would be restricted by the earnings cap under approved pension schemes and for those with less than 20 years' service to retirement who would be unable to obtain a maximum approvable pension. However, these opportunities are at the expense of the generous tax reliefs available to approved schemes, some or all of which will not be available to unapproved schemes. Guidance Notes on the tax treatment of top-up pension schemes were published in August 1991 by the Inland Revenue: these Notes have been used in parts of this Chapter.

5.2 Summary of effects of changes

(1) The major change is that benefits from 'approved' and 'unapproved' schemes no longer need to be considered in aggregate. In the past, membership of an unapproved scheme would render invalid membership of the approved scheme.
(2) The changes focus attention on the definition of 'retirement benefit schemes': this expression will generally be assumed to include a conventional occupational scheme or arrangement set up under trust and approved by the Inland Revenue for tax purposes. However, other arrangements may also fall within the meaning of this expression. For example, an insurance policy taken out by an employer on the life of a 'keyman' in the organisation might be regarded as an

unapproved pension scheme if the employee can expect that it will be assigned to him on retirement — a form of 'golden handshake'. (A keyman policy is one which pays out benefits to the employer in the event of the death of the keyman to provide a cushion until such time as the employer is able to employ another employee of similar calibre.)

(3) Employees will be taxed on contributions to 'funded' schemes at the time the contributions are paid. A scheme is 'funded' for these purposes when the payment is made 'with a view to provision of' benefits for the employee.

(4) In the case of unfunded schemes employees are taxed on the benefits they receive, but funded schemes can provide a full tax-free lump sum (although pensions are taxable).

(5) The tax treatment of contributions by employers to funded unapproved pension schemes is at the discretion of the local Inspector of Taxes. It is likely that in some cases these contributions will not be deductible expenses particularly where contributions are paid by private limited companies to schemes set up for members who are directors of those companies. The proposed changes to the maximum permissible funding rates that may be paid into typical directors' pension arrangements — to take effect towards the end of 1992 (see Chapter 7) — will make it more difficult for directors to make maximum use of the tax advantages of approved pension schemes, leading to more interest in unapproved schemes.

(6) The treatment of the National Insurance contributions (NIC) in respect of contributions by employers and benefits from unapproved pension schemes is not entirely clear, although it is possible that NIC will not be payable in many situations.

(7) Inheritance tax may be payable on the contributions to and the benefits from an unapproved scheme.

5.3 Retirement benefits scheme

One feature of the development of unapproved pension schemes is that more attention will have to be paid to the definition of 'retirement benefits scheme'. In the past employers generally knew when they were setting up a 'pension scheme' and approval was sought and obtained. In future the greater flexibility permitted by the amendment of Finance Act 1989, s 590(7) will permit the establishment of schemes which look less like a true pension scheme.

This focuses attention on what is a 'retirement benefits scheme' and what is not. This distinction is likely to be important as it may determine the tax treatment of both the contributions and the benefits.

A 'retirement benefits scheme' is 'a scheme for the provision of benefits consisting of or including relevant benefits'. (See ICTA 1988, s 611(1)). This definition makes it important to define the meaning of:

(1) 'Scheme'; and
(2) 'Relevant benefits'.

Scheme is defined by s 611(2) as including:

> 'Reference to a deed, agreement, series of agreements, or other arrangements providing for relevant benefits notwithstanding that it relates or they relate only to:
>
> (a) small number of employees, or to a single employee, or,
> (b) the payment of a pension starting immediately on the making of the arrangements.'

This definition is wide and is capable of encompassing many arrangments which would not perhaps be regarded as 'schemes' in the accepted sense. However, it is not as wide as it may at first appear because the word 'arrangement' must be read in the light of the preceding words 'deed' or 'agreement'. Both of these words denote a form of binding obligation (on the employer). It is possible that a letter from an employer promising a lump sum at retirement could constitute a scheme and that, theoretically at least, nothing in writing is needed at all. Following an Inland Revenue change of practice in October 1991 the Revenue now consider that an *ex gratia* pension or a lump sum may be capable of constituting a retirement benefit scheme.

The difficulty in deciding whether a 'scheme' exists is quite simply how far can the employer go in informing the employee and making any form of commitment without creating a scheme? The answer is not likely to be far, especially where the employee is continuing in employment and is thus working for his potential entitlement.

5.3.1 Relevant benefits

The second part of the definition of retirement benefits scheme is the definition of 'relevant benefits'. These are defined by s 612(1) as:

'Any pension, lump sum, gratuity or other like benefit given or to be given on retirement or on death, or in anticipation of retirement, or, in connection with past service, after retirement or death, or to be given on or in anticipation of or in connection with any change in the nature of the service of the employee in question, except that it does not include any benefit which is to be afforded solely by reason of the disablement by accident of a person occurring during his service or of his death by accident so occuring and for no other reason'.

One commentary on the definition says that 'relevant benefits ... are defined so widely that they could possibly be stretched to cover practically every kind of benefit paid or provided by an employer except remuneration paid during service'.

The only clear feature of the definition is that accidental death and disability benefits are not relevant benefits. However, this only applies to accidental death and disability benefits (although the accident need not have occured at work). It is clear that ordinary death benefits are relevant benefits although it is not clear whether disablement benefits generally are caught.

The answer probably depends on whether the individual can be said to have 'retired' and the better view is that there is a distinction between 'sick pay' (where the individual expects to return to work) which is not a relevant benefit, and a 'disability pension' or a lump sum disability benefit (where the individual does not expect to return to work) which are likely to be relevant benefits.

Finally it is not necessary for the creation of a scheme for there to be a direct contract between the employer and employee for the provision of the relevant benefits. Section 612(2) provides that references to the provision of relevant benefits include 'the provision of relevant benefits ... by means of a contract between the Administrator (of the scheme) or the employer or the employee and a third person'. The reference to the employee would appear to make it theoretically possible for an insurance policy effected by the employee himself to constitute a scheme providing relevant benefits. For this to be the case it is probably necessary for some employer involvement but this could be satisfied if the employer promised to pay the contributions for the employee. Of course, whether the Revenue would seek to extend the definition this far is doubtful.

5.4 Taxation of contributions — position of the employer

Contributions to an exempt approved scheme attract automatic tax relief for the employer by virtue of ICTA 1988, s 592(4). Contributions paid by the employer to an unapproved scheme do not qualify for relief automatically but *may* be relievable under the ordinary rules of Schedule D.

In order to be deductible, expenditure has to be in broad terms:

(1) incurred wholly and exclusively for the purposes of the business;
(2) not incurred for any other non-business purpose;
(3) expenditure of an income nature and not a capital nature;
(4) the expenditure must actually have been incurred.

These rules impact on expenditure on a pension scheme in the following ways:

(1) it is often difficult to argue that pension schemes for employees are wholly and exclusively for the purposes of the business;
(2) it is easy to imply a non-business purpose (eg a personal benefit) where the employees also have a significant shareholding in the company (or are relatives of such persons);
(3) it is often common to put in a lump sum to start a pension scheme (in order to make provision for past service) which could be regarded as a capital payment; and
(4) merely saving money or investing it may not be expenditure for these purposes.

5.5 Obtaining tax relief

As can be seen the test for obtaining tax relief is strict. The key features for schemes are:

(1) there is likely to be a need to put the assets of schemes beyond the reach of the company (perhaps directly in the hands of the employee or a trust for his benefit);
(2) there is likely to be a 'reasonableness' test in the level of benefits (ie it might become more difficult to justify high levels of pension as being wholly and exclusively for the purposes of the trade);

(3) deductibility is more likely in respect of arms length employees (ie non-shareholder directors) than employees with a proprietary interest or relatives of such persons;

(4) if the company merely sets up an accounting reserve to meet a liability under an unfunded scheme payments into the reserve are not regarded as expenditure and, therefore, are non-deductible;

(5) payments of lump sums and the purchase of annuities at retirement under unfunded schemes should be deductible if they satisfy the general rules for deductibility.

5.6 Taxation of contributions — position of the employee

'A payment made by an employer into a fund or by way of premium on an insurance policy is assessable upon the employee as an emolument of his office under the ordinary rules of Schedule E if the employee has an *absolute* right to his proportionate share of the fund'. (IR12 (1979), PN 23.1).

Thus, if an employee has an absolute right to benefit from a fund or policy the amounts paid in are taxable under ordinary principles and the specific rules relating to pension schemes do not apply. Those specific rules were introduced to catch a simple dodge. Rather than giving the employee an absolute right to benefit it was possible to make his benefits contingent on reaching retirement. This was actually quite common before Finance Act 1947 imposed the charge to tax on schemes where the employee's benefit was contingent.

This legislation is now contained in ICTA 1988, s 595. Subsection (1) deals with 'where, pursuant to a retirement benefits scheme, the employer ... pays a sum with a view to the provision of any relevant benefits for any employee (whether or not the accrual of the benefits is dependent on any contingency)'. These are what the Revenue call 'funded schemes' ie where the employer is actually making payments to provide the benefits.

However, s 595(1) is insufficient on its own to tax all situations where the employer has set up a scheme (ie made a commitment or promise of relevant benefits). If the employer did not fund in advance no tax would be payable.

Prior to Finance Act 1989, s 595(2) and (3) ICTA 1988 provided for the notional cost of providing the relevant benefit, based on actuarial principles, to be taxed in the hands of the employee. Section 596(A) now replaces these sections the consequence of which is that no charge will arise on 'unfunded' schemes but one would arise where the scheme is 'funded'.

The employee will be chargeable to tax where, to reiterate the words of s 595(1), the employer: 'pays a sum with a view to the provision of relevant benefits'. In effect this is the Inland Revenue's definition of 'funded schemes'.

The key question is what constitutes payment in this context. Clearly, merely setting aside money in the accounts of the employer does not constitute payment. However, does the purchase of a policy by the employer for the employee's benefit constitute a payment? Arguably it is a payment which, if made with a view to provide a benefit to the employee, is taxable in the hands of the employee. This could be so even if the employer is using the policy merely to save and not as the vehicle to provide the relevant benefits. At the other end of the scale, contributions to a trust holding a policy for the employee would constitute a payment and would be taxable in the hands of the employee.

The issue is, of course, linked with the question of the deductibility of the contribution in the hands of the employer and it seems theoretically possible for an employee to be taxed on the payment and for the contribution not to be deductible (ie the worst of all worlds).

This could apply where, say, a trust fund is established for the benefit of an employee to provide him with a pension but the employer can wind up the trust, or if the employee were a director or substantial shareholder of the company.

Where employers make contributions to unapproved pension schemes employees will not see any immediate benefits, but rather a tax charge, which could lead to pressure to increase employees' salaries. This in itself will be taxable and subject to employer's NIC (10.4%) giving considerable extra costs.

If an employer wants to meet the employee's tax liability on the contributions they may agree a grossing arrangement. The grossed-up equivalent of the actual chargeable contribution, and the tax figure, should then be included on the employer's pay record (form P11) for the pay period in which the contributions are paid. Contributions paid by an employer without a grossing arrangement should be notified by the employer at the end of the year to the Tax Office on a form P9D or P11D.

5.7 Taxation of the fund

In the case of unapproved unfunded schemes, there is by definition no fund but in the case of unapproved funded schemes, the scheme assets will not enjoy tax benefits available to exempt approved pension funds. Tax will be payable on investment income and on chargeable capital gains. However, if the fund is under a discretionary trust the additional tax normally applicable to such trusts will not apply as the exemption from this applies to all retirement benefits including unapproved ones. Even if the fund is established outside the UK tax will still be payable on dividends from UK companies and if the fund is eventually brought into the UK there may be a capital gains tax charge when the fund is distributed.

If the fund is invested in a life assurance policy, even if the policy is a qualifying policy, or any annuity policy there is a potential tax charge under new rules introduced in Finance Act 1989 (Schedule 9). If the policy is held by a company or under a trust set up by a company any investment profit realised from the policy is liable to corporation tax under the chargeable event legislation contained in ICTA 1988. In any case, the life assurance company's fund will be subject to tax as the policy will not form part of its pensions business exempt fund.

5.8 Taxation of lump sum benefits

Where the employee has an absolute right to the fund or insurance policy (and would be liable to tax under Schedule E), ie under a funded scheme, it appears that those benefits when paid as a lump sum would be tax free. This is purely based on the point of view that what is received as a lump sum is not a payment by the employer at all but the receipt of something to which the employee has already been absolutely entitled (and has been taxed upon).

Where this is not the case (ie the employee has not been taxed on the benefit) ICTA 1988, s 148 provides that tax under Schedule E is charged in respect of 'any payment (not otherwise chargeable to tax) which is made, whether in pursuance of any legal obligation or not, either directly or indirectly in consideration or in consequence of, or otherwise in connection with, the termination of the holding of the office or employment.' This would apply to tax on all payments (not otherwise taxable) from retirement benefit schemes were it not for a specific exemption.

Sections 188(1) and 189(b) provide this exemption. Section 188(1) provides an exemption for:

> '(c) a benefit provided in pursuance of a retirement benefits scheme ... where under Section ... 595 the holder of the office or employment was chargeable to tax in respect of sums paid, or treated as paid, with the view to the provision of the benefit'.

There is also a provision exempting payments from approved schemes.

Effectively ss 188(1)(c) and 189(b) operate to exempt all lump sum payments from funded unapproved schemes where tax is paid on the contributions. In the case of unfunded schemes there is no exemption and tax is payable on any lump sum payment.

5.9 Taxation of pensions

At present it is unlikely that any funded unapproved scheme would pay out a pension. If a pension is required, the better route for the employee is to take a lump sum and purchase a purchased life annuity. All pensions payable by the scheme will be taxed under the ordinary rules of Schedule E.

5.10 Inheritance tax

Inheritance tax is generally of little concern to approved pension schemes but is much more important in the case of unapproved schemes. First, it is possible for a liability of IHT to arise in respect of any contributions paid by a close company to a funded scheme if the contributions are not regarded as deductible business expense. For example, a close company could not transfer large amounts into an unapproved pension trust for the benefit of a shareholder director without the possibility of a deemed transfer of value being made by the participators in the company.

Most unapproved schemes are likely to be 'sponsored superannuation schemes' because even where the employee is charged to income tax under s 595(1), that tax does not cover the costs of setting up and running the scheme. For IHT, this means that unapproved schemes set up under trust may be sponsored schemes, if there are separately identifiable setting up and running costs and such schemes will fall within IHTA 1984, s 151. As a result, the normal IHT charges on settled property will not apply. So, for example, benefits paid out under such schemes will be free of any IHT trust charges.

Broadly, it is only death benefits that may be liable to IHT. Tax is chargeable if the benefit is expressed to be payable only to the deceased's estate. But commonly, death benefits may be paid at the employer's or scheme administrator's discretion to one or more of a specified group of possible beneficiaries as under approved schemes. In these cases IHT will not generally be payable if the employee's estate is excluded from this group. However, there remains the possibility of an inheritance tax gift with reservation (GWR) charge. Unlike tax approved schemes, where the GWR rules do not apply (see Inland Revenue press release of 9 July 1986) there remains the possibility of an IHT charge on benefits from an unapproved scheme if the employee is deemed by the Inland Revenue to have retained a benefit from the scheme.

5.11 National Insurance contributions

National Insurance contributions are payable on 'earnings'. These are broadly defined as 'any remuneration or profit derived from any trade business, profession, office or vocation'. It is not clear how payments into an unapproved scheme are treated.

Payments which are regarded as 'benefits in kind' are excluded for NIC purposes. This would include the circumstance where the employer pays a contribution on behalf of the employee under a policy taken out by the *employer*. Where the policy is taken out by the *employee*, the premiums would be regarded as 'earnings' and liable to NIC.

If the scheme is set up under trust it is likely that payments to the trustees would be 'benefits in kind' or not 'earnings' at all (in the same way as payments to existing approved schemes). There have been some special provisions relating to employee trusts, in recent years a number of employers made payments to discretionary trusts in order to avoid NIC. These exempting provisions have now been repealed which suggests that perhaps payments via trusts should be liable to NIC but the better view is that they are probably not 'earnings' at all.

Pensions are not themselves liable to NIC although the position of lump sums is not clear.

5.12 Social security legislation

An unapproved pension scheme may nevertheless be an occupational pension scheme for the purposes of the Social Security legislation. This defines an occupational scheme as:

> 'Any scheme or arrangement which is comprised in one or more instalments or agreements and which has, or is capable of having, effect in relation to one or more descriptions or categories of employments so as to provide benefits, in the form of, pension or otherwise, payable on termination of service, or on death or retirement'.

This is a very wide definition. It is significant as it brings into play the legislation relating to disclosure, etc, and all the other regulatory provisions, including the 'equal treatment' between men and women, preservation requirements and transferability.

This could pose an administrative overhead on unapproved schemes which is not counterbalanced by the tax advantages.

5.13 Uses of unapproved schemes

The Top Up Notes issued by the Inland Revenue suggest that there are three situations where an unapproved scheme is likely to be attractive.

(1) Where an employer wants to offer some employees a pension greater than two-thirds of final salary.
(2) Where the employee has not completed the full 20 years' service to qualify for a full two-thirds pension.
(3) Where the employer wants to pension earnings over £75,000 (in 1992/93).

The first situation is likely to be rare as few employers will want to offer a pension of more than two-thirds final salary as this is likely to be as much as the employer will want to pay or is able to afford. The second situation where employers wish to provide more for employees unable to obtain a full two-thirds final salary pension: is marginally more likely. (The maximum pension can now be provided only after 20 years whereas previously it was possible after ten).

In some circumstances employers may wish to recruit staff who will be affected by the £75,000 (indexed) earnings cap under an approved retirement benefits scheme, initially or at a later date. Employees who are already in existing schemes and are pre-1987 members or 1987–1989 members are less likely to wish to move jobs if they are earning or anticipate earning more than the £75,000 limit.

It remains to be seen, however, the extent of which employers will be forced to provide 'top-ups' to recruit staff. This may be more likely in industries with skills shortages than elsewhere. Also, companies who have one or more key employees whom they wish to tie in, eg computer experts, top salesmen, key executives, etc, may wish to provide top-up schemes. Small private companies could find the prospect of providing pensions for the key directors appealing but the availability of tax relief is crucial. The charge to tax on the employer's contribution as a 'benefit in kind' is a serious disadvantage for funded schemes (except perhaps in the case of death in service schemes where the premiums are smaller in relation to the emerging benefits). The alternative of an unfunded arrangement — where a lump sum is paid to the employee on retirement — while much more financially attractive offers little security for the employee.

5.14 Death in service benefits

The unattractiveness of unapproved pension schemes in relation to tax benefits is not so evident where the employer wishes to provide additional death in service benefits for an employee where there is a possibility of a substantial benefit compared with the tax liability.

Take an employee, aged 45 earning £100,000 who is a post 1989 member of an approved pension scheme and is subject to the earnings cap of £75,000. The scheme provides maximum approved death in service benefits as follows:

(1) A lump sum of four times capped earnings, ie £300,000.
(2) A pension for his widow payable on his death before retirement of £33,333 (2/3rds of his maximum approvable pension which is assumed to be £50,000). The widow's pension is assumed to be capitalised at a lump sum of £333,330 so that the total value of the death in service benefit amounts to £633,330.

The employer wishes to provide the above scale of death in service benefits in relation to total earnings of £100,000 which would have a capitalised value of £844,400. The difference which could be provided by an ordinary life assurance policy with a sum assured of £211,110 would be payable by the employer by means of an unapproved funded scheme written under a discretionary trust. The annual premium would amount to around £2,500 which would be regarded as income in the hands of the employee and subject to income tax. The contribution, however, could be regarded as a 'benefit in kind' and would escape National Insurance. The employer would obtain tax relief on the premiums.

On death the benefits would be paid to the trustees and distributed according to the trust provisions. The question of inheritance tax is still not clear but it is unlikely that tax would be payable as the unapproved scheme would be seen to have been 'sponsored' by the employer. However, 'sponsorship' will require more than payment of the premium by the employer: it is likely that this will be satisfied by separate and identifiable payments to meet expenses in setting up and administering the scheme.

The Finance Act 1989 charges to tax gains made by companies in respect of company-owned life policies and annuity contracts and those held in trusts set up by companies.

The gain is the difference between the premiums paid and the proceeds of the policy and in the case of a life assurance policy the gain on death is calculated by deducting total premiums paid. If a group policy is used, say, for a group of members, death benefits paid in respect of previous deaths may come into the computation for calculating the surrender value on a subsequent death. To avoid this, individual assurance policies should be used for each member.

5.15 Accounting for costs

Provisions for unfunded schemes made in company accounts are not allowable as business expenses but it may be possible to obtain allowance for deferred tax relief.

5.16 Future trends

As unapproved pension schemes are in their infancy (apart from ones set up inadvertently before Finance Act 1989) it is too early to point to any common approach by employers. Nevertheless, large employers profess to be interested in setting up unapproved pension schemes as they are keen to be able to offer an attractive financial package to high-flyers whom they may wish to recruit. However, it will be seen from this Chapter that the taxation of unapproved pension schemes gives rise to considerable disadvantages. Other options worth considering are as follows:

(1) By maximising the benefits under approved pension schemes in relation to earnings up to the cap, eg providing a maximum pension of 2/3rds of final remuneration after completion of 20 years' service, together with cost of living increases in pensions in payment: these benefit scales may be more generous than those for employees who are not subject to the cap.
(2) High earners could pay Additional Voluntary Contributions of up to 15% of their remuneration (subject to a cash limit of £11,250) in order to maximise benefits up to the cap.
(3) Rather than using a combination of approved occupational schemes and unapproved pension schemes (whether funded or unfunded), it may be worthwhile considering a personal pension scheme for the employee. Where earnings are high and the employee is young it is possible that personal pension plans might be able to provide higher benefits than under an approved pension scheme in any case, without having to resort to an unapproved scheme.
(4) Other 'benefits in kind' such as share option schemes or contributions to an employee's personal equity plan.

Offshore trusts

It may be possible to make a funded arrangement more tax efficient by establishing a trust offshore. If the offshore trust invests in non-UK assets it may be possible to avoid any UK income tax liability within the trust. There may also be savings in UK capital gains tax. However there are detailed anti-avoidance rules which apply to offshore trusts which would have to be considered. In addition, there may be additional costs in creating the offshore trust.

Table 5.1 Summary of tax position

	Funded	Unfunded
Employer's contributions	allowable as business expenses treated as a 'benefit in kind' and not subject to NI taxed in hands of employee	allowable as business expenses
Employee's contributions	paid out of taxed income, so no tax relief	not applicable
Growth of fund	subject to income tax and capital gains tax (with indexation allowance) at the basic rate of income tax	not applicable
Benefit payments	if lump sum, tax free if pension, subject to income tax (therefore an alternative)	lump sum or pension paid subject to income tax
Death benefits	free of inheritance tax under a 'sponsored' superannuation scheme	as for funded

6 Company directors

The Inland Revenue has for long regarded company directors — especially those with a controlling interest — as a special category for whom membership of an approved pension scheme will be permitted only subject to certain restrictions. In recent years, the Pension Schemes Office of the Inland Revenue has increased its monitoring of pension schemes with controlling director members.

The earnings cap (£75,000 in 1992/93) is likely to hit this particular group more than others.

The proposed changes to the maximum permissible contributions which may be paid into pension schemes (to take effect towards the end of 1992 — see Chapter 7) will make it more difficult for controlling directors to make maximum use of the tax advantages of approved pension schemes.

Directors of companies which are regarded for tax purposes as investment companies are ineligible to become members of a pension scheme approved by the PSO under their discretionary powers if they are controlling directors (see below) or are members of a family who together control more than 50% of the company (see Chapter 18). The PSO do not, however, object to such schemes for these directors if the investment company is the holding company for a group of trading companies for which it acts as coordinator.

The benefits which may be provided for a director who is described by the Inland Revenue as a *controlling director* are restricted as follows:

All members
The definition of 'final remuneration' and 'dynamised final remuneration' must not be based on one year only but must be averaged over a period of at least three consecutive years.

Pre-1987 and 1987-1989 members only
(1) The earliest normal retirement age is 60. This means that female controlling directors of schemes approved before 29 November 1991 are restricted to a normal retirement range of 60-70 and cannot retire on maximum benefits at age 55 (see Chapter 4, (4.4)).
(2) If the director defers drawing benefits beyond his normal retirement date the limits on pension and tax-free cash up to age 70 are the same limits as would have applied had he chosen the actual date of his retirement as his normal retirement date and there is no entitlement to the additional benefits described in Chapter 4, (4.15.4).
(3) For deferment beyond age 70, benefits based on final remuneration and service determined at age 70 may be increased by the greater of an actuarial increase and the increase in the RPI. Alternatively, full service to and final remuneration at the actual date of retirement can be taken into account, with an extra 1/60th of final remuneration given for each year of service after age 70 in excess of 40 years, up to a maximum of 45/60ths.
(4) If the cash lump sum is taken at the normal retirement date or later (but before age 70) during deferred retirement, the maximum deferred residual pension may only be increased by reference to the RPI up to age 70. Thereafter, it may be increased by the greater of an actuarial increase and the increase in the RPI.
(5) Normally lump sum death in service payments from a pension scheme are made at the discretion of the trustee of the scheme to a wide range of beneficiaries, free of inheritance tax. However, in the case of a controlling director, remaining in service on or after age 75, the rules of the pension scheme must provide either that any death in service payment is made automatically to the legal personal representatives, or is made to the surviving spouse and, if none, to the legal personal representatives.

Alternatively, the pension scheme may provide that the pension may not be deferred by the director once he attains the age of 75.

6.1 Controlling director — definition

There are currently two operative definitions of controlling director. The definition applicable to an individual director will depend on the date on which he joins the pension scheme. Therefore:

(1) A director joining a pension scheme *on or after* 1 December 1987 will be treated as a controlling director to whom the relevant above mentioned restrictions apply if he has at any time after 16 March 1987 and within ten years of retirement or leaving (pensionable) service been a director and either on his own or with one or more associates beneficially owned or been able to control directly or indirectly or through other companies 20% or more of the ordinary share capital of the company. 'Associate' means:
    (a) any relative or partner,
    (b) the trustees of any settlement in relation to which the director is a settlor,
    (c) the trustees of any settlement in relation to which any relative of the director (living or dead) is or was a settlor,
    (d) if the director has an interest in any shares or obligations of the company which are subject to any trust (or are part of the estate of a deceased person) the trustees of that trust (or the personal representatives of the deceased as the case may be).
'Either on his own or with one or more associates' means a director is treated as owning or controlling what any associate owns or controls, even if the director in question does not own or control any share capital himself. Benefits for a director who joined a pension scheme *before* 1 December 1987 to whom the above definition applies will be restricted to the definition of final remuneration which is based on an average of three or more consecutive years. None of the other restrictions will, however, be effective unless (2) below applies.
(2) A director who joined a pension scheme *before* 1 December 1987 will only be treated as a controlling director to whom all the relevant restrictions apply if he could at that date be described as a director who either alone or together with his/her spouse and minor children, is or becomes the beneficial owner of shares which when added to any shares held by the trustees of any settlement to which the director or his/her spouse had transferred assets carry more than 20% of the voting rights in the company providing the pension or in a company which controls that company.

The definition in (1) above applies to all members (irrespective of the date of joining the scheme) for the purpose of the certificates needed for controlling directors wishing to transfer benefits to a personal pension scheme.

6.2 Retained benefits

6.2.1 Controlling directors

Retained benefits cannot be disregarded for a controlling director, or a person who has been a controlling director in the ten years prior to first joining a scheme of the employer on or after 31 August 1991, even if earnings in the first year of scheme membership do not exceed 1/4 of the earnings cap at the date of entry.

Pre-1987 and 1987–1989 controlling directors
Benefits from all retirement annuity contracts and personal pension schemes must always be taken into account as retained benefits when calculating the maximum available under a company pension scheme or executive pension plan.

Post-1989 controlling directors
Benefits from retirement annuity contracts and personal pension schemes relating to previous employments or self employment can be ignored unless benefits from the company scheme are to be provided on an uplifted/accelerated accrual basis. Benefits from retirement annuity contracts and personal pension schemes relating to earnings from the same employment must always be taken into account, and treated as if they were further benefits provided by the company scheme.

6.3 Pensionable service

It may be possible by prior application to the Inland Revenue to pension the service of a director even although no remuneration is paid by the company. The reasoning appears to be that directors are included in the definition of 'employee' under ICTA 1988, s 612(1) and any employee can become a member of a retirement benefit scheme. Obviously the director will have to receive at least one year's remuneration on which to base the calculation of final remuneration.

6.4 Serious ill-health

Full commutation of a member's benefits for a cash lump sum may be permissible where the member is in serious ill-health such that the expectation of life is so short that it is measured in months rather than years. In the case of controlling directors, the prior agreement of the PSO must be obtained before a member's benefits are commuted on these grounds.

6.5 Continuous service/continued rights

Where a controlling director is a member of scheme set up by an employer which is later reconstructed (eg on a company takeover) there may be implications for the way in which 'pensionable service' is calculated. Neither continuous service nor continued rights will be granted on a move to employers associated only by a 'community of interest'. Continuous service may not be granted following a takeover unless the trade is treated as continuing for tax purposes by the Inland Revenue.

Also, in a centralised scheme for employers associated only by a community of interests, cross-subsidy is not permitted in relation to controlling directors: each employer must contribute only in respect of the controlling director's salary and service with that employer, and the benefits payable must also be calculated separately in respect of each employer, the applicable limits usually depending on the date of joining the relevant employer.

7 Funding methods

The techniques used for funding group pension schemes and individual pension arrangements differ considerably. Although this book is aimed primarily at the personal position of a company director or self-employed person whose benefits will normally be provided by means of an individual arrangement it is important to be aware of the differences in the techniques used as it is not uncommon for a director to receive benefits from a group pension scheme and also an individual pension arrangement.

7.1 Funding of group schemes

Most group schemes promise benefits related to final salary so that as salaries increase, so do prospective pensions: it is obvious therefore that it is difficult to quantify in advance the exact pension benefit and therefore the cost of providing it. Under group pension schemes, it is usual for employers to pay contributions which are expressed as a percentage of the total pensionable salaries of employees. This percentage, known as the 'funding rate' will be calculated by the actuary after making various assumptions of which the most important are:

(1) That salaries will increase uniformly at, say, 8% pa compound;
(2) That the yield on the fund will be, say, 9% pa compound after expenses;
(3) That mortality will be experienced in line with an appropriate mortality table;
(4) That the salary/age profile of the group will remain more or less constant;
(5) That the ratio of males and females in the scheme will remain constant;
(6) That persons retiring will be replaced by new entrants within a certain age range, usually at the younger ages.

In recent years funding rates have been affected by an external factor not allowed for in actuarial calculations: legislation changes, which have usually benefited scheme members but have resulted in increases in funding rates.

At least every three years, the actuary will check the actual performance of the fund against the assumptions made originally. If the assumptions have not been borne out in practice, an adjustment may have to be made to the funding rate.

If salaries have increased substantially, especially in periods of high inflation, without corresponding increases in the yield on the fund, there will be a deficit which may have to be made good by the injection of a lump sum.

However in recent years two factors have generated surpluses in some pension schemes, particularly those of large, public companies:

(1) The rate of pension fund growth has outstripped the growth in earnings.
(2) Pension schemes have made a profit out of early leavers. Large companies have shed large numbers of employees in recent years, many of whom will have been in the company pension scheme. As redundancy often works on the basis of 'last in, first out,' pension schemes have gained by having to provide minimal benefits for persons leaving service after a short period (see Chapter 20 for material on 'Surpluses') although recent legislation has, or will, improve the benefits of the 'early leaver'.

7.2 Funding individual arrangements

The funding of individual pension arrangements or Executive Pension Plans also involves making assumptions about salary growth and investment return, but these are related directly to the individual member concerned. The benefits to which he will be entitled will normally represent the proceeds of the fund at the end of the day and will therefore be a function of the contributions paid and the growth thereon: this differs from the final salary type scheme where the employer promises that benefits will be directly related to salary.

7.2.1 Funding for capital

The principle behind Executive Pension Plans is to accumulate capital in the hands of the trustees which can be used to purchase an annuity on retirement. The trustees purchase annuities at the most competitive rates available at the time of retirement from any life office — not necessarily the one which has been used to accumulate the capital before retirement. Thus the Executive Pension Plan can be split into two parts: the first part relates to the period when contributions are paid and invested in order to accumulate the maximum amount of capital, within Revenue limits, and the second part consists of buying an annuity with the accumulated capital.

The various ways in which capital can be accumulated are explored in Chapter 8.

The amount of capital needed at retirement depends on the annuity rates available at that time.

7.2.2 Annuity rates

The actual rate of annuity — or periodical payment by an insurance company in return for a capital investment — depends not only on the age of the person retiring, but on the following factors:

(1) whether the annuity is payable monthly, quarterly, or yearly;
(2) whether the annuity is level, or increases (or 'escalates') in payment; and
(3) whether it will be guaranteed for a minimum period of five or ten years or not guaranteed.

Annuity rates are also volatile as they relate directly to interest rates and also on the desire of an insurance company to come in or out of the annuity market. The following table is an example of annuity rates per annum for males and females based on a purchase price of £1,000 available in August 1992, although it does not represent the most competitive available at that time. It is assumed that the annuity is payable by quarterly instalments in advance and is payable for a minimum of five years and is based on an underlying interest rate of $8^{3}/_{4}\%$.

Table 7.1

	Male		Female	
Age	Level	5% esc.	Level	5% esc.
55	101.02	64.13	93.73	56.33
56	102.42	65.66	94.66	57.44
57	103.89	67.27	95.66	58.61
58	105.44	68.95	96.74	59.86
59	107.07	70.72	97.90	61.18
60	108.77	72.57	99.13	62.58
61	110.57	74.51	100.45	64.06
62	112.46	76.56	101.86	65.64
63	114.45	78.70	103.37	67.31
64	116.55	80.97	104.98	69.08
65	118.77	83.35	106.69	70.96
66	121.10	85.85	108.52	72.95
67	123.56	88.49	110.48	75.07
68	126.14	91.26	112.56	77.33
69	128.85	94.17	114.79	79.72
70	131.70	97.22	117.16	82.26
71	134.68	100.42	119.68	84.96
72	137.79	103.77	122.35	87.82
73	141.04	107.26	125.19	90.85
74	144.42	110.91	128.20	94.06

Annuities purchased by trustees of pension schemes are known as 'compulsory purchase annuities' and are treated as earned income. These contrast with 'purchased life annuities' which are available to individuals to purchase with their own money and which receive different tax treatment in that they are regarded as partly a return of capital which is tax-free with the balance being taxed as unearned income. (Since FA 1984 there is no longer any additional tax on unearned income.)

7.2.3 Salary increases

In order to calculate how much capital would be required at retirement, it is necessary to project current salary forward to retirement.

In March 1992 the Inland Revenue published proposals changing the rate at which salaries should be projected for funding purposes. For new schemes commencing towards the end of 1992 (although this could be delayed) salaries should increase at no more than 5.3% per annum compound. The earnings cap, £75,000 in 1992/93, should also be assumed to increase at this rate. Schemes set up before this date may continue to use the old projection of 8.5% per annum compound.

Example 7.1

A member, aged 40, subject to the more generous projection rate, proposing to retire at age 60 currently earning £18,000 pa, may have the cost of his benefits calculated on a projected final salary of £92,016.

Example 7.2

A director aged 30, proposing to retire at age 60, currently earning £65,000 and subject to the new basis may have the cost of his benefits calculated on a projected final salary of £353,000 (actual final salary would be £481,000 assuming increases at 6.9% pa but limited to the earnings cap increased at 5.3% pa).

7.3 Yield assumption

Having established the amount of capital required at age 60, it is then necessary to make an assumption about the return which will be earned on the investment to achieve that capital sum.

For schemes set up from towards the end of 1992 (possibly later) the PSO proposes a yield assumption of 1.6% in excess of that assumed for salary inflation, ie fund growth of 6.9% per annum. For schemes set up before then a yield assumption of only 0.5% per annum above salary inflation is acceptable.

7.3.1 Maximum permissible contributions — Inland Revenue changes

As stated above the Inland Revenue are proposing more realistic assumptions to be made about future salary increases and pension fund growth. Also, in future it may be possible to fund for pensions increasing in payment at only 5.3% per annum: prior to the introduction of the changes it was possible to fund for pensions increasing in payment at 8.5% per annum. The increase in the real rate of fund growth over salary inflation to 1.6% per annum and the reduction in the assumed increase in pensions in payment has the effect of reducing the input needed to fund maximum benefits at retirement. There is another change which has a considerable impact: in the past, maximum contributions were calculated on a 'level' basis. Under the new basis, contributions are assumed to increase in line with earnings, again reducing the initial contribution.

The following table shows a comparison of the 'old' and 'new' contribution levels in respect of males and females retiring at age 60, with no provision for widows' or widowers' pensions and where earnings are not affected by the earnings cap.

Table 7.2

Males age next	Old basis (approx) %	New basis (approx) %
30	87	25
35	92	30
40	100	40
45	113	55
50	140	87
55	226	181

Females age next	%	%
30	102	29
35	108	36
40	117	47
45	133	66
50	164	103
55	265	214

7.3.2 New schemes

The following example demonstrates the likely effect of the change on a new pension scheme set up for a director or key executive.

Example 7.3

Male aged 40 next with a salary of £50,000 and a retirement age of 60. The maximum regular annual contribution payable on the revised basis (40%) starts at £20,000 and, if earnings grow in line with the assumed rate of salary inflation of 6.9% per annum, rises to £75,960 just before retirement, as compared to a level 100%, ie £50,000 per annum currently.

Example 7.4

Female aged 35 next with a salary of £2,800 and a selected retirement age of 60. The maximum regular annual contribution payable on the revised basis (36%) starts at £1,008 and, if earnings grow in line with the assumed 6.9% per annum, rises to £5,344 just before retirement, as compared to the current £3,024 (108%) throughout.

Whilst the basis is quite different it should be understood that the objective remains the same, ie to build up a fund sufficient to provide a two-thirds pension at retirement.

7.3.3 Existing schemes

The current basis may continue for existing members (ie where funding started before the changes came into being). However if contributions are increased then the new, lower, basis must be used.

For example, if a new scheme is set up today for a male aged forty where the maximum contribution is 100% and this contribution is paid it may continue until such time as the new revised, escalating basis overtakes it.

7.4 Annual and special/single contributions — tax relief

7.4.1 The employer — regular contributions

Regular contributions to approved executive pension plans (being an exempt approved scheme) are deductible for tax purposes in the year of payment.

There are, however, circumstances in which regular contributions may be treated as single contributions (see 'The employer – single contributions' below) in which case tax relief could be spread for up to five years. Such circumstances include:

(1) Where a member is within three years of retirement age when the plan is set up (or five years in the case of a small self-administered scheme). In practice, the Revenue at present usually allows relief in the year of payment where regular contributions are payable and paid for at least three years, eg, if a director aged 63 next birthday starts a plan with a

retirement age of 65, regular contributions will be allowed each year as paid.

(2) Where a regular contribution plan is set up and the contribution is either reduced or stopped in a later year, the Revenue have discretion to go back and treat the previous contributions as single instead of regular.

7.4.2 The employer — single contributions

Payment of single premiums must be reported to the Inland Revenue if they exceed the greater of:

- £25,000 in total in the employer's financial year; and
- the total ordinary annual contributions paid by the employer in that year to all exempt approved schemes.

Tax relief will be spread evenly based on the following table:

Table 7.3

£25,000 – £50,000	2 year spread
£50,001 – £100,000	3 year spread
over £100,000	4 year spread

If the chargeable period is less than 12 months, the allowance will be given on a *pro rata* basis.

Example 7.5

Single premium of £66,000
£22,000 allowed in year of payment;
£22,000 allowed in year 2;
£22,000 allowed in year 3.

Example 7.6

Single premium of £66,000, initial chargeable period of 9 months
£18,000 allowed in year of payment (9/33rds);
£24,000 allowed in year 2 (12/33rds);
£24,000 allowed in year 3 (12/33rds).

Single contributions need not now be spread over a period of time if they are satisfied by an actuary as being made to finance cost of living pension increases for existing pensioners.

If an employer wishes to increase the maximum level of investment in the first year, it is common for a single contribution to be paid to provide past service benefits but in order to ensure tax relief is given in the year of payment this single contribution is matched by an equal annual contribution: the annual contribution will be lower than the maximum which would otherwise be allowed if a single contribution had not been paid.

The following table shows the approximate maximum levels of investment as a percentage of current salary which can be made at various ages in respect of an individual pension arrangement assuming that there are no retained benefits from earlier employment, that the individual can complete twenty years' service to retirement and that benefits will accrue on a pre-1989 basis. The percentages will vary from insurer to insurer but are unlikely to differ greatly.

Table 7.4

Age	SRA 65 All annual %	SRA 65 Annual & single %	SRA 60 All annual %	SRA 60 Annual & single %
29	18	17	25	24
34	21	20	30	29
39	26	25	40	38
44	34	32	55	52
49	48	44	87	79
54	74	67	181	150
59	154	128	—	—

The above table incorporates automatic escalation on the pension at 5.3% pa compound but ignores the cost of any death in service benefits or the provision of dependant's death in retirement benefits. Thus the absolute maximum levels for a complete pensions package will be higher. In the third and fifth columns it has been assumed that the member has sufficient years of past service to justify the payment of a single contribution in the first year equal to the regular annual contribution.

7.5 Dependant's death in retirement benefits

The amount of additional capital required to provide a widow's or widower's death in retirement pension varies according to the difference in ages between husband and wife. For example, if the wife is three years younger than her husband, between 15% and 20% additional capital would be required to provide the maximum widow's pension, whereas for the same age difference if a female director wishes to provide a widower's death in retirement pension for her husband, around 6% to 8% additional capital would be required to provide the maximum widower's pension.

7.6 Personal contributions

The maximum levels of contribution given above include any contributions paid personally by the employee or director from his own remuneration as follows:

(1) Any personal contributions which the employer requires the member to pay towards the cost of his benefits.
(2) Any Additional Voluntary Contributions (AVCs) which the member chooses to pay to top up his benefits within the employer's scheme.
(3) Any free-standing AVCs which the individual is free to make to a separate scheme of his choice (see Chapter 10).

Contributions in (1) and (2) above are fully tax deductible through the PAYE system but contributions under (3) above are paid net of basic rate tax with any higher relief given through the individual's tax assessment.

There is an overall limit on personal contributions of 15% of remuneration (subject to the earnings cap in the case of post-1989 members) in any one tax year.

7.7 Over-funding

As the maximum levels of contribution at the outset incorporate a projection of future salary, it is necessary to monitor the performance of the fund in relation to actual increases in salary, especially as retirement draws near, when a change in annuity rates upwards or downwards can seriously affect the provision of maximum benefits. If there is too much capital in the fund to provide the benefits promised, or the maximum levels of benefit, any excess must be returned to the employer and will be taxed as a trading receipt at a special rate of 40%. Alternatively, if there are other members in the fund it may usually be re-applied to purchase pensions for those other members. The changes in the basis of calculating the maximum contribution levels will reduce the likelihood of a build up of too much capital in the fund.

7.8 Death in service benefits

Under executive pension plans, lump sums and dependants' pensions are provided by means of a straightforward term assurance which normally ceases at retirement age.

The following table shows the approximate multiple of salary that can be provided at outset as a lump sum for a widow(er)'s death-in-service pension in addition to the four times salary life assurance benefit.

Table 7.5

Age of wife	Multiple of salary	Age of husband	Multiple of salary
up to 24	13	up to 23	13
25 to 34	12	24 to 32	12
35 to 42	11	33 to 39	11
43 to 48	10	40 to 45	10
49 to 54	9	46 to 51	9
55 to 60	8	52 to 56	8
61 to 67	7	57 to 62	7
68 to 69	6	63 to 67	6
		68 to 69	5

On death-in-service, any life assurance in excess of four times final salary is used to purchase a widow(er)'s death-in-service pension.

These multiples assume the member can complete at least 20 years' service to retirement age.

7.9 Annual and single premiums

Some insurance companies quote death-in-service benefits on the basis of single premiums. Thus, a premium paid at the beginning of a year will be sufficient to cover the cost of the risk for 12 months only. The following year, the same amount of cover will be slightly more expensive because the member will be one year older. Single premiums, therefore, involve an increase in cost for the same amount of cover.

Annual premiums, however, are level amounts paid throughout the term of the policy irrespective of any change in health and will be higher than single contributions in the early years, but less in later years.

7.10 Decreasing term assurance

Because the capital fund which is building up for retirement is normally returned in the event of death this itself will provide part of the required level of death-in-service benefit: some companies, therefore, are prepared to insure death-in-service benefits on the basis of a decreasing term assurance which provides the difference between the total desired level of death-in-service benefit and the amount building up under the fund.

This is a useful way of keeping the cost of life assurance requirements to a minimum especially in the case of older employees and directors.

8 Insured pension arrangements

Insured pension arrangements can be divided into four broad categories, as follows:

(1) With-profits policies;
(2) Unit-linked policies;
(3) Deposit administration policies;
(4) Unitised with-profits policies.

8.1 With-profits policies

Many insurance plans on the market fall into this category and are operated by traditional life offices, many of which have been in existence for over a century.

The pension policies are similar to with-profits endowment life assurance policies although life cover is generally optional. The policy will be either a pure endowment where a guaranteed capital sum will be payable on retirement, or a deferred annuity with a guaranteed annuity payable on retirement.

The pure endowment policy will be converted into an annuity at an annuity rate that may be guaranteed in the policy, whereas the deferred annuity policy may provide a guaranteed cash option. Most with-profits policies, however, offer an 'open market option' whereby the trustees may purchase an annuity on the open market from another insurance company.

An individual who is considering investing in a conventional with-profits policy will normally be offered a 'projected capital fund per £1,000 of annual contribution' made up of three elements:

(1) a minimum guaranteed amount payable at retiring age, plus
(2) an additional sum, which is not guaranteed, and which will depend on the actual results achieved over the full investment period. This additional 'bonus' (known as a reversionary bonus) is normally expressed as a percentage of the minimum guaranteed amount in (1) above and will usually benefit from a compounding effect, plus
(3) a final additional amount which will depend on economic and financial conditions prevailing at the time of retirement — known as a 'terminal bonus'.

Once a reversionary bonus has been declared by the insurance company, it cannot be subsequently removed even if future investment results fail to match expectations.

In recent years there has been a stabilising of reversionary bonuses and more emphasis on variations in terminal bonuses.

There is no such guarantee with terminal bonuses, however, as these are discretionary payments depending upon investment conditions when the policy matures.

In the event of the death of the member before retirement the policy may provide one of the following:

(1) No return of premiums paid.
(2) A return of the premiums paid without interest.
(3) A return of the premiums paid together with compound interest at around 3% to 6% pa.
(4) A return of the fund up to the date of death.

Obviously to the extent that the return on death is improved then the eventual benefits which may be received on retirement will be smaller. The fourth option set out above does not, of course, necessarily represent the face value of the policy including attaching bonuses but represents the 'value' of the policy as determined by the actuary.

The management charges made by the insurance company for issuing a with-profits policy and running the pension plan are not disclosed in the policy document, although sometimes a separate policy fee is specified in addition to the contributions.

It is only possible to monitor the performance of this type of contract when the policy is determined, for example, by analysing the amount paid in the event of death or the surrender value of the policy should it be discontinued on say, early retirement or should the policy actually mature at retiring age.

8.2 Unit-linked policies

The 1970s saw an upsurge of insurance companies offering policies on unit-linked principles. FA 1973 allowing controlling directors to have executive pension plans gave a timely boost to this business and today, most traditional life offices offer unit-linked policies as well as conventional with-profits policies. The unit-linked route has been so popular that companies which traditionally marketed only with-profits policies now also offer unit-linked policies.

Under a unit-linked policy, the investor is able to choose the investment sector in which he would like his contributions to be invested and he may switch between sectors from time to time. The contributions paid are used to buy units in one or more of the chosen investment sectors and the value of the units at any time is dependent on the value of the underlying investments.

On retirement, the units are encashed and the proceeds are used to purchase an annuity on the open market. No bonuses are declared and no guarantee attaches to the value of the units although most unit-linked policies actually state the investment charges.

8.3 Charging structures

The methods by which insurance companies take their charges for administering a unit-linked policy vary from one to another but will normally be based on one or more of a combination of the following principles.

8.3.1 Allocation to units

In most plans up to 100% of each contribution is allocated to units but sometimes there is a smaller allocation in respect of investment terms of ten years or less. The following table is fairly typical.

Table 8.1

Years to pension age from commencement of the contract	Allocation to units
10 or more	100%
9	99%
8	98%
7	97%
6	96%
5 and less	95%

Some insurance companies offer allocations in excess of 100% but often with the requirement that contributions have to be paid throughout the term, some give an increased rate of allocation, provided a proportion of the contributions payable within, say, the first ten years, have actually been paid, and some companies give a higher allocation to units in respect of contributions paid towards the end of the term of the contract.

8.3.2 Type of units

It is common to find the first one or two years' contributions allocated to 'capital' or 'initial' units, under which the insurance company takes an additional charge of between $3\frac{1}{2}$% and 6% pa of the value of the units. Subsequent contributions purchase 'accumulation' or 'ordinary' units under which all the income and growth from the underlying investment accrues to the planholders (except for the 'annual management charge — see below).

Another method of charging is where insurance companies allocate a reduced percentage of the first one or two years' contributions to 'accumulation' or 'ordinary' units. As an example, the insurance company may allocate between 25% and 85% of the first year's contribution depending upon the term of the contract.

Yet another method is for no explicit charge to be made in the first one or two years' contributions, instead all contributions are allocated to accumulation or ordinary units, but if contributions stop or reduce (a frequent event under pensions plans) a reduction is made to the fund at that time.

8.3.3 Management charges

In addition to the charges mentioned above, most insurance companies make a management charge which is expressed as a percentage of the total value of the units and might lie anywhere between 3/8% and 3/4% pa, although in recent years many insurance companies have started marketing unit-linked policies which have unlimited annual management charges or have the ability to increase management charges from, say, 3/4% pa to $1\frac{1}{2}$% pa at some stage in the future. Also, it is not uncommon in the case of property investments for the cost of buying, selling and managing properties, fees to independent valuers and other dealing costs to be borne by the fund.

8.3.4 Bid/offer prices

As with unit trusts, units are allocated on the basis of offer prices and are subsequently sold at lower bid prices when the policyholder takes his benefits. The difference between bid and offer prices is usually 5%.

8.3.5 Policy charges

In addition some companies take an initial instalment charge and a fixed policy amount in real terms every year (the initial amount will thus be increased every year in line with an index such as the National Average Earnings Index or Retail Prices Index) which actually reflects the cost of servicing the policy. This type of charge which applies in modern unit-linked policies compares favourably with the annual management charge shown above which can increase considerably as the fund accumulates especially in the later years of the contract.

Since July 1988, under LAUTRO rules, all insurance companies illustrating cash values must use standard assumptions on charges, expense deductions and future investment returns. This means that it is not possible to compare the impact of charges on the basis of illustrations of projected values.

However, insurance companies must illustrate the surrender (or transfer) values payable under the contract in years 1–5, based on the insurer's actual charges and assuming a rate of return of $10\frac{3}{4}$% pa. A comparison of these surrender values may give an indication of the charges under different contracts.

Since 1 July 1990 LAUTRO rules have required insurers to show the reduction in investment yield brought about by the charges under unit-linked contracts. (Under with-profits and unitised with-profits contracts only the effect of expenses need to be shown; expenses do not include the profits which will accrue to the insurer.) It is likely these rules will change in 1993.

8.4 Types of investment funds

Most companies offer separate property, equity, gilt-edged and cash funds, but the majority of investors choose the 'managed' approach where the insurance company itself invests each contribution in whatever proportions and between whichever different investment sectors it feels appropriate for the longer term. This normally means a mixture of property, equities and gilt-edged investments. Cash deposit funds or building society related funds are usually intended to be used as a means of consolidating gains (or losses) at or near retirement age. Policyholders need not direct all their contributions into one fund but will normally have the choice of investing in all funds or in any combination. In recent years, the investment funds available have been extended to include overseas areas such as North America and Canada, Japan, Hong Kong, Australia and Europe. Sometimes an international managed fund is available incorporating all these areas.

8.5 Deposit administration

In many respects, deposit administration contracts seek to combine the best features of conventional with-profits and unit-linked policies. The principle behind deposit administration is that, after deducting charges for administration, the policyholder has a deposit account with the insurance company — similar to a bank account — to which interest is added from time to time. The amount of interest that is actually guaranteed (if any) in the contract varies widely with some offices linking the rates to the building society lending rate and others crediting interest on a basis reflecting interest rates generally.

There are considerable variations in the method of charging expenses. For example, the credited interest rate may take account of expenses or a fixed policy amount may be deducted from the contribution before interest is credited, an annual charge may be made, or a lower interest may be applied to the initial contributions. The pension obtained from the accumulated fund at the time of retirement will depend on annuity rates prevailing at the time and therefore it is not normally guaranteed.

8.6 Unitised with-profits policies

The unitised with-profits policy is a variation on the conventional with profits policy, although it has the hallmarks of a unit-linked policy. However, there are a number of important differences: under unitised with-profits, there is no annual management charge and the unit prices are generally guaranteed to increase at a minimum rate of growth, eg 4% per annum although this price guarantee normally only applies at maturity or on early death. At any other time the unit price is not guaranteed and may be reduced by the actuary.

Investment performance is not reflected immediately but is smoothed over a period of years. The excess over the minimum guaranteed rate is added as a bonus which, once added, cannot be taken away.

The benefits are expressed in the form of units with bid and offer prices, allocation rates and initial charges, similar to unit-linked contracts.

Policyholders are permitted to switch into and out of the unitised with-profits fund although companies normally reserve the right to reduce the unit price on a switch-out and some do not allow switches-in within five years of the retirement date.

8.7 Comparisons of unit-linked funds

The most important factor determining the value for money which a unit-linked planholder will receive is the performance of the investment fund to which his plan is linked. How is he to assess the likely future performance of different life companies' investment funds?

Performance league tables are not by themselves the answer. The fact that one fund has performed particularly well over a period in the past — especially a short period — is no assurance that it will perform well in the period which matters to the new planholder, which is the future. Past performance over that period may have been the result of special circumstances which will not be relevant in the future.

The best solution is to look for the features which are likely to result in consistent long term performance. No one can guarantee future performance, but certain features can point to the likelihood of consistent long term performance, or act as a warning that future performance is likely to be volatile. The following checklist may be helpful.

- Does the fund have the benefit of a regular cash inflow?
- Has the fund a consistent long term performance record?
- How long has the fund been in existence?
- What is the size of the fund?
- How has the fund coped with market upheavals (eg in 1974/75 or 1987)?
- Is the fund broadly-based or is it a specialised fund?
- How have the company's other funds performed?
- Does the fund have continuity of investment management?
- Does the name of the fund reflect its composition?

The significance of these factors is analysed in detail below.

Does the fund have the benefit of an assured regular cash inflow?

Investment managers often state that nothing assists them more than the knowledge that there is a regular cash inflow, and nothing can harm investment performance more than a sudden drying-up of funds or worse still, a sudden need to liquidate investments to meet cash requirements of investors wishing to take out their money. A regular cash inflow makes it easy for an investment manager to change the weighting of investments in the fund without bearing the heavy costs of selling some shares in order to buy others. A sudden outflow can involve not merely the expense and the difficulty of selling shares on a falling market, but can force a fund to change its unit valuation from an 'offer price' to a 'bid price', which can reduce the unit price by 6% or 7% overnight. So a fund which shows up well in a short-term league table might still be highly vulnerable if it does not have a source of regular cash inflow.

When assessing the future prospect of a fund which has shown up well in a past performance league table, take the following other factors into account.

(1) If the table is for a relatively short term, check up on the

fund's performance over other periods, particularly long term periods. It is not uncommon for funds which are in the 'Top Ten' of this year's one-year performance tables to figure in the 'Bottom Ten' of next year's tables. What matters to a planholder is consistent, long term performance.

(2) How long has the fund been in existence? Many new funds have shown very good performance in their first year or two, only to lapse into disappointing performance in later years. Although many new funds have performed well in their early years, many other new funds have performed badly.

(3) Is the fund still a small fund? As there are a large number of small funds in existence, often with specialised investment policies, there are frequently a number of small funds near the top of the yearly league tables. The following year there may still be a number of small funds among the leaders, but they are quite likely to be different small funds. Any successful fund with a regular cash flow will soon become a large fund — and the real test is the ability to show consistent long term performance.

(4) How did the fund cope with market upheavals, for example in 1974/5 when share prices suffered the largest fall this century? A fund should be judged in bad conditions as well as good. Similarly, how did the fund cope with the 'Black Monday' crash in October 1987? Those which fell dramatically may eventually show significant increases from their low points.

(5) Does the fund have a broadly-based investment policy or is it a specialist fund? Specialist funds (invested in one type of share or one country) often lead the short term league tables because that type of share is in fashion during that year or that country's stock market has a good run for a year. These funds frequently fall sharply the following year; for example, over the last ten years there have been a number of specialist funds such as Commodities, Far Eastern and American funds in the Top Ten performance tables in one year but many of those same funds also appear in the Bottom Ten tables in other years.

(6) Where one fund of a life company or unit trust group shows up well in a performance table, how did the other funds managed by the same company or group perform over that period? Some life companies and unit trust groups have anything up to 40 different funds, so that a few of their funds will generally be in the upper levels of the league table in any one period, even if most of their funds do not perform

well — but of course no one knows in advance which of their funds will perform well.

In assessing the performance of property funds these additional factors should be considered.

(1) Is the fund large enough to include a broad spread of properties? Some small funds have in the past achieved very good performance for a year or two when invested in only two or three properties, including one 'special situation' property which gives the fund a non-repeatable boost to performance — and leaves it vulnerable to fall if there is a change in the marketability of that particular property (eg, a change in business conditions in that area, perhaps because one large factory closes down).

(2) Is the fund invested directly in property or in shares of property companies? Shares of property companies tend to be volatile, as exemplified by the October 1987 crash, whereas direct investment in property has a more stable history.

Does the life company offer a full range of broadly-based funds with consistent investment records?

When an individual (both a director and self-employed person) effects a unit-linked pension plan, he will want to know that he can use a low-cost switching facility to change the fund to which his plan is linked according to changes in his personal circumstances.

Do the funds have continuity of investment management?

Good past performance is not necessarily even a pointer to the future if the investment management has changed hands. Some smaller funds have changed hands on a number of occasions, and may well be sold on again in the future.

Does the name of the fund reflect its composition?

A property fund investor would probably expect it to consist of shops, offices, industrial units and cash. However, small 'property' funds could consist of a large amount of cash and only a few properties. A 'Managed' Fund might comprise a mixed portfolio of equities, properties, gilt edged securities and deposits or it might be largely concentrated in one sector in which case 'Managed' might really mean 'Managed Equity'.

9 Small self-administered schemes and insurance company hybrid schemes

Small self-administered schemes are similar to insured schemes in that the emerging benefits which may be enjoyed by the members are exactly the same, being governed by the same legislation and to a large extent the same Inland Revenue practice. In a self-administered scheme, however, the trustees, either directly or indirectly, are responsible for managing the investments and the administration of the scheme. This contrasts with an insured scheme where the trustees pay contributions to an insurance company which manages the scheme and is responsible for investing the contributions.

For many years, large organisations have tended to adopt the self-administered approach because they have felt that it could provide a better return and greater flexibility at lower cost than using insurance policies where control is left to the life office.

Under a small self-administered scheme (sometimes known as a captive pension scheme) the directors of a company are the sole or principal members of the scheme and also normally act as a scheme's trustees. They are then able to exert a considerable degree of control over the investments of the fund and the level of benefits provided. A small self-administered scheme is defined as a self-administered scheme with less than 12 members.

A scheme is defined as self-administered if some or all of the income and other assets are invested otherwise than in insurance policies. Scheme assets, of small amounts, held in a current account (whether interest-bearing or not) with a bank or building society for these purposes are not treated as an investment 'otherwise than in insurance policies'.

The proposals of the Inland Revenue to restrict the amount of contributions to earmarked money purchase schemes is likely to have a significant impact on the long-term attractiveness of these schemes for company directors (see also Chapter 7, Funding Methods).

9.1 Self-investment

The main attraction of self-administered schemes to directors is the scope to exercise wide investment powers available to the company through *self-investment* rather than *self-administration*.

Self-investment in areas which would assist the employer in its operations can be achieved through:

(1) loans to the company and/or its subsidiaries,
(2) the purchase of property from the company and/or its directors, or
(3) investment in a company's own shares.

The above areas will be considered in more depth later in this chapter.

9.2 Restrictions on self-investment

The Inland Revenue was concerned about some aspects of potential abuse and issued guidance on the approval of small self-administered schemes in February 1979 in the form of Memorandum 58. The Inland Revenue's major concern related to the problems which could arise if the potential beneficiaries under the trust decided to wind up the trust and distribute the assets amongst themselves. Under a normal pension scheme this would be a practical impossibility because there would be so many members and potential beneficiaries, and under a small insured scheme the insurance company could be expected to prevent this, but under a small self-administered scheme providing benefits for possibly only one person the enforced termination of the trust by all potential beneficiaries is a real possibility.

The Retirement Benefit Schemes (Restriction on Discretion to Approve) Small Self Administered Schemes (Regulations 1991) which were made on 15 July 1991 and came into force on 5 August 1991 limit the Inland Revenue's discretion relating to the approval of small self administered schemes and specify certain requirements for the approval of a SSAS.

Memorandum No 109 published in August 1991 (reproduced in Appendix 2) and Chapter 20 of the latest Inland Revenue Practice Notes (reproduced in Appendix 3) amplify the effects of the regulations.

The Social Security Act 1990 also introduced restrictions on self-investment by self-administered pension schemes to not more than 5% of the value of pension fund assets through the Occupational Pension Schemes (Investment of Scheme Resources) Regulations 1992. However, these restrictions are relaxed under small self-administered schemes provided that the following conditions are met:

(1) That all members of the scheme are trustees of the scheme (this is not as unwieldy as it seems because these schemes are generally only set up for a small group of people, normally the directors of the company), and the scheme requires the written consent of all members to any self investment.
(2) That the trust deed requires trustees' decisions on investment policy to be unanimous.
(3) That all members are party to investment decisions.

9.2.1 Investment of scheme funds

(1) Loans to scheme members or any other members with a contingent interest (eg relatives) are prohibited as is the purchase, sale or lease of any assets from or to scheme members or anyone connected with a scheme member.
(2) All loans have to be 'properly secured' which means that loans should be subject to a written agreement under which repayment can be legally enforced.
(3) In the first two years of establishment of the scheme all loans to the employer should not exceed 25% of the scheme's assets.
(4) In assessing the value of the fund for loan purposes any monies which have been assigned or transferred into the scheme have to be excluded during the first two years of the scheme's establishment.
(5) Loans to the employer should only be used for the normal trading activities of the employer.

9.2.2 Investment in property

(1) Investment in land or buildings may be a suitable investment where the members are many years from retirement, but the Inland Revenue may question investments where the property purchased is an important part of the employer's own commercial premises, and thus potentially difficult to realise.

(2) With regard to residential property, investments in residential property for use by, or leasing to, a director or shareholder or to the employer will not be approved unless the property is occupied by an arm's length employee (such as a caretaker).

(3) Investment in residential property may also be acceptable if it is occupied by someone unrelated to the members of the scheme (or to a person connected with a scheme member) in connection with his or her occupation of business premises (eg a shop with a flat above it) where those premises are held by trustees of the scheme as an asset.

9.2.3 Notification of transactions

The Regulations will require automatic notification of any transactions between the scheme and a 'connected person'. This is normally taken to include the principal employer, another employer which participates in the scheme, a company associated with the principal employer or participating employer because it is a subsidiary or it shares a common trade, shareholdings or directorships and scheme members, the member's husband and wife, a relative of the member or the relative's spouse.

This information has to be furnished to the Inland Revenue at the date of the transaction.

9.2.4 Pensioneer trustee

The Regulations require that all small self-administered schemes appoint a 'pensioneer trustee'. If this is not done the scheme will not be approved or existing approval will be withdrawn.

If the scheme ceases to have a Pensioneer Trustee the Inland Revenue must be notified in writing within thirty days and a replacement Pensioneer Trustee must be appointed within sixty days. Also, the Inland Revenue has to be given written notification of the name of the new Pensioneer Trustee within thirty days of appointment.

The main function of the 'pensioneer trustee' which currently is to prevent the premature winding up of the scheme other than in accordance with the approved terms for winding up in the scheme rules, will be extended to require the 'pensioneer trustee' to undertake to notify the Inland Revenue of any transaction undertaken by the scheme which, in his opinion, is likely to infringe requirements for approval.

9.2.5 Shares in the employer's company

If assets are acquired from the employer the Inland Revenue will wish to consult with the employer's Inspector of Taxes to determine

Small self-administered and insurance company hybrid schemes 109

whether tax avoidance is involved (in which case the scheme will not be approved) and whether the acquisition is part and parcel of a 'transaction in securites' to which s 703 ICTA 1988 applies.

9.2.6 Investments in works of art, valuable chattels, etc

Investments in such 'pride in possession' assets such as antiques, works of art, rare books, gold bullion, jewellery, etc are not permitted.

9.2.7 Borrowings

It is not uncommon for a scheme to borrow money to help finance the purchase of investment. Borrowings are limited to three times the amount of the employer's ordinary annual contributions to the scheme and three times the annual contributions paid by scheme members (excluding any additional voluntary contributions) plus 45% of the market value of the existing scheme investments.

'Ordinary annual contributions' means the smaller of:

(1) the annual average of the contributions paid by the employer in the three scheme accounting periods preceding the date on which the ordinary annual contribution is to be determined (or, where the scheme has been established for less than three years, the total amount paid to the scheme by the employer divided by the number of years since the scheme was established, and
(2) the amount of the annual contribution which has been advised by an actuary in writing within three years of the date on which the ordinary annual contribution is determined, and is necessary to secure the benefits payable under the scheme.

9.2.8 Provision of information

In addition to the general requirement in Paragraph 23 of JOM 58 that trustees of small self-adminstered schemes provide actuarial valuations every three years at least, schemes now have to volunteer other items of information relating to investments in the areas outlined above, together with an undertaking that the transaction does not infringe current Inland Revenue requirements.

9.2.9 Company loans

The scope for a small self-administered scheme to make available loans to assist the company represents a valuable and flexible facility.

The lenders, however (normally the directors as trustees of the scheme), should ensure that the employer has the ability to repay the loan. The following conditions apply:

(1) The loan should not exceed 50% of the total assets of the scheme (in the first two years 25% of the total assets excluding transfers received from other schemes).

(2) There should not be a regular pattern of lending back to the company part of successive employers' contributions.

(3) The loan should be on commercial terms at a realistic rate of interest: the Inland Revenue specify a rate of 3% pa above Clearing Bank Base Rate (unless the borrower can show in writing that he could have obtained a loan at less than this rate from another lender on otherwise similar terms). Interest must be charged and paid. The loan agreement should state the terms of the loan including the circumstances when the borrower would be in breach of the conditions of the agreement.

(4) The loan must be used for a genuine commercial purpose, for example, to purchase capital equipment or another specific capital requirement. Loans made solely to keep an ailing business afloat or to employers who are technically insolvent may lead to the withdrawal of approval of the scheme.

(5) Loans, being generally required on an unsecured basis, are normally made short-term. If the loan to the employer is to be on a long-term basis, the trustees may wish to take security, for example, a charge on company assets, such as property owned by the employer.

(6) The loan must be for a fixed term as agreed between the parties to the loan agreement. A series of 364 day loans (to enable interest to be paid to the Trustees gross without deduction of tax is not permitted). Also, it is not acceptable for the term to be longer than necessary.

9.2.10 Commercial property

If the trustees are considering investing pension fund assets in commercial property, the Revenue will normally want to be satisfied that:

(1) The trustees of the self-administered scheme buy the property at current market value, supported by an independent surveyor's valuation.

(2) The rental income should give a reasonable yield — currently 8% to 10% pa, again supported by the advice of an independent surveyor.

(3) In the long term at least half of the assets of the fund will

Small self-administered and insurance company hybrid schemes 111

be invested in assets not connected with the company, for example, arms length assets such as insurance policies, unit trusts, shares in publicly quoted companies, cash deposits, gilt edged securities.
(4) The property will be capable of being sold when liquid assets are required to provide retirement benefits for members of the fund or death benefits for their beneficiaries.

Other factors which the trustees will have to consider are:

(1) If the members are close to the normal retirement date, there may be insufficient time for the trustees to build up liquid assets and the only way in which they can provide the members with their benefits would be to sell the property which could cause problems if it were not readily saleable at the time.
(2) There should be adequate funds elsewhere so that the property would not have to be sold at an inopportune time to provide death benefits.
(3) The trustees of the self-administered scheme will normally have the powers in the trust deed to effect a short-term commercial mortgage to finance the initial purchase of a property which may well prove attractive because:
 (a) the company contributions to the scheme to enable the trustees to purchase the property and pay off the loan, will attract tax relief,
 (b) rental income paid by the employer to the trustees can be offset as an expense for the purposes of corporation tax,
 (c) rental income from the property accumulates tax free in the self-administered scheme, and
 (d) when the property is sold by the self-administered scheme trustees, they do not have to pay capital gains tax on the sale.

9.3 Company shares

Although the trustees of a small self-administered scheme may invest in shares of the company, this is not a common occurrence. The practice has been that most private companies operated by shareholding directors do not declare dividends or pay minimal dividends on ordinary shareholdings. This can cause problems when the trustees of a small self-administered scheme wish to acquire such shares because the Inland Revenue will want to be satisfied that the holding will represent a reasonable investment in terms of expected annual dividends whereas normally the directors will not wish to declare substantial dividends (although following the abolition of the investment income surcharge in the 1984 Finance Act the situation has changed slightly).

In considering the purchase of company shares, the trustees will have had to have ensured that:

(1) advance clearance has been obtained from the Inspector of Taxes as to whether or not the transaction gives rise to an assessment for income tax under ICTA 1988, s 703;
(2) there is a genuine commercial reason for the share transaction and it is not an exercise in tax avoidance;
(3) the shareholding in the company is taken into account when looking at the overall degree of self-investment, including loans;
(4) the shares have been professionally valued;
(5) the value of the shareholdings in the company is reasonable in relation to the overall value of the pension fund. In practice, this means that the Inland Revenue may object if it is proposed that more than, say, 10% of the pension fund is invested in company shares, although they may be prepared to agree a higher proportion if a sound case is put up;
(6) investments in the company shares should not exceed 30% of the issued share capital of the company; and
(7) shares in the company will have to be realised when the members retire and this may be difficult simply because shares in private companies tend not to be marketable.

9.4 Other Inland Revenue requirements

9.4.1 Pensioneer trustee

As stated above one of the trustees appointed must be a pensioneer trustee whose primary function is to ensure that the pension scheme is not wound up except in accordance with normal pension scheme practice, ie, that the assets would be distributed in the form of deferred pensions payable from normal retirement date. A pensioneer trustee is an individual or body widely involved with occupational pension schemes and known to the Inland Revenue who approve the appointment. It is generally accepted that the pensioneer trustee is jointly and severally liable for the administration of the trust with the other trustees although some pensioneer trustees have sought to limit their responsibilities to the primary function above.

Small self-administered and insurance company hybrid schemes

9.4.2 Investment strategy

Full details of the funding assumptions and the investment strategy must be submitted when Inland Revenue approval of the scheme is sought.

In addition to the initial actuarial report the Inland Revenue require subsequent actuarial reports every three years containing accounts and details of investments.

9.4.3 Inland Revenue scrutiny

As the Inland Revenue scrutinise the investment strategy adopted by the trustees of a small self-administered scheme to ensure that it is suitable, the trustees must satisfy themselves that the main purpose of the scheme is the provision of retirement benefits, rather than the avoidance of tax, and that any substantial investment in a particular area is appropriate to the benefits being provided for the members: in particular if all members are close to retirement, then purchasing a property may be regarded as inappropriate because of the possible problems in selling the investment to provide pensions.

9.4.4 Death in service benefits

If the death benefit formula provided under the scheme exceeds the value of the member's share in the assets of the scheme, then the balance of any death in service benefits promised must be insured with a life office.

9.4.5 Purchase of pensions

Up to within five years of a member retiring, his pension benefit may be paid directly out of the assets of a small self-administered scheme, but by the end of this five year period an annuity must be purchased by the trustees. This will be an important decision for the trustees as investment conditions may vary considerably during this period. However, unless inflation proofing is at the fixed rate of 3% pa the trustees may retain the right to pay any increases in pension in line with movements in the Retail Prices Index directly to the pensioner out of the plan assets.

9.4.6 Provision of information to Inland Revenue

The Inland Revenue must be notified of specified transactions on relevant Inland Revenue forms covering the following:

- Loans to Employer
- Acquisition or Disposal of Land

114 Allied Dunbar Pensions Guide

- Acquisition or Disposal of Shares
- Borrowing of Money
- Purchase or Sale from or to an Employer.

These transactions must be reported to the Inland Revenue within a period of 90 days from the date of acquisition or at the date when the scheme is submitted to the Inland Revenue if this is later.

9.5 Cost of setting up a small self-administered scheme

The costs involved in setting up a small self-administered scheme vary considerably depending on the services given. The services required in order to establish and run a small self-administered scheme include:

(1) **Documentation and Revenue negotiations.** These include drafting the definitive deed and rules, preparing undertakings for completion by the trustees, preparing announcements to members setting out benefits under the scheme. The documents will then have to be submitted to the Inland Revenue for approval and from time to time the employer will require advice in connection with the interpretation of the rules of the scheme and Inland Revenue practice.

(2) **Actuarial services.** These involve an initial actuarial report and triennial actuarial reports. From time to time, interim actuarial reports may be required, for example on company takeovers or if a claim is made on the scheme trustees, for example, on the death or early retirement of a member.

(3) **Pensioneer trusteeship.** See above.

(4) **Accounting and financial management.** This includes keeping records of assets and payments in and out of the scheme and how they are allocated between members; it includes, for example:
  (a) reconciling bank statements;
  (b) preparing audited annual accounts;
  (c) completing annual tax returns;
  (d) settling tax liabilities;
  (e) reclaiming any tax;
  (f) collecting dividends, interest and rental income.

The cost of obtaining all these services varies enormously from specialist to specialist and depends on the method of charging fees which can be either on a genuine time cost basis or as a percentage of the assets under management or even a combination of the two. The amount of work involved in setting up a small self-administered scheme tends to be the same whether £10,000 or £100,000 is being invested. These costs usually relate solely to the day to day administration and do not take into account the cost of managing the assets, such as the legal costs involved in purchasing property or the stockbroking costs incurred in managing an investment portfolio.

9.6 Key advantages and disadvantages of small self-administered schemes

The potential advantages include:

(1) The scope to assist company finances through self-investment in own company assets, particularly commercial premises used by the business.
(2) Loans to the company of up to 50% of the fund (or 25% during the first two years of the scheme's establishment). This requirement is also normally satisfied by policy loans available under executive pension plans offered by insurance companies — see below.
(3) The opportunity to achieve a high investment return where the directors have an interest or expertise in a particular investment sector.
(4) If the fund is large, the cost may be cheaper than under insured arrangements.
(5) The personal satisfaction of direct personal control over investment selection and administration of the scheme.

Disadvantages of self-administered schemes include:

(1) The cost of appointing outside specialists to provide actuarial reports, legal advice, pensioneer trustee services.
(2) The cost in terms of executive time required to manage investments and carry out trustee responsibilities.
(3) Most directors of small family companies are not likely to be expert in long term investment; they do not have the time, ability and resources to research markets in depth in order to maximise gains and minimise losses.
(4) The possible loss of control if company assets, such as properties, are switched to form part of a small self-administered plan. In particular a property which has been purchased by the small self-administered scheme from the company cannot

then be put up as security for loans to the company as it no longer forms part of a company's asset base.

(5) A small self-administered scheme is a common trust fund which means that the assets are held for the benefit of all the members (in practice, a small number of directors) as a whole. This contrasts with executive pension plans where assets are earmarked for each individual member.

Under a common trust fund, in the event of a claim being made by a beneficiary, for example, on the death of a member, the beneficiary will be entitled to a proportion of the assets of the common trust fund, say one-third. The trustees will then have to realise one-third of the fund in order to meet their liabilities to the beneficiary. This could cause problems for the trustees if the deceased member, when alive, had invested what he regarded as 'his share' of the fund in an area of investment which had shown poor returns, as the remaining two members of the scheme could have to subsidise the deceased member from other investments of the fund which had performed better.

The inability to earmark assets under common trust funds is a problem which has come to the fore over the past few years as more insurance companies have been prepared to set up and administer small self-administered schemes where a portion of the assets are invested in insurance policies.

These policies are, by their very nature, taken out by the trustees in respect of individual members of the scheme but they represent merely an investment vehicle on the part of the trustees. The proceeds of the policy are not earmarked for individual members.

This contrasts with a straightforward executive pension plan, which is not a common trust fund, and where the proceeds of each separate policy are indisputably earmarked for the member concerned.

9.7 Property purchase

Many small self-administered schemes are set up with a view to purchasing property (although it is now no longer possible for the scheme to purchase a property from the director(s)). The property may already be owned by the company, or it may be one which the director or the company is considering purchasing, and from which the company will operate. The following tables set out the pros and cons of the methods of property purchase.

Table 9.1: Property purchase by the director

Pros

(1) The property is separate from the company and can be sold independently

(2) The property does not have to be sold at retirement and could generate rental income which will supplement any pension received.

(3) When the property is sold by the director there will be a potential CGT liability but this should be substantially mitigated by the indexation allowance.

(4) The increasing value of the property could be used as collateral security for further ventures of a personal or corporate nature.

(5) If the director does not charge the company rent for the use of his property he will be entitled to business retirement relief usually from age 55 onwards.

(6) If the director uses the tax-free cash emerging from his pension plan to repay the capital he effectively obtains tax relief on the capital repayment.

(7) IHT relief for business property may be available.

Cons

(1) Additional life assurance will be required by the lender as collateral

(2) The director may have given personal guarantees to his company creditors so that the property is not necessarily free from creditors.

(3) When obtaining a loan to buy the property it is unlikely that the director will be able to obtain a 100% mortgage so that he may have to put up additional security such as his own private residence: this may be emotionally unacceptable, or may conflict with personal guarantees given to other lenders.

(4) If a full market rent is received from his company he will not be entitled to business retirement relief. A proportion of the business retirement relief is given if the rent received is less than the full market rent.

(5) The director may be unable to obtain a personal long term interest-only loan.

(6) Other directors may be unhappy about the property being owned by one director.

Table 9.2: Property purchase by the company

Pros

(1) It is the most natural place for the property to be held and the property can be used for future expansion.

(2) The company rather than an individual director, is much more likely to be able to obtain a loan if a substantial amount is involved.

(3) The company although paying interest and capital on the loan does not have to pay rent.

(4) Collateral life assurance is not necessarily needed. The death of one of the directors would not necessarily affect the loan (unless the deceased was a key man in the company).

(5) IHT relief for business property may be available.

(6) The method is simple.

Cons

(1) The company will probably be unable to obtain a loan on a long term interest-only basis. It is likely to be of a fairly short term with capital repayments every year.

(2) When the property is sold there will be a potential corporation tax liability on the gain and when the director sells his shares he will have a potential CGT liability. It may be possible to avoid this double tax charge if the company is sold as a whole, rather than individual elements of it.

(3) Although life assurance is not necessary as collateral security, it is advisable.

Table 9.3: Property purchase by the SSAS

Pros	Cons
(1) When the property is sold by the fund to provide the director with his retirement benefits there will be no CGT to pay.	(1) The SSAS is a common trust fund and the individual members will lose their personal investment choice; see above.
(2) The capital growth of the property will not increase the value of the director's shares for CGT and IHT purposes.	(2) Death, ill health, leaving service, early retirement could involve the trustees of the SSAS in having to sell the property, or obtain a loan at an inopportune time.
(3) If there are younger directors in the SSAS the property could effectively remain in the fund when older directors retire. There will be no need to sell the property if the share of the fund which belongs to the retiring director can be met from other SSAS assets.	(3) The Inland Revenue may not regard the investment as acceptable.
(4) The rent paid by the company to the trustees of the fund will reduce corporation tax liability.	(4) The property could not be used as collateral for future loans to the company.
	(5) The company would have to pay a commercial rent to the SSAS.
	(6) As an actuarial valuation of the fund is required every three years this will require a valuation of the property, an added cost.
	(7) If the SSAS borrows to purchase the property, it will be faced with high capital repayments so as to keep the term of the loan to a minimum: interest payable on the loan by the trustees does not rank for tax relief — the SSAS does not pay tax.

9.7.1 Property purchase — summary

Some companies make the mistake of setting up a small self-administered scheme to purchase a property, while the real aim should be to purchase the property on the most commercial and cost-effective terms to the company, with the pension fund as a secondary objective.

Example 9.1

The company are considering purchasing a property which will cost £200,000. Whilst it is feasible that a small self-administered scheme could be used to purchase the property, in practice this may be an unacceptable option as the cost of financing the project would be too expensive for the following reasons:

(1) The annual contribution to the SSAS would be around £50,000.
(2) The maximum loan which the trustees of the SSAS could obtain would be £150,000 (three times the regular annual contribution, averaged over the previous three years, if necessary, in line with Inland Revenue practice).
(3) The trustees now have £200,000 to purchase the property, assuming the lender is prepared to lend 75% of the valuation of the property. However in the case of an existing scheme, the facility to borrow an additional amount equal to 45% of scheme assets will assist the purchase.
(4) The directors of the company may have to increase their salaries and/or bonuses from the company in order to justify regular contributions to a SSAS of £50,000, affecting the directors' personal tax liability and the company's NIC liability.
(5) The company will have to pay a commercial rent to the SSAS for the use of the property, say, £16,000 per annum.
(6) Even with corporation tax relief on the annual contribution of £50,000 and rent of £16,000, and on the cost of the directors' remuneration, the total cost commitment may well be beyond the resources of the company.
(7) In order not to prejudice tax relief on contributions to the SSAS or to ensure that tax relief is not spread over a period of years the annual contribution would have to be maintained at £50,000.

An alternative method would be to regard the purchase of the property and the setting up of a pension scheme as two completely separate free-standing objectives. The property purchase would be financed by the directors or by the company on a long term basis which would reduce the strain on cash flow and a pension plan could be set up at modest levels. If, for various reasons, the company were unable to pay contributions to the pension plan this would not prejudice mortgage payments in respect of the property purchase and if the property had to be sold at an inopportune time it would not undermine the pension benefits of the directors and their beneficiaries.

9.8 Insurance-based hybrid schemes

Most insurance companies have adapted their own executive pension plans to match the flexibility of small self-administered schemes.

This is done quite simply by:

(1) Offering a fully-fledged small self-administered scheme on the basis set out above, but normally on condition that part of the assets of the fund be invested in an insurance policy (which may be a with-profits policy or a unit-linked policy). The balance of the fund will be invested by the trustees in other areas. The insurance company will then carry out either limited administration of the scheme or provide a full service including preparation of documents, negotiations with the Inland Revenue, accounting services, actuarial services and acting as pensioneer trustee.

The Inland Revenue and DSS regulations summarised above also apply to these schemes.

(2) An arrangement which is documented as a Small Self Administered Scheme but where the assets are invested solely in insurance policies is known as a 'deferred SSAS' or a 'Lossa' (a life office Small Self Administered arrangement). These arrangements were popular until the publication of memorandum 109 de-classified them as Small Self Administered Schemes. Until that time insurance companies marketed these arrangements as having the potential benefits of full Small Self Administered Schemes but with lower running costs while the assets consisted solely of insurance policies, there being no need for actuarial reports or for a Pensioneer Trustee.

(3) Offering a loan facility alongside its executive pension plan on the basis that this will normally satisfy the requirements of most directors of small family companies. Under this method the insurance company lends to the employer an amount currently not exceeding one half of the pension fund, taking as security the pension policy itself. The loan to the employing company must be for a genuine commercial purpose and interest will be payable at a commercial rate.

The loan must be repaid 12 months before the retiring age of the member. If the loan is not repaid the reduction by the insurance company in the member's benefits should be a last resort and in fact all legal processes should be pursued to obtain repayment of the loan before turning to the ultimate security, ie, the member's policy, where the tax free cash available on retirement will be reduced before any reduction in pension benefits.

The member must give his consent to the policy being used by the trustees as security, but in practice the member is a controlling director of the company directly involved in using the money borrowed from the insurance company for a commercial purpose. Under the DSS Regulations which restrict the amount of self-investment, the member has to be a trustee of the scheme.

The Inland Revenue require the insurance company to let them have copies of loan back documentation, to advise them of any case where it becomes necessary to reduce the member's benefits because the company has failed to repay the loan and to pass on information which will enable the Inland Revenue to check that the employers are using the loans for commercial purposes. As the funding of the scheme is through policies with the insurance company, the Inland Revenue do not require actuarial reports, and in practice the Inland Revenue do not normally stipulate the appointment of a Pensioneer Trustee, a requirement under small self-administered schemes.

As the loan made by the insurer to the company is normally long term, the company will pay interest to the insurer having deducted tax at basic rates and remitted it to the Inspector of Taxes. The insurer will then have to reclaim the tax from the Inland Revenue.

The following table, overleaf, shows the effect of setting up an executive pension plan for a director combined with a 50% loan back to the company.

Table 9.4

	No pension plan £	With pension plan £
Company		
Trading profits	300,000	300,000
Director's salary	(40,000)	(40,000)
Employer's NIC	(4,160)	(4,160)
Pension plan contribution	nil	(80,000)
Taxable profit	255,840	175,840
Corporation tax at 25/35%	(64,544)	(43,960)
Retained profits	191,296	131,880
Director		
Salary	40,000	40,000
Personal Tax	(10,279)	(10,279)
Employee's NIC	(1,699)	(1,699)
Net income	28,022	28,022
Total position		
Company's retained profits	191,296	131,880
Director's net income	28,022	28,022
Pension plan fund	nil	80,000
Retained	219,318	239,902
Personal and corporate taxes and NIC	80,682	60,098
Cash flow in first year		
Retained profits	191,296	131,880
Loan back from pension plan	nil	40,000
	191,296	171,880*

* less interest at a commercial rate.

Note

In arriving at the director's net income it has been assumed that he is married and pays tax at 1992/93 rates.

10 Topping-up group schemes

Most directors or senior executives have some form of retirement provision but very few enjoy benefits in line with the absolute maximum levels permitted by the Inland Revenue. The purpose of this chapter is to identify the ways in which existing benefits can be topped up either by the director himself or with the help of his company or a combination of the two.

The methods of increasing existing benefits depends to a large extent on the type of scheme from which the director's main benefits will emerge from and the date on which he joined it as this will determine whether he is classed as a pre-1987 member, a 1987–1989 member or a post-1989 member.

10.1 Group schemes

The vast majority of group schemes provide benefits related to final salary. For directors and senior executives this is likely to be 1/60th of final salary for each year of service as a member of a scheme: in the event of death a widow's or widower's death in retirement pension will be payable and in the event of death in service, there will probably be a lump sum payable of between twice and four times salary together with a spouse's death in service pension of one-half of the prospective personal pension. When in payment, the pension is likely to remain level or increase at a rate of around 3% pa compound. Retirement age is usually 65 for men and 60 for women. The following comparison table shows the benefits which a director who enters a scheme aged 35, earning £40,000 pa, is likely to receive under a typical group pension scheme compared with the maximum levels permitted.

Table 10.1

Benefit	Typical group scheme	Maximum benefits
Member's pension	30/60 × £40,000 = £20,000 pa	2/3 of £40,000 = £26,666 pa
Pension increases at	3%	In line with Retail Prices Index
Widow's pension	50% of member's pension = £10,000	2/3 of member's pension = £17,777 pa
Lump sum death benefit	£80,000	£160,000

In fact the difference between actual benefits received under a typical group scheme and the maximum benefits approvable are even greater than those set out above. Maximum benefits can be paid from age 60 rather than 65, total remuneration may be pensioned including such items as bonuses, commissions, director's fees, and the taxable element of fringe benefits: a typical group scheme will limit pensionable salary to basic salary only and will exclude fluctuating items. Thus there is usually plenty of scope for topping-up the benefits of a director or executive even if he is a post-1989 member and might be affected by the earnings ceiling of £75,000 (in 1992/93).

10.2 Additional voluntary contributions

The Inland Revenue allow contributions by members of up to 15% of their total remuneration. If the member is already paying normal contributions to the scheme of say, 5%, he may increase this by a further 10%. Since 26 October 1987, scheme members have a choice between investing AVCs through either:

(1) their employer's scheme (scheme AVCs or 'in house' AVCs); or
(2) free-standing AVCs.

The choice of investment vehicle for voluntary contributions is wide, including insurance contracts, building society and bank accounts and unit trusts. AVCs started after 8 April 1987 are not permitted to generate directly a lump sum but only pension.

(1) **Scheme AVCs** The whole of the member's additional contributions will be deductible from his/her pay before tax, thus giving relief from income tax at the highest rate (known as the net pay system).
(2) **Free-standing AVCs** This is a contract which is completely separate from any employer sponsored scheme, to which a scheme member can pay additional voluntary contributions. Tax relief is not given through the net pay system. Instead the individual obtains basic rate tax relief at source and claims any higher rate relief through his tax assessment. (For further details see 10.9.)
(3) **Added years** Public sector schemes often allow 'added years of service' to be purchased but very few private schemes adopt this approach since it requires a commitment on the part of the employer to underwrite salary inflation. For example, a voluntary contribution of 5% of salary might secure three or four years' additional pensionable service for a young member. If, however, his salary increases substantially later in life, the pension fund would have to meet the additional liabilities which have not been matched by the voluntary contributions paid by the member. From the point of view of the member, this would be very attractive but is unsatisfactory to the employer.

10.3 Augmentation under the group scheme

Most group schemes contain rules allowing the trustees to augment the benefits of selected individuals or groups and in recent years some large schemes have reduced surpluses in this way. Although this involves a financial commitment on the part of the employer, it may be attractive to the individual director, since the cost of the additional benefit can be lost in the group funding arrangements of the scheme. The employer will normally write to the director or key executive concerned advising him of the extent to which his benefits under the scheme are being topped-up. This method of augmentation does involve a loss of confidentiality, and in the case of directors of profitable family companies, will tend to be inflexible in dealing with tax problems. It is much more likely that the following method will be more suitable.

10.4 Topping-up through executive pension plans

The Inland Revenue permit categories of employees to have (effectively) two normal retirement dates: a director or executive could, for example, be a member of a group pension scheme with a normal retirement age of 65 when the majority of employees will retire, and also be a member of an executive pension plan arranged specially for him with a retirement age of 60 if this age is the best estimate of his date of retirement. For the purpose of deciding the maximum approvable benefits under the executive pension plan there must be taken into account the benefits payable under the main scheme on retirement at the supplementary scheme age, ie the benefits on early retirement.

When setting up a pension plan to top-up group scheme benefits, it is important to consider the status of the member, ie into what category does he fall: pre-1987, 1987–1989 or post-1989? (See 4.3.)

By combining an executive pension plan with a group pension scheme sufficient funds can be accumulated to provide:

(1) A full 2/3rds pension at 60 rather than at 65.
(2) Increases in dependants' benefits.
(3) Increases in pensions in line with increases in the cost of living.
(4) Increases in the tax-free lump sum up to the maximum permitted.

Further features of adopting the executive pension plan route are:

(1) Improved rights in the event of leaving service; if the director or executive leaves service, his benefits, (often in the form of an individual policy), can be transferred to his new employer (and even if it is not transferred, they continue to benefit from future growth).
(2) Improved death in service protection.
(3) The use of dynamised final remuneration (as explained in Chapter 4).
(4) Improved benefits on early retirement.
(5) The director will have greater control over the investment medium in which his contributions are invested and greater privacy over his retirement provisions.
(6) Items which are not normally pensionable, eg bonus, commission, are more easily handled under an executive pension plan.

(7) The employer may use it for discretionary payments in respect of certain directors from time to time, and as a benefit when recruiting executives who do not wish to join a group salary-related scheme.

The following example shows the extent to which a director could top-up his benefits.

Example 10.1

A is a member of a group pension scheme which provides him with 2/3rds of his final salary as a pension from the age of 65, having joined the scheme when he was 25, and is now aged 38. The scope for investment in an executive pension plan may be calculated as follows

Prospective pension at age 65 based on current basic salary	=	2/3 × £25,000
	=	£16,667 pa
Early retirement at age 60	=	35/60 × £25,000 × 0.7*
	=	£10,208 pa
Salary required to support this pension if he were entitled to maximum benefits at age 60	=	£10,208 ÷ 2/3
	=	£15,312
Non-pensioned basic salary	=	£25,000 – £15,312
	=	£9,688
Add other items averaged over three years, eg, bonus, taxable element of fringe benefits, say,		£2,000
Total non-pensioned remuneration		£11,688

*Early retirement actuarial factor to bring forward group scheme pension from age 65 to 60.

The approximate initial annual contribution, increasing at 6.9% pa thereafter, which could be paid to an executive pension plan in this example to provide a maximum member's pension is £4,400.

No allowance has been made for increasing any widow's pension or making provision for post-retirement increases in the group scheme pension.

10.5 Salary sacrifice

If a director's benefits are to be topped-up by means of a separate executive pension plan, which will require approval by the Inland Revenue in the usual way, the employer must contribute towards the costs. If the employer is unwilling to bear any additional expenditure, the employer's contribution can be made by the director giving up part of his salary voluntarily — a practice known as 'salary sacrifice'. Because the employer is paying a lower salary to the director, it has the funds to contribute to an executive pension plan. Amounts sacrificed in this way must be documented usually in the form of an exchange of letters, for example:

> Dear Mr X,
>
> This is to inform you that with effect from 1 October your salary will be reduced from £30,000 pa to £28,000 pa.
>
> Yours sincerely,
>
> For the Company ....
>
> I agree to this reduction in salary.
>
> Signed ....
>
> Director

It is essential that the letter makes no reference to the application of the foregone amount to pension contributions and that it is exchanged before the reduction in salary commences. Failure to observe these rules will almost certainly result in the treatment of the sacrifice as ineffective by the local Inspector of Taxes.

If the amount of salary sacrifice exceeds £5,000 pa notification should be sent direct to the Schedule E tax district. The Schedule E tax district will decide whether or not the sacrifice is an effective reduction of the employee's remuneration assessable to income tax.

If the director is considering paying personal contributions in addition to salary sacrifice the Inland Revenue will require that the employer's contribution is not a derisory proportion of the total — they will normally wish to see 10% of the total contribution paid by the employer.

The effect of salary sacrifice is that the director never receives the sacrificed salary so that he therefore cannot pay tax or National Insurance contributions on it, and the company obtains tax relief whether it pays a level of salary to the director or a lower level of salary plus a pension contribution. The director's salary must, however, be reduced for all purposes including his pensionable salary on which his pension benefits are calculated.

The following example shows how contributions may be paid:

Example 10.2

		Total contribution
Salary	£22,000	
Salary sacrifice	£ 2,000	£2,000 from employer
Revised salary	£20,000	
Personal contribution of, say, 15%	£ 3,000	£3,000 from employee
		£5,000

The employer will contribute £5,000 and deduct the member's share of £3,000 from his salary under a net PAY arrangement.

If, however, the company intend recouping the member's share in monthly instalments over a period of 12 months, then they are effectively giving him an interest free loan on a reducing basis which might be in breach of the Companies Act 1985, s 330 if the member is a director of a public company or of a company in a group which includes a public company. If there is any likelihood of such a breach then the employer should recoup the member's share in one lump.

10.6 Dividend waiver

The principle of dividend waiver is that the shareholder (who will be a working director or employee of the company) renounces in advance his entitlement to any dividend that may be declared in respect of his holdings so that he never becomes entitled to the dividend. The waiver should take the form of a unilateral deed under seal executed by the shareholder only. The waiver should be executed before payment in the case of an interim dividend and before declaration in the case of a final dividend. The waiver must relate only to dividends payable within 12 months of execution and there must be no connection between the dividend waiver and the provision of pension benefits.

10.7 Bonus sacrifice

Some employees are entitled to a bonus or commission which is calculated when the employer's accounts have been certified. For income tax purposes the bonus or commission is treated as accruing during the period to which it relates, for example by reference to annual, quarterly or monthly accounts. A bonus or commission sacrifice which is made after the end of the relative period is regarded by the Inland Revenue as retrospective and therefore as ineffective. The Inland Revenue take the view that the employee's entitlement is fixed at the end of the relative accounting period. When that point is reached the employee cannot sacrifice any part of his bonus or commission even though the exact amount may not be quantified until a later date.

However, the Inland Revenue is prepared to accept a reduction which is agreed sufficiently long before the year end so that the reduced annual sum is not less than the remuneration which has already accrued at the former rate. Ultimately, however, the question of whether or not a sacrifice is effective is a matter for the local Inspector of Taxes.

10.8 Effect of income sacrifice on National Insurance contributions

To the extent that an individual sacrifices income (whether salary, bonus, commission, etc) there will be a saving in the employer's National Insurance contributions.

Since 6 October 1985 National Insurance contributions have been payable by employers on all earnings (prior to that time they were limited to the Upper Earnings Level, which still applies to employees' National Insurance contributions).

Example 10.3

- An executive sacrifices a bonus of £10,000.
- The employer saves £1,040 in NIC.
- Employer's contributions to pension plan can be between £10,000 and £11,040.
- Net income sacrificed by executive £6,000 (assuming a 40% taxpayer).

Example 10.4

- The employer is prepared to spend £10,000 including National Insurance contributions.
- If the executive opts to receive a bonus he will obtain £9,058 gross, £5,435 net (assuming a 40% taxpayer).
- If the executive sacrifices his bonus the company will invest £10,000 in a pension plan for the director.

10.9 Free-standing AVCs

From 6 April 1988 the Social Security Act 1986 required employers to offer members of their occupational schemes the facility to pay Additional Voluntary Contributions to top-up their benefits, although many schemes had provided such facilities for years and had encouraged scheme members to take advantage of the tax-efficiency of AVC arrangements.

From 26 October 1987 a different type of AVC arrangement became available, known as a 'free-standing AVC'. This type of pension contract was introduced by the Finance (No 2) Act 1987 and has the following characteristics:

(1) It must be used to provide income in retirement only, not tax-free lump sums. This restriction also applies to scheme AVCs which started after 7 April 1987.
(2) Contributions are subject to the normal limits applying under occupational schemes approved under ICTA 1988, ss 590–612. There are two main restrictions:
   (a) The maximum contributions that may be paid by an individual amount to 15% of his remuneration (including any personal contributions which his employer may require him to pay under an occupational scheme or under a separate executive pension plan).
   (b) Benefits will also be subject to the normal limits applying under occupational schemes approved under ICTA 1988 (see Chapter 4), but broadly there is a maximum pension on retirement from all sources of two-thirds of final remuneration.
(3) The free-standing AVC scheme is completely separate from the employer's occupational scheme although there is liaison between the trustees of the employer's occupational scheme and the pension provider of the AVC, when benefits become

payable, eg on retirement. The trustees of the employer's scheme will inform the pension provider of the maximum benefits permitted under Inland Revenue rules, and the amount being provided under the employer's scheme. The balance may be provided by the free standing AVC scheme. If there is a surplus when benefits become payable it will have to be returned to the members minus a tax charge (see below).

(4) A significant change has been the lifting of the previous requirements that any AVCs had to be paid on a regular basis in order to attract tax relief. Prior to 6 April 1987 the Inland Revenue required AVCs to be paid for at least five years, or to retirement if earlier, in order to attract tax relief. From 6 April 1987 members have been permitted to vary the amount and timing of AVCs, making these arrangements even more flexible.

(5) They may be arranged through an extended number of pension providers which includes insurance companies, banks, building societies and unit trusts.

(6) Because contributions are paid directly by the individual to the pension provider, tax relief is not obtained in the same manner as tax relief on contributions to an occupational pension scheme or executive pension plan where the 'net pay arrangement' normally operates. Instead, the individual pays contributions net of basic rate tax, similar to the basis on which an individual obtains tax relief on mortgage interest payments on qualifying loans: for example an individual wishing to pay £100 per month to a free-standing AVC contract will therefore have to pay only £75 per month net to the pension provider who will reclaim the tax deducted, ie £25 per month from the Inland Revenue, and will credit the additional £25 per month to the contract (this example assumes basic rate tax relief of 25%). Any higher rate tax relief will be obtained by application to the Inland Revenue, ie through the individual's tax return.

10.9.1 Over-provision

If the combination of benefits under the main occupational scheme and the free-standing AVC provides excessive benefits the main scheme benefits are not reduced but the surplus arises under the free-standing AVC. The scheme administrator of the free-standing AVC must deduct tax at 35% of the surplus fund if the individual is a basic rate taxpayer. Assuming a surplus of £1,000, tax is deducted of £350 with £650 payable to the member. This amount, £650, is treated as income which has suffered basic rate tax (taken to be 25%). The net amount received by the individual of £650 has a grossed up equivalent of £867 but there is no further liability to tax in the case of a basic rate taxpayer. Even if the individual is not liable to tax the amount paid by the scheme administrator cannot be recovered. If the individual is a higher rate taxpayer, further tax at 15% is payable on the grossed up amount, in this case £130 further liability. In the case of a higher rate taxpayer, therefore, there is total tax to pay of £480, representing an effective tax rate of 48% on the surplus of £1,000.

10.9.2 Estimating benefits

An individual wishing to pay AVCs will wish to ascertain how much could be contributed to the free-standing AVC to top up the overall benefits to the Inland Revenue maximum. An indication of the scope for AVCs can be provided by the main scheme trustees or by the pension provider which runs the free-standing AVC. An individual wishing to pay contributions of £2,400 per annum or more must provide the free-standing AVC provider with information relating to his main scheme and previous retained benefits. The pension provider will then test the possibility of over-provision: if this is likely the pension provider will inform the intending contributor of the reduced level of contributions which should be paid to ensure that overall benefits do not exceed Inland Revenue limits. If contributions however, are less than £2,400 per annum the free-standing AVC provider does not have to carry out an initial check (but will do so should the contributions exceed £2,400 per annum in the future).

Although a disadvantage of the free-standing AVC scheme is the inability to take any of the emerging benefits in the form of a tax-free lump sum, in practice this problem may be overcome by looking at the combined benefits emerging from the free-standing AVC scheme and the individual's other pension arrangements. To the extent that an individual takes a tax-free lump sum from any pension scheme, his pension is bound to be lower: in practice, many pensioners reinvest any lump sum in other areas to provide additional income in order to maintain a reasonable standard of living. If, however, an individual is deterred from paying contributions to a free-standing AVC scheme because it does not provide a tax-free lump sum, he should investigate the rules of his main occupational scheme. Although it might provide a cash lump sum of, say, only 3/80ths of his final salary for each year of service, the rules will often contain powers of augmentation allowing the trustees to increase the tax-free lump sum (and other benefits) up to the maximum permitted by the Inland Revenue. The individual, therefore, could take increased cash from his occupational scheme leaving a lower income from that scheme which would be topped-up by the pension emerging from his free-standing AVC scheme.

Example 10.5

Company pension scheme provides:
a pension of £3,333 pa (20/60ths of pensionable salary of £10,000).
or
a reduced pension plus a cash lump sum of £7,500 (3/80ths of pensionable salary for each year of pensionable service, ie 60/80ths).

The Inland Revenue allow tax-free cash to be calculated using the greater of 3/80ths of pensionable salary for each year of pensionable service or 2.25 × the pension before commutation. Both methods would produce the same result. If the member contributes to a free-standing AVC scheme which produces an additional pension of £1,000 pa, this can be taken into account in the calculation. The member could then take £9,750 under the main company scheme as a cash lump sum (2.25 × £4,333).

10.9.3 Transitional arrangements

Finance (No 2) Act 1987 introduced changes affecting Additional Voluntary Contributions. Only new AVC arrangements entered into after 7 April 1987, including contributions to free-standing AVC schemes, are affected by the 'no commutation rule'. The following (which is an extract from Memorandum 87 published by the Inland Revenue on the subject) will *not* be affected:

(1) An arrangement whereby a contractual obligation was entered into before 8 April 1987, even if the first contribution had not been paid until after that date.
(2) Continuation of an arrangement following the re-organisation of an employer's pension arrangements, or the restructuring or sale of part or all of the employer's business.
(3) A change in the amount or timing of AVCs; examples are an increase in the percentage of salary being paid or a change from a monthly to annual payment basis.
(4) A break in contributions, provided that on recommencement the AVCs are paid to the original arrangement or to another arrangement which is part of the employer's scheme.
(5) A change in investment medium for the AVCs (eg a switch from an insurance contract to a building society deposit) provided that the new investments are held under an AVC arrangement first entered into before 8 April 1987.

11 State benefits

On 6 April 1978, the present state scheme started, following the Social Security Pensions Act 1975 and replacing the State Graduated Scheme. The scheme consists of two pensions — a basic old age pension and an earnings related additional pension (known as 'SERPS'). At that time employers with a good occupational pension scheme (providing pensions on a defined benefit basis) could 'contract out' of SERPS. Those employees who were contracted-out on this basis will receive the old age pension from the state and an additional earnings related pension from their occupational scheme.

In 1988 contracting-out on a money purchase basis through either an occupational pension scheme set up by the employer or a personal pension plan became available. Those employees who are contracted-out on a money purchase basis will receive the old age pension from the state and a 'protected rights' pension (see Chapter 12). Self-employed persons, however, are entitled only to the old age pension, not the earnings related pension (their National Insurance contributions are substantially lower than those paid by and on behalf of an employed person). The scheme has been the subject of amendments since its introduction, and this Chapter considers the scheme as it is (in amended form) and also the changes which took effect from 6 April 1988.

The Government has issued a consultative paper on the options for equalising the state pensions age for men and women, seeking comments by 30 June 1992. It is likely, however, to be a long time before any changes are introduced to state pensions.

11.1 Objective of the earnings related state pension

The single person's old age pension was around 25% of the national average earnings but now stands at around only 19%. (This is a result of increasing the old age pension in line with increases in the retail prices index rather than the national average earnings index, as applied previously.) The original objective of the earnings related part of the state scheme (which is not a funded scheme) was to increase the general level of state pension for single persons by a further 25% of national average earnings over a period of 20 years starting from April 1978. Thus, employed persons retiring in 1998 could expect to receive a full earnings related pension when they finally retired. Employed males who were over the age of 45 in 1978 and most working females over the age of 40 in 1978 will receive a proportion of the full pension depending upon the number of years that they participate before retirement and their own level of earnings.

The Social Security Act 1986, however, brought about major changes to the earnings related part of the state scheme (SERPS). These changes will result in the reduction in SERPS mainly for people retiring in the next century. The Social Security Act 1986, has also had a major impact on occupational schemes as it is simpler for employers to set up pension schemes to contract out of SERPS and it is also possible for individuals to decide whether or not to contract out of SERPS through the use of personal pension schemes (see Chapter 12).

11.2 State scheme contributions

Pensions are paid by levying National Insurance contributions on the working population on a 'pay as you go basis'. In 1974, the Government actuary estimated the potential liability of the enlarged state scheme and recommended an initial contribution rate of $16\frac{1}{2}\%$ of earnings, split 10% from employers and $6\frac{1}{2}\%$ from employees. The employer's contributions may be set against profits for corporation tax purposes but employee contributions are not tax deductible. (National Insurance contributions are collected through the PAYE system.)

National Insurance contribution rates incorporate other National Insurance benefits such as short-term sickness, National Health and redundancy payments. They do not therefore represent the actual cost of state pensions alone.

The following table sets out contracted-in and contracted-out National Insurance contributions payable by employers and employees from 1978 to 1990 inclusive.

Table 11.1

(National Insurance contribution rates)

			Contracted-out rates	
Tax Year	Employee %	Employer %	Employee %	Employer %
1978/79	6.50	10.00	4.00	5.50
1979/80	6.50	10.00	4.00	5.50
1980/81	6.75	10.20	4.25	5.70
1981/82	7.75	10.20	5.25	5.70
1982/83	8.75	10.20	6.25	5.70
1983/84	9.00	10.45	6.85	6.35
1984/85	9.00	10.45	6.85	6.35
1985/86 (to 6.10.85)	9.00	10.45	6.85	6.35
6.10.85 to 5.4.86 Earnings per week				
below £35.50	Nil	Nil	Nil	Nil
£35.50–£55.00	5	5	2.85	0.90
£55.00–£90.00	7	7	4.85	2.90
£90–£130.00	9	9	6.85	4.90
£130.00–£265.00	9	10.45	6.85	6.35
6.4.86 to 5.4.87 Earnings per week				
below £38.00	Nil	Nil	Nil	Nil
£ 38.00 to £ 60.00	5	5	2.85	0.90
£ 60.00 to £ 95.00	7	7	4.85	2.90
£ 95.00 to £140.00	9	9	6.85	4.90
£140.00 to £285.00	9	10.45	6.85	6.35
6.4.87 to 5.4.88 Earnings per week				
below £39.00	Nil	Nil	Nil	Nil
£ 39.00 to £ 65.00	5	5	2.85	0.90
£ 65.00 to £100.00	7	7	4.85	2.90
£100.00 to £150.00	9	9	6.85	4.90
£150.00 to £295.00	9	10.45	6.85	6.35
6.4.88 to 5.4.89 Earnings per week				
below £41.00	Nil	Nil	Nil	Nil
£ 41.00 to £ 70.00	5	5	3	1.2
£ 70.00 to £105.00	7	7	5	3.2
£105.00 to £155.00	9	9	7	5.2
£155.00 to £305.00	9	10.45	7	6.65

6.4.89 to 3.10.89				
Earnings per week				
below £43.00	Nil	Nil	Nil	Nil
£ 43.00 to £ 75.00	5	5	3	1.2
£ 75.00 to £115.00	7	7	5	3.2
£115.00 to £165.00	9	9	7	5.2
£165.00 to £325.00	9	10.45	7	6.65
4.10.89 to 5.4.90				
Earnings per week				
below £41.00	Nil	Nil	Nil	Nil
£ 41.00 to £ 70.00	2% on first	5	2% on first	1.2
£ 70.00 to £105.00	£41.00 plus	7	£41.00 plus	3.2
£105.00 to £155.00	9% on	9	7% on	5.2
£155.00 to £305.00	remainder up to £305.00	10.45	remainder up to £305.00	6.65
6.4.90 to 5.4.91				
Earnings per week				
below £46.00	Nil	Nil	Nil	Nil
£ 46.00 to £ 80.00	2% on first	5	2% on first	1.2
£ 80.00 to £125.00	£46.00 plus	7	£46.00 plus	3.2
£125.00 to £175.00	9% on	9	7% on	5.2
£175.00 to £350.00	remainder up to £305.00	10.45	remainder up to £305.00	6.65
6.4.91 to 5.4.92				
Earnings per week				
below £52.00	Nil	Nil	Nil	Nil
£ 52.00 to £ 85.00	2% on first	4.6	2% on first	0.8
£ 85.00 to £130.00	£52.00 plus	6.6	£54.00 plus	2.8
£130.00 to £185.00	9% on	8.6	7% on	4.8
£185.00 to £390.00	remainder up to £390.00	10.40	remainder up to £390.00	6.6
6.4.92 to 5.4.93				
Earnings per week				
below £54.00	Nil	Nil	Nil	Nil
£ 54.00 to £ 90.00	2% on first	4.6	2% on first	0.8
£ 90.00 to £135.00	£54.00 plus	6.6	£54.00 plus	2.8
£135.00 to £190.00	9% on	8.6	7% on	4.8
£190.00 to £405.00	remainder up to £405.00	10.40	remainder up to £405.00	6.6

Notes:

1   The table shows the rates payable according to the band in which the employee's earnings fall. If the employee earns less than the Upper

Earnings Limit the above rates apply to all earnings. If the employee earns over the UEL then the employer's rate is 10.40% on all earnings. The employee's rate, up to 4.10.88, was 9% on all earnings up to the UEL, but from 4.10.89 was reduced to 8% on earnings up to the LEL plus 9% on the remainder between LEL and UEL. For an occupational scheme which is contracted-out the contributions between the Lower and Upper Earnings Limits are reduced — see Note (3) below. The Lower and Upper Earnings Limits are set out in Table 11.2 below.

2   An Employer's Surcharge applied at the following rates between April 1978 and October 1984:

1978/79, 1979/80, 1980/81, 1981/82: 3.5%
1982/83   : 2.0% (approximately)
1983/84 to 1.8.83   : 1.5%
1983/84 from 1.8.83   : 1.0%
1984/85 to 1.10.84   : 1.0%

3   The reduction in NIC where the individual is contracted-out is currently 2.00% (employee), 3.80% (employer), in respect of earnings between the UEL and LEL. For years 1978/79 to 1982/83 the reduction was 2.50% and 4.55% respectively and for the years 1983/84 to 1987/88 the reduction was 2.15% and 4.10% respectively.

11.3 Upper and lower earnings limits

There is a ceiling on earnings for National Insurance purposes known as the upper earnings limit. The lower earnings limit corresponds roughly with the flat rate pension for a single person while the upper earnings limit is around seven times the lower earnings limit: both limits are adjusted in April each year. Table 11.2 sets out upper and lower earnings limits for 1978 to 1992 inclusive.

Table 11.2

Earnings Limits

Tax year	Lower Earnings Limit £ pa (a)	Upper Earnings Limit £ pa (a)
1978/79	910	6,240
1979/80	1,014	7,020
1980/81	1,196	8,580
1981/82	1,404	10,400
1982/83	1,534	11,440
1983/84	1,690	12,220
1984/85	1,768	13,000
1985/86	1,846	13,780
1986/87	1,976	14,820
1987/88	2,028	15,340
1988/89	2,132	15,860
1989/90	2,236	16,900
1990/91	2,392	18,200
1991/92	2,704	20,280
1992/93	2,808	21,060

Note

(a) 52 times the weekly amount

11.4 Qualifying conditions

SERPS is paid as part of the old age pension, and the qualifying conditions are therefore the same, namely that the individual:

- has reached pensionable age (65 males, 60 females); and
- has retired from regular employment (see below); and
- satisfies the contribution condition (in SERPS terms, this is the requirement that the Class 1 National Insurance contributions paid in at least one tax year from 1978/79 onwards generate a 'surplus' — see 11.6 below).

11.5 Employment beyond pensionable age

An individual who is continuing to work after reaching pensionable age will usually still be regarded as having retired from regular employment if the employment falls within no more than one of the following:

(1) the work does not normally involve more than 12 hours per week; or
(2) the work is 'occasional' (ie no normal weekly commitment).

Individuals will automatically be treated as having retired on attaining the age of 70 (males) or 65 (females) if they have not already done so. The individual will still need to submit a claim for SERPS even on attaining the age of 70/65.

Widow(er)s
A widow(er) may also be able to claim SERPS benefits based on the contribution record of the deceased spouse (see widow(er)s benefits).

11.6 Amount of pension

The total earnings figure on which SERPS depends is calculated as follows:

(1) Earnings on which Class 1 National Insurance contributions have been paid in each tax year commencing 1978/79 are calculated.
(2) Each earnings figure is then 'revalued' by increasing it by a percentage reflecting the increase in national earnings since the tax year concerned (no revaluation takes place for the tax year in which age 64 (males) or age 59 (females) is attained).
(3) Each annual figure is then reduced by the lower earnings level applicable to the tax year in which age 64 (males) or 59 (females) is attained.
(4) The resulting reduced amounts represent the 'surplus' for each of the tax years in question.

11.7 Annual rate of SERPS

11.7.1 Pre-April 1988 calculation

The annual rate of SERPS is then determined according to the tax year in which the individual retires as follows:

(1) **Retirement in 1998/99 or earlier.** The total of 1/80th of each of the surpluses as calculated above.
(2) **Retirement in 1999/2000 or later.** SERPS will be based on a maximum of 20 years of earnings on which NIC have been

144 Allied Dunbar Pensions Guide

paid. Employees who make NIC for more than 20 years will receive an earnings related pension based on the **best** of 1/80th of each of the surpluses for each of the best 20 years, giving a maximum pension of 25% of surpluses.

11.7.2 Post-April 1988 calculation

(1) **Retirement in 1998/99 or earlier:** the total of 1/80th of each of the surpluses as calculated above.

(2) **Retirement in 1999/2000 — 2008/09:**

$\frac{25\%}{N}$ of the surpluses for the tax years 1978/79 to 1987/88 inclusive,

plus

$\frac{20 + X\%}{N}$ of the surpluses for the tax years 1988/89 onwards.

(3) **Retirement in 2009/10 onwards**

$\frac{25\%}{N}$ of the surpluses for the tax years 1978/79 to 1987/88 inclusive,

plus

$\frac{20\%}{N}$ of the surpluses for the tax years 1988/89 onwards.

Where:

N = the number of tax years in the pensioner's working life after 5 April 1978

X = 0.5 for each tax year by which retirement precedes the tax year 2009/10

and may be reduced in respect of tax years after 5 April 1978 in which:

(a) contributions or earnings were credited in order to enable a person to satisfy contribution conditions, or
(b) the pensioner was precluded from regular employment by responsibilities at home;

but not to the extent that N would fall below 20.

11.7.3 Major differences

The two major differences between the original and modified bases are:

(1) The reduction in the level of SERPS from a maximum of 25% to 20% in respect of surpluses for the tax years 1988/89 onwards (with a sliding scale for ten years); and
(2) The removal of the 'best 20 years' rule which will have the effect of reducing the level of earnings/surpluses on which SERPS is calculated.

Example 11.1

Person retiring in 2006/07 with a working life (since 1978/79) of 28 years.

Original basis: 1.25% of surpluses for the best 20 of the 28 years (ie the worst eight years are ignored), giving a total of 25% of surpluses.

Revised basis: $\frac{25\%}{28}$ of the surpluses for tax years 1978/79 to 1987/88 inclusive plus

$\frac{(20 + 1.5\%)\%}{28}$ of surpluses for the tax years 1988/89 onwards, giving a total of 22.75% of surpluses.

11.8 Increases during payment

The amount of SERPS benefit is increased each year by the state (along with the basic old age pension) in line with increases in the Retail Prices Index.

11.9 Deferred pension

If an individual, on reaching pensionable age, is still in regular employment (see above) or defers claiming the state pension, additional pension benefits will accrue at a rate of 1/7th % for each full week deferred.

The maximum period of deferment is five years to age 70 (males), 65 (females), and no further NICs are payable by the individual during this period (although employers' Class 1 NIC continues for as long as the employment continues with no upper age limit). The maximum additional pension which may be earned over a full five years' deferment is approximately 37%.

If any social security benefits (except attendance allowance, mobility or benefit for a child) are received, or an unemployability supplement is paid with a disablement pension in any week, no additional pension will accrue for that week.

Any additional pension earned by deferment may also be inherited by a widow(er) on the individual's death.

11.10 Widows' benefits

The availability of any SERPS benefits in the event of a husband's death is dependent on:

- the husband's age at date of death, and
- the widow's age at date of husband's death, and
- whether any children under the age of 19 are resident with the widow.

The following paragraphs show the various benefits which may be claimed and should be read in conjunction with the following notes:

Notes
(1) Widow's payment, a lump sum of £1,000, cannot be claimed if:
 (a) the widow was over age 60 when her husband died and he was then over age 65 and then entitled to a retirement pension (this does not include a retirement pension which has been deferred), or
 (b) the 'contribution conditions' are not fulfilled.
(2) Widowed Mother's Allowance is payable immediately on bereavement until the youngest child ceases to be dependent.
(3) Where SERPS is claimed on the contribution record of the late husband in order to supplement the contribution record of the widow, the maximum benefit will be that which a single person could have earned by paying maximum contributions.
(4) Widow's Pension will continue to be paid after age 60 unless the widow retires and she will automatically be treated as having retired at age 65. When she retires, widow's pension will be replaced with retirement pension.
(5) Both Widowed Mother's Allowance and Widow's Pension will cease permanently if the widow remarries, and will be suspended if she lives with another man as his wife.
(6) Where SERPS is 'inherited' from a deceased husband, the current amount is 100% of the SERPS earned up to the date

of the husband's death, but will be reduced to 50% of this amount if the husband dies after 5 April 2000.

11.11 Husband dies leaving children

The benefits payable to the widow are:

(1) Widow's Payment (but see Note 1 above);
(2) Widowed Mother's Allowance and SERPS based on husband's contribution record; followed by
(3) A Widow's Pension based on her age at the time the Widowed Mother's Allowance ends as follows:

Table 11.3

Widow's age	Widow's pension
Over 60	Basic and SERPS on own and/or husband's contribution records (see Note 3).
55–60	(a) Basic and SERPS on husband's contribution record payable to age 60; then (b) Basic and SERPS on own and/or husband's contribution records (see Note 3) but with a minimum of the pension payable immediately before age 60.
45–54	(a) Basic and SERPS on husband's contribution record, reduced by 7% for each year (or part) by which widow's age falls short of 50, payable to age 60; then (b) Basic and SERPS on own and/or husband's contribution records (see Note 3) but with a minimum of the pension payable immediately before age 60.
Under 45	(a) No further benefit to age 60; then (b) Basic and SERPS on own contribution record.

11.12 Husband dies leaving no children

The benefits payable to the widow are:

(1) Widow's Allowance (but see Notes (1) and (2) above); followed by
(2) A Widow's Pension based on her age *at the time of her husband's death* as follows:

Table 11.4

Widow's age	Widow's pension
Over 60	Basic and SERPS on own and/or husband's contribution records (see Note 3).
55–60	(a) Basic and SERPS on husband's contribution record payable to age 60; then (b) Basic and SERPS on own and/or husband's contribution records (see Note 3) but with a minimum of the pension payable immediately before age 60.
45–54	(a) Basic and SERPS on husband's contribution record, reduced by 7% for each year (or part) by which widow's age falls short of 50, payable to age 60; then (b) Basic and SERPS on own and/or husband's contribution records (see Note 3) but with a minimum of the pension payable immediately before age 60.
Under 45	(a) No further benefit to age 60; then (b) Basic and SERPS on own contribution record.

11.13 Widowers' benefits

11.13.1 Original basis

A widower may only claim any SERPS based on his late wife's contribution record if:

(1) both he and his wife had reached pensionable age before she died; and
(2) he had retired from regular employment.

The maximum SERPS a widower may inherit is such that, when added to his own SERPS entitlement, it does not exceed the maximum SERPS an individual would be entitled to based on maximum contributions.

11.13.2 Modified basis

The amount of SERPS which a widower may inherit from his late wife will be 50% of that calculated on the original basis, if she dies after 5 April 2000.

11.14 Summary of state pensions

Table 11.5

Basic Old Age Pensions

From	Single person £ per annum	Married couple £ per annum
13 November 1978	1,014.00	1,622.40
12 November 1979	1,211.60	1,939.60
24 November 1980	1,411.80	2,259.40
23 November 1981	1,539.20	2,462.20
22 November 1982	1,708.20	2,732.60
21 November 1983	1,770.60	2,834.00
26 November 1984	1,861.60	2,979.60
25 November 1985	1,991.60	3,187.60
28 July 1986	2,012.40	3,221.40
6 April 1987	2,054.00	3,289.00
6 April 1988	2,139.80	3,426.80
6 April 1989	2,267.20	3,629.60
6 April 1990	2,438.80	3,905.20
6 April 1991	2,704.00	4,329.00
6 April 1992	2,815.80	4,508.40

Table 11.6 sets out the projected pension (SERPS and basic old age) for single persons as a percentage of salary on retirement at age 65 (men), 60 (women).

Table 11.6

Age Males	Females	£7,000	£8,000	£9,000	£10,000	£15,000	£21,060	£25,000	£40,000
16		52.2	48.2	45.0	42.5	35.0	30.7	25.9	16.2
17		52.2	48.2	45.0	42.5	35.0	30.7	25.9	16.2
18		52.2	48.2	45.0	42.5	35.0	30.7	25.9	16.2
19		52.2	48.2	45.0	42.5	35.0	30.7	25.9	16.2
20		52.2	48.2	45.0	42.5	35.0	30.7	25.9	16.2
21	16	52.3	48.2	45.1	42.6	35.1	30.8	25.9	16.2
22	17	52.3	48.3	45.2	42.7	35.2	30.9	26.0	16.3
23	18	52.4	48.4	45.3	42.8	35.3	31.0	26.1	16.3
24	19	52.4	48.4	45.3	42.8	35.4	31.1	26.2	16.4
25	20	52.5	48.5	45.4	42.9	35.4	31.1	26.2	16.4
26	21	52.6	48.6	45.5	43.0	35.5	31.2	26.3	16.4
27	22	52.6	48.6	45.5	43.1	35.6	31.3	26.4	16.5
28	23	52.7	48.7	45.6	43.1	35.7	31.4	26.5	16.5
29	24	52.8	48.8	45.7	43.2	35.8	31.5	26.5	16.6
30	25	52.8	48.8	45.7	43.3	35.9	31.6	26.6	16.6

150 Allied Dunbar Pensions Guide

31	26	52.8	48.9	45.8	43.3	35.9	31.6	26.6	16.6
32	27	52.8	48.9	45.8	43.3	35.9	31.6	26.6	16.7
33	28	52.9	48.9	45.8	43.3	35.9	31.6	26.7	16.7
34	29	52.9	48.9	45.8	43.3	35.9	31.7	26.7	16.7
35	30	52.9	48.9	45.8	43.4	36.0	31.7	26.7	16.7
36	31	52.9	48.9	45.8	43.4	36.0	31.7	26.7	16.7
37	32	52.9	49.0	45.9	43.4	36.0	31.7	26.7	16.7
38	33	52.9	49.0	45.9	43.4	36.0	31.8	26.8	16.7
39	34	53.0	49.0	45.9	43.4	36.0	31.8	26.8	16.7
40	35	53.0	49.0	45.9	43.5	36.1	31.8	26.8	16.8
41	36	53.0	49.0	46.0	43.5	36.1	31.8	26.8	16.8
42	37	53.0	49.1	46.0	43.5	36.1	31.9	26.9	16.8
43	38	53.0	49.1	46.0	43.5	36.2	31.9	26.9	16.8
44	39	53.1	49.1	46.0	43.6	36.2	31.9	26.9	16.8
45	40	53.1	49.1	46.1	43.6	36.2	32.0	26.9	16.8
46	41	53.1	49.2	46.1	43.6	36.3	32.0	27.0	16.9
47	42	53.1	49.2	46.1	43.7	36.3	32.1	27.0	16.9
48	43	53.2	49.2	46.2	43.7	36.3	32.1	27.0	16.9
49	44	53.4	49.5	46.4	44.0	36.7	32.4	27.3	17.1
50	45	53.6	49.7	46.7	44.3	37.0	32.8	27.6	17.3
51	46	53.8	50.0	46.9	44.5	37.3	33.1	27.9	17.4
52	47	54.1	50.2	47.2	44.8	37.6	33.4	28.1	17.6
53	48	54.3	50.4	47.4	45.0	37.8	33.7	28.4	17.7
54	49	54.5	50.6	47.7	45.3	38.1	34.0	28.6	17.9
55	50	54.7	50.9	47.9	45.5	38.4	34.3	28.9	18.0
56	51	54.9	51.1	48.1	45.7	38.6	34.5	29.1	18.2
57	52	55.0	51.2	48.3	45.9	38.9	34.8	29.3	18.3
58	53	55.2	51.4	48.5	46.1	39.1	35.0	29.5	18.4
59	54	55.2	51.4	48.5	46.1	39.1	35.0	29.5	18.4
60	55	54.4	50.6	47.6	45.2	38.1	34.0	28.6	17.9
61	56	53.7	49.8	46.8	44.3	37.1	32.9	27.7	17.3
62	57	53.0	49.0	45.9	43.4	36.0	31.8	26.8	16.7
63	58	52.2	48.2	45.0	42.5	35.0	30.7	25.9	16.2
64	59	51.5	47.4	44.2	41.6	34.0	29.6	25.0	15.6

Table 11.7 shows the Married Couples' Additional Amount as a percentage of salary.

Table 11.7

Salary £7,000	£8,000	£9,000	£10,000	£15,000	£21,060	£25,000	£40,000
24.2	21.2	18.8	16.9	11.3	8.0	6.7	4.2

Notes to Tables 11.6 and 11.7

(1) The age shown is the age attained on the birthday falling within the 1992/93 tax year.
(2) It is assumed that salary, Lower Earnings Limit, Upper Earnings Limit and Old Age Pension all increase at the same rate.
(3) Amounts assumed. Lower Earnings Limit £2,808
    Upper Earnings Limit £21,060
    Old Age Pension £2,815.80
    Married Couples'
    Additional Amount £1,692.60
(4) The self-employed will only receive the Old Age Pension and where applicable the Married Couples' Additional Amount.
(5) Females who are younger than 24 will receive up to $\frac{1}{2}\%$ less.
(6) The figures assume that individuals have been in contracted-in employment since 1978 or age 16 if later.
(7) The Married Couples' Additional Amount assumes the wife is unable to claim state scheme benefits in her own right.

11.15 Adequacy of state pensions

The combination of the basic flat rate pension and the earnings related pension will provide reasonable benefits for employees earning up to national average earnings (approximately £14,800 per annum). For employees whose earnings are above the national average there are serious inadequacies including:

(1) The inability to obtain a pension on earnings which exceed the upper earnings limit.
(2) The maximum additional state pension obtainable of 20% to 25% of revalued earnings is substantially less than the maximum pension which could be provided from an occupational scheme or an executive pension plan.
(3) The state does not allow any part of the pension to be commuted for a tax-free lump sum.
(4) The state does not provide any lump sum benefits in the event of death in service or after retirement.
(5) The state makes no provision for benefits to be payable on early retirement.

The major advantage of the state scheme, however, is the degree of inflation-proofing provided.

In view of the above limitations it is advisable to top-up state benefits through executive pension plans (particularly in the case of directors who are able to fund for maximum benefits) and through personal pension schemes which have the added advantage of being able to contract out of SERPS which is particularly beneficial for younger employees (see Chapter 12).

11.16 DSS leaflets

In general the calculation of state benefits is a complicated exercise especially as so many conditions attach to the benefits. In practice the benefits themselves will probably be inadequate so that the need to top-up state benefits through private provision, eg by membership of an occupational scheme or through a personal pension scheme, is of paramount importance, particularly in relation to widows'/widowers' benefits.

The DSS publish a number of leaflets describing state benefits and these are essential reading for anyone who wishes to comprehend fully all the conditions which apply. The principal leaflets are:

'A Guide to Retirement Pensions' ref NP46 and 'New Pensions Choices', refs NP 40, NP 41, NP 42.

By completing BR 19 'Retirement Pension Forecast' the DSS will provide an individual with an estimate of his state benefits. These quotations will be of particular use to individuals who are considering contracting-out of SERPS through a personal pension.

11.17 Contracting-out

This chapter has concentrated mainly on benefits provided under the State Earnings Related Pension Scheme. The next chapter looks at how it is possible to contract-out of SERPS.

12 Contracting-out of the State Earnings Related Scheme

Contracting-out of SERPS may be achieved either through membership of an occupational scheme set up by the employer or by taking out a personal pension scheme. However contracting-out through a personal pension scheme was not possible before 1 July 1988.

Since 6 April 1978 it has been possible for occupational schemes to contract-out. However this can be achieved on either a defined benefit or money purchase basis; the latter was not available before 6 April 1988. Around one-half of the working population are members of contracted-out occupational pension schemes. Many of these schemes which had been in existence prior to 1978 provided worthwhile benefits so that in 1978 they required only fine-tuning to enable them to meet the original conditions for contracting-out.

These conditions were two-fold: the scheme had to provide a reasonable level of benefits generally, known as 'requisite benefits', and, at the very least, the scheme had to match SERPS by providing 'Guaranteed Minimum Pension', ie the pension which an individual would have received from SERPS if he had never been contracted-out.

The basic minimum conditions which had to be satisfied were as follows:

(1) The occupational pension scheme had to provide pensions based on an accrual rate of 1/80th of final salary (or average salary revalued in line with National Average Earnings) for each year of contracted-out service subject to a maximum of 40 years (a 'requisite benefit').
(2) There had to be a widow's pension payable on death either

before or after retirement of at least 1/160th of the employee's final salary for each year of contracted-out service (a 'requisite benefit').
(3) The occupational scheme had to meet certain minimum requirements laid down by the Occupational Pensions Board.
(4) The pension in respect of a member and the widow's pension in respect of a deceased member must never have fallen below the Guaranteed Minimum Pension.
(5) Employees leaving service before retirement age would enjoy revaluation of their Guaranteed Minimum Pensions between leaving and retirement age.

12.1 Abolition of requisite benefit test

From November 1986, occupational schemes no longer had to satisfy the requisite benefit test referred to in the previous paragraph. It is now sufficient for schemes to provide Guaranteed Minimum Pensions for contracting-out purposes. This is particularly beneficial for occupational schemes which have a younger age distribution because the Guaranteed Minimum Pension is considerably lower than requisite benefits. Under the requisite benefit test an individual aged 25 would have been provided with a pension of 40/80ths, ie 50%, of his total salary on retirement at 65. The Guaranteed Minimum Pension, which matches SERPS, amounts to a maximum of 25% of earnings between the lower and upper earnings levels. Whilst the removal of the requisite benefit test has made it easier for employers to contract-out of SERPS, in practice the pensions payable to individual members will, in many cases, do no more than match SERPS. However, most occupational schemes, particularly those set up prior to November 1986, provide a level of benefits greater than SERPS.

Where an occupational scheme is used to contract out of SERPS the employer and employee pay National Insurance contributions at contracted-out rates. In 1992/93 the employer pays 10.40% of an employee's earnings up to £2,808 per annum and above £21,060 per annum and 6.60% of earnings between these two limits. An employee pays 2% of earnings up to £2,808 per annum and 7% of his earnings between £2,808 per annum and his actual earnings or £21,060 per annum, whichever is the lower. By being contracted-out there is a saving in National Insurance contributions of 5.8% of band earnings (the earnings between the lower and upper earnings levels): it is split 2% to the employee and 3.8% to the employer. Of course the employer has to contribute to the scheme and generally the member will be asked to contribute also. Where the age distribution of the scheme is young an employer can set up an occupational scheme providing only Guaranteed Minimum Pensions at virtually no cost because the reduction in National Insurance contributions is more or less equal to the cost of the scheme. The benefits from the scheme, however, are virtually no better than SERPS.

12.2 Guaranteed minimum pensions

12.2.1 Original basis

The GMP and widow's GMP mirror SERPS and are calculated as follows:

Retirement in 1997/98 or earlier: $1\frac{1}{4}\%$ of the total of earnings factors (see Chapter 11 for a description of earnings factor).

Retirement in 1998/99 or later: $25\%/N$ of the total of the earnings factors.

12.2.2 Revised basis

Retirement in 1997/98 or earlier:

$1\frac{1}{4}\%$ of the earnings factors for the tax years 1978/79 to 1987/88 inclusive, plus 1% of the earnings factors for the tax years 1988/89 onwards

Retirement in 1998/99 onwards:

$\frac{25\%}{N}$ of the earnings factors for the tax years 1978/79 to 1987/88 inclusive, plus

$\frac{20\%}{N}$ of the earnings factors for the tax years 1988/89 onwards.

Where 'N' is the number of contracted-out tax years in the pensioner's working life after 5 April 1978 and 'retirement' is age 65 (men), age 60 (women).

12.2.3 Major difference

The major difference between the current and revised bases is the reduction in the accrual of GMP from a maximum of 25% to 20% in respect of earnings for the tax years 1988/89 onwards.

Example 12.1

Person retiring in 2006/07 with a contracted-out working life (since 1978/79) of 28 years.

Original basis:	$\frac{25\%}{28}$ of earnings factors for the 28 years (ie 25% of the total earnings factors).
Revised basis:	$\frac{25\%}{28}$ of earnings factors for the tax years 1978/79 to 1987/88 inclusive,
plus	$\frac{20\%}{28}$ of earnings factors for the tax year 1988/89 onwards.

12.3 Deferred GMP

If an individual continues in employment beyond state pensionable age, the scheme may provide for the GMP to be postponed for any period of continued employment.

The member's consent will, however, be required for any postponement beyond five years after state pensionable age or where the continuing employment is not that to which the scheme relates.

Where GMP is deferred, the amount is increased by 1/7% for each full week of deferral. Unlike SERPS, the minimum period of deferral before an increase is payable is just one week, and GMP may be deferred for longer than five years.

12.4 Widow's GMP

Since the abolition of the requisite benefit test on 1 November 1986, it has only been necessary for a contracted-out scheme to provide members with a widow's GMP of half the member's GMP, whether the member dies before or after pensionable age.

The widow's GMP must be payable for any period for which a widow's pension, widowed mother's allowance or retirement pension based on the deceased member's contribution record is payable.

A widow's GMP can only be paid to the widow and not to any other dependant.

The amount of total pension benefits a widow may inherit will be calculated in the same way as for the member's own pension, ie SERPS is calculated as if the member had never been contracted-out and then reduced by the amount of any GMP payable.

12.5 Increases during payment

The amount of GMP payable will be increased each year (along with the basic old age pension) in line with prices. In respect of the GMP attributable to earnings factors for tax years prior to 1988/89, this increase is provided by the state. However, in respect of GMP attributable to earnings factors for the tax years 1988/89 or later, it will be necessary for the occupational scheme to increase the GMP each year by the lesser of:

(1) the increase in the general level of prices; and
(2) 3%.

As the GMP is not provided by the state, the total amount of increase to be paid by the state is calculated as follows:

(1) An amount of SERPS is calculated as if the employee had never been contracted-out. This provides a base figure on which all future increases will be based.
(2) The amount of 'revalued' SERPS is then reduced by the amount of any GMP payable (including any increases to GMP provided by the scheme).
(3) The net amount is then paid each week along with the basic old age pension.

This method also allows SERPS to be calculated where the individual is entitled to both an element of SERPS and GMP as a result of not having been contracted-out for his entire working life.

12.6 Contracting-out after 1988

The Social Security Act 1986 has resulted in an increase in the number of contracted-out people because:

(1) Since 1 July 1988 individuals have been allowed to effect a personal pension scheme and contract-out. Any person acting before 6 April 1989 was allowed to contract-out retrospectively

from 6 April 1987. The DSS will pay into the personal pension scheme a rebate in National Insurance contributions. The rebate is a flat-rate rebate, ie it is not age- or sex-related, and as a result favours the young. However, in order to reduce the numbers of people ceasing to contract-out and opting back into SERPS, the Government may eventually introduce an age- and sex-related rebate. The payment of an additional incentive of 1% to personal pensions for persons over age 30 from 1993/94 is a step in that direction.

(2) Since 6 April 1988 employers have been allowed to contract-out through occupational schemes which provide benefits on a money-purchase basis. Prior to that time employers could contract-out only if the scheme provided benefits on a defined benefit basis, as described above.

12.7 Contracting-out through personal pensions

About one-half of the working population are not members of an occupational scheme which means that their only benefits on retirement will come from the State Earnings Related Pension Scheme, and old age pension.

Employees not in pensionable employment were eligible for retirement annuity contracts between 1956 and 30 June 1988. Nevertheless the number of employees taking out retirement annuity contracts was insignificant. Personal pension schemes, which became available on 1 July 1988 and are very similar to retirement annuity contracts (both of which are covered fully in Chapter 14) have the added advantage of allowing individuals to contract-out. This has resulted in a substantial increase in the number of individuals taking out personal pension schemes. The increase has come from younger people as the rebate in National Insurance contributions, which is flat-rate, rather than age- or sex-related, is particularly beneficial for young people.

12.8 Mechanics of contracting-out through personal pension schemes

The individual, having examined the options open to him (see below for 'Who should contract-out'), decides he wishes to contract-out. The process which will follow this decision is as follows:

(1) The individual and the pension provider will complete a Joint Notice which is sent to the DSS. The employer will continue to deduct National Insurance contributions at the contracted-in rate. The employer need not necessarily be aware of the employee's decision. Individuals wishing to contract-out through personal pension schemes will either be in non-pensionable employment or will be members of a contracted-in occupational pension scheme.

(2) At the end of the tax year the DSS, having been informed by the Inland Revenue of the National Insurance contributions paid during the tax year, will pay directly into the personal pension scheme a sum calculated as follows:
 (a) the contracted-out rebate, plus
 (b) an incentive payment (see below), if appropriate.

(3) The rebate for 1992/93 is 5.80% of band earnings. However, the employee's share, 2.00%, will be grossed up by the DSS to take into account tax relief at basic rate (25%) so that the actual percentage will be 6.47%, giving a total of 8.47% of band earnings where the 2% incentive is due.

(4) A change in legislation in 1989, to allow members to take protected rights benefits from age 60 under a COMP scheme to prevent sex-discrimination in favour of females, may presage a similar change to personal pension schemes in years to come.

(5) For the quinquennium starting in 1993/94 the rebate will reduce to 4.80% of band earnings. The employee's share, 1.80% will be grossed up by the DSS for basic rate tax relief, giving a total of 5.40% if income tax is at 25%. In addition, an incentive may be payable at a new lower rate of 1% so that the maximum for the tax year 1993/94 will be 6.40% of band earnings. (It is not currently the Government's intention to pay the 1% incentive to COMP schemes.)

The contributions paid by the DSS will constitute 'protected rights', and will be separated from any other contributions paid by the employee and/or employer, and will be subject to the following conditions:

(1) Protected rights may be used to provide a pension only in retirement, from State pensionable age (65 men, 60 women), there being no provision for early retirement.

(2) It will not be possible to take protected rights in the form of a cash lump sum.

(3) As a move towards a reduction in sex discrimination, protected rights must buy annuities on a unisex and unistatus basis.

This means that there must be no discrimination between males and females and single and married people (in practice, this will mean a downward movement in annuity rates for men). Unisex/unistatus rates, however, do not have to be used in respect of annuities purchased in the event of the death of the member whilst in service before state pensionable age.

(4) The annuity must be increased by the lower of the increase in the Retail Prices Index and 3% per annum. This also applies to any widow's/widower's annuity.

(5) Protected rights do not have to provide a Guaranteed Minimum Pension. If at State pensionable age protected rights purchase benefits lower than what SERPS would have provided if the individual had not been contracted-out, the State will not make up the shortfall. However, any excess benefits the individual.

(6) An open-market option must be available.

An individual may have a series of personal pension schemes but only one of these schemes may accept the rebate from the DSS.

When personal pensions started on 1 July 1988 it was possible to use them to contract-out retrospectively from 6 April 1987 provided that the individual had not already been contracted-out by reference to an occupational scheme during that period.

However, an election to contract-out for a particular tax year must now be made by 5 April of that year.

12.9 The 2% incentive

Initially the Government offered a 2% incentive to encourage contracting-out of SERPS. The incentive is currently 2% of band earnings and originally was to be payable for five years from 6 April 1988. It was, however, then extended to six years for those taking out personal pension schemes contracted-out retrospectively to 6 April 1987. In the case of personal pension schemes and money purchase occupational pension schemes which are contracted-out, the incentive benefits the member. In the case of a defined benefit occupational scheme the incentive, in practice, benefits the employer.

In order to qualify for the 2% incentive an individual can take out an 'appropriate' personal pension scheme, ie one which is used for contracting-out purposes, or become a member of a newly contracted-out occupational scheme. For this purpose 'newly contracted-out' means a money purchase scheme contracted-out from 6 April 1988, or a final salary contracted-out scheme which has been contracted-out for the first time after 31 December 1985.

Under personal pension schemes the incentive is paid automatically by the DSS. Under occupational pension schemes, however, incentive payments must be claimed at the end of each tax year. Payments from the DSS are normally made between June and October in any tax year in respect of the previous tax year. The regulations relating to eligibility for the incentive can be complicated and expert advice should be sought.

The Government have announced that an incentive will continue to be paid after the initial 2% ends. The new incentive will be 1% of band earnings but will only apply to anyone over age 30. It will be paid during the years 1993/94, 1994/95, and 1995/96, after which the contracting-out process will be further reviewed. The new 1% incentive will apply to personal pension plans only.

12.10 Who should contract-out?

Currently, the emphasis is in favour of contracting-out at the younger ages. The decision to contract-out will have to be reviewed regularly, especially when changes in rebate are announced — every five years.

The break-even point in 1992/93 is around age 50 for males, and age 43 for females, on the assumption that growth in the personal pension scheme will exceed the increase in national average earnings by 2.5% per annum and that the 2% incentive applies. If this incentive does not apply the ages drop to around 46 and 40.

In 1993/94 the reduction in rebate and incentive payments will have the effect of reducing the break-even point to around 46 for males and 40 for females if the new 2% incentive applies.

Employers are permitted to pay contributions to their employees' personal pension schemes thereby meeting a requirement or wish to provide retirement benefits but without having to undertake the responsibilities and administration of an employer's in-house occupational scheme. The bulk of the administration is carried out by the DSS as it will pay directly into the personal pension scheme the flat-rate rebate in respect of those individual employees who have chosen to contract-out. There is no need for the employer to rearrange his payroll systems to deduct National Insurance contributions at the contracted-out rate.

12.11 Contracting-out through money purchase schemes

Contracting-out on a money purchase basis is beneficial to small businesses which would like to offer employees a remuneration package which includes a good pension on retirement, and which wish to use the scheme for contracting-out purposes but not take on the open-ended liability inherent in a scheme which guarantees benefits on retirement. (Even the removal of the requisite benefit test does not remove the open-ended commitment from a scheme providing Guaranteed Minimum Pensions, although this guarantee might not be a heavy burden.)

It has been possible for employers to contract-out on a money purchase basis since 6 April 1988. As with occupational schemes operating on a defined benefit basis, the employer and employees pay National Insurance contributions at the contracted-out rate (see Table 11.1). This means a reduction in National Insurance contributions amounting to 5.8% of band earnings (split 2% employee, 3.8% employer). From 1993/94 the National Insurance contributions will be reduced by 4.80% (split 3% employer, 1.80% employee.) This saving in National Insurance contributions will be the minimum payment paid to the occupational scheme — it may be virtually the only contribution into the scheme. Although this contribution is merely a re-direction of what would have been paid to the DSS, employers may consider that this route is worthwhile in fostering good employer/employee relations. Whatever other benefits are provided under the scheme in respect of additional contributions paid by the employee and employer, the benefits generated by the reduction in National Insurance contributions will secure 'protected rights' and will be subject to the conditions described above.

The fact that a contracted-out money purchase scheme does not have to provide an ultimate guarantee on retirement means that many more employers have been prepared to contract-out. The only 'guarantee' which will apply is the requirement that the saving in National Insurance contributions is directed into this scheme to secure 'protected rights'.

In the case of a controlling director of a company it may be advisable not to contract-out of SERPS but to use an executive pension plan to provide the maximum approvable pension of two-thirds of final salary. In this way the overall benefits on retirement will exceed two-thirds of remuneration because SERPS will be paid in addition as it does not count towards the two-thirds limit. However, if a controlling director, or employee, contracts-out through an occupational scheme (of any description) the overall maximum potential benefits will be lower because the equivalent of SERPS is provided within the scheme and therefore within the normal two-thirds limit.

Alternatively, the director or executive could take out a personal pension scheme to contract out personally: the sole permitted contribution will be from the DSS — no contributions may be paid by the individual or his employer. Because this scheme is being used as SERPS replacement the protected rights within it may be in addition to the maximum benefits available under the executive pension plan.

12.12 The effects of contracting-out on employers' schemes

The facility to contract-out through a personal pension scheme applies not only to individuals who are in non-pensionable employment and those who are in contracted-in occupational schemes but also to members who leave their existing occupational schemes. From 6 April 1988, the Social Security Act 1986 has prevented employers insisting that employees join their occupational pension schemes (except schemes providing death in service benefits only) and also allows members of schemes to opt out, in favour of personal pensions, or even back into the State Earnings Related Pension Scheme. Prior to 6 April 1988 most employers required employees to join their schemes as a condition of service, and usually prevented members leaving their schemes unless they left service.

The second relaxation has not resulted in large numbers of members opting out of occupational schemes in favour of personal pensions because the employer is not bound to pay a contribution into the individual's personal pension scheme. Although the member may obtain greater flexibility under the personal pension scheme he is likely to consider that the cost of sacrificing the employer's contribution is too great. However, other factors may come to bear on the decision: if the individual considers that he is unlikely to remain with the employer for long or that he intends to move from job to job regularly in order to widen his experience he may be better off with a personal pension scheme which is fully portable.

Before making a decision to opt out of an occupational scheme, especially one which relates benefits to final salary, the member will have to consider very carefully the benefits which he will be giving up. These include not just the pension itself but widow's pensions, death in service benefits and escalation of pensions payment.

While it is unlikely that many good schemes will see a large number of members leaving in favour of personal pensions, it is more likely that schemes will not be able to expect the same number of new entrants as in the past. Regrettably, there is evidence that significant numbers of new entrants to schemes have decided not to join occupational schemes; some are relying purely on SERPS and have not even taken out a personal pension scheme. Higher take-home pay (because they do not have to pay the member's contribution under the occupational scheme) is seen as the immediate 'benefit' to the employee. As it is not possible to make it a condition of service that new employees join the scheme, inevitably employers will recruit individuals who are in favour of personal pension schemes and as the years go by there will be an increasing number of individuals who have been contributing to personal pension schemes in the past. Failure to attract new members to a final salary scheme will result in the average age of the scheme increasing so that the cost as a percentage of payroll is likely to increase (although the cost will of course be related to a smaller number of members and a smaller payroll). Although it is still too early to say exactly what effect this legislation will have on occupational schemes, it is likely that some employers will actually pay contributions to the personal pension schemes of individuals who have opted out in favour of this route. Some employers will also allow individuals to opt back into the occupational scheme at a later date, perhaps imposing an age limit of, say, 40. If employers allow individuals to opt back into the occupational scheme, then only future service in the scheme is likely be pensioned.

The initial resistance to personal pensions by employers running occupational schemes is beginning to diminish and more employers will offer a money purchase alternative to a final salary scheme either by running a separate money purchase scheme for new employees or by contributing to the personal pension schemes taken out by individual employees.

The 1991 Annual Survey of Occupational Pension Schemes by the National Association of Pension Funds shows that where there was automatic entry to schemes, around 89% of those eligible actually joined: where new entrants had to apply for membership, the take-up rate was reduced to 78%.

Around two-thirds of employers allow employees who have opted-out of schemes to be re-admitted later. Around 38% of schemes provided death in service for employees who opted-out.

Only 5% of employers are willing to contribute to personal pension schemes.

12.13 Contracting back into SERPS

Persons approaching the pivotal ages when contracting-out ceases to be attractive (see para 12.10 above) should consider informing the DSS that they no longer wish to be contracted-out. This is done by sending a completed form APP 2 'Cancellation Notice' to the DSS. A member of a COMP scheme will have to approach his/her pension scheme trustees to find out their options, which might include switching into a 'not contracted-out' category of membership whilst remaining in the scheme.

13 Executive pensions and inheritance tax planning

Lump sums on death payable under retirement benefit schemes, approved under ICTA 1988, ss 590–612, retirement annuity contracts approved under ICTA 1988, ss 619–627 *(ICTA 1970, s 226)* and personal pension schemes approved under ICTA 1988, ss 630–655, are largely free of inheritance tax. The methods of inheritance tax planning through retirement annuity contracts and personal pension schemes are set out in Chapter 14. This chapter deals with the use of executive pension plans in assisting a director in passing on his company to future generations without saddling his family with inheritance tax liabilities.

The Finance Act 1989, however, has lessened the effectiveness of executive pension plans for inheritance tax planning in the case of directors who would be categorised as 'post-1989 members' because of the cap on earnings.

In general terms a director should try to make provision for his spouse through the inter-spouse exemptions: all life-time gifts and property left by one spouse to the other on death are exempt from inheritance tax (although there is a restriction if the donor spouse is domiciled in the UK but the donee spouse is not).

In order to make provision for future generations, however, it is advisable to use death benefits arising from an executive pension plan. The rules of a pension scheme which has been designed specifically for controlling directors and key executives will contain a list of persons to whom the lump sum benefit may be paid such as the director's spouse, children, dependants and other individuals whom he has nominated. The rule will give the trustees power to pay to such one or more of the persons specified as they may in their discretion choose. Ideally the rules should also allow the trustees to pay monies to a separate trust (outside the trust governing the executive pension plan) for the benefit of the deceased's children: the trust could also provide for sums to be lent to the widow or widower for immediate needs.

Since the trustees exercise their discretion as to who will receive the benefit after the director's death, it cannot form part of his freely disposable estate for inheritance tax purposes, and the pension plan is exempt from the normal charging provisions relating to discretionary trusts because it comes within IHTA 1984, s 58(1)(*d*).

The director will normally indicate his preference to the trustees in advance of his death by completing a nomination form or expression of wish letter although this will not bind the trustees who may decide to disregard his wishes.

As the trustees are often fellow directors, for example, his wife, or the limited company itself, the director may be reasonably happy that his wishes will be complied with and by this simple device he can pass to his children and grandchildren considerable sums which will escape inheritance tax altogether.

13.1 Deferring retirement

A director who defers his retirement may have benefits paid in the event of his subsequent death on either of the following bases:

(1) The usual death in service benefit of a lump sum equal to four times final remuneration (subject to the earnings cap of £75,000 in 1992/93 for post-1989 members) together with a refund of his own personal contributions plus growth; or
(2) The benefits based on the assumption that he had retired on the day before his death, ie, a lump sum payment equal to five years pension payments, which is the usual guarantee period attached to pensions.

Although in both situations the payment will be free of inheritance tax, where the guarantee under the pension itself is more than five years, the guarantee payments as they fall due must be paid to the deceased's estate — it is not possible to commute them.

In addition, a widow's or widower's pension can also be paid in either circumstance which would of course be free of inheritance tax.

13.2 Personal contributions

As the object of the exercise is to pass as much capital to the next generation free of inheritance tax, basis (1) above will normally be the most favourable. In fact, a director who is setting up an executive pension plan should, where there is a need, ensure that part of the contributions are paid in the form of personal contributions from his own salary to maximise death in service benefits. If he already has an executive pension plan in existence where the contributions are paid wholly by the employer, then if necessary, he should take a larger salary from the company enabling him to pay personal contributions and reduce the employer's contributions appropriately. The following example and table show the effect of paying personal contributions.

Example 13.1

Current position
(1)   Director's remuneration = £30,000
    Company's contribution to executive pension plan = £8,000 pa
    Company's total expenditure in remuneration and pensions = £38,000 pa
    Maximum lump sum death in service benefit which can be provided under the plan = £120,000 (4 × £30,000).

Alternative position
(2)   Director's revised remuneration = £35,295
    Director's personal contribution under PAYE = £5,295 (15% of £35,295)
    Director's taxable remuneration of £30,000
    Company's contribution to executive pension plan = £2,154 pa
    Company's total expenditure in remuneration and pensions = £38,000 pa
    Maximum lump sum death in service benefit which can be provided under the plan = £141,180 (4 × £35,295) *and* £5,295, plus growth, for each year of payment

Notes
(1)   The director's remuneration has been increased by 17.65%, a factor that can be applied to any level of remuneration.
(2)   Since October 1985 the removal of the Upper Earnings Level for the purposes of National Insurance Contributions payable by employers means that any increase in remuneration increases the NIC. In this example the extra NIC would be 10.40% of £5,295, ie £551 which is included in the company's total expenditure above.
(3)   Where the director is a post-1989 member the lump sum will be restricted to four times capped remuneration, so the above method of increasing the lump sum through the use of personal contributions is of even greater value (although the personal contribution will also be restricted to 15% of capped remuneration).

Table 13.1

A member of an executive pension plan has an initial salary of £10,000 pa, which increases by 8½% pa. He pays personal contributions of 15% of salary. The lump sum that could be paid free of inheritance tax on death in service is shown below, assuming pension fund growth of 10% pa net. The member is not subject to the cap on earnings applicable to post-1989 members.

At the end of:	4 × salary death in service benefit £	Increasing additional cover £	Total permissible cover £
5 years	60,140	10,480	70,620
10 years	90,430	32,270	122,700
15 years	135,980	74,710	210,690
20 years	204,480	153,980	358,460
25 years	307,470	297,840	605,310

13.3 Restrictions on 20% directors

In March 1979, the Inland Revenue, through Memorandum No 59, limited the ability of a 20% director to ensure that monies could be paid to succeeding generations free of capital transfer tax, the forerunner of inheritance tax. If he is still in service at the age of 75, then in the event of his subsequent death the lump sum payable must be made either to the legal personal representatives, or to the surviving spouse, or in the absence of any surviving spouse, to the legal personal representatives.

If however, the member had retired and died during the first five years following his retirement, and there was a five year guarantee attaching to his pension, then the value of the outstanding pension instalments may be paid to the trustees who can then pay them at their discretion to the usual range of beneficiaries.

13.4 Options at retirement

On reaching normal retirement date, it is possible to:

(1) take all the benefits, ie cash and pension,
(2) defer all the benefits and continue working, or

(3) take the tax-free lump sum, but defer the pension benefits (provided that the director is not classed as a post-1989 member).

From an inheritance tax point of view, however, taking cash and deferring pension is not to be recommended as this effectively triggers the director's retirement for the purposes of determining future benefits. In the event of his subsequent death while still working with the company, he will be regarded as having retired on the day before he died.

Example 13.2

Salary at date of death £24,000.
Maximum pension is £16,000 per annum or a reduced pension of around £12,000 per annum plus a tax-free cash sum of £36,000.

(1) If tax-free cash of £36,000 has been taken the maximum death benefit will be 5 × the reduced pension of £12,000 per annum, ie £60,000.
(2) If all benefits have been deferred the maximum death benefit will be calculated on the normal death in service basis, ie 4 × salary, ie £96,000.

The difference between the two bases is magnified where the length of time between the taking of tax-free cash and death is increased.

13.5 Continuation facilities

Term assurance is the usual means of providing death in service benefits under executive pension plans. However if the director takes his benefits on retirement, or if he leaves service, death in service benefits will usually cease. Most executive pension plans offer an option to the director to convert the term assurance into an ordinary life assurance policy, for example, a whole of life policy in his own name, without the need to produce medical evidence. The whole of life policy will be a personal contract where contributions are paid by the director himself at the rate applicable to his age when he effects the contract. Thus, a director is able to convert term assurance to permanent insurance. These policies can be written in trust and can provide a way of mitigating inheritance tax liability for the rest of his life. If he takes his pension from his pension plan the cost of the whole of life policy may be met from the pension payments.

13.6 Summary

Executive pension plans, although appearing to emphasise the word 'pension' should not be looked at in this narrow sense. They offer flexibility for the director who wishes to build up his business rapidly over the short term and sell out, as benefits can be provided on early retirement from age 50 onwards, or more commonly, they can be used for the director who has virtually no intention of ever retiring from the business.

In the latter situation the director is almost certain to build up an inheritance tax problem. Thus an executive pension plan is unlikely to ever provide a pension simply because he will continue to take an income from the company and defer taking his pension benefits although for directors categorised as post-1989 members, this facility is not available beyond age 75, by which time benefits under the executive pension plan must be taken. What he requires, however, is an effective means of transferring capital to succeeding generations to enable them to pay inheritance tax and to continue the business if they wish. A pension plan is an extremely tax-efficient way of building up this capital.

A group pension scheme will very rarely provide this degree of flexibility — in fact, it should not really be used as a tax planning vehicle. Traditionally a group pension scheme should be regarded as a means of providing an adequate standard of living in retirement, whereas the executive pension plan provides not only deferred pay, but also a tax planning medium.

14 Personal pension schemes and retirement annuities

14.1 Background

Traditionally, retirement annuities were the means by which the self-employed provided for retirement. The term 'self-employed retirement annuity' (the common generic title for these contracts) is misleading as it suggests that eligibility was confined to one group: in fact persons in non-pensionable employment may have taken out these contracts although the vast majority were self-employed.

1 July 1988 saw a considerable development in the legislation surrounding retirement annuities and their successors, personal pension schemes. From 1 July 1988 personal pension schemes, introduced by the Finance (No 2) Act 1987 and now incorporated in ICTA 1988, Chapter IV, came into force and no new retirement annuities (governed by ICTA 1970, ss 226–228 now incorporated in ICTA 1988, Chapter III) were available from that date.

Personal pension schemes are similar to retirement annuities but there are important differences, notably the facility to use the former to contract out of the earnings-related part of the State pension scheme (see Chapter 12).

Retirement annuities taken out before 1 July 1988 may continue beyond that date, and may be concurrent with personal pension schemes. In order to distinguish between the two contracts a 'retirement annuity' denotes an ICTA 1988, ss 618–629 contract and a 'personal pension scheme' denotes an ICTA 1988, ss 630–655 contract.

Because many people contribute to both types of contract, and the interaction of the two can be significant, both types are described in this chapter.

14.1.1 How personal pension schemes and retirement annuities work

Under the terms of a personal pension scheme which is effected between the individual and the pension provider (which can be an insurance company, friendly society, bank, building society or unit trust company), the individual pays contributions in order to secure benefits in the form of pension and a tax-free lump sum. The contributions may be payable:

(1) annually on a level basis, or with provision for increases each year,
(2) monthly, but with provision for increases to be made, or
(3) as single contributions.

Personal pension schemes often have the facility to convert from a monthly to an annual basis, and vice versa, and also to take additional single contributions from time to time.

If the personal pension scheme is used for contracting-out of the State Earnings Related Scheme (SERPS) contributions will also be paid by the Department of Social Security (DSS). Personal pension schemes may also take contributions from an employer: the employer's contributions will be treated as a deductible business expense like an employer's contributions to an approved retirement benefits scheme.

The contributions excluding any paid by the DSS are subject to maximum limits arising from the legislation (set out below).

Retirement annuities, the forerunners of personal pension schemes, work in a similar way except that they cannot be used to contract-out of SERPS, so that they will not receive contributions from the DSS, and nor can they accept contributions from an employer.

14.1.2 Comparison of personal pension schemes and retirement annuities

Although full information on the differences between retirement annuity contracts and personal pension schemes is given throughout this chapter, a brief comparison of the major differences is set out in the following table.

Table 14.1

	Retirement annuity	Personal pension scheme
Benefit ages	Between 60 and 75	Between 50 and 75
Basis of calculating tax-free cash	3 × the annuity remaining after cash has been taken	25% of fund used to provide the member's pension*
Facility to carry back/carry forward contributions	Yes	Yes
Ancillary benefits eg life assurance, waiver of contribution	Yes	Yes
Ability to contract-out	No	Yes
Cash limit	£150,000 (unless effected before 17 March 1987)	None
Tax relief on contributions at source	No	Yes, for employed only
Ability to accept employer's contributions	No	Yes
Facility to accept transfers from other schemes	No **	Yes
Facility to pay transfer to other schemes	Yes	Yes
Ability to write in trust	Yes	Yes
Open market option available	Yes	Yes

* Any part of the fund which consists of 'Protected Rights' will have to be excluded for this purpose when the scheme was taken out after 27 July 1989. In the case of a scheme taken out before 27 July 1989 although Protected Rights do not have to be excluded, any part of the fund which is used to buy a widow's or widower's annuity may have to be excluded, meaning that, in practice, around 20% of the total fund may be taken in cash.

** Except other retirement annuities.

14.1.3 Benefits

Income in retirement

The sole purpose of the personal pension scheme is to provide an annuity in retirement commencing at any time between the ages of 50 and 75 but an annuity can be drawn regardless of whether or not the individual is working. Indeed it is possible to stagger the benefits over that period either by having a series of separate schemes or one scheme within which there are a number of arrangements which provide for the benefits to be paid at intervals.

The facility to take benefits under a personal pension scheme from age 50 compared with age 60 under a retirement annuity was a welcome improvement although in practice it is unlikely to be seen as a sufficient reason for stopping contributions to a retirement annuity in favour of a personal pension scheme. Most planholders will not have had the opportunity of building up sufficient funds to provide a worthwhile income at age 50.

Lump sums

Generally, up to one quarter of the fund accumulated in a personal pension scheme may be taken as a tax-free lump sum. The retirement annuity legislation restricts the maximum tax-free lump sum to three times the remaining pension after the cash has been taken. Although more complicated than the personal pension scheme legislation this method usually provides more tax-free cash.

These options are very valuable as they give the member the flexibility of having more tax-free money in his hands, but if he is more interested in income he can use the tax-free cash to buy a purchased life annuity (ICTA 1988, s 656) which is taxed only on the interest content.

Assuming a retirement fund of £100,000 the amounts which could be taken in the form of a tax-free cash sum are as follows:

Table 14.2

	Age	Personal pension scheme	Retirement annuity
Males	60	£25,000	£25,800
	65	£25,000	£27,800
	70	£25,000	£30,400
Females	60	£25,000	£23,900
	65	£25,000	£25,400
	70	£25,000	£27,400

Notes

(1) Under the retirement annuity the tax-free cash increases as age increases, and differs according to sex.

(2) It will be seen that a retirement annuity (which will have been effected before 1 July 1988) will give a higher proportion of tax-free cash sum than a personal pension scheme. Of course there is nothing to prevent an individual paying contributions to both contracts concurrently (within the overall maximum contribution limits).

(3) Under a retirement annuity the Inland Revenue allows the tax-free lump sum to be calculated on the most favourable basis (ie annually in arrears without guarantee), eg as the highest annuity available is one payable annually in arrears, the lump sum will be calculated as if this type of annuity had been selected. After the lump sum has been taken, the balance of the fund can be used to provide an annuity on a different basis, normally payable quarterly or monthly in advance, guaranteed for 5 years.

(4) In arriving at the tax-free cash under the retirement annuity an underlying interest rate of $8\frac{3}{4}\%$ has been assumed. If interest rates were lower, the tax-free cash under the retirement annuity could be lower than £25,000 at younger ages.

(5) If an open market option is exercised under a retirement annuity and transferred to a personal pension scheme, tax-free cash will be limited to 25% of the fund.

Example 14.1

A fund of £100,000 built up under a personal pension scheme might provide an income payable in monthly instalments throughout the life of a man aged 65, guaranteed for five years of £11,700 per annum, but subject to tax at, say, 25%, leaving a net income of £8,775 per annum.

Alternatively the fund could be taken in the form of a tax-free lump sum of, say, £25,000 plus a reduced income of £8,823 gross, netting down to £6,617: the cash of £25,000 could be used to buy a purchased life annuity. Part of the annuity is regarded as a return of the purchase price — known as the capital content — and is not subject to tax: the balance is interest and is subject to tax.

The cash lump sum of £25,000 could be used to buy a purchased life annuity of say, £2,941. Of this, £1,444 is interest and would be taxed (leaving a net income of £2,580 for a basic rate taxpayer).

The combination of the two net annuities is £9,197, an increase of £422 over the income obtained if the whole fund is used to buy an annuity. This demonstrates the benefit of taking advantage of the tax-free lump sum even if income is a priority.

14.1.4 Open market option

Retirement annuities usually permit an 'open market option' where the accumulated fund can be transferred, when the benefits are being cashed, to another insurance company. The policyholder will take advantage of the open market option if another insurance company offers annuity rates better than those of the original insurance company. The policyholder will normally be given an indication of the insurance companies who are at the top of the market and monies will pass from insurer to insurer (not through the policyholder). Sometimes the policyholder will incur a penalty if the monies are transferred to another insurance company.

Under retirement annuities, when the open market option is exercised, the new insurance company issues a 'substituted contract' to provide the pension *and* the tax-free lump sum. Thus the whole fund is transferred from the first insurance company to the second: cash is not paid by the first company with the pension paid by the second. There is no objection, however, to a transfer of only part of the value of the planholder's benefit under the contract. In that event, both the original and the substituted contracts must limit the tax-free lump sum by reference to the pensions payable under the respective contracts.

Since 1 July 1988 no new retirement annuities can be effected including substituted contracts. This means that if an open market option is exercised monies must be transferred from the retirement annuity either to another retirement annuity (which must have been effected before 1 July 1988) or to a personal pension scheme and subject to its rules which include, inter alia, a limitation on the tax-free cash to 25% of the fund used to provide the member's pension.

Personal pension schemes and retirement annuities 179

Personal pension schemes arranged through banks, building societies and unit trusts are not allowed to provide pension benefits on retirement directly: the underlying funds after tax-free cash has been paid have to be transferred to an insurance company which then provides the annuity.

Personal pension schemes arranged through insurance companies have to offer the right to a transfer as a condition of approval.

14.1.5 Types of pension available

On taking the benefits from the personal pension scheme or retirement annuity, the member will normally have various options including the facility to take a reduced pension on his own life but which will continue in the event of his death to the spouse. For example, £100,000 would at the time of writing, purchase the following types of annuity on the open market for a man aged 65. These annuities are not necessarily at the top of the market as annuity rates change frequently. (Further comments on this topic are given in Chapter 19.)

Table 14.3

Type of Annuity	Amount per annum
Single life annuity payable annually in arrear	£13,100
Single life annuity payable monthly in advance	£12,200
Single life annuity payable monthly in advance but for a minimum of five years	£11,900
Single life annuity payable monthly in advance but for a minimum of ten years	£11,200
Single life annuity payable monthly in advance for a minimum of five years, increasing each year by 3% pa compound	£970
Joint life annuity, during the lives of the man and his wife, aged 62	£960

14.1.6 Death before taking benefits

The amounts payable vary widely between different contracts but the choices include:

- No return of contributions (rare).
- Return of contributions without interest.
- Return of contributions with interest at around 4%.
- Return of the accumulated fund.

Example 14.2

Return on death after various periods of years, where the annual contribution is £1,000

	After 10 years £	After 20 years £	After 30 years £
No return of contributions	—	—	—
Return of contributions without interest	10,000	20,000	30,000
Return of contributions with interest at 4% pa compound	12,486	30,969	58,328
Return of accumulated fund, assuming unit growth of 10% net of charges	14,439	50,037	139,919

14.1.7 Life cover

Personal pension schemes allow life assurance to be provided through an authorised insurance company, under ICTA 1988, s 637. The advantage of paying contributions to a policy approved under this section as opposed to an ordinary life assurance policy of a similar class, is that the contributions for the former are fully deductible from earnings for income tax purposes. Under ordinary life assurance policies, however, no tax relief is given to policies effected following the 1984 Budget (although policies effected before that time benefit from tax relief at 15%, reducing to 12½% from 1989/90).

The relief under a s 637 policy in 1992/93, is at 25% of the contribution for an employee who pays tax at the basic rate of 25% so that the net outlay would be only 75% of the contribution payable. For the self-employed and higher rate taxpayers higher rate relief will be given as appropriate, but relief will be at only 20% on the part of their taxable earnings subject to the 20% band.

Example 14.3

The annual cost of providing £100,000 worth of life cover up to age 60 for a male non-smoker aged 29 would amount to around £24 per month gross, £18 net for a 25% taxpayer under a s 637 policy. For a 40% taxpayer, the net annual cost of the s 637 policy would drop to £14.40 per month.

It is possible to assign s 637 policies with the result that they are often used to provide collateral security where the individual is borrowing money; they are also used for partnership assurance.

Life assurance may also be provided under the retirement annuity legislation (ICTA 1988, s 621 (1)(*b*)) provided that the policy was effected before 1 July 1988. These policies may also be assigned.

14.2 Personal pension schemes in more detail

The relevant legislation is ICTA 1988, Chapter IV, ss 630–655 (an extract is contained in Appendix 3). Under a personal pension scheme various types of benefit may be provided within the scheme rather than by means of separately approved contracts as applies to retirement annuity contracts under ICTA 1988, ss 620–621. In this way a personal pension scheme is rather similar to an approved retirement benefit scheme. The benefits that may be provided within the scheme are as follows:

(1) An annuity must be payable by an authorised insurance company chosen by the member. The annuity may commence between the ages of 50 and 75. However, earlier commencement than age 50 is possible in the event of permanent incapacity or where earlier retirement ages are agreed for special occupations.
(2) A lump sum may be provided for the member provided it is payable when the annuity is first payable (it is not possible to provide for a lump sum alone). It must not exceed one-quarter of the value of the retirement benefits provided for the member.
(3) A dependant's annuity may be provided for the surviving spouse or dependants if pension provision is being made for the member.
(4) Life assurance may be provided by an authorised insurance

company on the death of the individual before he attains the age of 75. (This is the same as the benefit allowed under ICTA 1988, s 621(1)(*b*) for retirement annuities set up before 1 July 1988.)

14.2.1 Existing retirement annuities

The relevant legislation is found in ICTA 1988, ss 618–629: an extract from the legislation is contained in Appendix 3.

It has not been possible to take out a retirement annuity approved under the above legislation since 30 June 1988 but contracts already in existence at that time may continue in force and will be able to accept subsequent increases in contributions (provided that the contract is sufficiently flexible). Contracts taken out from 1 July 1988 will be personal pension schemes approved under ICTA 1988, ss 630–655.

Three types of benefit can be provided within the retirement annuity legislation:

(1) A retirement annuity approved under s 620, having for its main object the provision of an annuity in old age, but with provision for commutation of part of the annuity for a lump sum. Contracts effected on or after 17 March 1987 must limit the lump sum to £150,000. (This £150,000 limit may be raised by Treasury Order.) The annuity may commence between the ages of 60 and 75. However, earlier commencement is possible in the event of permanent incapacity or where earlier retirement ages are agreed for special occupations.

(2) A dependant's annuity approved under s 621(1)(*a*). This is a contract which provides an annuity for the wife or the husband of the individual or for any one or more dependants of the individual.

(3) Life assurance approved under s 621(1)(*b*). This is a contract the *sole object* of which is the provision of a lump sum on death of the individual before he attains the age of 75. The lump sum can be paid in instalments to provide income for dependants.

14.2.2 Earnings and eligibility

For the purpose of a personal pension scheme 'relevant earnings' is defined in s 623(2) and means:

(1) Emoluments chargeable under Schedule E from an office or

employment held by the individual. This includes benefits in kind and emoluments from an employment which are paid in accordance with a profit-related pay scheme, but excludes anything arising from the acquisition or disposal of shares or an interest in shares or from a right to acquire shares (share option schemes) and anything in respect of which tax is chargeable by virtue of s 148 ('golden handshakes').

(2) Income from property which is attached to or forms part of the emoluments of any such office or employment held by him.

(3) Income which is chargeable under Schedule A, Schedule B or Schedule D and is immediately derived by him from the carrying on or exercise by him of his trade, profession or vocation either as an individual, or in the case of a partnership, as a partner personally acting therein. In practice income under Schedules A and B will be investment income and will not constitute relevant earnings.

(4) Income treated as earned income by virtue of ICTA 1988, s 529 (patent rights).

(5) Earnings from certain commercial lettings of furnished holiday accommodation, although assessed to tax under Schedule D Case IV, will be treated as a trade for the purposes of s 623(2) and regarded as relevant earnings.

'Relevant earnings', do not include:

(1) Any remuneration as director of a company whose income consists solely or mainly of investment income and the individual, either alone or together with any other persons who are or have been at any time directors of the company, controls the company.

(2) Any remuneration from a company in which the individual was a controlling director in the year of assessment or has been a controlling director of the company at any time in the ten years immediately preceding that year of assessment and where the individual is in receipt of benefits under a superannuation scheme of the company or where benefits have been transferred from that superannuation scheme into a personal pension scheme.

These exclusions prevent a controlling director of a company pensioning his service through an occupational pension scheme, retiring and taking his benefits and then continuing to receive an income from that company which is pensioned by means of a personal pension scheme.

However for the purposes of an existing retirement annuity, relevant earnings can include share options and 'golden handshake' payments from non-pensionable employment and the pensioning of earnings of a director who is already in receipt of a pension from that company.

In summary, membership of a personal pension scheme can be extended to:

(1) Persons holding an office or employment which is not pensionable (but *not* controlling directors of investment companies).
(2) Persons engaged in business on their own account.
(3) Partners engaged in a trade, profession or vocation.

An occupation or office or employment is pensionable if an individual is a member of a relevant superannuation scheme from which he expects to receive retirement benefit. 'Relevant superannuation scheme' is defined in s 645(1), and is one which provides relevant benefits as defined in s 612 and is established by someone other than the individual but the following points should be noted.

Membership of a scheme which provides lump sum life assurance benefits only on death before age 75 or some lower age and, or an annuity to the surviving spouse or a dependant does not make the occupation count as pensionable. An occupational pension scheme which provides a cash lump sum on retirement would be regarded as 'pensionable' preventing membership of a personal pension scheme or a retirement annuity contract. If, however, the scheme provides in addition to life assurance benefits a widow's or dependant's pension this would render the occupation pensionable for *retirement annuity purposes* (unless extra statutory concession A38 applies).

The following points are also relevant for the purposes of both personal pension schemes and retirement annuities:

(1) A scheme does not have to be insured, or even funded at all. A formal promise to an employee of a pension to be paid when he reaches pension age, with no previous provision made for it is a sponsored superannuation scheme (although it may be regarded as an unapproved pension scheme — see Chapter 5).
(2) An employee may not supplement his employer's scheme,

Personal pension schemes and retirement annuities 185

however inadequate, by a personal pension scheme, or retirement annuity.
(3) Membership of an overseas scheme which is not approved in the UK is regarded as pensionable employment for the purposes of the retirement annuity legislation but does not preclude membership of a personal pension scheme.
(4) Where an employee is covered by a permanent health insurance arrangement providing only for the continuation of what in effect is long term sick pay up to state pension age, or if earlier, the normal retirement date of the employee (the employee remaining in the service of the employer until the date when the PHI contract ceases to provide benefits), such an arrangement will not be regarded as pensionable employment.
(5) Membership of the state pension scheme is not regarded as pensionable employment.

The relevant earnings for an employee or director taxed under Schedule E would be his actual earnings during the fiscal year beginning on 6 April and ending on 5 April, but for a self-employed individual relevant earnings for the year of assessment will usually be based on the earnings in his accounting year which ended in the previous fiscal year. This preceding year basis of assessment under Schedule D, however, may not apply in the opening years and closing years of the business.

14.2.3 Net relevant earnings

Although it is necessary to have relevant earnings to be eligible to pay contributions to a personal pension scheme or retirement annuity, the tax efficiency of the arrangement depends on having *net* relevant earnings. The contributions which an individual may pay are calculated with reference to net relevant earnings (see ICTA 1988, s 646(*b*) and s 623).

Net relevant earnings means the amount of relevant earnings less business expenses including any deductions in respect of losses or capital allowances.

Personal charges as alimony, charitable covenants and non-business interest do not reduce net relevant earnings.

14.2.4 Allowable maximum

In arriving at an individual's net relevant earnings for the purposes of a personal pension scheme, any amount in excess of the allowable maximum is ignored.

Table 14.4

The allowable maximum amounts are:

Tax year	Amount
1988/89	none
1989/90	£60,000
1990/91	£64,800
1991/92	£71,400
1992/93	£75,000

There is no allowable maximum for the purposes of a retirement annuity contract.

14.2.5 Associated employments

For the purposes of a personal pension scheme, if an individual has earnings from two or more employments which are associated and both are non-pensionable the earnings are aggregated for the purposes of assessing net relevant earnings and the earnings cap (see examples (1) and (2) below).

If one of the employments is pensioned through an Occupational Pension Scheme or Executive Pension Plan the earnings from the second employment on which contributions may be based is restricted to the excess of the earnings cap over the pensionable earnings (see example (3) below).

However if an individual has two sources of earnings, one from employment which is pensioned and the other from self-employment then the pensionable earnings may be disregarded (see example (4) below).

Example 14.4

(1)	Non-pensionable earnings from Job A	£60,000
	Non-pensionable earnings from Job B	£20,000
	Total non-pensionable earnings	£80,000
	Capped NRE from Job A plus Job B	£75,000
(2)	Earnings from Job A fully pensioned through Personal Pension Scheme	£60,000
	Non-pensionable earnings from Job B	£20,000
	Capped NRE from Job B	£15,000

(3)	Earnings from Job A pensioned through	
	Occupational Pension Scheme	£60,000
	Non-pensionable earnings from Job B	£20,000
	NRE from Job B	£15,000
(4)	Earnings from Job A pensioned through	
	Occupational Pension Scheme	£60,000
	Earnings from self-employment	£20,000
	NRE	£20,000

Personal pension scheme and retirement annuity contributions themselves, although requiring to be deducted in order to arrive at total income for tax purposes, are not deductible for the purposes of arriving at net relevant earnings.

Where a husband and wife both have net relevant earnings, the maximum contribution that each may pay is determined by reference to their separate net relevant earnings. The fact that the husband and wife may be taxed on a joint basis or may have chosen separate taxation or assessment, prior to independent taxation in 1990/91, is irrelevant. For the purposes of determining contributions to personal pension schemes and retirement annuities, they are looked at separately (s 644(1) and s 623(1) respectively).

The net relevant earnings in the year of assessment in which the annuity commences, or in which a personal pension scheme providing a lump sum on death terminates, are the earnings for the *whole* of the year.

14.2.6 Summary of calculation

Those in non-pensionable employment (taxed under Schedule E) will normally have no deductions to make from their relevant earnings: their gross earnings from their employment will be their net relevant earnings and all deductions (such as tax, National Insurance contributions, alimony, covenants and interest) whether or not allowable for tax are ignored.

In the case of an approved personal pension scheme any employer's contributions are not regarded as emoluments of the employment chargeable to Schedule E income tax.

The self-employed (taxed under Schedule D) have to make the following deductions from their gross profits in order to arrive at their net relevant earnings:

188 Allied Dunbar Pensions Guide

(1) all expenses incurred in earning the profits, such as rent, rates, business interest, employee's salaries, etc;
(2) losses, whether
   (a) incurred in the current tax year, or
   (b) incurred in a previous tax year and carried forward to set against profits in the current tax year under ICTA 1988, s 385(1) or
   (c) incurred in a previous tax year, relieved against other income under s 380, and not yet deducted from net relevant earnings;
(3) capital allowances.

Personal mortgage interest and covenants to charity can be ignored.

14.2.7 Capital allowances and Business Expansion Schemes

Only capital allowances relating to the trade reduce net relevant earnings. The special capital allowances on small workshops introduced in FA 1980 and 1981 did not usually reduce NRE because the income to an investor in a small workshop (as opposed to the person renting it and working in it) is investment income. Investments in Business Expansion Schemes and Enterprise Zones are personal investments and do not reduce NRE.

14.2.8 Interest

Interest payable on money borrowed to buy into a partnership or buy shares in a close company is statutorily deductible, but it does not reduce NRE because it is money laid out for a personal purpose. The principle appears to be that interest on money borrowed for the purpose of running the business, which is deductible on normal accounting principles as an expense and not prohibited under ICTA 1988, s 74 reduces NRE while interest paid on money borrowed for personal purposes which is specifically allowable under ICTA 1988, Part IX does not reduce NRE.

This gives some scope for tax planning because a partnership, for instance, could provide extra finance for work in progress either by the partners applying to increase their business overdraft or by an individual partner borrowing money in a personal capacity to buy into (or increase his share in) the partnership. The money would be available for the partnership's business purposes either way but interest on the first loan would reduce the NRE of the partners concerned, while that on the second would not.

Personal pension schemes and retirement annuities 189

14.2.9 Maximum contributions (as a percentage of net relevant earnings)

The contributions which may be made from the tax year 1989/90 onwards, to a personal pension scheme are:

(1)

Age on 6 April	Maximum contribution	1989/90 £	1990/91 £	1991/92 £	1992/93 £
Up to 35	17.5%	10,500	11,340	12,495	13,125
36 to 45	20.0%	12,000	12,960	14,280	15,000
46 to 50	25.0%	15,000	16,200	17,850	18,750
51 to 55	30.0%	18,000	19,440	21,420	22,500
56 to 60	35.0%	21,000	22,680	24,990	26,250
61 to 74	40.0%	24,000	25,920	28,560	30,000
Maximum contributions for life assurance		3,000	3,240	3,570	3,750

(Monetary limit)

(2) up to 5% of net relevant earnings for life assurance/dependants pension contracts are included in the maximum contributions above, as is the cost of waiver of contribution benefit,
(3) where a personal pension scheme is used for contracting-out purposes, the minimum contributions made by the Secretary of State (in effect, the DSS) are payable in addition to the maximum contributions above,
(4) for the tax year 1988/89 there was no monetary limit and the maximum contributions were the same as for retirement annuity contracts, as below.

Contributions which may be made to retirement annuity contracts for earlier tax years are:

Year of birth	% for tax years 1982/83 to 1986/87
1934 or later	17½
1916 to 1933	20
1915	21

The contributions which may be made for the tax year 1987/88 onwards to a retirement annuity contract are:

Age on 6 April	Maximum contributions
Up to 50	17.5%
51 to 55	20.0%
56 to 60	22.5%
61 to 74	27.5%

Note: All the above figures are inclusive of any contributions for life assurance and waiver of contribution benefit.

14.2.10 Interaction of contributions to personal pension schemes and retirement annuities

Many people who contribute to existing retirement annuities also wish to take advantage of the higher contribution limits available under personal pension schemes. However, special conditions apply in these circumstances.

The maximum amount that may be paid to a personal pension scheme includes any contributions being paid to a retirement annuity contract; if the latter is to continue this may mean that no contributions can be paid to the personal pension scheme.

Table 14.4 Tax year 1992/93 Scope for contributions to Personal Pensions (if maximum paid to retirement annuity contract)

Ages

NRE	35 or less RAC	PP	36-45 RAC	PP	46-50 RAC	PP	51-55 RAC	PP	56-60 RAC	PP	61-74 RAC	PP
Up to £75,000	17.5% £14,000	Nil	17.5% £14,000	2.5% £1,000	17.5% £14,000	7.5% £4,750	20% £16,000	10% £6,500	22.5% £18,000	12.5% £8,250	27.5% £22,000	12.5% £8,000
£80,000	£15,750	Nil	£15,750	Nil	£15,750	£3,000	£18,000	£4,500	£20,250	£6,000	£24,750	£5,250
£90,000	£17,500	Nil	£17,500	Nil	£17,500	£1,250	£20,000	£2,500	£22,500	£3,750	£27,500	£2,500
£100,000		Nil		Nil								
Earnings above which PP contribution is Nil	£0		£85,714		£107,142		£112,500		£116,666		£109,090	

Notes
(1) If NRE is £116,666 or higher then it can be seen that if maximum RA contributions have been paid, there is *no* scope for a PP contribution *regardless of age*.
(2) If an RA contribution is paid at a level lower than the maximum, then a PP can be used to top-up (but only to PP maximum).

Example 14.5

An individual aged 53 has net relevant earnings of £80,000. He currently contributes 20% to a retirement annuity contract, ie £16,000.

He wishes to top up through a personal pension scheme in 1992/93 where the maximum contribution is £22,500 (30% of £75,000).

As £16,000 is already paid to the retirement annuity he has scope to pay £6,500 to the personal pension scheme.

Example 14.6

An individual aged 48 has net relevant earnings of £120,000. He currently contributes 17.5% to a retirement annuity contract, ie £21,000.

He is unable to top up with a personal pension scheme as the maximum contribution to a personal pension scheme is £18,750 (25% of £75,000), which is less than his contribution to the retirement annuity contract.

Further examples showing the scope for contributions to a personal pension, if the maximum contributions are being paid to a retirement annuity, are contained in Table 14.4 opposite.

14.2.11 Overfunding

The personal pension scheme must make provision, under ICTA 1988, s 640, to ensure that the member's and any employer's contributions to the arrangement, in aggregate, do not exceed the permitted maximum. Any excess must be repaid to the contributor, as appropriate.

Excess contributions to retirement annuity contracts are not expressly prohibited under ICTA 1988 but insurers will not knowingly accept excess contributions from policyholders.

14.2.12 Tax relief

Contributions under approved personal pension schemes and retirement annuity contracts are treated as deductions from relevant earnings before their assessment to income tax. For the self-employed, the deductions are effective in the year of assessment in which they are paid (subject to the carry back provisions described later) rather than in the business year. Income tax relief is obtained at the highest tax rates paid by the individual on any part of his income. If the amount of the contribution exceeds the part of the income attracting tax relief at the highest rate, the remainder of the contribution attracts tax relief at the next highest rate and so on. For the self-employed and higher rate taxpayers relief will be given at only 20% on the part of their earnings subject to the 20% band.

Example 14.7

If an individual's taxable earned income in 1992/93 amounted to £30,000, a contribution to a personal pension scheme or retirement annuity contract of £8,000 would attract tax relief of:

£6,300 at 40% =   £2,520
£1,700 at 25% =   £ 425
                   £2,945

The tax relief obtained can be affected by the amount of investment income of an individual. For example, if net relevant earnings, (ie earned income) in 1992/93 amounted to £10,000 and investment income amounted to £20,000, a contribution of £1,750 (17½% of net relevant earnings of £10,000) would reduce taxable earnings and effectively obtain tax relief at 40%.

The fact that deductions such as personal pension scheme contributions are applied to income before allowances has some favourable and unfavourable implications.

Income for the purposes of calculating age allowance is income after deduction of the contribution, so that the net income (after tax relief) is looked at when arriving at the abatement of the age allowance (on the £1 for every £2 basis) when it exceeds the statutory level (£14,200 for 1992/93).

On the other hand, personal allowances are given on an actual basis, with no provision for carrying forward unused allowances from one year to the next. This means that tax relief on a personal pension scheme or retirement annuity contribution may be wasted if the income would have been covered by personal allowances, or investments in Business Expansion Schemes so that no tax would have been payable in any case. In the case of a person who is assessed to tax under Schedule E, however, contributions to a personal pension scheme may only be paid net of basic rate tax in which case the benefit of the personal allowance is not lost.

14.2.13 Pension relief at source

Under retirement annuities, contributions are paid gross and tax relief is given later. In the case of an employee this will normally be done by an adjustment to his tax coding.

Contributions to personal pension schemes by employed persons (but not the self-employed) are paid net of basic rate tax. The scheme administrator (in the case of an insured personal pension scheme this will be the insurance company itself) has to accept the net payment in the same way as if no deduction had been made and will recover the amount withheld from the Inland Revenue. If the individual is a higher rate taxpayer the difference between the actual rate of tax and the basic rate of tax may be reclaimed later when the individual completes his tax return and will normally result in an adjustment to the individual's tax coding. This system is known as 'PRAS' or 'pension relief at source'.

This system is similar to the MIRAS (Mortgage Interest Relief At Source) system and represents a considerable cash-flow advantage over the system used under retirement annuity contracts. Even when the employed individual's earnings would not be chargeable to tax because they are low, or have been reduced for tax purposes by personal allowances, contributions are still paid net of basic rate of tax. The basic rate of tax is 25% (in 1992/93) even though the first £2,000 of income is taxed at 20%.

14.2.14 Carry forward/carry back facilities

It is possible for eligible persons to take advantage of two valuable facilities to maximise pension contributions and obtain the best possible taxation advantages on those contributions. The facilities are generally referred to as 'carry forward of unused relief' and 'carry back provisions'.

14.2.15 Carry forward of unused relief

(1) This facility enables a planholder to pay a higher contribution than normally available for the current year in order to catch up for missed contributions from previous years.
(2) Tax relief is, however, available against the current year, *having no effect on tax paid in past years*, and will therefore be calculated according to current tax rates. It is important to

note that tax relief is only available up to the level of tax payable on earned income for the current year. Thus there is no tax relief available upon payments in excess of the level of taxable earnings, except where contributions are paid to personal pension schemes by employees taxed under Schedule E: these contributions are payable net of basic rate tax, and the sum of the contributions for the current year and previous years may not exceed the net relevant earnings in the current year even though taxable earned income will be lower than NRE as a result of personal allowances and mortgage interest relief. However, tax relief is at the highest rates, reflecting any investment income and income from pensionable employment.

(3) If the individual pays more than the year's normal maximum contribution in order to take advantage of this facility, then his local Tax Inspector will automatically refer back over the previous six years in order to discover any unused relief which can be carried forward to absorb the excess contribution. Under a personal pension scheme a special form has to be completed, form PP42, and submitted to the tax inspector. Unused relief will only be carried forward from previous years after the maximum contribution has been paid for the current year.

14.2.16 Carry back provisions

(1) A contribution (or part of a contribution) may be carried back to the tax year preceding the year of payment, regardless of the date of assessment and regardless of whether or not there are relevant earnings in the year in which the contribution is paid. A contribution cannot be carried back more than one year, except that if there were no net relevant earnings in the preceding tax year then the contributions may be carried back one further year. However, contributions may never be carried back more than two years.

(2) Carrying back a contribution in this way means that it will be treated for tax purposes exactly as if it had been paid in the year to which it is carried back and the maximum contribution is based on the limits for that year, ie the normal maximum for that year plus any unused relief from the six previous years.

Thus a contribution paid in 1992/93 and carried back to 1991/92 would, for tax relief purposes, be allowed against the 1991/92 tax bill (subject to the limits applicable to 1991/92) and could include an amount relating to missed contributions carried forward from 1985/86.

14.2.17 Mechanics of carry back

In order to carry back a contribution to the *previous* tax year, the following procedures must be followed:

(1) The contribution must be received by the pension provider before 6 April in the *current* tax year.
(2) An election must normally be made in writing to the Inspector of Taxes before 6 July following the tax year in which the contributions were made.
(3) The contract must have been issued by 6 April in the *current* tax year.
(4) An election for carry back may be made in the middle of a tax year. Normally, the Inland Revenue treat all methods of payment (annual, monthly or single) alike for tax relief purposes. Under a personal pension scheme an election to carry-back has to be accompanied by a completed Inland Revenue form PP43.

It is important to be aware that the Inland Revenue adhere very strictly to these rules.

14.2.18 Carry back — effect of status

The fact that self-employed persons pay contributions to a personal pension scheme on a gross basis but employed persons pay on a PRAS basis (ie 'Pension Relief At Source' — which is net of basic rate tax) raises questions as to how contributions should be paid if contributions are to be carried back to a previous year when the status of the individual was different, eg self employed today, employed last year. The following Table sets out the procedure.

14.2.19 Administrative requirements

In March 1988 the Inland Revenue published guidance notes on personal pension schemes. These include the administrative requirements which have to be carried out by the individual and by the pension provider. The individual when applying to the pension provider has to provide details of his name and address, national insurance number, the Inspector of Taxes office dealing

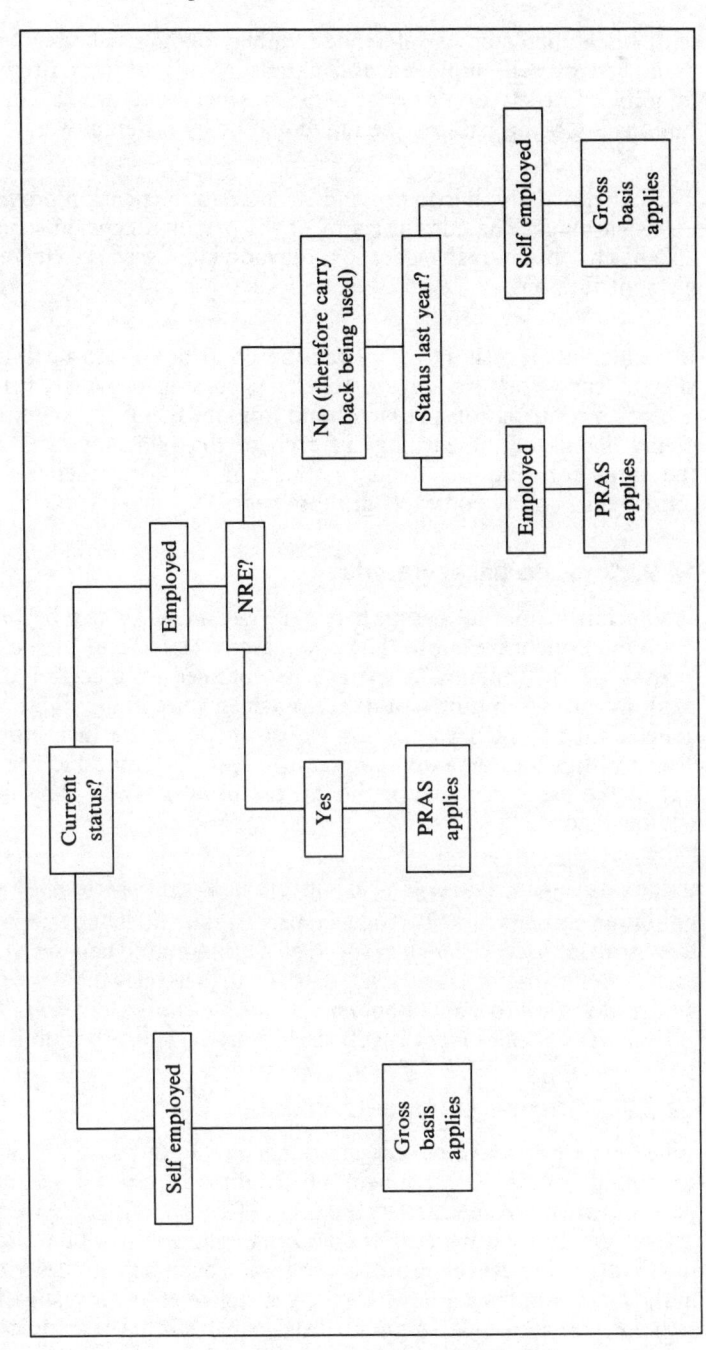

Personal pension schemes and retirement annuities 197

Table 14.5

```
                        Current status?
                       /              \
              Self employed          Employed
                    |                    |
              Gross basis              NRE?
              applies                /      \
                                   Yes      No (therefore carry
                                    |        back being used)
                                  PRAS              |
                                  applies      Status last year?
                                               /              \
                                          Employed          Self employed
                                              |                    |
                                           PRAS              Gross basis
                                           applies           applies
```

with his affairs and its reference number for him, whether he is employed or self-employed and details of any other retirement annuity contracts or personal pension schemes to which contributions are being paid by the individual or by his employer.

The individual also has to provide evidence to the pension provider of his earnings. The administrator of the personal pension scheme also has to obtain fresh evidence if the individual wishes to increase his contributions.

If the individual wishes to carry back his contributions to a previous year or carry forward unused relief the pension provider, before accepting contributions, has to obtain from the member a statement giving details of the earnings in each of the years involved and the total contributions paid to personal pension schemes and retirement annuity contracts in those years.

14.2.20 Late assessments

In the fairly unusual case where an assessment to tax becomes final and conclusive more than six years after the end of the tax year to which it relates, relief may be obtained on a contribution paid within six months of the assessment becoming final and conclusive, provided an election is also made to the Inspector of Taxes within the same six months in respect of any relief arising out of the assessment, even though the usual six-year time limit will have gone.

Relief is given in the year in which the contribution is paid and not in the earlier years. This special provision entitles the tax payer to absorb unused relief in respect of a year more than six years earlier, only insofar as it related to *extra* net relevant earnings, which have only become apparent *because of the assessment*. The current year's entitlement is still set against the contribution first.

14.2.21 Investigation settlements

Where incorrect returns and accounts are found to have been submitted, offers in settlement of liability to tax, interest and penalties are often accepted by the Inland Revenue without a formal assessment. In the absence of the assessment, it would not be strictly possible to make use of the provisions for later assessments described in the previous paragraph where the year to which the investigation settlement related ended more than six years prior to the settlement.

The Inland Revenue operate a special practice which applies to all investigation settlements where the letter of offer is made after 6 April 1981. This practice enables an individual to pay a contribution and make an election as described in the previous section within a period of six months from the date of the letter from the Inland Revenue accepting the offer. Relief is granted against tax in the year in which it is paid. The individual is not obliged to pay during that period the maximum contribution applicable for the year in which the excess contribution is paid. He has in the usual way, until the end of the following tax year in which to pay that maximum contribution.

14.3 Specific benefits under personal pension schemes and retirement annuity contracts

14.3.1 Death benefits

Personal pension schemes and existing retirement annuity contracts
Death benefits are largely assimilated with ordinary life assurance policies, in that they can be written in trust using similar procedures and with similar inheritance tax consequences, except that they are treated more favourably.

Where the contract also provides for a pension, this remains under the control of the policyholder and he will continue to decide when and how to take his pension (within the limits imposed by the legislation) and in unit-linked contracts, for example, whether to switch or change the combination of investment funds at his disposal. The pension in payment and the tax-free cash sum are still required by law to be personal to the policyholder and cannot be assigned.

14.3.2 Flexible trusts

It is possible to write death benefits emerging from personal pension schemes and retirement annuity contracts in a form of flexible trust which provides for:

(1) **an immediate beneficiary** to whom it is intended benefits should go on death immediately after setting up the trust, and
(2) **a class of potential beneficiaries** with a power of appointment

under which the death benefit may be appointed to any potential beneficiary, in addition to or to the exclusion of the current immediate beneficiary.

The power of appointment (revocable or irrevocable) is exercised by the policyholder during his life or by the trustees within 79 years from the commencement of the trust, although the appointment has to be made within two years of death to avoid inheritance tax liability.

The policyholder's lifetime power of appointment is subject to the exception that appointments back to the planholder himself must be made by at least two trustees (or whom he may be one).

It is desirable to have a second trustee in addition to the policyholder himself so that the death benefit can be paid to the surviving trustee without waiting for Probate.

14.3.3 Inheritance tax implications

Regular contributions
Under personal pension schemes and retirement annuity contracts, regular contributions on which tax relief is obtained are ignored for inheritance tax purposes on the principle that they are paid primarily to provide the planholder with a personal benefit (his pension) and that the death benefit, which has been gifted to the trust beneficiaries, is incidental. Additional contributions paid from time to time, for example, to pick up unused relief, or putting an existing contract in trust, are treated differently.

Under ICTA 1988, s 621 regular contributions for life assurance contracts and the life assurance benefit within a personal pension scheme, are not ignored because by definition they are not paid to provide a personal benefit, but to provide the in-trust death benefit, but in virtually every case they will be exempt as normal expenditure out of income.

Proceeds on death
Payment will be made on death to the trustees who will use the money in accordance with the trust provisions. Normally they will pass the money to the immediate beneficiary under the trust chosen by the planholder. Since the money is paid to the trustees and not to the deceased's estate, there is no inheritance tax liability.

Discretionary trusts

Provided the trust has been drawn up correctly and, in effect, is the same as the type of trust used for retirement benefit schemes approved under ICTA 1988, ss 590–612, the normal rules for discretionary trusts do not apply, ie there are no exit charges or ten year periodic charges, as it will fall within IHTA 1984, s 58(1)(*d*). Also, there is no 'interest in possession' so that there is no charge to inheritance tax should there be any change in the destination of the death benefits away from the person nominated by the member during his lifetime, provided this occurs within two years of death.

Interest in possession trusts

Under this type of trust the chosen beneficiary or beneficiaries have an immediate entitlement to any income produced by the trust. This means that for inheritance tax purposes the beneficiary is treated as owning the capital and it is included in his estate. In an interest in possession trust every appointment of a potential beneficiary to immediate entitlement involves the reduction (or disappearance) of the entitlement of the current immediate beneficiary. For example, if (a) alone is entitled to the benefits and (b) and (c) are appointed in addition, then (a), (b) and (c) are each entitled to a one-third interest and the interest of (a) who is previously entitled to the whole benefit, has been reduced by two-thirds. If (b) and (c) had been appointed to the whole interest to the exclusion of (a), his interest would have disappeared altogether.

On each such occasion, the value of the policy is treated as passing for inheritance tax purposes as a potentially exempt transfer to the extent that the current immediate beneficiary's entitlement is reduced. The tax is calculated on the personal 'meter' of the beneficiary from whom the benefit was switched but it is payable by the trustees. There will be no inheritance tax to pay if the beneficiary losing his interest survives for seven years.

On lifetime appointments, the value switched is the market value of the death benefit and this will usually be too small to attract inheritance tax. The value will only be significant in the exceptional case where the planholder is in such poor health that a benefit payable on his death is imminent enough to make it attractive to a notional buyer of the policy.

If appointments are made in the two years after the planholder's death, the value switched will be the actual death benefit paid, and in that case there may well be inheritance tax payable, unless the appointment is to the planholder's spouse which would be exempt.

Protected rights

Some personal pension schemes will have discretionary trust provisions contained in the rules of the scheme. Other personal pension schemes will allow individual trusts to be declared of the death benefit, as with retirement annuities described above. If the personal pension scheme is used to contract out, the protected rights, which cannot be assigned, can still be subject to discretionary disposal provisions in accordance with the rules, with nominated beneficiaries.

14.3.4 Putting existing policies in trust

Declaring a trust of an existing retirement annuity policy or personal pension is also in principle a gift for inheritance tax purposes, the value transferred being the market value of the death benefit unless the immediate beneficiary is the planholder's spouse, in which case the transfer will be exempt because it is between spouses.

Non-regular contributions to a personal pension scheme, or to a retirement annuity contract, eg an additional contribution in respect of unused relief carried forward from previous years, are treated in the same way.

In practice, however, such transfers are likely to be treated as negligible unless the planholder dies from natural causes within two years of making the declaration of trust. In these cases, the Capital Taxes Office of the Inland Revenue may treat the market value at the time of the transfer as a transfer made at the time of the declaration with inheritance tax being payable at death rates. On the other hand, if the declaration had not been made, the entire fund value (not its market value at the date of the declaration) would have fallen into the estate on death and been chargeable at the death rates. So while it will sometimes be difficult to say whether a declaration will be liable to precipitate a charge to inheritance tax and at what level, as a general rule, it is true to say that planholders have something to gain by declaring trusts of their policies and little or nothing to lose.

Retirement annuity contracts, including life assurance contracts under s 621 and personal pension schemes, should be written in trust. If they are not written in trust then the planholder is missing out on an obvious way of passing monies to beneficiaries free of inheritance tax, and the pension provider will not be able to pay out the proceeds until probate has been granted. It is essential, therefore, when considering retirement planning, to ensure that the pension provider is able to offer a suitable trust and should any existing policies not be written in trust to put them into trust.

Deferring benefits

From age 50 (or age 60 in the case of a retirement annuity) a policyholder may elect to take retirement benefits. Where the policyholder does not take benefits at the specified age and has still not done so when he or she dies, the Capital Taxes Office may consider that the failure to take retirement benefits before death gives rise to a charge to inheritance tax. This may arise where there is prima facie evidence that the policyholder's intention was to increase the estate of someone else — ie the beneficiaries of the death benefit. The CTO will look closely at arrangements where the policyholder became aware that he or she was suffering from a terminal illness or was uninsurable and at that time or after that time the policyholder took out a new policy and:

(1) assigned the death benefit on trust;
(2) assigned on trust the death benefit of an existing policy;
(3) paid further contributions to a single premium policy or increased contributions to a regular premium policy where the death benefit had been previously assigned on trust; or
(4) deferred the date for taking retirement benefits.

A claim by the CTO is unlikely to be pursued where the policyholder survived for two or more years after making these arrangements, or where the death benefit was paid to the policyholder's spouse and/or dependants.

14.3.5 Disability benefits

The past few years have seen an increase in the number of life offices offering different types of disability cover. Most offer a *waiver of premium benefit* while a few offer disability incomes and incapacity pensions.

Waiver of premium benefit

This benefit protects the planholder's commitment to pay pension contributions during disability at minimal cost. Under personal pension schemes it is possible to obtain a waiver of premium benefit in respect of both the investment content and the life assurance element.

Each life office offering waiver of premium benefit naturally has its own embellishments but some characteristics are common to most of them:

(1) the waiver of premium element tends to cost around 2% to 6% of the premium, depending on age at entry and sex;
(2) the waiver of premium element is a risk premium, and is not invested in order to provide retirement benefits, so that it is not normally returnable in the event of death;
(3) the waiver of premium element is considered as part of the premium under retirement annuities and personal pension schemes and the whole contribution including the waiver of premium element is eligible for tax relief;
(4) during periods of incapacity, the planholder is unlikely to have net relevant earnings, which is sometimes raised as an objection to the whole concept of waiver of premium benefit. The difficulty, however, falls away because premiums are not paid for the period in which the waiver of premium comes into operation so that the question of the life office accepting premiums or the planholder getting tax relief on them, does not arise. The life office does not *pay* the contributions, it *waives* the contributions.

The benefit is usually only available to those not over age 55 at entry and normally ceases at age 60 or 65. There is usually a deferment period of three to six months, during which disability has to exist before the waiver of premium benefit comes into operation.

Interest in this benefit has grown considerably since the advent of mortgages alongside pensions (see Chapter 18).

Example 14.8

A man aged 33 takes out a personal pension plan paying £1,000 pa with a pension age of 65 without waiver of premium benefit.

At the end of the second year he falls ill, and having no net relevant earnings, is unable to pay his third annual contribution. He recovers and restarts contributions in the fourth year.

His fund at 65 will be approximately £240,000. If he had opted for waiver of premium benefit, his fund at 65 would be approximately £261,000, a difference of £21,000.

The above figures are based on a typical unit-linked contract and assume an annual growth rate of 12% after charges.

Disability incomes and incapacity pensions

Section 620(4)(*b*) and s 634(3)(*c*) of ICTA 1988 allow for annuity payments to commence on incapacity: this means permanent incapacity — long term incapacity is insufficient. This type of benefit should not be confused with permanent health insurance.

Insurance companies normally issue contracts containing a provision for the annuity to come into payment early in the event of incapacity; the annuity may be based on the premiums paid or, alternatively, there may be an insured element, in which case the life office will have charged an extra premium for what is an extra benefit in that should the planholder become disabled, the income which he receives will be more than that which could have been generated by the premiums actually paid.

14.3.6 Tax treatment of pensions

Pensions payable under retirement annuity contracts and personal pension schemes to:

- the planholder
- the planholder's dependant under the continuation of a joint life pension
- the planholder's dependant under a nomination

are taxed as earned income. (The only situation in which the above pensions are taxed as investment income is where the contributions under a retirement annuity contract from which the pension arises were not all completely relieved for tax.)

Following FA 1984 which removed the investment income surcharge, the fact that a pension or part of it is taxed as investment income is no longer very relevant. Before FA 1984, the investment income was subject to the investment income surcharge if it exceeded the threshold — £7,100 for the year 1983/84.

Where a planholder dies during the period for which his pension is guaranteed (normally five years), the remaining guaranteed instalments (the right to which will have passed under the planholder's will) are taxed as investment income.

If a married woman received income from a personal pension scheme or retirement annuity prior to 6 April 1990 which was taxable as investment income, she was unable to set her wife's earned income allowance against it, and it was taxed in her husband's hands. Under independent taxation, however, she is able to set her own allowance against her investment income.

Prior to 6 April 1990, a married woman receiving a pension from a retirement annuity contract in her own right — from a policy on her own life under which she had paid contributions herself — was entitled to set the wife's earned income relief against it. She was also so entitled if the pension derived from her late husband's policy and she was named in the contract as an annuitant (s 619(1)); for example, if he died on pension and the pension continued to be paid to her because he had chosen a joint life pension.

14.3.7 Overseas aspects

The overseas aspects of retirement annuities and personal pension schemes can be split into two parts, the first relating to foreign earnings and whether or not they constitute relevant earnings and so support contributions; the second is the effect on the payment of a pension to a planholder living abroad at the time.

Overseas earnings
These may be treated in one of four ways.

(1) UK residents are in principle liable to tax on earnings from all sources, including foreign earnings, and any such earnings which are liable to tax are correspondingly potentially relevant earnings.

(2) Such foreign earnings, (prior to FA 1984) whether taxable under Schedule D or Schedule E, were eligible for a 25% deduction for tax purposes. The eligibility for the deduction depended upon periods actually spent abroad engaged in the activities giving rise to the overseas earnings. Where overseas earnings were taxable, but with a 25% reduction, the whole of the overseas earnings (not just 75% of them) constituted relevant earnings in respect of which a retirement annuity contribution could be paid.

FA 1984 reduced, with effect from 1984/85, the 25% rate of relief to $12\frac{1}{2}\%$ for the UK residents working and trading abroad and abolished the deduction altogether for subsequent years. The previous rules, outlined above, may still be relevant for the purposes of calculating contributions which are to be carried forward from previous years to a current period.

(3) If virtually the whole year is spent abroad, Schedule E taxpayers may be eligible for a 100% deduction (the 100% deduction does not apply to Schedule D taxpayers): this was not affected by FA 1984.

The principle of the 100% deduction is exactly the same as that of the 25% deduction and the whole of overseas earnings derived from non-pensionable employment constitutes relevant earnings. A contribution to a retirement annuity or personal pension scheme may be effected in respect of the whole of it, despite the fact that effectively no tax would be payable in these circumstances on the overseas earnings. The 100% allowance is not itself a deduction in arriving at net relevant earnings although it may be a competing allowance against the same income and consequently a contribution should only be paid if the individual has another source of relevant earnings taxable in the UK. However, an employee who is entitled to a 100% allowance may have relevant earnings and may so contribute to a personal pension. He will pay contributions net of basic rate tax. It appears that current Inland Revenue practice is not to recoup tax deducted at source by these employees, so there is a distinct planning opportunity.

(4) Where a UK resident takes a job abroad with a foreign employer which will involve him in actually living abroad, as opposed to a job with a UK employer which usually involves spending long periods abroad, then he will usually become non-resident for tax purposes. In that case, his foreign earnings will be outside the UK tax net altogether, there will be no question of their being liable to UK tax and, as a result, he will not be eligible for a contribution in respect of those earnings to a retirement annuity or to a personal pension scheme.

Foreign emoluments

Foreign emoluments are defined in ICTA 1988, s 192 as emoluments of a person not domiciled in the UK from an office or employment under or with any person, body of persons, or partnership resident outside and not resident in the UK. Such emoluments (prior to FA 1984) were reduced by 25% or by 50% and charged to tax under Schedule E. If such emoluments are relevant earnings, the calculation of net relevant earnings will take into account the whole rather than the reduced amount after the 25% or 50% deduction.

As a result of FA 1984 employees domiciled overseas and working for non-resident employers ceased to qualify for the 50% and 25% deductions from earnings. Special transitional relief protects those who already qualified or were in transit to the UK on 13 March 1984, although those people who had been resident in the UK for nine out of the last ten years ceased to qualify for relief on 5 April 1984. Again, these provisions may be relevant for the purposes of calculating contributions which are to be carried forward from previous years to a current period.

Payment of pensions

Pensions payable from a UK source, including the pension emerging from a retirement annuity and from a personal pension scheme, are in principle liable to UK tax regardless of the residence of the pensioner.

In practice the position is governed by the double tax agreement, if any, in operation between the UK and the pensioner's country of residence. Most modern DTAs provide that private pensions (as opposed to ones paid by the Government to former civil servants) are liable to tax in the country of residence and therefore not in the country of origin.

Where this situation applies, the life office can obtain permission from the Inland Revenue to pay the pension gross.

If permission has not been obtained to pay a gross pension, the pension provider will adopt its normal procedure which applies to UK residents and deduct tax at basic rate from the instalments of pension.

14.4 Specialised occupations

The Inland Revenue permits a pension age lower than age 50 under personal pension schemes and 60 under retirement annuity contracts in the case of occupations where early retirement is customary. The following is the list of early retirement ages which have been agreed by the Inland Revenue.

Table 14.6

Profession or occupation	Minimum retirement age
Air Pilots	55*
Athletes (appearance and prize money only)	35
Badminton Players	35
Boxers	35
Brass Instrumentalists	55*
Circus animal trainers	50
Cricketers	40
Croupiers	50
Cyclists (Professional)	35
Dancers	35
Distant Water Trawlermen	55*
Divers (Saturation, Deep Sea and Free Swimming)	40
Firemen (Part-Time)	55*
Footballers	35
Golfers (tournament earnings)	40
Inshore Fishermen	55*
Inter Dealer Brokers	50
Jockeys	
— Flat Racing	45
— National Hunt	35
Martial Arts Instructors	50
Models	35
Moneybroker Dealers (excluding Directors and Managers responsible for dealers)	50
Moneybroker Dealers (Directors and Managers responsible for dealers)	55*
Motorcross Motorcycle Riders	40
Motor-cycle Road Racing Riders	40
Motor Racing Drivers	40
Newscasters (ITV)	50
Nurses, Physiotherapists, Midwives or Health Visitors who are females	55*
Off-shore Riggers	50
Psychiatrists (who are also maximum part time specialists employed within the National Health Service solely in the treatment of the mentally disordered)	55*
Real Tennis Players	35
Royal Marine Reservists (non-commissioned)	45
Royal Naval Reservists	50
Rugby League Players	35
Rugby League Referees	50
Singers	55*

Speedway Riders	40
Squash Players	35
Table Tennis Players	35
Tennis Players	35
Territorial Army Members	50
Trapeze Artists	40
Wrestlers	35

Note: Under personal pension schemes there is provision to take benefits between ages 50 and 75 so that individuals falling within those professions or occupations, and marked with an asterisk, may prefer a personal pension scheme if they wish to have access to benefits earlier than age 55.

From time to time new occupations and professions are added to the list, usually as a result of representations made by a trade body or professional association.

An individual falling into one of the above categories has the option of paying contributions into a personal pension scheme which will provide for benefits to commence at the earlier pension age shown above: he is entitled to defer the benefits in the usual way.

The earlier pension ages are intended to benefit individuals who fall into one of the specialised occupations. If the individual's job changes to one which would not fall into one of the above categories, he should stop paying contributions to the original contract and divert future contributions to a separate personal pension scheme which will specify the normal range of pension ages, 50 to 75.

An individual who falls into one of the above occupations but was not aware of the earlier pension ages or where they have been reduced since he effected his original contract, may nevertheless take benefits at the earlier pension age provided that he can show that his occupation fell into one of the above categories at the time he took out the contract.

Although the earlier pension ages may appear to be attractive to an individual whose occupation is such that his earning capacity will drop considerably after an early age, this does not necessarily mean that his retirement income will be adequate because the period of time during which he is contributing will be short, whereas the period during which he will be receiving an income will be long.

Example 14.9

A deep-sea diver, with high earnings, pays £5,000 pa for fifteen years, to a personal pension scheme starting when he is 25: at age 40 he has built up a fund of £156,630 (assuming growth of 10% pa after charges) which provides him with immediate benefits of a £37,306 tax free lump sum plus a level income of £11,647 pa.

It will be seen from the above example that even though the earning capacity may have been high, the contributions are restricted to $17\frac{1}{2}\%$ up to age 35 and 20% between ages 35 and 40 with the result that the emerging benefits are unlikely to be adequate so that additional provision will have to be made elsewhere to supplement the income. By age 55, the income will be worth around £4,900 if inflation over the fifteen year period is 6% pa.

14.4.1 Lloyd's underwriters

The ability to pay a contribution and to elect to have it treated as having been paid in the previous year does not necessarily assist Lloyd's Underwriters who are generally unable to establish net relevant earnings until several years have elapsed.

FA 1982, s 37 relating to Lloyd's Underwriters extended the carry back provisions of the retirement annuity legislation: the provision enables a contribution to be treated as paid in the last year but two, ie, three years (*not* up to three years). This special carry back cannot be used in conjunction with the ordinary carry back nor can it be used in conjunction with the carry forward of unused relief. So, for example, a contribution paid in the tax year 1992/93 could be treated as having been paid in the tax year 1989/90 and relieved against tax for that year, provided that an election had been made. A similar facility is available under personal pension schemes (s 641(2)).

This section relates only to Lloyd's Underwriters who are 'working names' and are therefore charged to income tax in respect of their underwriting activities, and also to employees of underwriting agencies whose earnings include a commission.

14.4.2 Doctors and dentists

It may seem surprising that a large section of this chapter is devoted to doctors and dentists, but the reason for this is that considerable planning opportunities are available to this section of the community through personal pension schemes and retirement annuities. A

212 Allied Dunbar Pensions Guide

doctor or dentist is likely to be a member of the NHS Superannuation Scheme. The opportunities available however, depend upon whether he is assessed to tax under Schedule E or under Schedule D.

Doctors and dentists assessable under Schedule E

A doctor or dentist who is in salaried employment in the NHS will be assessable to tax under Schedule E and pays a contribution of 6% of his remuneration to the National Health Service Superannuation Scheme (NHSSS). He is eligible for tax relief on these contributions under ICTA 1988, s 594. As his job is pensionable, the remuneration is not relevant earnings for the purpose of personal pension schemes and existing retirement annuity contracts.

It is possible that such an individual may have private earnings, assessable under Schedule D. For instance, it is common for a hospital doctor to carry out private consultancy work which will normally be non-pensionable and would be regarded as relevant earnings. Retirement annuity contracts and personal pension schemes may be effected within the usual limits in respect of these non-pensionable earnings (see the earlier part of this chapter dealing with provisions relating to people with more than one job).

Doctors and dentists assessable under Schedule D

A doctor or dentist who is engaged in the NHS and who is assessable under Schedule D is a self-employed person. He is in the unusual position of being a member of a sponsored superannuation scheme, the NHSSS. Thus although he is not an employee, he is nevertheless a member of a pension scheme. The contribution which he pays to the NHSSS does not rank for tax relief. There is, however an extra-statutory concession (A9), reproduced in Appendix 5, under which the Inland Revenue is normally prepared to allow such contributions as deductions from the earnings assessed to tax.

A practitioner assessed under Schedule D has three options in relation to the tax treatment of personal pension scheme contributions and any retirement annuity contributions and NHSSS contributions which he pays: the following is a reproduction with permission of a note produced by the Inland Revenue Pension Schemes Office on the subject. The note also applies unchanged in respect of personal pension schemes taken out from 1 July 1988.

Personal pension schemes and retirement annuities

Medical or dental practitioners assessed under Schedule D
Retirement annuity relief for the year of assessment 1983/84

1   For the year 1983/84 a practitioner will have three options in relation to the tax treatment of any retirement annuity premiums and National Health Service Superannuation Scheme contributions which he pays—

    (*A*)   to claim retirement annuity relief up to the statutory maxima by reference to his net relevant earnings, both from National Health Service and private practice; this option will preclude any concessional relief on his NHS Superannuation Scheme contributions;

    (*B*)   to claim concessional relief on NHS Superannuation Scheme contributions against his NHS earnings, and to claim in addition retirement annuity relief up to the statutory maxima by reference to non-NHS earnings only;

    (*C*)   to claim concessional relief on NHS Superannuation Scheme contributions, and to claim in addition retirement annuity relief up to the amount of the largest premium on which tax relief was allowed for any of the 3 years 1969/70, 1970/71 and 1971/72, but with a restriction if necessary to keep the total relief (on NHS Superannuation Scheme contributions and retirement annuity premiums taken together) within the pre-1971 statutory limits.

2   In the preceding paragraph —

    (*a*)   'statutory maxima' means the present limits of $17\frac{1}{2}\%$ (or the higher figures for older persons) plus any unused relief for earlier years.

    (*b*)   'pre-1971 statutory limits' means 10% and £750 and the other figures corresponding thereto in sections 227 and 228 Income and Corporation Taxes Act 1970.

    (*c*)   'NHS earnings' will be computed by multiplying the amount of NHS Superannuation Scheme contributions paid in the year of assessment by 100/6.

    (*d*)   'non-NHS earnings' means the remainder of the profits as assessed under Schedule D.

3   If NHS Superannuation Scheme contributions are inflated because of an addition for 'added years', only the normal annual NHS contributions should be used when computing NHS earnings for the purposes of Option 1(B) above.

4   The total relief to be kept within pre-1971 statutory limits under option 1(C) must be based on total NHS Superannuation Scheme contributions, including those relating to 'added years' and retirement annuity premiums taken together.

Special Note

A doctor or dentist holding a full or part time hospital appointment is an employee and the remuneration therefrom is assessed under Schedule E. Generally speaking, such an office would be pensionable (see Part 2 of the booklet relating to NHS Superannuation). If the individual is also in receipt of fees from a private practice assessed under Schedule D then he is able to pay retirement annuity premiums and claim relief to the extent of the statutory maxima as in 2(a) above.

Although the total benefits from the NHSSS and retirement annuities under basis (A) might exceed the maximum benefits approvable by the Inland Revenue [see Chapter 4] the individual's benefits under the NHSSS would not be restricted by the Inland Revenue.

Example 14.10

(1) Option (A)

A GP has net relevant earnings of £38,000. His NHS contributions (excluding any for added years) amount to £1,600.

NHS Pensionable Earnings (included in the NRE of £38,000) are £26,666 (1,600 × 100/6).

A GP can claim retirement annuity relief or personal pension scheme relief in relation to NRE of £38,000, provided that he does not claim tax relief on his NHS contributions of £1,600 and on any contributions for added years.

(2) Option (B)

In the above example the non-NHS earnings amount to £38,000 — £26,666, ie £11,334 on which he may claim retirement annuity relief or personal pension scheme relief without giving up relief on his NHS contributions.

Notes
(1) In some circumstances NHS pensionable earnings are more than NRE because the former is a multiple of NHS contributions paid in the actual tax year whereas NRE represents adjusted profits in the accounting period which ended in the previous tax year.
(2) NHS pensionable earnings may be lower than NRE even although there are no genuine private earnings because NHS Pensionable Earnings are an average.

Added years — Personal pension schemes
A practitioner who is considering increasing his pension benefits will normally have the option of:

(1) Paying additional voluntary contributions to purchase added years under the NHSSS.
(2) Paying contributions to a personal pension scheme, either in respect of his total net relevant earnings under option (A) or in respect of any non-NHS earnings under option (B).
(3) A combination of the two.
(4) Paying contributions to a retirement annuity contract taken out before 1 July 1988.
(5) Paying additional voluntary contributions to a freestanding scheme (only available if he is claiming tax relief on his NHSSS contributions).

Under option (B), it would be possible for the practitioner to buy added years under the NHSSS and also pay maximum retirement annuity or personal pension scheme contributions in respect of any non-NHS earnings. If, however, the practitioner opts for option (A) he will be precluded from claiming concessional relief on his NHS contributions, *including* those to buy added years so that the cost might become prohibitive.

Other factors which have to be considered are as follows:

(1) the NHSSS currently inflation-proofs pensions;
(2) contributions for added years are limited to 9% of NHS pensionable earnings because the maximum personal contribution that can be paid to an approved scheme amounts to 15%;
(3) the personal pension scheme, or existing retirement annuity contract affords greater flexibility in taking the benefits: benefits from separate contracts may be phased over a period of years between 50 and 75 (60 and 75 under the retirement annuity contract) regardless of whether or not the practitioner is working or has completely or partially retired; the personal pension scheme gives even greater flexibility in allowing benefits to be taken between 50 and 75;
(4) life assurance under ICTA 1988, s 637 can be provided with full tax relief on the contributions.

Retired practitioners
A doctor or dentist who has retired from the NHS but is continuing to practise privately, full-time or part-time, is eligible to contribute to a retirement annuity and/or personal pension scheme.

Carry back provisions

A doctor or dentist is entitled in the usual way, to pay a contribution and elect under ICTA 1988, s 619(4)(*a*) or s 641(1)(*a*) to have it treated as having been paid in the previous tax year. If he wishes to carry back in this way and use option (B), whereby he does not claim tax relief on his NHSSS contributions, a complication arises because he will probably have claimed tax relief on those NHSSS contributions already, as an expense against his profits. Nevertheless he may effectively 'unclaim' that relief and pay a personal pension scheme contribution and/or retirement annuity contribution in respect of net relevant earnings under option (B). If he is using option (A) there will be no problem, as he will not have claimed tax relief on his NHSSS contributions in the first place.

14.5 Benefit levels

This chapter, so far, has dealt with technical matters such as eligibility, the meaning of 'net relevant earnings' and how to obtain tax relief in the current year and previous years, but it is important not to lose sight of the principal purpose of retirement annuities and personal pension schemes, namely to provide a worthwhile income in retirement.

In practice, the only way of doing this within the legislation is to contribute the maximum tax-relievable contributions allowed. Many people, however, do not contribute anything like the maximum contributions because they are not aware of the effect that inflation will have on their current pension planning.

The following table shows the benefits emerging from a typical personal pension scheme at age 60 based on:

- contributions commencing at 10% of income, but not increasing in line with increases in income, and
- contributions starting at 10% of income and continuing at that level in line with salary increases.

The table is based on an initial income level of £10,000 pa, and assumes that income increases by $8\frac{1}{2}$% pa to age 60, and that fund growth amounts to 10% pa after charges.

Table 14.7

Man aged	Projected income at age 60	Projected level pension produced by £1,000 pa investment contribution	
		level	Indexed at $8\frac{1}{2}\%$ pa
24	£181,032	£24,965 (13.8%)	£78,774 (43.5%)
29	£120,395	£15,550 (12.9%)	£43,567 (36.2%)
34	£ 80,068	£ 9,578 (12.0%)	£23,513 (29.4%)
39	£ 53,249	£ 5,782 (10.9%)	£12,254 (23.0%)
44	£ 35,413	£ 3,364 (9.5%)	£ 6,052 (17.1%)
49	£ 23,551	£ 1,815 (7.7%)	£ 2,719 (11.5%)

The table clearly demonstrates the importance of keeping pension provision under regular review and of planning for retirement many years before the event — in fact, it may be rather daunting to some people. The above figures however, could be increased by 75% if maximum contributions were made, (or at least doubled for a man over age 50); in addition contributions could be paid representing unused relief carried forward from previous years.

The most important figures in the above table are not the projected incomes on retirement and the projected pensions emerging from the pension plan, but the relationship between the two, for example, the individual aged 39 retiring at age 60 will receive an income from his personal pension of either 13% or 24.6% of his final income depending upon whether or not he has increased contributions throughout the previous twenty years.

The following table shows the pension emerging from a personal pension scheme as a *percentage* of final income in retirement. Income at retirement and the benefits under a personal pension scheme may appear extremely high in relation to today's earnings but in relation to final earnings, they may well be a very small percentage. The pension is based on contributions of 10% of income throughout, (ie an increasing contribution) on the same assumptions as the previous table.

Table 14.8

Age	Males Pension age 60	Males Pension age 65	Females Pension age 60	Females Pension age 65
24	43.5%	56.1%	39.7%	50.4%
29	36.2%	47.5%	33.0%	42.7%
34	29.4%	39.5%	26.8%	35.5%
39	23.0%	32.1%	21.0%	28.8%
44	17.1%	25.1%	15.6%	22.6%
49	11.5%	18.7%	10.5%	16.8%
54	6.2%	12.6%	5.6%	11.3%

The purpose of this table is to show what a future pension will be *worth* rather than showing the pension as a sterling amount.

The pensions are level: pensions increasing at $8\frac{1}{2}\%$ pa compound would be approximately *one half* of the pensions illustrated.

Example 14.11

A man aged 39 paying contributions of 10% of his income throughout could expect to receive an income of 23.0% of his income at age 60.

If he requires 50% of his income to live on, the contribution level required, as a percentage of his income is as follows:

$$\frac{50.0}{23.0} \times 10 = 21.7\%$$

14.6 Other schemes for partners

14.6.1 Retired partners' annuities

A partner who has made no provision for income through the retirement annuity or personal pension scheme legislation may nevertheless receive a pension from his firm on retirement.

Such a pension, because of old age or ill-health, will normally be treated as a charge for basic and higher rates of tax on the earned income of the paying partners under ICTA 1988, s 683(1) although it cannot be deducted from the investment income except to the extent that the pension exceeds the allowable limits under ICTA 1988, s 628.

Personal pension schemes and retirement annuities

In order for the pension to be regarded as earned income at the hands of the recipient, under the provision of s 628, it must be within the allowable limits, ie not more than 50% of the average profits of the retiring partner for the best three out of the last seven years prior to his retirement during which he had devoted substantially the whole of his time to acting as a partner.

The payment must be in accordance with the partnership agreement or a supplementary agreement. The firm may make increases in the pension paid to a former partner in order that it may keep pace with inflation, as measured by the retail prices index for the December preceding the year of assessment for which the revised pension is to be paid compared with the December in the year of assessment in which he ceased to be a member of the partnership. It is permissible for the pension to continue for a widow or dependant.

Payments made by continuing partners to a retired partner do not reduce the net relevant earnings of the former.

There are several disadvantages in relying on a pension from the firm:

(1) The pension is usually limited to a period of, say, ten years simply because the continuing partners are unlikely to commit themselves to continue paying a pension for the life of a retired partner or even the life of his dependant.
(2) If several of the retiring partners leave the firm either on death or on retirement, the pension liability could be too great a burden on the continuing partners which might result in the dissolution of the partnership or a reduction in the pension paid to the retired partners. In fact it may be difficult for the firm to enter into mergers with other firms which might otherwise be desirable or it may prevent new partners from joining the firm.
(3) The continuation of the pension paid to the retired partner will depend on the continued success of the firm over which the retired partner has no control.

14.7 Self-managed schemes for partners

Prior to the introduction of personal pension schemes on 1 July 1988, a few insurance companies had introduced a variation on the retirement annuity contract whereby contributions were paid by a number of partners to the insurance company which would issue a policy to the partners as policyholders in an approved retirement annuity contract. The insurance company was the beneficial owner of the investments. The partners had an influence on the investment of the policies in a similar way to a self-managed or personalised life assurance mini-bond to the extent that the insurance company was prepared to take account of the preferences for investment as expressed by the policyholders. The partners could invest only in approved investments for the retirement annuity fund, but these could include, for example, approved quoted investments or, more commonly, the premises occupied by the partnership.

The main attraction of these schemes was the possibility of transferring property owned by the partnership into the retirement annuity or using the funds built up to purchase a property from which the partnership would operate.

Under the personal pension scheme legislation this is no longer possible. Inland Revenue practice on 'self investment' is now much more restricted and is contained in their 'Memorandum 101', dated October 1989, an extract of which follows:

Part I   Investment of members contributions

1. In his Budget statement the Chancellor proposed that personal pension scheme (PPS) members should have the opportunity to become more involved in decisions about how their contributions are invested. This Memorandum contains the further guidance promised in paragraph 59 of Memorandum No 99.
2. This guidance applies to all personal pension schemes, regardless of the type of provider (bank, building society, friendly society etc), which wish to give members a degree of investment choice.
3. Decisions on the extent of choice which scheme members can have are matters for each scheme to decide. There will be no Revenue requirements on this point. Some schemes may choose to limit individual involvement to selecting the parameters of the investment portfolio, leaving the selection of particular investments to a fund manager. On the other hand, others may give the members a direct say as to the specific investments to be held and when they should be bought or sold.

Range of acceptable investments

4. The SFO will, therefore, now consider for approval schemes whose rules allow members to choose, if they wish, how their contributions should be invested. Investments available can be any of the following.

Stocks and shares (eg equities, gilts, debentures etc.) quoted on the UK Stock Exchange including securities traded on the Unlisted Securities Market.

Stocks and shares traded on a recognised overseas stock exchange.

Unit trusts and investment trusts.

Insurance company managed funds and unit-linked funds.

Deposit accounts.

Commercial property.

Part II   Use of scheme funds

5. There will need to be some controls on investment activities and the way in which the scheme is administered. This is because the sole purpose of an approved PPS must be the provision of annuities or lump sums as required by Section 633 of the Taxes Act. So, from the date of this Memorandum it will be a condition of approval for all personal pension schemes, irrespective of the type of provider, that the documents must contain provisions expressly prohibiting investments of the types described in paragraphs 6 to 8 below.

Loans

6. Scheme funds must not be used to provide loans to members or any persons connected with a member. Further, no loan from any source made to an individual who is a member of the scheme should in any way affect the return on the investments representing that member's interest in the scheme.

Other investments

7. Schemes must not, except in the circumstances described in paragraph 8, enter into any investment transactions with a member or any person connected with a member. The acquisitions by the scheme of a member's commercial property or portfolio of stocks and shares are such transactions, as is the subsequent acquisition by the member of any of the scheme's assets. All transactions in quoted UK or overseas securities should take place through a recognised stock exchange.

8. Schemes must not hold directly as an investment residential property or land connected with such a property, or personal chattels capable in any way of private use. This does not apply to commercial land and property (subject to paragraph 7 above). Where commercial property is leased to a business or partnership connected with the member, the scheme rules should ensure that the lease, including the rent payable, is on commercial terms determined by a professional valuation.

Connected transactions

9. For the purposes of paragraphs 6 to 8 above a person is connected with a member if that person falls within the definition of connected persons in Section 839 of the Taxes Act. The duty of ensuring that a transaction is not one with a connected person must be placed on the scheme administrator.

Transactions completed before the issue of this Memorandum

10. Investment transactions which conflict with the requirements in paragraphs 6 to 8 above, but which were completed by an approved (or provisionally approved) scheme before the issue of this Memorandum will not normally be treated as giving rise to unapprovable benefits.

Existing schemes

11. Schemes which have already received full approval will be required to amend their rules accordingly, and should submit appropriate amendments to this Office. In the meantime no transactions as described in paragraphs 6 and 8 above should be entered into.

12. Schemes which have received provisional approval will be required to include the new restrictions in the rules before substantive approval is given. In the meantime the administrator's undertaking that the scheme does not make provision for any benefit other than those mentioned in the Taxes Act should be regarded as preventing any of the transactions described in paragraphs 6 to 8 above.

13. Schemes which have already submitted rules, and which are capable of, but have not yet received provisional approval in all respects except for paragraphs 6 to 8 above will be granted provisional approval on the understanding that the administrator will interpret his undertaking as in paragraph 12 above.

New schemes

14. The rules should contain the restrictions in paragraphs 6 to 8 above before provisional approval can be given. The form of application for approval (SFPP1) will be amended in due course to require an indication of where in the scheme documents the new restrictions are to be found. In the meantime applications should include in part 3 of the SFPP1 a note showing which rules contain these provisions. If rules have already been executed without these provisions this Office may be prepared to grant provisional approval upon receipt of an assurance from the administrator that he will interpret his undertaking as in paragraph 12 above.

Model rules

15. The model rules coded IMR/APP/88 and IR/PP/88 will be amended in due course to incorporate provisions permitting members' investment choice and the restrictions described above.

When personal pension schemes first started in July 1988 new providers such as banks, building societies and unit trusts were permitted to offer them, not just insurance companies. The above guidelines show the extended choice available to individuals by allowing all providers to offer members the facility to decide exactly how their fund can be invested. In effect the member can take advantage of a 'portfolio management' type service if this is offered by the pension provider.

The scheme may borrow to purchase a commercial property and there is no restriction on the amount (as applies to small self-administered schemes for directors — see Chapter 9 — where borrowings are limited to three times the ordinary annual contribution to the scheme plus an amount equal to 45% of scheme assets).

It will be seen that loans and other transactions with scheme members and their associates are banned. Loans to the employer/company and unsecured loans generally are not permitted (in contrast to small self-administered schemes for directors where the scheme trustees may make an unsecured loan — generally for a short period — and to the company). Although investment in commercial property is allowed and the property may be used in connection with the member's (or his associate's business), because of the prohibition on transactions with the member it will not be possible for the member to transfer to his personal pension scheme an *existing property* owned by his business. If a property is bought on the open market by the personal pension scheme and then leased back to the member's business the terms of the lease and the level of rent must be on commercial terms.

As with small self-administered schemes run by small limited companies, investments in residential property or 'pride in possession' assets is not permitted.

The above guidelines also prohibit any associated loans from a third party, eg a bank, where the return on the member's personal pension scheme fund would be affected. Under similar arrangements operated within the retirement annuity legislation it was not uncommon for a loan to be granted to a member on condition that a switch was made from his investment fund into another fund where the future return was linked in some way to the rate of interest charged on the loan. This is prohibited under personal pension schemes offering these facilities.

The documentation required for self-managed schemes is similar to that required for personal pension schemes offered by other providers although the paperwork will increase significantly if investments are made outside insurance company pension funds. Actuarial valuations are not required at inception or for continued approval (as applies under small self-administered schemes for directors) but regular fund valuations will be needed from time to time.

14.7.1 Friendly societies

Having their own friendly society enables a group of partners to make retirement provision with all the advantages normally enjoyed under an insured arrangement. By avoiding an insurance company the partners will hope that their expenses will be lower. They will, however, incur expenses in setting up their friendly society. The main steps to be undertaken are:

(1) At least seven partners of the same firm will be required to establish the arrangement, and the group will have to be approved by the Chief Registrar of Friendly Societies.
(2) A set of rules will have to be submitted to the Registrar who will need to be satisfied that suitable accounting systems will operate.
(3) A policy document will need to be approved by the Inland Revenue.
(4) Audited annual returns will have to be made to the Registrar.

Further changes to the legislation affecting friendly societies will come into force when the Friendly Societies Act 1992 takes effect.

Self-managed investments of this nature will require professional advice, especially as the effort involved in the above process is likely to be time consuming. They will also have to comply with the provisions of the Trustee Investment Act 1961 which requires at least 50% of the fund to be invested in 'narrow-range' investments — mainly government securities.

15 Tax planning hints through pensions

This chapter contains brief notes on ways of using pension schemes in order to achieve not only retirement income for the member and his family, but also a means of overall tax planning.

The first part of this chapter deals with executive pension plans and the second half with personal pension schemes and existing retirement annuity contracts. It is suggested, however, that the whole of the chapter is read by both the company director and the self-employed person, because they may well change status throughout their careers. Indeed, it is not uncommon for persons to have income from limited companies and also from sole proprietorships or partnerships, in which case executive pension plans, personal pension schemes and retirement annuity contracts may be used concurrently.

15.1 Executive pension plans: planning hints

(1) Ensure that employers' contributions are paid by the end of the accounting period otherwise tax relief will be lost — there is no provision for carrying back pension contributions.

(2) Pension contributions can create, or augment a trading loss which can be carried back one year or carried forward indefinitely.

(3) A trading loss (possibly caused by payment of a pension contribution) can be set against chargeable gains in the same year or in the previous year.

(4) Special, one-off contributions can be paid to purchase past service benefits, although tax relief will normally be spread over a period not exceeding four years. Try to match the single contribution with a regular annual contribution of a like amount in order to obtain tax relief in the year of payment.

(5) Any personal contributions paid by the director (not exceeding 15% of remuneration) are relieved in the fiscal year in which they are paid (not the company's accounting year). Thus any personal contributions should be paid by 5 April in any year. Since 6 April 1987 it has been possible to vary the amount and timing of any additional voluntary contributions.

(6) Apart from specialised occupations the earliest normal retirement date that you may specify under an executive pension plan is age 60. This, therefore, is normally the best possible date to choose even if you are considering working on beyond this date. Having chosen age 60, you may still defer the benefits if you continue working. A normal retirement date of age 60 is the earliest date at which you are entitled to take maximum benefits from your pension plan, ie a pension of 2/3rds of your final salary, part of which you may exchange for a maximum tax-free lump sum of $1\frac{1}{2}$ times your final salary.

If however, you choose a normal retirement date of 65, but subsequently decide to retire at, for example, age 63, you will not be entitled to maximum benefits even although you may well have completed 20 years' service by age 63. You will be treated as going on early retirement with resulting limitations on your maximum benefits.

The only exception to this recommendation is that if you can only complete 20 years' service with the company by say, age 63 and are proposing to fund for maximum benefits, then you should choose a normal retirement date of 63.

(7) Although you cannot choose a normal retirement date before age 60, it is still possible to take substantial benefits from age 50 onwards on early retirement from the company.

If you are classed as a 'post-1989 member' of an executive pension plan you will be entitled to a pension of 2/3rds of your final (capped) remuneration from age 50 onwards if you have completed 20 years' service by that date, so that if funds are available, an executive pension plan could provide maximum benefits from an early age. However, advance funding by the employer is not permitted in these circumstances; contributions may only be paid into the executive pension plan to provide the maximum benefits at age 60 but in the event of immediate early retirement at age 50 the shortfall may be provided by means of a one-off contribution into the plan at that time or in the case of a large group occupational scheme the required amount to provide the maximum pension could be drawn from the fund.

(8) As maximum benefits are related to 'final remuneration' which is usually based on the average of the best three consecutive years' remuneration in the last 12 years before retirement (whether normal retirement or early retirement), ensure that you pay yourself remuneration at higher levels for at least three consecutive years in the period. These three consecutive years do not necessarily have to be the *last* three: for example, they may be the levels of remuneration in the 12, 11 and ten years prior to retirement increased in line with the Retail Prices Index, up to retirement.

(9) If you are classed as a pre-1987 member of an executive pension plan, it is possible to fund purely for the tax-free lump sum of 1½ times final remuneration if you can complete 20 years' service: on reaching normal retirement date (ideally age 60 for the reasons set out above) the whole of the pension fund can be taken in the form of a tax-free lump sum but you can continue working for the company. There is no necessity to retire, but you cannot receive any further lump sum retirement benefits, and any death benefits will have to be calculated as if you had retired before your death. Pre-1987 membership is particularly valuable because it is possible to fund for a 2/3rds pension over ten years rather than 20 years under post-1987 membership.

(10) If the remuneration which you draw from the company is less than the upper earnings limit (currently £21,060), the 'tax' saving by taking a lower salary is not just the basic rate of income tax but also the saving in National Insurance contributions.

Example 15.1

Current situation

Director draws remuneration of £23,000

Alternative

Director draws reduced remuneration of £20,000

Company pays £3,000 to an executive pension plan.

Personal tax saving	= £750.00	(25% of £3,000)
Personal NIC saving	= £ 95.40	(9% of £1,060)
Company's NIC saving	= £312.00	(10.4% of £3,000)
	£1,157.40	

Thus £3,000 is invested at a net cost of £1,842.60 (£3,000 — £1,157.40 saving).

---

(11) Because of the effect of compound interest, it is the early years' pension contributions which generate most of the pension fund as the following examples show, so that provided profits permit, it is preferable to pay contributions in the early years rather than waiting until retirement approaches:
    (a) A director pays contributions of £3,000 pa for ten years between ages 40 and 50 and builds up a fund of £106,887 at age 60, assuming 10% growth net of charges.
    (b) Another director pays contributions of £1,500 pa between the ages of 40 and 60 and builds up a fund of £78,205 assuming 10% growth net of charges.

(12) The pension fund represents an additional source of borrowing: up to one-half of the pension fund (normally in respect of controlling directors) may be loaned back to the company for a genuine commercial purpose. This type of loan, which may be on a long-term, interest only basis, can be a useful addition to short-term bank loans.

(13) Personal loans to the director can be arranged alongside pension plans. Banks and building societies are prepared to lend on an interest only basis, long term, usually on the security of property with capital being repaid at retirement. The tax-free lump sum which emerges from the pension fund has been built up in a tax-free fund and tax relief has been given on

the pension contributions so this represents an extremely tax efficient way of repaying a mortgage (see Chapter 17).

(14) Where pension fund contributions are paid out of company profits, which lie between £250,000 and £1,250,000, tax relief is obtained at marginal rates. The rates of corporation tax for 1992/93 have been set at the following levels:

Over £1,250,000	33%
Up to £250,000	25%
Marginal rate	35%

(15) If you own a property, for example, a commercial property which is used by your company, resist the temptation to transfer it to a self-administered pension fund which you may set up. Apart from incurring a possible CGT charge on the disposal of the asset, and conveyancing costs and stamp duty, you will be converting a capital asset over which you have personal control into earned income. When the trustees of the self-administered scheme sell the property it will be paid to you largely in the form of earned income with only a proportion of the total pension fund assets being paid to you in the form of tax-free cash.

(16) Following the Finance Act 1984 which abolished the investment income surcharge, you may consider taking dividends from the company, rather than salary as your personal tax position will be the same but National Insurance contributions will be avoided. The disadvantages in taking this course of action are:
  (a) by not taking salary, you will not be able to pay pension contributions;
  (b) any periods of service with the company which were not salaried cannot be pensioned at a later date;
  (c) State Earnings Related Pension may be lost;
  (d) the payment of a dividend by the company may form a base for valuing the company and this may have an adverse effect on future inheritance tax;
  (e) if the company is paying corporation tax at other than the 'small companies rate' (ie it has taxable profits over £250,000) the saving in National Insurance contributions may be balanced by higher corporation tax (because dividends, unlike salary, are not tax deductible). Thus, there would be no financial advantage in taking dividends.

The following table shows a comparison of effective tax rates using £10,000 of profits to provide benefits for a director. In the case of the last column the figures show for simplicity, that one-half of the £10,000 available profits are paid into an executive pension plan.

Table 15.1

	Salary	Dividend (Corp Tax at 25%)	Dividend (Corp Tax at 35%)	Salary plus Executive Pension Plan
Company outlay	£10,000	£10,000	£10,000	£10,000
Salary	(£ 9,058)	—	—	(£ 4,529)
NIC	(£ 942)	—	—	(£ 471)
Executive pension plan	—	—	—	(£ 5,000)
Taxable profits	Nil	£10,000	£10,000	Nil
Corporation tax	Nil	(£ 2,500)	(£ 3,500)	Nil
Dividend	—	(£ 7,500)	(£ 6,500)	—
ACT payable (25/75 of dividend)	—	£ 2,500	£ 2,166	—
Cash retained in company	Nil	Nil	Nil	Nil
Director's income (gross)	£ 9,058	£10,000	£ 8,666	£ 4,529
Income tax at, say, 40%	(£ 3,623)	(£ 4,000)	(£ 3,466)	(£ 1,811)
Company's NIC	(£ 942)	—	—	(£ 471)
Balance of Corp Tax	—	Nil*	(£ 1,334)	—
Tax and NIC	£ 4,565	£ 4,000	£ 4,800	£ 2,282
Effective 'tax' rate	45.7%	40%	48.0%	22.8%

*Corporation tax less ACT already paid

(17) If you are classed as a pre-1987 member or a 1987–89 member you may, on retirement, opt to be treated as a post-1989 member. Although you would be subject to the post-1989 rules relating to the earnings cap, years of service required to achieve maximum benefits and lump sum restrictions you may still be better off, especially if you are proposing to retire early from age 50 onwards.

(18) Remuneration received in the form of unit trusts (popular when it was possible to avoid National Insurance contributions by paying remuneration this way) can be treated as pensionable provided that the scheme rules permit and that remuneration

is assessable to tax under Schedule E. This element of remuneration is treated as 'fluctuating emoluments' and so must be averaged with other P11D earnings over a period of at least three years.

15.2 Personal pension schemes and retirement annuity contracts: planning hints

Contributions do not have to be paid by the end of your accounting period in order to attract tax relief; contributions are relieved in the tax year in which they are paid, or the previous tax year.

Even although you may not have paid contributions in previous years, you can carry forward the unused reliefs for up to six years, and by using the carry back facility you can effectively carry forward unused relief for seven years.

Although you may have retired having sold your business, there may still be scope for paying personal pension scheme contributions and carrying them back one year or in some circumstances, two years, to a period when you were in business in order to obtain a tax refund.

If on reaching retirement you have sources of capital and/or income, you should exhaust these before drawing on your pension benefits simply because the pension fund does not pay tax and will usually grow faster than your other investments. Arrange to pay contributions into a series of separate personal pension schemes or into one scheme which consists of a number of 'arrangements' or 'contracts' so that you can phase your retirement benefits in stages between the ages of 50 and 75.

To the extent that you defer your benefits, you are deferring an increasing capital sum which in the event of your death, can be returned to a wide range of beneficiaries free of inheritance tax (provided the policy is written under a suitable trust).

If you are considering increasing contributions use an existing retirement annuity where possible, rather than a personal pension scheme. The reason for this is a retirement annuity gives a higher proportion of the fund in the form of a tax-free lump sum —

see Chapter 14. However, the retirement annuity has to be sufficiently flexible to take increases in contributions.

Consider making use of personal loans alongside existing retirement annuities and personal pension scheme (see Chapter 17).

The life assurance benefits under the retirement annuity and personal pension scheme legislation can provide substantial amounts free of inheritance tax, provided the policy is written under a suitable trust. The contributions attract tax relief up to the highest rate on earned income, whereas ordinary life assurance policies taken out since March 1984 do not attract tax relief. This type of policy can be used to provide life cover for your family and also business associates, for example, co-partners.

By taking advantage of the ability to carry forward unused relief from previous years you can reduce current tax liability substantially. For example, you may carry forward unused relief from previous years when you were paying tax at lower rates to the current year when you may be paying tax at higher rates.

If you are already paying maximum contributions for yourself and you employ your wife, you should set up an executive pension plan for her: the contributions that you may pay to an approved pension scheme of that nature are generally much higher than the contributions that you could pay to your own personal pension scheme or retirement annuity contract (see Chapter 14). If your wife works in your business, you can pay her a salary which will be a deductible expense, provided, of course that her employment can be justified. Traditionally, the level of remuneration paid to the wife of a partner will be set at a figure which is below the lower earnings limit (and therefore not be subject to National Insurance contributions) and also lower than the personal allowance (and not taxable in her hands, provided she does not have other income).

Example 15.2

Current situation

Taxable earnings (top slice)	£10,000
25% tax	2,500
Net	7,500

Revised situation

Taxable earnings		£10,000
Wife's salary £2,808		
Pension plan contribution £936		3,744
Taxable earnings		6,256
25% tax		1,564
Husband's net income		4,692
Add back wife's salary		2,808
Total net income		7,500

The pension plan has been set up for the individual's wife at no reduction in net spendable income.

The above example has an added advantage for the sole proprietor or partner in that as profits have been reduced by £3,184, this may also have the effect of reducing the employer's Class 4 National Insurance contributions (6.3% of profits between £6,120 and £21,060 in 1992/93). When the benefits are taken from the executive pension plan at retirement, they will be taxable as earned income but effectively tax-free as the wife's earned income relief continues in retirement and can be set against the wife's pension.

16 Leaving service benefits

16.1 Preservation of benefits

Much of the publicity relating to pension schemes over the past few years has related to the treatment of members who change their jobs. Until 1975, many pension schemes provided nothing for the job mover whether he was dismissed for misconduct, was made redundant or left of his own accord.

The Social Security Act 1973 altered the benefits of early leavers considerably with effect from 6 April 1975. Schemes had to provide benefits at or after normal retirement age for scheme members who attained age 26 and who left service having completed five years of scheme membership. The Social Security Act 1985 removed the age 26 qualification. The Social Security Act 1986 reduced the service qualification to two years from 6 April 1988 and provided for 5% revaluation of that part of the early leaver's preserved pension (from a final salary scheme) which related to service after 1 January 1985 in respect of early leavers after 1 January 1986.

The Social Security Act 1990 extended this requirement to revalue preserved pensions in respect of *all* service for leavers after 1 January 1991.

The options normally available to the employee are set out below, although some of the options may not be granted either as a result of the preservation requirements under the Act or because the employer's pension scheme does not provide some of the options.

The options are as follows:

(1) A deferred pension (sometimes known as preserved, paid up or frozen pensions) may be provided, payable when the member reaches normal retirement age, although early and late retirement options will be permitted.

(2) A deferred annuity may be purchased from an insurance company which issues s 32 annuities, sometimes called 'buy-out plans'.
(3) The assignment by the trustees of the original scheme of an employee's individual pension policy to a new employer.
(4) A cash transfer of the member's rights under the original scheme to the new employer's pension scheme but not via the member.
(5) A cash transfer of the member's rights under the original scheme to a personal pension scheme.
(6) A refund to the employee of his contributions to the pension scheme.
(7) The assignment by the trustees of the original scheme of an employee's individual pension policy to the employee personally, subject to the provisions of the original scheme.
(8) Again, in the case of an individual policy scheme, the policy may continue to be held by the trustees and will participate in any future growth. If the original trust deed allows, it may be possible for separate trustees to be appointed to hold the leaver's individual policy.

16.2 Deferred pensions

A deferred pension is generally limited to a proportion of the employee's total final remuneration at the date of leaving his employment. For pre-1987 members and 1987–1989 members the maximum proportion under Inland Revenue limits is two thirds of the fraction obtained by taking the number of actual years of service over the number of potential service which the employee could have achieved at normal retirement age.

Example 16.1

An employee aged 45 who is a pre-1987 member leaves the service of a company having completed twenty years service. His salary on leaving is £22,000. He was a member of a scheme providing a pension of 1/60th of his final salary for each year of service at age 65. His deferred pension payable from age 65 will be £7,333, ie 20/60ths of £22,000, subject to statutory revaluation which is generally 5% (see below). His maximum deferred pension is:

$$\text{Total remuneration} \times \frac{\text{Actual service to date of leaving}}{\text{Potential service to age 65}} \times 2/3 = \text{Deferred pension}$$

The deferred pension must be revalued in line with the cost of living between the date of leaving and normal retirement age, subject to a maximum of 5% pa. Assuming the deferred pension of £7,333 is revalued at 5% pa it will amount to £19,456 pa at age 65.

For post-1989 members the maximum proportion is $1/30$ th of total remuneration for each year of service to the date of leaving, subject to an overall limit of 2/3rds of salary.

Example 16.2

An employee aged 45 who is a post-1989 member leaves the service of a company having completed 15 years service. His salary is £30,000. He was a member of a scheme providing a pension of 1/60th of his final salary for each year of service at age 65. The deferred pension from age 65 will be £7,500 pa, ie 15/60ths of £30,000, subject to statutory revaluation. His maximum deferred pension is:
Total remuneration × actual service to date of leaving × 1/30th. Again, this maximum pension must be increased in line with the cost of living between the date of leaving and normal retirement date.

Defined benefit company pension schemes which are contracted out of the earnings related part of the state scheme must protect against inflation the guaranteed minimum pension (the proportion of the deferred pension which would have been provided by the state if the employee had not been contracted out). The methods of revaluing the GMP between the date of leaving and the date of retiring are as follows:

(1) full revaluation in line with movements in earnings levels (known as s 21 orders), or
(2) revaluation at 5% pa compound together with the payment of a limited revaluation premium to the National Insurance fund which will then undertake to cover increases in excess of 5% pa, or
(3) revaluation at a fixed rate of at least $7\frac{1}{2}$% pa compound, with effect from 6 April 1988. (Any GMP preserved by fixed rate revaluation before 6 April 1988 is revalued at $8\frac{1}{2}$% pa.)

Part of the pension may be exchanged for a lump sum on reaching normal retirement date. The maximum lump sum is calculated on the same basis as for early retirement (see Chapter 4).

In the case of a former employee dying before reaching normal retirement age, the scheme may provide benefits for a widow or dependants, in which case maximum benefits are calculated as on death in service.

16.3 Problems of the early leaver

16.3.1 Frozen pensions

For a long time anyone who left their job — and their final salary scheme — before reaching pension age lost out on their pension benefits because their pension was frozen at the date of leaving (except to the limited extent of revaluation of the GMP under a contracted-out scheme).

The Social Security Act 1985 provided protection for the early leaver:

(1) The proportion of a deferred pension which relates to pensionable service with the employer from 1 January 1985 must be revalued in line with increases in the Retail Prices Index or 5% per annum if lower. This resulted in little immediate improvement in early leavers' benefits in the short term as no account was taken in respect of service with the employer before January 1985. (With some schemes, particularly large ones where the trustees wish to use up surpluses, the revaluation was applied in respect of service before January 1985.)
(2) The Social Security Act 1990 has now extended this requirement so that the revaluation must apply to all service for any scheme member leaving the employer's service on or after 1 January 1991.

The following example shows the effect of the Social Security Acts in providing for revaluation at 5% per annum. It assumes that an individual has four jobs, each providing a pension of 1/80th of final salary for each year of service. Without revaluation the combined total pensions would be £20,080 pa, approximately less than one half of the pension which would have been payable had the employee remained in the first job for 40 years, ie 40/80ths of £87,548 = £43,774 pa. With revaluation, the pension is increased by around one third.

Example 16.3

	Age on leaving	Salary on leaving		Frozen pension entitlement	Pensions revalued at 5% pa
Job 1	35	£10,000	$\frac{10}{80}$ =	£ 1,250	£ 5,402
Job 2	45	£20,610	$\frac{10}{80}$ =	£ 2,576	£ 6,835
Job 3	55	£42,478	$\frac{10}{80}$ =	£ 5,310	£ 8,649
Job 4	65	£87,548	$\frac{10}{80}$ =	£10,944	£10,944
				£20,080	£31,830

Note: It has been assumed that salary increases at $7\frac{1}{2}$% pa and that the whole of the deferred pension is revalued at 5% pa.

16.4 Section 32 annuity

Rather than providing deferred benefits under the scheme as above, the trustees may purchase from an insurance company chosen by the member a deferred annuity in the name of an employee.

FA 1981, s 32 enabled such annuities to be purchased: this may be an attractive option to pension scheme trustees and those leaving or thinking of leaving an employer. A series of s 32 annuities may be purchased with different insurers allowing benefits to be taken in stages.

The maximum pension and the maximum tax-free cash lump sum permitted by the Inland Revenue will be endorsed on the policy issued by the insurer. These benefits may be increased between the date on which the transfer is made into the s 32 annuity policy and retirement in line with increases in the retail prices index subject to a maximum of 5% pa. The projected benefits payable under such a policy should be carefully examined and compared with the alternative deferred pension.

A s 32 policy effected without the consent of the member now has to contain an option allowing the member to surrender or assign the policy in exchange for another s 32 policy, eg of the member's own choice, a personal pension scheme or an occupational pension scheme.

The s 32 annuity itself may include an open-market option and power to surrender the policy and transfer it to a new scheme including a personal pension scheme. The GMP within the s 32 policy may also be transferred to a new scheme.

Benefits (pension *and* tax free cash lump sum) may be taken from age 50 onwards, but not later than age 75, regardless of whether or not the policyholder has retired or is continuing to work. These benefits may include the GMP element.

On death, before taking benefits, the policy may provide for a lump sum to be paid equal to four times remuneration on leaving the previous scheme, increased in line with increases in the RPI up to 5% pa, up to the date of death.

16.5 Personal pension plans

An individual leaving his employer's scheme also has the option of transferring his benefits into a personal pension plan. Although a personal pension plan is generally only available to the self-employed or to those in non-pensionable employment there is an exception: an individual who is in a pension scheme can take out a Personal Pension Plan which is funded by the transfer from another scheme.

This new option may be more flexible than the s 32 annuity described above because the transferred benefits will be subject to the personal pension legislation allowing ongoing contributions to be paid by the member if he has net relevant earnings and also any subsequent transfer payments. If the individual was a member of a contracted out defined benefit scheme the transfer will include a Guaranteed Minimum Pension (GMP). On transferring into the personal pension there will no longer be any need for the guarantee to continue, but 'protected rights' will have to be provided instead. These protected rights benefits must not be paid until the member reaches State Pensionable Age (currently 65 for men, 60 for women) although the non-protected rights benefits may be paid in stages between the ages of 50 and 75 regardless of whether or not the policyholder has retired or is continuing to work.

On death before taking benefits, one quarter of the value of the plan may be paid as a lump sum with the balance being paid as a widow's or widower's pension. If there is no dependant, the whole amount may be paid as a lump sum.

However, before benefits may be transferred to a personal pension scheme the trustees of the employer's scheme must provide certificates as required in Inland Revenue regulations, as follows:

(1) **A Controlling Director's/High Earner's Certificate**
This certificate is required only in respect of a person who is a controlling director, or was a higher earner (defined as earning £75,000 or more in 1992/93), at any time during the ten years prior to the date in which the transfer value is applied for. The certificate must confirm that the transfer value does not exceed the cash equivalent of the maximum benefit that could have been paid under the transferring scheme.

The basis of the calculation may result in an apparent surplus which would be subject to tax if returned to the employer. (The calculation basis is strict in that it assumes that earnings will increase at only 5% pa between the date of leaving and normal retirement date and that the pension will increase at 3% pa in payment.) The possibility that the individual member may lose in this way will act as a deterrent against transferring where a surplus is identified.

(2) **A Cash Sum Certificate**
This certificate applies only in respect of a person who is a controlling director or high earner (as defined above) or who is over age 45 at the date that a right to a transfer value is applied for. This certificate must state the maximum cash lump sum payable under the transferring scheme at normal retirement date based on salary and service at the date of leaving.

The maximum cash sum that may be paid from a personal pension scheme arising from the transfer payment is the lesser of 25% of the accumulated fund (excluding any 'protected rights' if the personal pension plan was effected on or after 27 July 1989) or the certified cash amount increased in line with increases in the Cost of Living Index between the date of transfer and the date benefits are taken under the personal pension scheme.

For persons under age 45 who are not controlling directors or high earners there may be opportunities to transfer into a personal pension scheme in order to increase the amount of cash lump sum at retirement.

16.5.1 Assignment of an individual policy under an executive pension plan

Where benefits were provided under an insured individual arrangement, it is possible for the policy to be assigned to a new employer, although this is regarded by the Inland Revenue as a new scheme set up by the new employer. In the case of an individual who leaves to set up his own company, the 'new employer' will effectively be the individual himself. When a policy is assigned in this way, the surrender penalties often associated with the following option may be avoided.

16.5.2 Transfer values

When an employee leaves one employment to take up another employment, his benefits under the original pension scheme may be transferred to the new pension scheme (if it meets standards laid down by the DSS and Inland Revenue) provided the new employer scheme is willing and able to accept a transfer value. Alternatively the trustees may pay the transfer value to an insurance company of the employee's choice to buy a s 32 annuity or to a personal pension scheme as described above. Alternatively the employee can choose a combination of both. However, it is not possible for the transfer value to be paid direct to the individual.

16.5.3 Right to a transfer value

An employee has a right to a transfer value if he left his previous employer's scheme on 1 January 1986 or later and he was in that scheme long enough to qualify for benefits — normally two years (five years before 6 April 1988). There is no right to a transfer value if the employee is already receiving a pension from the previous scheme or if he has less than one year to go before reaching the previous scheme's pension age.

Although trustees are not obliged by law to pay a transfer value if the employee left before 1 January 1986 most schemes will pay a transfer value to an approved scheme.

16.5.4 Calculation of transfer values

A transfer value is the current cost of providing the benefits to which the employee was entitled under his former scheme and is based on the value of the benefits on the date the transfer value is requested. The transfer value must take into account any increases, statutory or otherwise, that would apply to the benefits if they were to continue to be preserved within the scheme.

In calculating transfer value schemes, trustees must have regard to a Guidance Note published by the Institute of Actuaries (reference GN11) which ensures that members of defined benefit schemes exercising a right to a transfer value can be assured that it reflects the reasonable expectation of benefits otherwise available on withdrawal and ensures that incoming and out-going transfers are dealt with consistently.

The assumptions used in the calculations, however may be overriden by the transfer regulations which affect controlling directors and high earners, as described above.

Transfer values are a constant source of difficulty as the amount which is transferred from one scheme to another depends on various assumptions, for example:

(1) whether the former scheme provides benefits on a final salary or money purchase basis;
(2) whether the deferred pension otherwise available in the former scheme will be increased between the date of leaving and retirement;
(3) if a transferred payment is regarded by the receiving scheme as purchasing an additional number of years service (added years), it is usually found that the purchased years will be less than the years of service actually obtained by the employee in the former pension scheme.

However the introduction of personal pension schemes resulted in improved transferability generally.

In some of the large private sector companies, as well as for those in the public sector there is a special basis for calculating higher transfer values between schemes which are members of the 'transfer club'. This ensures that employees moving between member organisations lose less on transferring: in some cases, pensionable service is deemed to continue without a break.

The European Court decision in the *Barber* case which makes it unlawful to discriminate between males and females in relation to pensions has caused employers to examine the benefits payable under their schemes and the dates on which those benefits become payable. The effects on schemes resources can be considerable; some employers are considering equalising pension ages at 60 (the date at which females usually retire) and some are considering equalising at age 65 (the date on which males usually retire). Until this reassessment has taken place a member *may* wish to defer taking a transfer value; if benefits are eventually equalised at age 60 the value of the preserved benefits of a male member may improve although if benefits are equalised at age 65 the value of the preserved benefits of a female member may reduce.

Another factor which may cause a member to delay taking a transfer value is where there is a surplus of scheme assets over liabilities, part of which is likely to be required under forthcoming legislation to increase pensions in payment in line with increases in the cost of living, or 5% per annum, if lower. A preserved pension which currently does not increase in payment but which is later improved as a result of the distribution of a surplus will have an increased transfer value. (In practice, however, many defined benefits schemes already provide for increases in payment on part of the pension, and indeed the GMP element already has to increase at 3% per annum.)

16.6 Refunds of members' contributions

Currently, no refund can normally be made if the employee has completed two years membership of a pension scheme. 1991 Regulations on preservation removed the option to take a refund of pre-April 1975 contributions as part of short-service benefits. This option had previously been available to early leavers whose pensionable service ended on or after 28 February 1991. Regulations permit trustees to buy-out benefits for leavers who have completed between two and five years membership.

Any refund may include interest on the contributions. If a refund of contributions is made to a former employee (except in the event of his death), the administrator of the scheme has to account to the Inland Revenue for tax at the rate of 20% on the contributions (including any interest) repaid to the member.

16.7 Which schemes may permit a transfer value?

Table 16.1

Previous scheme	PPP	Occ MP	Occ FS	R Ann	FSAVCs	s 32
Personal Pension Plan (PPP)	✓	✓	✓	✗	✗	✗
Occupational-Money Purchase (Occ Mp)	✓	✓	✓	✗	✗	✓
Occupational-Final Salary (Occ FS)	✓	✓	✓	✗	✗	✓
Retirement Annuity[1] (R Ann)	✓	✓	✓	✓	✗	✗
FSAVCs	✓	✓	✓	✗	✓	✓
Section 32[2]	✓	✓	✓	✗	✗	✓

[1] A transfer may only be taken from a retirement annuity by endorsing the policy accordingly.

[2] A transfer from a s 32 is only allowed if the previous scheme rules permit. Transfers out of s 32s established before October 1983 are not permitted.

16.8 Effects of Social Security Act 1990

The Social Security Act 1990 made a number of significant changes to occupational pension schemes, including:

(1) Occupational pension schemes providing benefits on a defined benefit basis will have to guarantee pension increases in line with increases in the Retail Prices Index (RPI), subject to a maximum of 5% per annum. At the time of writing, this had not taken effect.
(2) Early leavers are entitled to revaluation of all of their deferred pensions, including the portion which accrued before 1 January 1985.
(3) Self investment by pension schemes is limited to 5% of the scheme assets (see Chapter 9).
(4) A number of measures were introduced to help the individual

member: the setting up of a 'Pensions Ombudsman', the development of the role of the Occupational Pensions Advisory Service (OPAS) in providing a conciliation service between scheme members and scheme trustees, and the establishment of a register of occupational and personal pension schemes to provide a tracing service for scheme members.

16.8.1 Defined benefit schemes

The requirement that defined benefit schemes will have to guarantee pension increases applies to pension benefits which accrue after an 'Appointed Day'. (This has been delayed pending clarification of certain issues relating to equalisation of benefits between males and females.) This increase in payment is known as 'Limited Price Indexation' (LPI) as it means increases in line with the RPI but subject to a maximum of 5% per annum.

LPI will not apply to guaranteed minimum pensions payable under contracted out schemes as they already benefit from increases in payment. Also, LPI will not apply immediately to any pension benefits relating to service before the 'Appointed Day'. However, should a surplus arise in the pension scheme, the scheme must use the surplus to guarantee pension increases for benefits accruing before the 'Appointed Day'.

16.8.2 Money purchase schemes

The measures in the Act do not apply to personal pensions or to money purchase occupational pension schemes.

16.8.3 Deferred pensions

Prior to the Social Security Act 1990, the preserved pension of an early leaver from a defined benefit occupational scheme was subject to limited revaluation: the amount of preserved pension accruing in respect of pensionable service from 1 January 1985 would be subject to increases at the lesser of increase in the Retail Prices Index and 5% per annum. The Social Security Act 1990 extended the compulsory revaluation of the preserved pension in respect of pensionable service accrued up to 31 December 1984 from 1 January 1991.

16.9 Golden handshakes

Following the issue of a Statement of Practice by the Inland Revenue in October 1991, care must be taken to distinguish between *ex gratia* payments on retirement (or death) and 'golden handshakes' made under s 148 as described below.

If there is an 'arrangement' to make an *ex gratia* payment to a director or employee, and the recipient is not a member of a tax approved scheme of the employer, the payment may receive tax approval from the Revenue and be treated as a relevant benefit. If these conditions are not met, then the payment may be treated as emerging from an unapproved pension scheme.

16.9.1 Application of the 'golden handshake' legislation

Section 148 only applies to payments 'not otherwise chargeable to tax'. Consequently, a payment made under the terms of a contract of service or in respect of services (past, present or future) will be taxable as an emolument under the normal Schedule E rules. It is still, therefore, as important as it was before FA 1981 to ensure that the documentation of the golden handshake is carefully worded so as to avoid reference to past services.

Statutory redundancy payments are taxed under the golden handshake provisions rather than the provisions of Schedule E by ICTA 1988, s 572. The Revenue have also agreed that non-statutory redundancy payments will be taxed in the same way provided there is a 'genuine' redundancy. The Revenue will be satisfied that the redundancy is genuine if:

(1) the payment is only made on account of redundancy as defined in Employment Protection (Consolidation) Act 1980, s 81;
(2) the employee has been in continuous service for at least two years;
(3) the payments are not made to selected employees only; and
(4) the payments are not excessively large in relation to the employee's earnings and length of service.

On the other hand, certain payments which are not taxable under Schedule E are also exempted from the charge in s 187. The main examples of these payments are:

(1) payments made on the death of the employee or the termination of his employment on account of injury or disability;

(2) considerations for certain restrictive covenants;
(3) payments made under certain approved pension schemes in the UK and abroad; and
(4) certain payments made by Royal Warrant or Order in Council to members of the forces.

The amount of the redundancy payment which is exempt from taxes in the hands of the employee is £30,000.

16.9.2 Close companies

Two problems arise in connection with golden handshakes made to directors who are shareholders of close companies or members of their families:

(1) the non-tax deductibility of the payment from the company's point of view; and
(2) the possibility of the payment being treated as a distribution.

Unlike contributions to an exempt approved scheme, golden handshake payments will only be allowed as a deduction for the purposes of Schedule D if it is allowed by the Inspector in accordance with the normal 'wholly and exclusively' rule. It may be that in normal 'arm's length' cases that payment will not be allowed because, for example, the payment is made in conjunction with a cessation of trade or winding-up. In the case of a close company, however, it must be very likely that the payment will be disallowed as being a payment made for the personal benefit of the director or his family.

Potentially more serious, however, is the possibility of the payment being treated as a distribution under ICTA 1988, s 209. It seems that in cases where the distributor holds nearly 100% of the share capital it will very likely be treated as a distribution.

On the other hand there is a good chance of the question of a distribution not being raised if:

(1) the individual has put in genuine service of the quality and length that would have recommended him for a severance payment were he an arm's length employee;
(2) the shareholding is modest (say around 5%); and
(3) the amount involved is modest (up to £25,000).

Where, as will be common, the case falls between these two extremes, all that can be said is that the payment should not be made while the recipient is still a controlling shareholder and that if de-control is possible, the higher the former shareholding and the more recently de-control took place, the more likely it is that the inspector will treat it as a distribution.

16.9.3 Pensioning 'golden handshakes'

If the employment from which the golden handshake is payable is already pensionable, the payment may not be included in remuneration for the purposes of providing additional retirement benefits through augmentation or voluntary contributions by the employee.

If the employment was not pensionable the individual will be entitled to contribute to a personal pension scheme. However, the golden handshake payment must be excluded from earnings for this purpose. No such restriction applies if the individual has a retirement annuity contract (which must have been in existence on 29 July 1988), in these circumstances the taxable element golden handshake payment may be included in the definition of 'net relevant earnings'.

16.10 'Hancocks'

A Hancock annuity is now little more than a way of describing the outright purchase of an immediate or deferred annuity for an employee at the time of or after his retirement, or for the widow, widower, or dependant of a deceased employee.

The name is derived from the case of *Hancock* v *General Reversionary and Investment Co Ltd* (1918) TTC 358 which established that the payment by an employer to purchase an annuity for an employee on his retirement is an allowable expense in the year in which it is paid and is not regarded as additional remuneration to the employee.

The only aspect in which the Hancock precedent may provide a better position than the legislation now provides is that it will not require relief on the payment to be spread forward if it is more than the employer's ordinary annual contribution (see Chapter 6). In such cases, it is understood that the Revenue will direct that the scheme be approved as an exempt approved scheme if they feel that the relief should be spread forward, so the advantage is more apparent than real.

The Hancock procedure is now the only method of providing a pension for an employee or director who has attained age 75. Since Finance Act 1989 it has not been possible to accumulate funds within an approved pension scheme and provide benefits after age 75, and under personal pension schemes and retirement annuities benefits must be taken by age 75.

17 Pension loans

The past few years have seen a dramatic increase in the number of institutions promoting loans alongside pension plans.

The ingredients of a pension loan are as follows:

(1) The individual effects a pension plan which has the following favourable tax advantages:
   (a) income tax is saved on contributions at the highest rate paid on earned income,
   (b) the contributions accumulate free of UK income and capital gains taxes, and
   (c) at retirement age a substantial part of the benefits may be taken in the form of a tax-free lump sum.
(2) A bank or building society, or the insurance company itself, lends money to an individual on a basis similar to an endowment mortgage — interest is paid on the loan throughout the term and the capital is repaid at the end of the term. The lending institution will normally take as security a property owned, or about to be bought by the individual.
(3) The tax-free lump sum emerging from the pension plan may be used to repay the loan. In this way the borrower has effectively obtained full tax relief on his capital repayments as opposed to the usual method of paying them out of net income.
(4) The balance of the pension plan provides a lifetime income.
(5) The borrower will probably effect a life policy to cover the loan repayment in the event of his death before retirement. In the case of a person who has an existing retirement annuity policy or personal pension scheme the associated life assurance benefit which may be provided is an attractive option because tax relief at the highest rate on earned income is granted and because the policy can be assigned to the lender.
(6) However, pensions legislation does not permit a pension plan to be used as security for a loan and the policy provisions

or pension scheme rules will state that it cannot be assigned by the member.

17.1 Comparing costs

Although the contributions for the pension plan may be considerably higher than those for a repayment mortgage or a low-cost endowment assurance, when tax relief is taken into account the net result is that there is often little difference between the pension related loan and the non-pension related loan. Since the Finance Act 1984 which removed tax relief on ordinary life assurance policies, low-cost endowments have become less attractive. The higher the tax bracket of the borrower the cheaper the pension mortgage becomes.

It has been said by the detractors of pension-related loans that as the cash lump sum is used to pay off the capital at the end of the term the individual's retirement benefits are being reduced. In fact, the tax advantages of pension schemes will result in many people enjoying an additional income in retirement, by default. An individual who is currently contributing £100 per month to an endowment insurance policy taken out since March 1984 does not enjoy any tax relief. An equivalent net contribution to a pension plan will result immediately in £133 per month being invested, assuming the individual is a 25% tax payer. When the benefits of tax-free growth within the pension fund are added, the pension fund at the end of the term would be significantly higher than the endowment fund. This fund may be taken partly in the form of a tax-free lump sum, with the balance being used to provide an income. The tax-free lump sum can be used to repay the loan.

The only circumstances in which a pension-related mortgage might be said to reduce retirement income would be where an individual arranges a loan on an interest-only basis with the intention of using the cash lump sum from an existing pension plan to repay the capital but without making any additional pension provision, for example through Additional Voluntary Contributions. However, in practice most pension-related loans are arranged on the basis that pension contributions will be increased, or started.

A pension-related loan alongside a retirement annuity contract or personal pension scheme must result in income in retirement even after the loan is repaid. The reason for this is that it is not possible to fund solely for a cash lump sum. Under a retirement annuity the amount which may be taken in a form of a cash lump sum is three times the annuity which remains after the cash has been taken, and therefore varies according to retirement age and sex. On retirement at age 65 a male could expect to receive approximately 28% in the form of a cash lump sum, on annuity rates prevailing in August 1990 (for other ages see Chapter 14). This means that if the cash lump sum amounts to £30,000 (sufficient to repay the loan), the total fund would be £107,000.

Under a personal pension scheme one quarter can be taken in the form of a cash lump sum, regardless of age and sex. This means that if the cash lump sum amounts to £30,000 (ie is of sufficient size to repay a loan), the total fund would be £120,000 and the cost would be 12% higher than that under a retirement annuity contract. It will be seen, therefore, that an existing retirement annuity, because it is likely to generate more cash lump sum than a personal pension scheme, requires less outlay if the cash lump sum is to be used to repay a loan. In either case, if the cash lump sum is used to repay a loan the bulk of the fund remains to provide an income.

Some personal pension schemes can be particularly useful as they can provide more than one quarter in the form of a tax free lump sum: ones taken out before 27 July 1989 and used for contracting-out can include in the overall fund of which one quarter is taken the fund built up by DSS contributions — the 'protected rights fund'.

For example: assume that the protected rights fund amounts to £100,000, and the fund generated by personal contributions amounts to £33,333. One quarter of the total fund amounts to £33,333. The protected rights fund of £100,000 is not being eroded and the additional contributions generate tax free cash.

If the cash lump sum of £33,333 were to be used to repay a loan the outlay will be much lower than in the examples in the previous paragraphs because the individual does not have to fund for the pension benefits in addition — they have been financed by DSS contributions.

In summary, existing retirement annuity contracts, and personal pension schemes used for contracting out purposes but to which additional contributions are paid are likely to be tax-efficient methods of repaying loans at retirement, but certain personal pension schemes taken out before 27 July 1989 are particularly useful.

17.2 Recent developments

Traditionally, loans of all descriptions have been arranged on the basis that there is a fixed term, although there is often provision to extend the term of the loan. From the point of view of tax planning, however, it may be worthwhile to extend the loan indefinitely especially if the loan is one on which interest payments qualify for tax relief. Also, having to repay a significant amount of capital at the end of the term may cause cash flow problems for the borrower, even though he might have built up sufficient monies to repay the loan, by means of personal investments including pension funding.

A recent development in this field has been the introduction of 'the lifetime loan'. As with any conventional loan, the normal criteria have to be satisfied at the outset as to status, earnings, suitability of security, etc but the loan may be continued until death. The borrower, however, must effect a life assurance policy which is assigned to the lender so that in the event of his death the lender obtains repayment of the loan.

At one time lenders were only prepared to advance monies on an interest only basis to individuals whose pension benefits would emerge from an individual policy such as an executive pension plan: from the point of view of the lender the benefits of an ear-marked policy could be easily identified. However, many lenders are now prepared to arrange interest-only loans for individuals whose pension benefits will emerge from group pension schemes (where benefits are not usually ear-marked individually but form part of a common trust fund). The lender will usually require a copy of the benefit statement which is provided for the scheme member by trustees. This statement should confirm that the amount of cash lump sum which is likely to emerge is at least equal to the required loan. The lender may want to see future statements to confirm that the individual is still a member of the pension scheme.

17.3 Loan purposes

If the loan is for a qualifying purpose, tax relief will be obtained on the interest provided interest is paid. Examples of qualifying loans are as follows:

(1) to purchase a main residence in the UK (the maximum loan for tax relief purposes is currently £30,000);

(2) to purchase a share or interest in a partnership;
(3) to contribute capital or loan monies for the use of a partnership;
(4) to purchase shares in a closed company or to make loans to such a company for business purposes;
(5) to purchase plant and machinery for use in a partnership or business;
(6) to purchase or improve land or buildings which are let at a commercial rent for at least 26 weeks during the year in which the interest was paid. Interest paid can only be offset against rent and cannot be deducted against general income.

If the loan is for business purposes, then the interest is deductible from business profits under ICTA 1988, s 74. If, however, the loan is taken for the purpose of a main residence or is taken by an individual for putting into a partnership or close company the interest is offset against personal income and not business profits. To the extent that interest is deductible from business profits, the net relevant earnings on which an individual can contribute to a retirement annuity will be reduced. Personal interest, however, does not reduce net relevant earnings.

17.3.1 Unsecured loans

Unsecured loans are normally only available to those who are professionally qualified and at the discretion of the lender which probably is well acquainted with the tax and business affairs of the individual and is already lending to the individual.

17.3.2 Interest rates

In the past the interest rate charged on a pension mortgage would often be around 1% more than under a straightforward repayment mortgage, (although if the amount being borrowed was substantial, the differential might drop).

Recent developments have been lower interest rates for larger mortgages and increasing competition to reduce or even reverse the differentials between capital repayment loans and interest-only loans such as endowment or pension-related loans.

Some institutions are prepared to lend to individuals, subject to financial underwriting and the taking of security, on the basis that interest can be rolled up or deferred, with the unpaid interest added to the loan outstanding.

17.4 Personal loans — differences under executive pension plans for directors

The preceding paragraphs related generally to loans which may be obtained by an individual who has effected a retirement annuity policy or personal pension scheme. A director, or executive, however, who is contributing to an approved retirement benefit scheme — an executive pension plan — and who is proposing to use the tax-free cash emerging from his fund to repay loan capital, will have these additional factors to consider.

(1) If the plan is arranged for the purpose of getting a loan, the Companies Act 1985, s 330 may be infringed. This section specifically prohibits companies making or procuring loans to directors. To avoid infringing the Companies Act and to avoid jeopardising approval of the pension plan by the Inland Revenue, the setting up of the plan should not be dependent upon obtaining a loan. The sole purpose of the pension plan should be the provision of 'relevant benefits'.

(2) Any collateral life assurance will have to be effected by an ordinary life assurance policy; the life assurance associated with an executive pension plan will not be satisfactory because it cannot be assigned to a lender and in any case, the destination of the benefits on the death of the member is at the discretion of the trustees.

(3) It is not possible to have a waiver of premium benefit in respect of any contributions paid into an executive pension plan so that in the event of sickness or disability contributions to the plan (in particular those payable personally by the member) are likely to stop or reduce. Consequently the fund at retirement will be lower.

18 Various aspects of executive pension plans

18.1 Investment companies

An investment company is a company the income of which would be treated as investment income for tax purposes if it were the income of an individual. A company which is treated for tax purposes as an investment company will not be able to set up a pension plan and obtain approval under the Inland Revenue's discretionary power under ICTA 1988, s 591 if the membership includes 20% directors or controlling directors of that employer or directors who while not owning 20% of the shares themselves, or being controlling directors, are members of a family together controlling more than 50% of the shares.

Since controlling directors of investment companies are prohibited from contributing to personal pension schemes (see Chapter 14), this effectively prevents such individuals from making any pension provision except through a scheme approved under ICTA 1988, s 590 which requires the Inland Revenue to approve a scheme if it meets the more stringent conditions of that section. Very few directors would be happy with the benefits which may be provided under that section, and very few life offices are prepared to write s 590 schemes.

The only benefits which can be provided under s 590 are a pension of 1/60th of final remuneration for each year of service (part of which may be exchanged for a lump sum which does not exceed 3/80ths of final remuneration for each year of service) and a widow's pension which does not exceed 2/3rds of a member's pension and is payable only on death in retirement. There is no sliding scale of accelerated accrual, and no death in service benefits are allowed, including a refund of any contributions made by a member. Remuneration which can be pensioned under s 590 is limited as the Schedule E income which a director can receive from an investment company is usually very low.

There is no Revenue objection to the provision of retirement benefits for employees and non-controlling directors of investment companies.

18.2 Service companies

Professional firms sometimes establish service companies to provide clerical staff, accommodation, and administrative services for the firm, the directors of the company usually being partners in a practice.

The question then arises as to the possibility of providing the partner who is also a director of the service company with additional pension benefits through an executive pension plan in respect of his Schedule E earnings as a director.

While in principle this is acceptable, the Inland Revenue are not prepared to approve schemes for such directors where the benefits are geared to a level of remuneration exceeding the amount allowed by the local Inspector as a trading expense of the company. The local Inspector will in turn, generally take the view that the duties which the director performs for the company are minimal and so the remuneration allowable as a trading expense of the company will be correspondingly very small — as his other profit earning activities are in his capacity as partner of a firm. It will be seen that in most cases, the amount of additional pension which can be provided for a partner/director will be insignificant, although there may of course be exceptions, where the facts of the case warrant them; for example, it may be possible to show as a matter of fact that the main duties, of, say, a staff partner related properly to the service company and should be remunerated from the service company.

Once again, there is nothing to prevent service companies from providing pension benefits in the usual way for its employees.

18.3 Special occupations — retirement dates

There are a number of occupations where a reasonable case may be made out for a normal retirement date earlier than the normal range of 60 to 70. Because of the particular characteristics of the occupation, it may be possible for certain jobholders to agree with the Inland Revenue a retirement date in the range 50 to 55, eg airline pilots, advertising executives, money dealers and trawlermen.

However, an earlier normal retirement date is not automatic simply because the individual follows one of these occupations (as is the case with the special occupations for which early retirement dates can be chosen under retirement annuity contracts and personal pension scheme — see Chapter 14) and a case has to be put up to the Inland Revenue for each executive pension plan detailing the exact nature of the work.

If the Inland Revenue accept that a normal retirement date of 50 to 55 is appropriate in a particular case, they will normally insist that benefits have to be taken at normal retirement date and cannot be deferred if the individual works on, whether in the same or another occupation.

18.4 Retirement dates below age 50

There are also a number of occupations which cannot be continued much beyond the mid-30s and for these the Inland Revenue may agree to much earlier normal retirement dates — even as low as 35. The occupations to which this applies are usually limited to professional sportsmen and women, for example;

>Professional footballers (normal retirement date, 35)
>Professional tennis players (normal retirement date, 35)
>Professional cricketers (normal retirement date, 40)

If an early normal retirement date is chosen, severe restrictions will be placed on the benefits — in particular:

(1) the pension is limited to 1/60th of final salary for each year of service;
(2) the cash lump sum is limited to 3/80ths of final salary for each year of service;

(3) no early retirement is allowed, except through incapacity;
(4) late retirement is restricted to five years; for example, a footballer still playing in his forties must receive his benefits from the pension plan at age 40;
(5) if the member takes on some other occupation with the same employer, for example, a footballer becoming a coach or manager, he must still take his benefits at his normal retirement date.

18.5 International aspects of executive pension plans

(1) The basic rule is that if an employee is effectively chargeable to UK tax under Case I or II of Schedule E, then the employer can provide executive pension plans benefits for him or her.
(2) The benefits of a tax-approved executive pension plan are available to employees who are resident, but not necessarily domiciled in the UK, eg the Swiss-domiciled manager of the UK-based agency of a US corporation.
(3) The only exception to the above rule is the provision by a *UK resident employer* of executive pension plan benefits for an employee who is both resident and domiciled outside the UK, eg the Spanish sales manager of a UK-based company, who is a Spanish national and lives in Spain ordinarily.

18.5.1 Definitions

(1) United Kingdom means England, Scotland, Wales and Northern Ireland — it does not include the Channel Islands, the Isle of Man or the Republic of Ireland.
(2) Domicile refers to the country which is a person's natural home, and for most people would be their country of birth.
(3) Residence for tax purposes is determined by a number of criteria such as the length of time spent in the country during a fiscal year.
(4) Foreign emoluments describes remuneration paid by an employer who is not *resident* in the UK to an employee who is not domiciled in the UK. If a UK resident receives foreign emoluments, he will be assessable to tax under Schedule E on their full amount.
(5) An overseas employer is one who is not resident in the UK for tax purposes and whose trading profits are, if at all, assessable to UK tax only to the extent that they arise from a branch or agency in this country.

18.5.2 Overseas employer with UK resident employees

The Inland Revenue will tax-approve an executive pension plan established by an overseas employer conditional upon:

(1) the appointment of a UK resident person as 'administrator' of the pension plan, who will be responsible for ensuring that Inland Revenue requirements are met. It is usual for the trustee of the executive pension plan to act as the administrator.
(2) an undertaking to exclude from the pension plan UK-domiciled employees who qualify for full income tax relief on account of the length of time spent overseas.

In establishing an executive pension plan, the overseas employer should give critical consideration to whether it is the most suitable vehicle for the particular employee.

(1) For employees who are both UK-resident and -domiciled, there is no alternative to a UK tax-approved pension plan.
(2) For employees who are not UK-domiciled, much will depend on how long they will be resident in the UK. For highly mobile employees who are unlikely to remain in the UK sufficiently long to build up a significant benefit, clearly the executive pension plan is not satisfactory as a retirement savings medium. The position is quite different for the long-term expatriate resident in the UK, in view of the fact that even after the additional restrictions imposed by the 1985 and 1987 Finance Acts, the tax treatment of and benefits emerging from UK pension plans are attractive in comparison to that likely to be available in the country of domicile.

Other aspects which may affect an overseas employer's consideration of whether to provide retirement benefits through a UK tax-approved pension plan are:

(1) Concern about the obligations, liabilities and expense involved in establishing a UK pension plan, especially where the overseas employer is unfamiliar with UK pensions legislation, and where the business connection is either in its early stages or not intended to be long-term in nature.
(2) The overseas employer may be unable to obtain relief in respect of its contributions to the pension plan from its home tax authorities, so that relief will be confined to its UK profits, if any.

(3) The overseas employer may be subject to restrictions which prevent it contracting with a UK insurer or remitting contributions to the UK. Also the inconvenience of having to comply with accounting requirements under domestic legislation (eg in the United States) covering pensions provisions for employees of overseas subsidiaries may deter overseas employers from establishing UK pension plans.

18.5.3 Offshore plans

Overseas employers with multi-national representation often prefer to adopt a global strategy in relation to retirement provision for overseas employees. They may accordingly establish an offshore plan in a tax-efficient area, eg the Bahamas, or else include their overseas employees in parallel plans to those established for the corporation's home-based employees.

The advantages of this strategy are:

(1) Uniform benefits can be provided for all employees regardless of where they are stationed at any time.
(2) The problem of having to comply with local national legislation on retirement provision and social security can be mitigated.

The disadvantages are:

(1) Tax relief may not be available on either the employer's contributions or the fund. Conversely, the employee may be taxed on the employer's contribution paid for his/her benefits.
(2) Depending on the employee's country of residence at retirement
 (a) the pension benefit may be subject to double taxation
 (b) the pension may be secured in an unsatisfactory currency
 (c) the emerging benefit may be completely inappropriate. In many countries lump sum benefits on retirement are the norm, and in other countries there are ultra-generous state pension benefits (eg some Latin-American states) giving rise to the problem of over-provision.

18.5.4 Corresponding approval

If it can be shown to the Inland Revenue's satisfaction that a pension plan established offshore for an employee receiving foreign emoluments 'corresponds' in terms of ICTA 1988, s 596(2), then tax relief will be permitted on the employee's contributions to the plan. This means that the benefit structure of the offshore pension plan must be similar to the structure of a pension plan approved under ICTA 1988, s 591. The Inland Revenue are particularly concerned to prevent the encashment of benefits by an employee on leaving service, or in other circumstances before retirement, and may require an undertaking from the plan administrator in that regard.

If the employee continues to be resident in the UK after his retirement, the pension payable from the offshore plan will be assessable under Schedule D, Case V, but only on 90% of the amount of the pension (ICTA 1988, s 65).

18.5.5 Section 614 plans (known previously as section 218 plans)

A half-way house to a full offshore pension plan, which is operated by some UK based multi-national corporations for employees who are resident overseas, is a plan established under ICTA 1988, s 614. A s 614 Plan enjoys exemption from UK taxation on its investment income in respect of pensions paid in the UK, but is otherwise a much less flexible pensions vehicle than a genuine offshore plan established outside the UK.

18.5.6 UK resident employer with overseas resident employees

Persons who are not resident in the UK, but who are directly employed and remunerated by a UK employer, can be included in a pension plan approved under ICTA 1988, s 591. Even where an employee ceases to be employed directly by the UK employer, and is in fact employed either by an overseas subsidiary or else on contract to other employers (but so that his movements are still controlled by the UK employer) he or she can remain in the UK pension plan for a period of up to ten years.

18.6 Pensioners resident abroad

The questions that arise when a pensioner is resident abroad generally relate to the payment of the cash sum and the pension from the UK scheme. As far as the cash payment is concerned, problems will only arise if there are exchange controls in force at the time of retirement (there are none at present) in which case Bank of England permission will be needed to effect the transfer abroad. There is no problem about paying pensions abroad but their taxation needs greater consideration. The position is that as a general rule, all pensions must be paid from the UK under deduction of Schedule E tax under the PAYE system. There is no general exemption for pensioners resident abroad even where they have worked abroad, but exemption can be granted if the last ten years' service in respect of which the pension is paid was abroad or half the total service and at least ten out of the last twenty years service was abroad. Alternatively, exemption may be due under a double taxation agreement under which the pension is taxed in the country of residence — such DTAs exist with most of the major countries in the West to which pensioners are likely to go, but *not* the local tax havens — the Channel Islands and the Isle of Man. Where a DTA applies, the Inspector of Foreign Dividends is able to authorise gross payments at source.

18.7 Overseas transfers

It may be possible to transfer benefits from a UK pension arrangement to an overseas arrangement, or vice versa. In general, such transfers can only be made with the prior agreement of the UK Inland Revenue, and considerable information may be needed, depending on the circumstances. There may also be tax implications for the individual, and requirements set by the overseas authorities.

The UK Inland Revenue are particularly concerned to ensure that transfers to and from overseas are made only in circumstances where a person is or has been genuinely resident and working abroad. Agreement to a transfer from overseas will therefore usually only be given if the member has been employed in the overseas employment to which the proposed transfer relates for at least two years.

Similarly, a transfer can only be made to an overseas arrangement in the individual's country of residence and confirmation is needed that the person has no intention of returning to the UK and understands that the transfer is permanent.

Reciprocal arrangements exist for transfers between the UK and the Isle of Man, the Channel Islands and the Republic of Ireland, which qualify or set aside some of the requirements for transfers to and from overseas. There are also special arrangements for transfers to the pension scheme for staff of the European Communities.

19 Retirement options — investment considerations

It is not the purpose of this chapter to deal with generalised aspects of retirement, but solely with some of the investment considerations which arise when benefits are paid under pension plans.

The options available at retirement have already been discussed in previous chapters — they differ according to whether benefits are paid from an executive pension plan, retirement annuity or personal pension scheme. Investment considerations however, are similar for both:

- Should the benefits be taken wholly in the form of a pension?
- Or should the maximum tax-free lump sum be taken with a reduced pension?
- What type of pension should be taken, level, escalating, single life or joint life?

An indication of the different types of annuity purchased by a fund of £100,000 at age 60 is given in Chapter 14 (and is repeated below), as is the effect of using tax-free cash emerging from a pension plan to buy a purchased life annuity which is taxed only on the interest portion.

19.1 Types of pension available

On taking the benefits from a personal pension scheme or a retirement annuity, the policyholder will normally have various options including the facility to take a reduced pension on his own life but which will continue in the event of his death to the spouse. For example, £100,000 would purchase the following types of annuity on the open market for a man aged 65. These annuities are not necessarily at the top of the market as annuity rates change frequently.

Table 19.1

Type of annuity	Amount per annum
Single life annuity payable annually in arrear	£13,100
Single life annuity payable monthly in advance	£12,200
Single life annuity payable monthly in advance but for a minimum of five years	£11,900
Single life annuity payable monthly in advance but for a minimum of ten years	£11,200
Single life annuity payable quarterly in advance for a minimum of five years, increasing each year by 3% pa compound	£970
Joint life level annuity, during the lives of the man and his wife, aged 62	£960

19.2 Purchased life annuities

As an example, a fund of £100,000 built up under a personal pension scheme would provide an income payable in monthly instalments in advance throughout the life of a male aged 65, guaranteed for five years, of £12,600 per annum, but subject to tax as earned income at, say 25% leaving a net income of £9,450 per annum.

Alternatively, the fund could be taken in the form of a tax-free lump sum of £25,000 plus a reduced income of £9,470 (gross), £7,102 (net); the cash of £25,000 could be used to buy a purchased life annuity of £3,060 of which £1,500 is interest and would be taxable as unearned income. The net income would be £2,685. The combination of the two net annuities amounts to £9,787, an increase of £337 per annum.

A further alternative is sometimes available under personal pension schemes and retirement annuities — the option to take a unit-linked annuity. The planholder may choose a pension which varies with the value of the units, in for example, a managed fund, a property fund, an equity fund, a gilt edged fund, a fixed interest deposit fund, and overseas funds.

The pension is expressed as the value of a fixed number of units determined at the time that benefits start to be drawn and depending upon the age of the planholder and upon mortality experience at the time.

When each pension payment falls due, the amount of pension is calculated by applying the bid price of the units on the due date to the fixed number of units calculated at the commencement of the pension.

The value of the units, and hence the pension, rises to the full extent of the income plus the capital growth of the fund (after charges) in any year so that the growth potential of the pension is maximised. The initial pension, however, starts off at a much lower amount than the level pension. If a unit price goes down, so will the pension.

The following table shows the history of a unit-linked pension for a man aged 65 secured by a fund of £1,000 commencing on 1 May 1971 and the subsequent payments in successive years compared with level and escalating pensions.

Table 19.2

Date	Unit-linked (annuity)		Sterling annuity	
	Pension managed fund	Pension property fund	Level	Escalating at $8\frac{1}{2}\%$
1.5.71	£ 66.29 pa	£ 66.29 pa	£124.41 pa	£ 67.28 pa
1.5.72	£ 90.15	£ 79.09	£124.41	£ 73.00
1.5.73	£ 92.19	£ 94.41	£124.41	£ 79.20
1.5.74	£ 93.75	£105.64	£124.41	£ 85.94
1.5.75	£ 104.33	£103.70	£124.41	£ 93.24
1.5.76	£ 129.71	£132.19	£124.41	£101.17
1.5.77	£ 146.46	£146.47	£124.41	£109.77
1.5.78	£ 176.24	£181.06	£124.41	£119.10
1.5.79	£ 228.15	£211.01	£124.41	£129.22
1.5.80	£ 230.38	£258.22	£124.41	£140.20
1.5.81	£ 293.54	£297.80	£124.41	£152.12
1.5.82	£ 329.23	£341.80	£124.41	£165.05
1.5.83	£ 432.89	£361.49	£124.41	£179.08
1.5.84	£ 505.61	£398.38	£124.41	£194.30
1.5.85	£ 600.95	£436.85	£124.41	£210.81
1.5.86	£ 777.97	£465.62	£124.41	£228.73
1.5.87	£ 926.90	£520.12	£124.41	£248.17
1.5.88	£ 932.33	£634.88	£124.41	£296.26
1.5.89	£1090.83	£787.78	£124.41	£292.15
1.5.90	£1133.24	£864.83	£124.41	£316.98
1.5.91	£1267.38	£794.85	£124.41	£343.92
1.5.92	£1387.00	£772.48	£124.41	£373.15

In deciding what type of annuity the planholder should take he will have to consider the following factors:

(1) is he in bad health, in which case would it be better to opt for a higher level pension rather than a lower escalating or unit-linked pension?
(2) is there a history of longevity in the family, in which case might he opt for the lower escalating pension?
(3) if he opts for the unit-linked pension and it drops in value, will he have other income to fall back on?
(4) does his wife has an income in her own right — if not should he perhaps opt for a joint life last survivor pension?
(5) if he opts for a lower escalating or unit linked pension, how long will it take to overtake the level pension in real terms?
(6) It will be seen from the figures in Table 19.1 that the difference in an annuity with a five year guarantee compared with an annuity with no guarantee is only £300 pa (cf £11,900 and £12,200). Similarly, the difference in an annuity with a ten year guarantee compared with an annuity with no guarantee is only £1,000 pa (cf £11,200 and £12,200). It may be worthwhile taking this reduction in view of the benefit payable should death occur during the guaranteed period.

19.3 Investing the cash lump sum

If the lump sum is taken and is not to be spent immediately, the following investment areas are available depending upon whether the individual is concerned to increase his current income or is investing with a view to producing an income at some stage in the future.

19.4 Increasing current income

Individuals investing to increase current income will normally be looking at a range of 'money' investments including bank deposits, building societies and fixed interest securities such as gilts. Of these investments, deposit accounts of any kind, whether bank, building society or national savings are rarely appropriate because the level of income is variable, and unpredictable, and the capital base generating the income is fixed. Such investments should be regarded as a store for uninvested cash which may be required at short notice; in other words, as an alternative current account.

Fixed interest securities such as gilts do have a role for investors seeking income because the income flow is predictable and guaranteed. Once again, it might be unwise for an investor to put more than a small percentage of his investment in such an area since guarantees, contrary to popular belief, still represent an investment risk. Investments giving a guaranteed income as such should only be used as a major part of the portfolio if the need for income is very short term.

Individuals seeking a long term rising income with capital appreciation should consider investing a reasonable portion of their lump sum in asset-backed investments such as unit trusts and insurance bonds, specifically these which invest in companies with good dividend records.

Unit trust Personal Equity Plans (PEPs) offer tax free income and capital growth and, therefore, the first tranche of long term capital should ideally be invested in a PEP, up to the current minimum.

In the past, higher rate taxpayers were less interested in receiving investment income and would be more interested in achieving capital growth in order to make use of the CGT exemptions. If a higher rate taxpayer invested in a spread of low yielding unit trusts, there was a reasonable chance that even in the short term one or more of the funds would show a gain, hence giving the investor scope for profit taking within the CGT exemptions. Following the 1988 Budget which reduced the top rate of tax on both income and capital to 40%, higher rate taxpayers are now less likely to distort their investment decisions by trying to reduce income and increase their returns through capital growth.

Taking withdrawals from insurance bonds is also a popular way to supplement income in a tax efficient way. Insurance bonds have the further advantage that they have a wider spread of underlying investments than unit trusts, which enable the investor to have some exposure to property or take advantage of the managed fund concept.

To summarise: for individuals who are seeking income, then income producing PEPs, unit trusts and insurance bonds provide a very high quality secure source of income which is expected to rise in the future. Income can be received on regular dates throughout the year.

19.5 Producing income in the future

Most planholders who are already taking benefits from pension plans are less likely to require income in the future, but they may wish to provide income for succeeding generations. If this was the case, a broad spread of equities should protect the real value of an investment, while providing a reasonable income and should form a part of the investment portfolio of any prudent investor.

20 Pensions — the future

In recent years there have been a number of developments which will result in legislation which will affect the running of occupational schemes considerably. They are:

(1) The European Community (EC) directive on equal treatment for men and women in pension schemes.
(2) The Financial Services legislation and its effects on pension scheme trustees.
(3) Social Security Act 1985: disclosure of information.
(4) Personal pension schemes.

20.1 Equal treatment for men and women in pension schemes

20.1.1 The EC

The European Community Council Directive (86/378) of 24 July 1986 requires member states to have legislation on their statute books by 30 July 1989 providing for equal treatment of men and women in occupational pension schemes with effect from 1 January 1993. This was achieved in the UK by Social Security Act 1989. The Act gives right of access to schemes for part-time employees many of whom are women. The Act prevents schemes providing 'bridging' pensions for men who retire early, before state pension age because these pensions are not available to women.

Equal treatment means that there must be no sex discrimination under occupational pension schemes either directly or indirectly by reference in particular to marital or family status. It is unlikely, however, that the principle of equal treatment will be fully operational by 1993 as the Directive postpones its application to pensionable age and dependants' benefits until Member States apply the principle to State Social Security arrangements.

Also, the Directive does not apply to

(1) Schemes with only one member.
(2) The benefits paid by defined contribution schemes (such as Executive Pension Plans).
(3) Options available under occupational pension schemes (eg, cash commutation of pension).

Although the Directive prohibits different contribution levels for males and females, implementation of this provision is deferred until 1999.

The process has, however, been hastened by a series of references to the European Court of Justice, including the *Bilka-Kaufhaus* case, the second *Defrenne* case, and, most importantly, the *Barber* case. The theme common to the Court's decision in all these cases is that 'pensions are pay' and are therefore subject to the provisions of Article 119 of the Treaty of Rome (the Equal Pay Article). The concern with which the decision in the *Barber* case was received initially has been followed by resignation as a further series of cases (*Coloroll, Ten Oever*, and *Moroni*), intended to provide clarification of the *Barber* decision's degree of retrospectivity, await the judgment of the Court.

20.1.2 Equalisation of state pension ages

One of the key issues which will have to be resolved in the 1990s is the inequality of state pension ages in the UK (60 for women, 65 for men). Until this is resolved it will be very difficult for occupational pension schemes to implement equal treatment as most schemes are integrated with state pensions in some way. While there is a powerful lobby in the UK for a facility to take state benefits during a 'decade of retirement', expense considerations appear to be driving the Government towards a common retirement age of 65.

20.2 Investor protection

The need to restore public confidence in the security of pension schemes following the Maxwell affair is likely to result in further legislation.

A House of Commons Social Security Select Committee Report on the operation of Pension Funds has made a number of recommendations, including the following:

(1) Trust law should be replaced by a Pensions Act, as the legal basis for Occupational Pension Schemes.
(2) An independent trustee should be appointed for Occupational Pension Schemes for the purpose of holding Pension Fund assets.
(3) The Occupational Pensions Board should be given responsibility for the co-ordination and supervision of the regulations of Occupational Pension Schemes.
(4) A compensation scheme should be established.

On 8 June 1992, Peter Lilley, the Secretary of State for Social Security, announced the setting up of a committee to review pensions law. The committee is chaired by Professor Roy Goode QC, and is to report back within 12 months.

In addition, employees of the various Maxwell companies have indicated that they intend to sue the UK Government on the grounds that it failed to implement properly an EC directive requiring all Member States to set up funds to pay wages arrears to employees of insolvent employers. It is currently not clear whether or not the National Insurance Fund is responsible for meeting the pension benefits of employees made redundant on their employer's insolvency.

20.3 Insured pension schemes

The high level of regulation applying to insurance companies makes it unlikely that the problems suffered by the Maxwell pension schemes could occur under insured pension arrangements:

(1) The Insurance Companies Act 1982 gives the Department of Trade and Industry considerable powers to monitor and control the affairs of insurance companies; these powers have been exercised to withdraw an insurer's authority to issue business.
(2) The Policyholders Protection Act 1975 established the mechanism under which a compensation scheme financed by a levy on insurance companies operates.
(3) The Insurance Ombudsman Bureau established by the insurance industry. The Ombudsman can require an award of up to £100,000 to be paid in compensation, and the decision is binding on the insurance company. There are currently over 270 member companies in the scheme.
(4) The Financial Services Act 1986 is the foundation of the

massive framework of regulation which affects all aspects of an insurance company's business. The Self-Regulatory Organisation (SRO) which covers most insurers is the Life Assurance and Unit Trusts Regulatory Organisation (LAUTRO). SROs are approved by the Securities and Investments Board (SIB). In the event that a policyholder is ineligible for compensation under the terms of the Policyholders Protection Act 1975, he or she may qualify under the LAUTRO indemnity scheme. In addition, policyholders may qualify for compensation under the Investors' Compensation Scheme established by SIB and financed by a levy on insurance companies.

(5) The regulations relating to disclosure of information made pursuant to the Social Security Pensions Act 1975 apply to all pension schemes. These regulations have recently been amended to extend the information which trustees and providers must give to scheme members.

(6) Members of all pension arrangements may seek redress from the Pensions Ombudsman.

20.4 Personal pension schemes

The next few years could show a marked shift towards defined contribution schemes in general, and increasing use of personal pensions schemes as job mobility increases. The Finance Act 1989 has already limited the attraction of occupational schemes for job movers. In the United States the trend is towards preference for investment choice and portability offered by plans controlled by the participants, and away from salary related schemes with their ever-increasing regulatory and administrative burdens.

20.5 Divorce

There has been considerable discussion in the press about the possibility of legislative clarification on the valuation and apportionment of pension benefits on divorce. It is not yet clear what approach will be taken by the Government.

Appendix 1 Glossary of terms

This glossary provides an explanation of expressions commonly used by pension scheme practitioners.

Accrual rate The fraction of earnings for each year of service which forms the basis of pension entitlement in a final salary or average salary scheme. For example, '1/60th' for each year of pensionable service.

Accrued benefits The benefits in respect of service up to a specific date calculated in relation to current earnings or projected final earnings. Sometimes known as accrued rights.

Accrued rights premium (ARP) State scheme premium payable when a scheme ceases to be contracted out in respect of a member who has not reached state pensionable age, and for whom a guaranteed minimum pension is not being preserved in any other way.

Actuarial certificate A certificate given by an actuary, especially a certificate in respect of the solvency test required by the Occupational Pensions Board for contracted out schemes.

Actuarial valuation An investigation into whether or not a pension scheme has sufficient assets to meet its liabilities. The investigation is usually to assess the degree of solvency of the scheme.

276 Allied Dunbar Pensions Guide

Added years	This is a method of increasing a member's benefits where additional periods of pensionable service are provided, especially when a transfer payment has been made from a previous scheme. Sometimes members have the option of paying additional voluntary contributions in order to purchase added years, for example, an additional 3/60ths of final remuneration.
Additional component	The State earnings related pension above the *basic component*.
Additional voluntary contributions	Contributions, (AVCs), over and above a member's normal contributions (if any), which a member may pay in order to secure additional benefits.
Administrator	The person regarded by the Pension Schemes Office and, where relevant, the OPB as being responsible for the management of the pension scheme. Often the trustee or employer or a committee of management.
AEI	Average Earnings Index.
Bridging pension	A pension which bridges the gap between early retirement and normal retirement when the State pension becomes payable. There are considerable doubts as to the effect of bridging pensions following the decision of the European Court in *Barber* v *GRE*.
Buy back terms	An expression used to describe the payment of a *state scheme premium* especially when a scheme ceases to be contracted out.
Buy out plans	The purchase by pension scheme trustees of an insurance policy (a s 32 annuity) in the name of the beneficiary who gives up his entitlement to benefits under the scheme on leaving service.

Glossary of terms 277

Comp
The abbreviation for a contracted-out money purchase scheme which became available from 6 April 1988.

Continuation option
Where a member leaves a pension scheme which also provided life assurance benefits, the insurance company underwriting those benefits will often give him or her the facility to continue cover under a life assurance policy, without having to provide evidence of health. There is normally a time limit of one month after leaving the scheme for the facility to be taken up.

Contract out
Where an occupational pension scheme is used to provide its members with a level of benefits replacing part of the earnings related state scheme benefits that they *would* have enjoyed had they not been members of a contracted-out scheme. Contributions to the state scheme in respect of employees who are contracted out are lower.

Contracting-out certificate
Provided the conditions relating to contracting-out have been satisfied, the Occupational Pensions Board issue a certificate to an employer.

Contributions equivalent premium (CEP)
A type of state scheme premium which may be paid when a member leaves an occupational pension scheme after a short period of contracted out employment. The state scheme then takes over the obligation to provide the member with his **Guaranteed Minimum Pension**.

Controlled funding
A type of funding commonly used in connection with insured final earnings schemes, where the contributions are assessed to the liabilities of the pension scheme as a whole rather than for individual members.

278 Allied Dunbar Pensions Guide

Deductive amount A reduction in pension or pensionable earnings in order to achieve a degree of integration with the state scheme.

Deposit administration A type of insurance policy where contributions, after expense charges, are accumulated and to which interest and/or bonuses are added. The interest usually reflects prevailing interest rates or building society lending rates.

Director Special rules apply to persons classed as directors (normally of private limited companies).

A 20% director is one who either on his/her own or with one or more associates beneficially owns or is able to control directly or indirectly or through other compares 20% or more of the ordinary share capital of the company.

Discretionary scheme A scheme where employees to be included are selected by the employer on a purely discretionary basis. The discretion normally extends to benefits and contributions for each members.

Dynamisation The index linking of earnings for determining *final remuneration* for the purpose of Inland Revenue limits. The term is sometimes also used to describe escalation or indexation.

Earnings Cap The maximum amount of earnings that may be pensioned, and in respect of which a member may make personal contributions under an occupational scheme, currently £75,000 (1992/93). Also, the maximum earnings in respect of which contributions may be paid to a personal pension scheme in 1992/93.

Equivalent pension benefit (EPB)	The benefit which must be provided for an employee who was contracted out of the former graduated pension scheme (sometimes known as the Boyd-Carpenter scheme).
Executive pension plan	A scheme for selected directors or employees.
Exempt approved scheme	An approved scheme established under an irrevocable trust and thus enjoying the tax relief specified in the Finance Acts.
Expression of wish	Where a member makes a nomination indicating his wishes as to the destination of death benefits to the trustees of the scheme. They are not bound by the nomination, however.
Final salary scheme	A pension scheme where the benefit is calculated with reference to the member's pensionable earnings at or around retirement or leaving service.
Fixed revaluation rate	The rate by which a final salary contracted-out scheme may revalue the **guaranteed minimum pension** where a member's contracted out employment ceases. An alternative to **s 21 orders**.
Free cover	The maximum amount of death benefit which an insurance company covering a group of lives is prepared to underwrite for each individual without requiring evidence of health.
Freestanding AVC	An additional contribution, by a member of an occupational scheme, to another scheme which is completely separate. The total of the individual's contributions to both schemes is limited to 15% of remuneration.

Guaranteed annuity option	Where the proceeds of an insurance policy may be used to buy an annuity at a rate guaranteed in the policy which may also include an open market option.
Guaranteed minimum pension	The minimum pension which a contracted-out scheme must provide. The state benefits payable in respect of a contracted out employee are reduced by the amount of the guaranteed minimum pension.
Hancock annuity	A type of immediate annuity purchased by an employer when an employee retires.
Industry-wide schemes	Multi-member schemes set up by a number of employers operating in a similar industry, eg the printing industry. Members moving between employers within the scheme are deemed to have continuous service.
Integration	Where a pension scheme is designed to take into account part or all of the state scheme benefits.
LAUTRO	The life assurance and unit trust regulatory organisation.
Joint notice	A document which is completed by an individual and a pension provider and sent to the DSS stating that the personal pension scheme entered into by the individual is to be used for contracting-out of SERPS and requesting the DSS to remit the minimum contribution to it.
Letter of exchange	A letter which constitutes the formal setting up of an individual pension arrangement which comes into effect when the employee acknowledges its receipt in writing.

Glossary of terms

Limited price indexation (LPI) — Under the Social Security Act 1990, defined benefit schemes will be required to guarantee pension increases in line with increases in the Retail Prices Index (RPI), subject to a maximum of 5% per annum. At the time of writing this requirement had still not taken effect.

Limited revaluation premium — A type of state scheme premium which may be paid when a member ceases to be in contracted out employment in return for which any revaluation of guaranteed minimum pension above a specified level (currently 5%) is provided by the state scheme.

Lower earnings limit — The minimum amount which must be earned before contributions become payable to the state scheme. Once the limit is exceeded, contributions are payable in respect of earnings both above and below the limit. The level is approximately the same as the basic single person's pension.

Market level indicator — An index giving a weighted comparison of values of fixed interest securities and equities, and used to adjust the amount of state scheme premiums.

Money purchase scheme — A scheme where benefits are directly determined by the value of contributions paid in respect of each member as opposed to a scheme which provides benefits related to earnings.

New code — The code of approval of occupational pension schemes which was introduced by FA 1970, Ch II, Pt II.

Normal retirement date — The date at which a member of a pension scheme normally becomes entitled to receive his retirement benefits.

Old code	The code of approval of occupational pension schemes which applied before the passing of FA 1970: approval under the old code ended on 5 April 1980, if it had not already been replaced by new code approval.
Paid up benefit	A preserved benefit secured for an individual member under an insurance policy where premiums have ceased to be paid in respect of that member.
Pension Schemes Office	The Inland Revenue branch which deals with the approval of pension schemes.
Pensionable earnings	The earnings on which benefits and/or contributions are calculated. Pensionable earnings may differ from actual remuneration in that they may exclude various items such as bonuses, overtime, commission and directors' fees.
Pensioneer trustee	An individual widely involved with pension schemes and accepted by the Inland Revenue as being a trustee of a small self-administered scheme.
Pensioner's rights premium	A type of state scheme premium which may be paid for a member or pensioner over state pension age, when a scheme ceases to be contracted out in return for which the state scheme will take over the obligation to provide his guaranteed minimum pension.
Practice notes	The vast majority of occupational pension schemes are approved by the Inland Revenue under their discretionary powers which are embodied in the publications IR 12 (1979); *Occupational Pension Schemes: Notes on Approval Under Finance Act 1970 As Amended by the Finance Act 1971* and updated considerably in IR 12 (1991)

to take into account the numerous changes in practice which have occurred since 1987. Further publications describe PSO practice on personal pension schemes, free standing AVC schemes and simplified schemes.

Protected rights That part of a personal pension scheme or contracted-out money purchase scheme that represents the fund accumulated by contributions paid by the DSS. These rights are separated from any other benefits built up by the member's or the employer's contributions, as restrictions are imposed on the options available in respect of protected rights.

Purchased life annuity An annuity purchased privately by an individual where instalments of annuity are subject to tax only in part (ICTA 1988, s 656).

Relevant benefits Any benefits given in connection with the termination of service except for benefits given only in the event of accident (see ICTA 1988, s 612).

Requisite benefits The scale of benefits which, prior to November 1986, a pension scheme had to provide as one of the conditions to allow it to contract-out. Requirements were, that the member's personal pension had to be based on his final pensionable salary or his average pensionable salary revalued in line with the growth in earnings generally, and in most cases the pension had to build up at a rate of at least $1\frac{1}{4}\%$ of pensionable salary for each year of contracted-out employment. Additionally, if the employee died leaving a widow who would qualify for a state scheme widow's pension or widowed mother's allowance, she had to receive a pension from the scheme equal to at least $5/8$% of the husband's pensionable salary for each year he was in contracted-out employment. Although this requisite benefit test has been removed in order for a scheme to be contracted-out it must still provide benefits not less than Guaranteed Minimum Pensions.

Retained benefits Retirement or death benefits in respect of an employee's earlier service with a former employer or an earlier period of self-employment.

SSAP 24 The abbreviation given to the accounting standard 'Statement of Standard Accountancy Practice'. It refers to the statement which has been issued by the accountancy bodies concerning accounting for pension costs in company accounts: certain items of information must be disclosed about a company's pension arrangements, eg the results of the most recent actuarial valuation and the long term contribution rate required to meet the cost of pension benefits.

Salary sacrifice An agreement, normally in the form of an exchange of letters between an employer and an employee where the employee gives up part of his salary. The employer is then able to make a corresponding increase in his contribution to the pension scheme.

Section 21 orders Orders issued each year in accordance with s 21 of the Social Security Pensions Act 1975, setting out the rates of increase to be applied in the earnings factors on which the additional component and GMP are based. This revaluation is based on the increase in national average earnings.

Glossary of terms

Self-administered scheme A scheme where the assets are invested by the trustees or through an external investment manager in media other than purely insurance policies.

Simplified scheme A money purchase scheme specially designed by the Inland Revenue to speed up the process by which pension schemes are approved. Provided the benefits are exactly as set out in specimen documents produced by the Inland Revenue and membership excludes controlling directors, scheme approval will follow automatically.

Special contributions Contributions paid by the employer (or, rarely, by a member) for a limited period or as a single payment to provide augmented benefits for a member or to meet deficiencies in funding levels.

State pensionable age The age from which pensions are normally payable by the state scheme, currently 60 for women and 65 for men.

Superannuation funds office (SFO) The former name for the Pension Schemes Office.

Top hat scheme An alternative term for the executive pension plan.

Transfer payment A payment made by the trustees of one pension scheme to the trustees of another when a member leaves employment to enable the receiving pension scheme to give additional benefits.

Unit-linked pension scheme Usually an individual arrangement where the amount of retirement benefits is related to the units in an investment fund and the value of the fund varies according to the value of the units.

Upper earnings limit The amount of earnings (approximately seven times the lower earnings limit) on which contributions are payable to the state scheme.

Vested rights The benefits under the scheme to which a member is unconditionally entitled if he were to leave service including related benefits for dependants.

Waiting period Period of service which an employee may have to serve before being entitled to join a pension scheme.

Appendix 2 Memorandum No 109 (August 1991)

Small self-administered schemes (issued by the Inland Revenue Superannuation Funds Office)

Introduction

1 The Inland Revenue's discretionary practice in relation to the approval of Small Self-Administered Schemes (SSAS) has continued to develop since the mid-1970s when such schemes first began to emerge. General guidance as to the special requirements for the approval of these schemes was set out in Memorandum No 58 which was issued in February 1979. The Memorandum is only a general guide as to how the Inland Revenue is likely to exercise its discretion in particular circumstances. It has always been made clear that further conditions could be imposed to meet the facts of particular cases or more generally in the light of further experience in dealing with such schemes.

2 The fact that the Inland Revenue has discretionary powers under the law means that it is not possible to lay down hard and fast rules of general application. Strictly each case requires individual consideration based on its own facts and merits. This is particularly burdensome in the area of SSAS where, because of the usual close identity of interests between the employer, the trustees and the scheme members, it is necessary to monitor carefully transactions between the parties and to establish that the purpose of a particular investment is bona fide for the sole purpose of providing relevant benefits. Parliament has therefore approved Regulations to limit the Board's discretion and to specify certain requirements for the approval of SSAS.

3 These Regulations, The Retirement Benefit Schemes (Restriction

on Discretion to Approve) (Small Self-Administered Schemes) Regulations 1991 (SI 1991 No 1614) were made on 15 July 1991 and came into force on 5 August 1991. Copies are obtainable from HM Stationery Office. In this Memorandum references to regulations are to these regulations.

4 The effect of the regulations is to restrict the power of the trustees of a SSAS to borrow money and to make and dispose of certain investments. They also require the scheme administrator to provide information and documents to the Superannuation Funds Office (SFO).

5 The purpose of this Memorandum is to highlight the main points of the regulations and explain some other aspects of SFO practice in relation to SSAS. Memorandum No 58 has not yet been cancelled (see however paragraph 21). Where the regulations or this Memorandum overlap Memorandum No 58, the new provisions will prevail.

Definition of a Small Self-Administered Scheme

6 Regulation 2 contains definitions of terms used in the regulations including 'Small Self-Administered Scheme'. This is defined as a self-administered scheme with less than 12 members.

For this purpose, a scheme is defined as self-administered if some or all of the income and other assets are invested otherwise than in insurance policies. Scheme monies held in a current account (whether interest-bearing or not) with a bank, building society, etc, for incidental purposes will not be treated as an investment 'otherwise than in insurance policies'.

The second leg of the definition provides that a scheme will not be regarded as a SSAS unless at least one of the members is related

(i) to another member, or
(ii) to a trustee of the scheme, or
(iii) (where the employer is a partnership) to a partner, or
(iv) (if the employer is a company) where a member or a person connected with that member has been a controlling director of the company at any time during the preceding 10 years.

Notwithstanding this definition the SFO may, under their discretionary powers, apply the same restrictions and requirements to a self-administered scheme with 12 or more members (for example where rank and file employees have been introduced into the scheme as 'makeweight' members with insignificant benefits, simply to increase the number of members to 12 or more).

Some small schemes (generally administered by life offices) are documented to permit self-administration but scheme monies are wholly invested in insurance policies from the outset. These schemes have commonly been known as wholly insured LOSSAs or as deferred SSASs. Such schemes do not fall within the regulation definition of a SSAS. As soon as the trustees of such a scheme invest other than in insurance policies, then the scheme will immediately become a SSAS and subject to the requirements of the regulations. The SFO must be notified at once if this happens and details of the non-insured investment should be supplied.

Previously those schemes described in the previous paragraph have not been required to submit full-scale actuarial valuations provided their only investments were insurance policies with one life office. This dispensation was given on the understanding that a short report was provided every three years covering remuneration and contribution details of each member in the preceding three-year period and also confirmation that the scheme remained fully insured with one life office. Such reports and confirmation are no longer required. As explained above when such a scheme becomes self-administered the SFO must be informed.

Pensioneer trustee

7 Regulation 2 also defines 'pensioneer trustee'. The criteria for being accepted as a pensioneer trustee remain as set out in Memorandum No 58. Regulation 9 requires that in the event of a scheme ceasing to have a pensioneer trustee the SFO must be notified in writing within 30 days and a replacement pensioneer trustee must be appointed within 60 days. The regulation also requires that the SFO should be given written notification of the name of the new pensioneer trustee within 30 days of appointment. A copy of the document(s) removing and appointing pensioneer trustees should be sent to the SFO.

Restriction of board's discretion

8 Regulation 3 prohibits the approval of a further SSAS of a particular employer if one has previously been approved but not wound up. If an employer has an approved SSAS that is being wound up the SFO cannot approve another SSAS for that employer until winding up is complete and the scheme has ceased to exist. If an employer who wishes to establish a SSAS has been participating in another employer's approved SSAS, it will be necessary for him to withdraw from the latter before his own SSAS can be approved. Regulation 3 also sets out the general restriction of discretion to approve a SSAS unless its rules conform with regulations 4 to 10.

Scheme borrowing

9 Regulation 4 restricts any borrowing by the trustees of a SSAS to not more than 45% of the market value of the scheme investments plus three times the ordinary annual contribution and three times the annual amount of the contributions paid by scheme members (excluding AVCs).

For this purpose 'ordinary annual contribution' means the *smaller* of:

(i) the average annual amount of the contributions paid to the scheme by the employer in the three scheme accounting periods preceding the date on which the ordinary annual contribution is to be ascertained (or, where at that date the scheme had been established less than three years, the total amount of contributions paid to the scheme by the employer divided by the number of years since the scheme was established (a part year counting as one year)), and

(ii) the amount of the annual contribution which has been advised by an actuary in writing within three years of the date on which the ordinary annual contribution is to be ascertained, as that necessary to secure the benefits payable under the scheme.

The borrowed money must be used to benefit the scheme. If the money is on-lent to the employer (or any associated company) the trustees must receive a higher rate of interest than they have to pay to obtain the finance.

Purely as a work saving measure, the SFO will not require to be notified of temporary borrowings for a period not exceeding six months where the aggregate amount borrowed does not exceed the lesser of 10% of the market value of the fund or £50,000 and the borrowing is repaid at or before the due date. If a borrowing is 'rolled over' into a further term it is outwith the concession and must be reported (see paragraph 19).

Scheme investments

10 Regulation 5 prohibits among other things investment by trustees in personal chattels other than choses in action. A 'chose in action' is something which is not corporeal, tangible, movable or visible and of which a person has not the present enjoyment but merely a right to recover it (if withheld) by action. Choses in action are permitted investments and include:

Company shares	Financial futures
Copyrights	Commodity futures
Deposit Accounts	Traded options

The following assets are personal chattels which are *not* choses in action and are therefore prohibited investments:

Antiques	Furniture
Works of Art	Fine wines
Rare books	Vintage cars
Rare stamps	Yachts
Jewellery	Gold bullion
Gem stones	Krugerrands
Oriental rugs	

The above lists are given simply by way of example and are not comprehensive. Trustees who are uncertain as to whether a particular investment is a chose in action should consult their professional advisers before making the investment.

Residential property

11 Regulation 5 prohibits investment in residential property except where it is for occupation by:

  (i) an unconnected employee as a condition of employment (eg a caretaker), or
  (ii) someone unrelated to the members of the scheme (or to a person connected with a scheme member) in connection with his or her occupation of business premises (eg a shop, with an integral flat above) where those business premises are held by the trustees as a scheme asset.

Shares in unlisted companies

12 Regulation 5(1)(c) limits a scheme's investment in an unlisted company to not more than 30% of the shares (as defined) in that company. This restriction is intended to limit the scope for tax avoidance which exists when an exempt approved pension scheme operates through its 'own' company. Any attempt to circumvent the effect of the 30% limit, for example by means of dividend waivers by other shareholders will prejudice the approval of the scheme.

Transactions with scheme members

13 Regulation 6 bans loans to scheme members or anyone connected with a scheme member and regulation 8 prohibits the purchase, sale or lease of any assets from or to scheme members or anyone connected with a scheme member.

Loans to the employer and associated companies

14 These are permitted subject to the conditions contained in regulations 6 and 7.

(i) *amount*
First the 50% limit on self-investment (viz loans to and shares in an employer company and any associated company) has been reduced to 25% for the first two years of the scheme's existence. And second the 25% is to be applied to the value of the fund *exclusive* of transfers received from other schemes ie the 25% relates to the funds contributed by the employer and scheme members and any investment income or gains from the investment of these contributions. The 25/50% test is to be applied at the date that money is loaned (or shares acquired).

(ii) *purpose*
The borrower must use the borrowed money only for business purposes. In other words the money must be used to benefit the borrower's trade or profession. The money should not be on-lent nor should it be used for some purely speculative purpose such as the purchase of shares or other investments. A holding company is however permitted to make or manage share investments in its 51% trading subsidiaries.

(iii) *term*
The loan must be for a fixed term. The length of the term is a matter for the parties to the loan agreement but it should be realistic. It is not acceptable for a series of 364 day loans to be made (simply to enable the interest to be paid to the trustees gross without deduction of tax) when in reality there is no real intention to repay the loan for say three years. Nor is it acceptable for the term to be longer than necessary — scheme funds should not lodge unnecessarily with the employer.

(iv) *rate of interest*
Loans must be at a commercial rate of interest. Commercial rate is not defined in the regulations. The SFO will maintain its long established practice and accept an interest rate equivalent to Clearing Bank Base Rate (CBBR) plus 3%

as satisfying the 'commercial rate' test. This rate will be accepted for both secured and unsecured loans. The SFO will be prepared to consider a lower rate of interest only if written evidence is produced to show that the borrower can obtain a loan *on similar terms* from a bank or other arm's length financial institution at a rate below CBBR plus 3%.

(v) *loan to be on commercial basis*

It is a Revenue requirement that the commercial rate of interest (see (iv) above) must be charged *and paid*. It is also a requirement (regulation 6(3)) that the loan document must provide for the loan to be repaid immediately in certain circumstances including that where the borrower is in breach of the conditions of the agreement.

The regulations apart, the SFO require pension scheme trustees to act in the best interests of scheme members in their capacity as members of the pension scheme and not as employees, shareholders etc. If they fail to do so the SFO are likely to take the view that the scheme is not being properly administered and that exempt approval should be withdrawn. Examples of the sort of actions which might lead to withdrawal of approval are:

(*a*) loans solely to keep an ailing business afloat,
(*b*) loans to employers who are technically insolvent,
(*c*) the failure of trustees to take all legal steps open to them to enforce the repayment of a loan to an employer in the circumstances described in regulation 6(3).

As a rule loans should not be made to the employer (or any associated company) unless the trustees would be prepared to lend the same amount on the same terms to an unconnected party of comparable standing.

(vi) *'roll over' of loan*

The regulations do not preclude an outstanding loan from being 'rolled over' into a fresh loan agreement. For the future the SFO will not, however, agree to a loan being 'rolled over' more than twice. Where a loan is 'rolled over' after the regulations have taken effect the new loan will be subject to the conditions in regulations 6 and 7. The 'roll over' of unpaid interest into a new loan will not be permitted.

Back to back loans

15 Any attempt to circumvent the longstanding ban on loans to members or the restrictions on loans to employers by entering into arrangements by which the scheme loans money to an unconnected

party on the understanding for instance that reciprocal loans will be made by that party (or an associate) to the employer or a scheme member will have serious consequences. The SFO will enquire about loans to allegedly unconnected companies or individuals. If it comes to light that the parties are indulging in back to back loans or other arrangements to avoid the restrictions on loans the SFO will not hesitate to withdraw approval, if necessary retrospectively, from the schemes involved.

Application of the regulations

16 *New schemes and schemes not yet approved*
   (i) From 5 August 1991, the date on which the regulations came into force, the SFO cannot approve a SSAS unless its governing documentation takes account of the requirements of the regulations.
   (ii) However as a transitional measure a SSAS established before, but not approved by, 5 August 1991 may retain investments made before 15 July 1991 provided they are acceptable under previous SFO practice. Such investments may be disposed of by the trustees in due course to whoever they wish (including scheme members and their relatives) provided that the disposal is on an arm's length basis at full market value in accordance with current SFO discretionary requirements. It is emphasised that in all other respects the requirements of the regulations must be fully observed with effect from 5 August 1991. The scheme rules must be amended to take account of the regulations, before approval can be granted.

Existing approved schemes
   (iii) Under section 591A Income and Corporation Taxes Act 1988 (introduced by section 35 of the Finance Act 1991), those SSAS approved before 5 August 1991 have three years from that date to amend their rules to accord with the regulations otherwise they will cease to be approved. Investments made before 15 July 1991 may be retained provided they are acceptable under previous SFO practice. Such investments may be disposed of by the trustees in due course to whoever they wish (including scheme members and their relatives) provided that the disposal is on an arm's length basis at full market value in accordance with current SFO discretionary requirements. It is emphasised that in all other respects the requirements of the regulations must be fully observed with effect from 5 August 1991. For the future the Board's discretionary practice will be adapted to reflect the spirit and content of the regulations.

Model rules

17 The Standard Section of SFO has produced a package of model rules that may be used to incorporate the requirements of the regulations into scheme documents. These rules may be used by any SSAS irrespective of whether or not it has been documented using agreed model rules. The package does not include a provision for retaining assets acquired before the regulations came into effect. Where such a provision is appropriate it should be individually drafted to meet the particular circumstances of the scheme.

Copies of the package will be issued to all practitioners who are negotiating or have agreed model SSAS rules with SFO. Copies are also available free of charge by writing to the Standards Section of SFO.

Rule amendments

18 Rule amendments to take account of the regulations should be submitted to SFO in the normal way. If the amendments are entirely in accordance with the package of model rules (see paragraph 17) this should be stated. Use of the SFO package will avoid detailed rule examination and should lead to earlier agreement.

Information and documents

19 The regulation 9 requirement to notify the removal and appointment of pensioneer trustees is covered at paragraph 7 above. Regulation 10 provides that the scheme administrator must, within 90 days of certain specified transactions, furnish information and documents to the SFO. The information and documents are as specified on the relevant forms supplied by the SFO. Copies of the relevant forms are attached. Supplies of the new forms are being issued automatically to large users. Otherwise supplies may be obtained by writing to the Supplies Section, Room 0407 at the above address or by telephoning extension 4254. The SFO have no objection to practitioners producing their own supplies of these forms. The forms are as follows:

- SF 7012 details of the acquisition or disposal of land (this term includes buildings and other structures),
- SF 7013 lending of money to an employer (including associated companies),
- SF 7014 acquisition or disposal of shares in the employer, associated companies or unlisted companies,
- SF 7015 the borrowing of money,

SF 7016   purchase from an employer or associated company of any asset other than land or shares, or the sale of any asset of the scheme to an employer or associated company.

The SFO will continue to issue forms SF 191/4 when making enquiries concerning investments made before the regulations take effect.

Compliance

20   Failure to comply with the regulations in any way, including arrangements to circumvent particular conditions or requirements, and failure to provide information or documents by the due dates will jeopardise a scheme's tax approved status.

Practice notes

21   The revised Practice Notes when published later this year will contain a detailed explanation of both the effect of the regulations and Inland Revenue practice in relation to SSAS. Memorandum No 58 will then be cancelled.

Form 7012

SMALL SELF-ADMINISTERED SCHEMES
Information required under The Retirement Benefit Schemes (Restriction on Discretion to Approve) (Small Self-administered Schemes) Regulations 1991

Name of Principal Employer..

Name of Scheme ....

SFO reference   SF......./ ....

	SCHEME INVESTMENTS: Property or land acquisitions (or disposals)	
1	Date of purchase/sale *(state which)*	
2	Address of property	
3	Description of property	
4	Purchase/sale price and interest in property (freehold or leasehold)	
5	Name of vendor/purchaser and whether 'connected' ie a relative or business associate of a member, trustee or employer	
6	If property purchased leasehold, and vendor is 'connected', was any part of the vendor's interest in the property retained by him?	
7	Name of lessee (if any) and whether 'connected'	
8	Length of lease and rent payable	
9	Details of any associated agreement concerning the property or otherwise involving any member of the scheme or any connected person	
10	Details of any trustees' borrowing to finance the purchase (see also form SF 7015)	

Signed (by or on behalf of administrator) ....

Capacity in which signed   ....

Notes on completion
1. Administrators of small self-administered schemes are required to furnish to the Board of Inland Revenue the relevant information and documents *within 90 days* after the trustees in their capacity as such have acquired (or disposed of) any land or buildings.
2. If the vendor/purchaser is 'connected' (see question 5) please enclose a copy of an independent valuation of the property. Similarly, if the lessee is 'connected', a copy of an independent valuation of the rental value is required, and a copy of the lease. As a concession further time may be allowed for production of the copy of the lease.   SF 7012

Form 7013

SMALL SELF-ADMINISTERED SCHEMES
Information required under The Retirement Benefit Schemes (Restriction on Discretion to Approve) (Small Self-administered Schemes) Regulations 1991

Name of Principal Employer..

Name of Scheme ....

SFO reference   SF......./..................................

SCHEME INVESTMENTS: Loans to employer and associated companies	
1	Name of borrower
2	Date of loan
3	Amount
4	Rate of interest
5	Purpose of loan *(full details are required 'cash flow' is **not** sufficient)*
6	Term of loan and any repayment conditions
7	Total value of fund at date of loan
8	The amount invested in loans and shares in the employer and associated companies, at date of loan. *(Note: The 25%/50% limit applies to loans and shares combined.)*

Signed (by or on behalf of administrator) ....

Capacity in which signed   ....

Notes on completion
1. Administrators of small self-administered schemes are required to furnish to the Board of Inland Revenue the relevant information and documents *within 90 days* after the trustees in their capacity as such have loaned money to an employer (or any associated company).
2. A copy of the loan agreement is required and this should be submitted with the completed questionnaire.

SF 7013

Form 7014
SMALL SELF-ADMINISTERED SCHEMES
Information required under The Retirement Benefit Schemes (Restriction on Discretion to Approve) (Small Self-administered Schemes) Regulations 1991

Name of Principal Employer..

Name of Scheme ....

SFO reference   SF......./ ....

	SCHEME INVESTMENTS: Shares in an employer company (or associated company) or an unlisted company	
1	Name of company	
2	Type and number of shares concerned	
3	Date of purchase/sale (state which) and purchase/sale price	
4	Name of vendor/purchaser and whether 'connected' ie a relative or business associate of a member, trustee or employer	
5	Total Issued Share Capital (ISC)	
6	Where shares purchased by scheme, vendor's beneficial interest (as a % of ISC) prior to sale	
7	Trustees' reason for acquiring shares	
8	Date and reference number of any clearance under s 707 ICTA 1988	
9	Total amount invested in loans to or shares in the employer company or associated company prior to this transaction *(the 25%/50% limit applies to loans and shares combined)*	

Signed (by or on behalf of administrator) ....

Capacity in which signed   ....

Notes on completion
1. Administrators of small self-administered schemes are required to furnish to the Board of Inland Revenue the relevant information and documents *within 90 days* of any acquisition (or disposal) by the trustees in their capacity as such of shares in an employer, associated company or unlisted company.
2. 'Unlisted company' means a company which is not officially listed on a recognised stock exchange within the meaning of section 841 ICTA 1988.
3. If the vendor/purchaser is 'connected' (see question 4) and the shares were purchased/sold privately, the following are required:—
   (a) Full details of the calculations used in valuing the shares, and a copy of any professional valuation or advice obtained.
   (b) Copies of the most recent accounts of the scheme, and the last three years' accounts of the company.
   (c) Details of any associated agreement with anyone connected with the scheme to purchase or sell shares in the company.

SF 7014

Form 7015

SMALL SELF-ADMINISTERED SCHEMES
Information required under The Retirement Benefit Schemes (Restriction on Discretion to Approve) (Small Self-administered Schemes) Regulations 1991

Name of Principal Employer..

Name of Scheme ....

SFO reference   SF......./................................

	SCHEME BORROWING	
1	Date of borrowing	
2	Amount	
3	Rate of interest	
4	Purpose of borrowing	
5	Repayment date	
6	Name and address of lender	
7	Total value of fund at date of borrowing	
8	Total amount of employer contributions to the above scheme in the last three completed accounting years of the scheme (or since commencement, if the scheme has not been in existence for three years)	
9	Total amount of employee contributions to the scheme (as a condition of membership) in the year ended 5 April prior to the date of borrowing	

Signed (by or on behalf of administrator) ....

Capacity in which signed   ....

Notes on completion
1. Administrators of small self-administered schemes are required to furnish to the Board of Inland Revenue the relevant information and documents *within 90 days* after the trustees in their capacity as such have borrowed money for any reason.
2. If the lender is 'connected', a copy of the loan agreement should be submitted with the completed questionnaire.
3. As a concession, no report need be made of temporary borrowings for a period not exceeding six months where the aggregate amount borrowed does not exceed the lesser of 10% of the market value of the fund or £50,000 and the borrowing is repaid at or before the due date. If a borrowing is rolled over into a further term it is outwith the concession and must be reported.

SF 7015

Form 7016

SMALL SELF-ADMINISTERED SCHEMES
Information required under The Retirement Benefit Schemes (Restriction on Discretion to Approve) (Small Self-administered Schemes) Regulations 1991

Name of Principal Employer...

Name of Scheme   ....

SFO reference   SF......./...................................

	SCHEME INVESTMENTS: Miscellaneous acquisitions and disposals	
1	Description of asset	
2	Date of purchase/sale (state which) and purchase/sale price	
3	Name of vendor/purchaser and whether 'connected', ie a relative or business associate of a member, trustee or employer	
4	If the asset has been leased to anyone please give brief details and state whether the lessee is 'connected'	

Signed (by or on behalf of administrator) ....

Capacity in which signed   ....

Notes on completion
1. Administrators of small self-administered schemes are required to furnish to the Board of Inland Revenue the relevant information and documents *within 90 days* after the trustees in their capacity as such have acquired, leased or disposed any asset from or to an employer or associated company. Transactions involving property and shares should not be reported on this form.
2. If the vendor/purchaser is 'connected' (see question 3) please enclose a copy of an independent valuation of the asset. Similarly, if the lessee is 'connected', a copy of an independent valuation of the rental value is required, and a copy of the lease.

SF 7016

Appendix 3 1991 Inland Revenue Practice Notes

Part 20: Small self-administered schemes

Introduction

20.1 As the term indicates, a small self-administered scheme is a self-administered scheme with a small number of members. The Inland Revenue's discretion to approve a small self-administered scheme is limited by The Retirement Benefit Schemes (Restriction on Discretion to Approve) (Small Self-Administered Schemes) Regulations 1991 (SI 1991 No 1614). References in this Part to 'regulations' are to those regulations and the guidance in this Part should be read in conjunction with those regulations. The regulations define a small self-administered scheme as a self-administered scheme with less than 12 members where at least one of those members is connected with another member, or with a trustee or an employer in relation to the scheme. The Inland Revenue may also require a scheme with 12 or more members to be treated as a small self-administered scheme and to comply with the special requirements set out in this Part. An example would be a scheme established primarily for a few family directors, to whom were added some relatively low-paid employees with entitlement to a very low level of benefits, included as makeweights to bring the total membership to 12 or slightly more. Conversely it will not be necessary to apply 'small scheme' treatment to a scheme with less than 12 members if all the members are at arm's length from one another, from the employer and from the trustees.

20.2 The reasons why the Inland Revenue consider special requirements necessary for the approval of such schemes are:

(a) Under trust law which evolved before the advent of pension schemes, a trust with one or a few beneficiaries is susceptible

to being broken regardless of the terms in which the trust is constituted.
(b) The funding of a self-administered scheme for a few members is difficult because the small membership limits the extent to which statistical fluctuations can be smoothed out (eg for mortality).
(c) Small self-administered schemes are usually established to provide benefits for directors. Often the scheme members control the employer company and are also trustees of the scheme. This multiplicity of roles can face a trustee with a conflict of interests leading to actions concerning the scheme being taken for reasons other than the provision of benefits on retirement.

20.3 The special requirements thus fall into three categories viz:

(a) control of the format of the trust,
(b) control of funding, and
(c) control of investments.

The trust

20.4 The regulations restrict the Board's discretion to approve a small self-administered scheme to one whose governing documentation contains provisions requiring one of the trustees to be a 'pensioneer trustee'. A pensioneer trustee is an individual or body recognised by the Inland Revenue as being widely involved with occupational pension schemes and having dealings with the Superannuation Funds Office, who has given an undertaking to that Office that he or she will not consent to any termination of a scheme of which he or she is trustee otherwise than in accordance with the approved terms of the winding-up rule.

20.5 Where a corporate body wishes to be recognised as a pensioneer trustee it is normally essential for the directors, or a majority of them, to be acceptable as such in their own right. The acceptable directors should have the power to direct how the corporate trustee will vote in any proceedings of pension scheme trustees.

20.6 The object of the appointment of a pensioneer trustee is to block any proposal that the trust should be terminated and the funds distributed among the members. It is, however, accepted that trustees have no power to resist such a proposal if all the persons having an interest under the trust are agreed in requiring this action (*Saunders* v *Vautier* (1841)). Such a consensus is unlikely in the context of a typical pension scheme where, even if the number of members is small, the existence of further contingent beneficiaries can rarely be excluded.

20.7 The trust provisions of an approved small self-administered scheme must be framed to allow the pensioneer trustee to fulfil his or her function. Thus a provision which allows trustees to act on majority rather than unanimous decisions must be qualified so as not to apply in relation to the termination of the scheme. A scheme subject to Scottish law must expressly require the pensioneer trustee's concurrence in any decision about the scheme's termination.

20.8 A pensioneer trustee should not act as such in any scheme of which he or she is a member. Similarly a corporate trustee should not act in that capacity for a scheme for its own employees. A pensioneer trustee must not be connected with a scheme member, any other trustee of the scheme or any employer in relation to the scheme.

20.9 If a pensioneer trustee ceases to be qualified to act as such or ceases to be a trustee of the scheme, regulation 9 requires the trustees or the remaining trustee or trustees to:

(a) notify the Board in writing within 30 days of such cessation;
(b) within 60 days of the cessation to appoint a successor as a pensioneer trustee; and
(c) within 30 days of the appointment, to notify the Board in writing of the name of the successor.

A copy of the document(s) removing and appointing pensioneer trustees should be sent to the Superannuation Funds Office.

20.10 The Inland Revenue reserves the right to withdraw pensioneer trustee status should the circumstances warrant it.

20.11 It is not permissible for an approved small self-administered scheme to secure a member's benefits against particular trust assets. There is no objection to the calculation of the amount of the member's benefits being notionally linked to the value of particular assets but the trust provisions must ensure that the member's entitlement to benefit is against the funds of the trust as a whole.

20.12 Regulation 3 prohibits the Board from approving a small self-administered scheme in respect of an employer where that employer already has such a scheme approved by the Board to which it was or is entitled to pay contributions, and that scheme has not been wound-up. Thus if more than one employee is to be pensioned through this medium they should all be included in one scheme. Where an employee is employed by several companies in a group of associated companies, one centralised small self-administered scheme may be established in which all the relevant companies participate (see paragraphs 21.3 and 21.4 in this context) or, alternatively, each employer may set up its own small self-administered scheme to provide benefits for the employee based on his or her salary and service with it alone.

20.13 The scheme rules should provide that lump sum benefits payable on death (including any lump sum payable under a pension guarantee) are, except where paragraph 11.12 applies, to be distributable at the trustee's/administrator's discretion among a wide class of beneficiaries.

Funding

20.14 An approved small self-administered scheme, like any other approved scheme, must comply with the general funding principles set out in paragraph 13.1. The more specific requirements of Part 13 are, however, qualified as described in paragraphs 20.15 to 20.20.

20.15 An approved small self-administered scheme is required to obtain an actuarial valuation of its assets and liabilities at its inception and thereafter at intervals no greater than three years. A copy of each actuarial report must be submitted to the Superannuation Funds Office.

20.16 No contributions to be paid to the scheme unless justified by the latest actuarial report. It is not permissible to make contributions when money is available irrespective of the needs of the scheme (it is a popular misconception that a scheme may hold a general reserve equal to one year's ordinary annual contribution).

20.17 All death benefits, insofar as they exceed the value of the member's interest in the fund based on his or her accrued pension and other retirement benefits, must be insured.

20.18 When a pension becomes payable under the scheme it must be secured from the outset by the purchase of a non-commutable, non-assignable annuity from a life office. The annuity should be in the name of the trustees.

Where, however, the pension is guaranteed for no more than five years and there is a lump sum guarantee payment contingently payable on the member's death at the discretion of the trustees (see paragraph 20.13), the rules may permit the purchase of the annuity to be made at or before the expiry of the guarantee period.

20.19 A prospective widow's/widower's reversionary pension should be secured by the purchase of a contingent annuity at the same time as the member's own pension is so secured. If, however, the pension is payable to whichever person is the member's spouse when the member dies (ie the entitlement is not limited to the current spouse at the time of retirement), its purchase may be deferred until the death of the member.

20.20 Any cost of living increases granted in respect of a pension already secured in accordance with paragraphs 20.18 and 20.19 above should be secured with a life office as soon as they are awarded. Where scheme rules provide for pension increases at a fixed rate of up to 3% pa compound (paragraph 9.4(a)), the increases should be secured when the basic pension is secured.

Investments

20.21 The Inland Revenue's interest in the investments of a small self-administered scheme flows from the statutory condition of approval that a scheme should be 'bona fide established for the sole purpose of providing relevant benefits' (section 590(2)(a)). The concern is that tax exempt investments held for the provision of the scheme benefits should not be of a kind or used in such a way as to produce a non-relevant benefit for the beneficiaries or the employer.

20.22 The regulations contain requirements in relation to the power of the trustees of small self-administered schemes to:

(a) borrow money,
(b) hold certain assets as investments,
(c) lend money and purchase shares, and
(d) purchase, sell or lease assets.

The regulations restrict the Board's discretion to approve such a scheme to one whose governing documentation contains requirements complying with the regulations in relation to (a) to (d) above. The only exception is where at the date on which the regulations were made, the scheme was in existence and either had not been submitted to the Board for approval or was before the Board awaiting approval. In these circumstances approval will not be precluded by reason of provisions in the scheme's documentation which allow the trustees to retain as an investment of the scheme:

(a) personal chattels other than choses in action (see paragraph 20.40),
(b) residential property other than is described in paragraph 20.38, or
(c) shares in an unlisted company which carry more than 30% of the voting power in that company or entitle the trustees to more than 30% of any dividends declared by that company (see paragraph 20.42),

provided that such an investment was held by the trustees prior to the date on which the regulations were made and was acceptable under previous Inland Revenue discretionary practice. Similarly, a provision in the scheme's documentation authorising the trustees to:

(d) continue to lend money or retain shares in an employer or any associated employer, where that money was being lent or the shares were being held prior to the date on which the regulations were made and when the money was first lent or the shares were acquired, the scheme had been in existence for two years or less and the 25% restriction but not the 50% restriction described in paragraph 20.26 was exceeded, or
(e) sell assets held by them immediately before that date to a member of the scheme or to any person connected with a member of the scheme,

will not prevent approval being given. It should be noted, however, that in relation to (e), the sale must be on an arm's length basis at full market value.

20.23 It is a condition of approval that when actuarial reports are submitted to the Superannuation Funds Office (see paragraph 20.15) they must be accompanied by a statement detailing how the funds of the scheme are invested. This enables the Inland Revenue to monitor whether the bona fides of the scheme are being maintained.

The Board's discretion to approve a small self-administered scheme is restricted to one whose governing documentation contains

Appendix 3 1991 Inland Revenue Practice Notes

provisions complying with regulation 10. Regulation 10 requires the scheme administrator to provide to the Board, within a period of 90 days after the transaction taking place, information and documents relating to any transaction by the scheme trustees in their capacity as such involving:

(a) the acquisition or disposal of land including buildings and other structures,
(b) the lending of money to an employer or an associated employer,
(c) the acquisition or disposal of shares in an employer or an associated employer,
(d) the acquisition or disposal of shares in an unlisted company,
(e) the borrowing of money, and
(f) the purchase, sale or lease from or to an employer, or any associated employer, of any asset other than one as described in (a), (c) or (d).

The information and documents required are as may be specified on the relevant form supplied by the Superannuation Funds Office. The relevant forms are:

SF 7012 for details of the acquisition or disposal of land (including buildings and other structures),
SF 7013 for the lending of money to an employer or associated employer,
SF 7014 for the acquisition or disposal of shares, in the employer, associated employers or unlisted companies,
SF 7015 for the borrowing of money,
SF 7016 for the purchase from, or sale or lease to an employer, or any associated employer, of any asset other than as described in (a), (c) or (d) above.

Specimens of these forms are included in Appendix [2]. Supplies of these forms are available from the Superannuation Funds Office. Alternatively, practitioners may print their own supplies provided they are identical in all respects with the Inland Revenue forms.

Apart from the requirements of regulation 10, when requested, scheme administrators should provide full details of any transaction to the Superannuation Funds Office. The following paragraphs contain details of the various restrictions which are imposed on scheme trustees by the regulations in relation to their powers as described in (a) to (d) of paragraph 20.22 together with some guidance on Inland Revenue views and requirements on particular aspects of investment.

20.24 The Inland Revenue will not necessarily regard any form of investment as consistent with approval just because it is within the trustees' powers and not prohibited under the terms of the regulations. In general the Inland Revenue do not interfere in the way trustees invest trust monies except:

(a) where tax avoidance is suspected, or
(b) where an investment appears to be irreconcilable with the bona fides of the scheme having regard to the sole purpose requirement and the scheme's cash needs for purchasing annuities.

For example, investment in land or buildings may be a good long-term investment when the members are many years from retirement but becomes less appropriate as their retirement approaches. This is particularly so if the property purchased is an important part of the employer's own commercial premises and thus potentially difficult to realise.

20.25 Regulation 6(1) prohibits scheme trustees from making loans to a member of the scheme or to any person, apart from an employer or any associated employer, who for the purposes of the regulations is connected with a member of the scheme. Thus if a scheme is to be approved, its trust documents should specifically preclude loans to such individuals or persons. The reason why this prohibition is considered necessary in small self-administered schemes in particular is because of the possibility (arising from the less than arm's length relationship of all the parties) that such a loan would become, in reality, a charge on the retirement benefit, or that the pension scheme would be used in this way so as to avoid the tax liability arising on loans direct from a close company to its 'participators'.

20.26 Regulation 7 restricts trustees' investment in assets of an employer company during the first two years from the date the scheme was established, to 25% of the market value of its assets which are derived from contributions made to it by an employer and the members since it was established. After the end of the two-year period the figure increases to 50% of the market value of all the assets of the scheme. In this context investment means both loans to, and the purchase of, shares in the employer company and any associated employer whether or not they participate in the scheme. The Inland Revenue also apply these limits in relation to loans to, or shares in, other persons connected with a scheme through a member, trustee or an employer. It is not possible to provide a comprehensive definition of a connected party in this context, but broadly it includes:

(a) an individual who is a business associate of a member of the scheme, or of a trustee or employer in relation to the scheme, or who is a relative of a trustee or employer,
(b) a partnership where one of the partners is connected as in (a) with a member of the scheme, trustee or employer, and
(c) a company in which a director or influential shareholder (ie one who controls 20% or more of the voting shares in the company) is connected as in (a).

An individual is connected with a corporate trustee or employer if he or she is a relative or business associate of any director or influential shareholder (as defined in (c) above) of the trustee or employer company. For practical purposes a 'business associate' means a partner in a partnership, a fellow director of a company, or a fellow influential shareholder in a company. A director of a company is regarded as a business associate of an influential shareholder of the same company and vice versa. Forms SF 7013, SF 7014 and SF 7016 (headings suitably amended where necessary) should be used to provide details of loans to, shares (acquired and disposed of) in, or purchases, sales or leases from or to connected parties other than an employer or associated employer. The required documentation should accompany the completed forms.

20.27 Subject to paragraph 20.26 and Social Security legislation, a scheme may lend funds to an employer or any associated employer but if it is to be approved, Regulation 6 requires that such lending may only be made for the purposes of the borrower's business (broadly an activity other than that of making or managing investments, except that a holding company is permitted to make or manage share investments in its 51% trading subsidiaries) and that the loan is:

(a) for a fixed term,
(b) at a commercial rate of interest, and
(c) evidenced by an agreement in writing which contains all the conditions on which it is made and provides for immediate repayment of the loan if the borrower:
   (i) breaches the conditions of the agreement,
   (ii) ceases to carry on business,
   (iii) becomes insolvent, or

if repayment is required to enable the trustees to pay benefits which have already become due under the scheme.

The Inland Revenue will also expect these requirements to be met where a loan is made to connected persons other than an employer or associated employer as described in paragraph 20.26.

20.28 Loans should not be of such an amount and frequency as to suggest that the employer is only partly funding the scheme while claiming a tax deduction for the total pension contributions. Regulation 6 requires that a loan must be for a fixed term. The length of the term is a matter for decision between the parties to the loan agreement but it should be realistic. It is not acceptable for a series of 364 day loans to be made when in reality the intention is that the employer will not repay the loan for, say, three years. Nor is it acceptable for the term to be longer than necessary — scheme funds should not lodge unnecessarily with an employer.

20.29 It is an Inland Revenue requirement that the commercial rate of interest (see paragraph 20.27(b)) must be charged and paid. The commerciality of the interest will not be questioned if it is at least 3 per cent above the Clearing Banks' Base Rate and an interest rate on this basis will be acceptable for both secured and unsecured loans. The Superannuation Funds Office will be prepared to consider a lower rate of interest only if written evidence is produced demonstrating that the borrower can obtain a loan on similar terms from a bank or other arm's length financial institution at a rate below Clearing Banks' Base Rate plus 3 per cent.

20.30 Quite apart from the requirements of the regulations, the Superannuation Funds Office require scheme trustees to act in the best interests of scheme members in their capacity as scheme members and not as employees, shareholders etc. If they fail to do so the Superannuation Funds Office are likely to take the view that the scheme is not being properly administered and that exempt approval should be withdrawn (see Part 19). Examples of the sort of actions which might result in this course of action being taken are:

(a) loans made solely to keep an ailing business afloat,
(b) loans to employers who are technically insolvent,
(c) the failure of trustees to take all available legal steps to enforce the repayment of a loan to an employer in the circumstances described in paragraph 20.27(c).

As a rule loans should not be made to an employer or any associated employer unless the trustees would be prepared to lend the same amount on the same terms to an unconnected party of comparable standing.

20.31 The regulations do not prohibit an outstanding loan from being 'rolled over' into a fresh loan agreement. The Superannuation Funds Office will not, however, agree to a loan being 'rolled over' more than twice nor to the 'roll over' of unpaid interest into a new loan. Where a loan is 'rolled over' it must satisfy the conditions described in paragraphs 20.26 to 20.30.

20.32 Any attempt to circumvent the ban on loans to members and connected persons or the restrictions on loans to employers by entering into arrangements whereby the scheme loans money to an unconnected party on the understanding for instance that a similar loan will be made by that party (or an associate) to the employer or a member, will almost certainly lead to withdrawal of approval from the scheme(s) involved.

20.33 Trustees of schemes sometimes wish to borrow funds to enable them to acquire particular assets. Regulation 4 restricts trustees' borrowing so that at the time of any borrowing the aggregate amount borrowed does not exceed the total of:

(a) three times the ordinary annual contribution paid by the employers,
(b) three times the annual amount of the basic or contractual contributions paid by the scheme members in the year of assessment ending immediately before the time of borrowing, and
(c) 45 per cent of the market value of the investments held for the purposes of the scheme.

For the purpose of regulation 4, ordinary annual contribution . . . means the smaller of:

(i) the average annual amount of the contributions paid to the scheme by the employers in the three accounting years of the scheme immediately preceding the date of the borrowing, or where at that date the scheme had been established less than three years, the total amount of contributions paid to the scheme by the employers divided by the number of years since the scheme was established (a part year counting as one year), and

(ii) the amount of the annual contributions which, within the period of three years immediately preceding the date of the borrowing, an actuary has advised in writing would have to be paid in order to secure the benefits provided under the scheme.

Monies borrowed by trustees must be used to benefit the scheme. Thus if the borrowed monies are on-lent to the employer (or any associated employer) the trustees must receive a higher rate of interest than they have to pay to obtain the finance.

As an administrative relaxation, the Superannuation Funds Office do not require notification of short term borrowings for a period not exceeding six months where the aggregate amount borrowed does not exceed the lesser of 10 per cent of the market value of the fund or £50,000 and the borrowing is repaid at or before the due date. If, however, the borrowing or part of it is rolled over into a further term it must be reported.

20.34 Regulation 8 prohibits the direct or indirect purchase by scheme trustees of an asset from a member of the scheme or any person, apart from an employer or any associated employer, connected with a member of the scheme. For this purpose, the purchase of an asset by the trustees will not be regarded as being an indirect purchase from a member of the scheme or connected person if at the time of purchase three or more years have passed since the asset was owned by the member or connected person. Regulation 8 does not preclude the scheme trustees purchasing an asset from an employer or any associated employer but it requires that such purchase may only be made:

(a) after the trustees have obtained independent professional advice in writing, and
(b) in accordance with that advice.

Although the purchase of an asset from an employer or an associated employer is permissible, the Superannuation Funds Office will need to be satisfied that it is consistent with the scheme's approval. The Superannuation Funds Office should, whenever possible, be advised in advance of any such proposed transactions. The Superannuation Funds Office will generally need to consult the appropriate Inspector of Taxes to determine whether tax avoidance is involved and whether the acquisition is part and parcel of a 'transaction in securities' to which section 703 might apply. Trustees may wish to satisfy themselves that the vendors have obtained clearance under section 707 (from the Inland Revenue Compliance and Collection Division) before making such an acquisition. If such clearance cannot be given or if tax avoidance is involved, the transaction will not be consistent with the scheme's approval.

20.35 Subject to the exception explained in paragraph 20.22, regulation 8 prohibits the direct or indirect sale by the trustees of a scheme asset to a member of the scheme or any person, apart from an employer or any associated employer, connected with a member of the scheme. For this purpose, the sale of a scheme asset by the trustees will not be regarded as being an indirect sale to a member of the scheme or connected person, if the purchase by the member or connected person took place three or more years after the sale by the trustees. Regulation 8 does not preclude the sale by the trustees of a scheme asset to an employer or any associated employer but such a sale may only be made subject to the conditions described in (a) and (b) of paragraph 20.34.

20.36 Regulation 8 permits scheme documentation to provide for the lease by the trustees of scheme assets to an employer or any associated employer but only where the conditions described in (a) and (b) of paragraph 20.34 are satisfied.

20.37 Regulation 8 prohibits the trustees from leasing any scheme assets to a member of the scheme or any person, apart from an employer or any associated employer, connected with a member of the scheme.

20.38 Regulation 5 prohibits scheme trustees from investing in residential property other than:

(a) residential property which is, or is to be, occupied by an employee who is not connected with his or her employer and who is required as a condition of employment to occupy the property, or
(b) residential property which is, or is to be, occupied by a person, other than a scheme member or a person connected with a scheme member, in connection with that person's occupation of business premises (for example, a shop with an integral flat above) where those business premises are held by the trustees as a scheme asset.

In relation to (a) above, an employee is connected with his or her employer in circumstances where:

(i) the employer is a partnership and he or she is connected

with a partner (viz is the partner's spouse, or is a relative, or the spouse of a relative, of the partner or the partner's spouse) in the partnership, or
(ii) the employer is a company and he or she or a person connected with him or her (viz in this context the spouse, or a relative, or the spouse of a relative, of the employee or the employee's spouse) is, or at any time during the preceding ten years has been, a controlling director of the company.

For the purposes of regulation 5, the scheme trustees are not regarded as indirectly holding as an investment residential property other than as is described in (a) and (b) above where they hold as an investment units in a unit trust scheme:

(i) which is an authorised unit trust scheme within the meaning of section 468(6), or
(ii) where all the unit holders would be wholly exempt from capital gains tax or corporation tax (otherwise than by reason of residence) if they disposed of their units,

and the trustees of the unit trust scheme hold such property as an investment subject to the trusts of the scheme.

20.39 Investment by scheme trustees in holiday property is not regarded as being consistent with approval.

20.40 Regulation 5 prohibits scheme trustees from investing in personal chattels other than choses in action (or, in Scotland, movable property other than incorporeal movable property). A 'chose in action' is something which is not corporeal, tangible, movable or visible and of which a person has not the present enjoyment but merely a right to recover it (if withheld) by action. Examples of personal chattels which are prohibited investments include works of art, jewellery, vintage cars, yachts, gold bullion etc. Examples of choses in action which are permitted investments include company shares, copyrights, financial futures etc. If scheme trustees are uncertain as to whether a particular investment would be acceptable, they should consult their professional advisers before making the investment.

20.41 There is no objection in principle to a scheme joining with other parties to make a single investment (eg in a property) provided that the other parties do not include a member of the scheme or any person, apart from an employer or any associated employer, connected with a member of the scheme. The trustees should not, however, allow any restriction of the scheme's freedom to realise its investment how and when it wishes.

20.42 It is not necessarily inconsistent with approval for the trustees of a scheme to enter into trading activities but, as explained in paragraph 17.10, any profits are outside the protection of section 592(2). There have been, however, instances of scheme trustees either setting up a trading company or acquiring a controlling interest in such a company either directly or indirectly in order to convert non-tax exempt trading profits into tax exempt dividends. This is not consistent with approval and therefore regulation 5 prohibits scheme trustees from investing in the shares of an unlisted company which:

(a) carry more than 30% of the voting power in the company, or
(b) entitle the shareholder to more than 30% of any dividends declared by the company.

20.43 An approved small self-administered scheme may not exercise any provision for full commutation of an employee's pension on grounds of exceptional circumstances of serious ill-health without the specific prior agreement of the Superannuation Funds Office.

20.44 Scheme documentation should provide that, if an employer goes into liquidation without a successor, the scheme is to be wound-up or partially wound-up as appropriate. The proceeds are to be used in accordance with the documentation to purchase or transfer the accrued benefits. Any surplus is to be returned to the employer (see Part 13).

Appendix 4 ICTA 1988, ss 590-612, 618-655 and Schedule 23 (as updated by FA 1991)

590 Conditions for approval of retirement benefit schemes

(1) Subject to section 591, the Board shall not approve any retirement benefits scheme for the purposes of this Chapter unless the scheme satisfies all of the conditions set out in subsection (2) below.

(2) The conditions are—

- (a) that the scheme is bona fide established for the sole purpose of providing relevant benefits in respect of service as an employee, being benefits payable to, or to the widow, widower, children or dependants or personal representatives of, the employee;
- (b) that the scheme is recognised by the employer and employees to whom it relates, and that every employee who is, or has a right to be, a member of the scheme has been given written particulars of all essential features of the scheme which concern him;
- (c) that there is a person resident in the United Kingdom who will be responsible for the discharge of all duties imposed on the administrator of the scheme under this Chapter;
- (d) that the employer is a contributor to the scheme;
- (e) that the scheme is established in connection with some trade or undertaking carried on in the United Kingdom by a person resident in the United Kingdom;
- (f) that in no circumstances, whether during the subsistence of the scheme or later, can any amount be paid by way of repayment of an employee's contributions under the scheme.

(3) Subject to subsection (1) above, the Board shall approve a retirement benefits scheme for the purposes of this Chapter if the scheme satisfies all the conditions of this subsection, that is to say—

(a) that any benefit for an employee is a pension on retirement at a specified age not earlier than 60 and not later than 75, which does not exceed one-sixtieth of the employee's final remuneration for each year of service up to a maximum of 40;

(b) that any benefit for any widow or widower of an employee is a pension payable on his death after retirement such that the amount payable to the widow or widower by way of pension does not exceed two-thirds of any pension or pensions payable to the employee;

(c) that no other benefits are payable under the scheme;

(d) that no pension is capable in whole or in part of surrender, commutation or assignment, except in so far as the scheme allows an employee on retirement to obtain, by commutation of his pension, a lump sum or sums not exceeding in all three-eightieths of his final remuneration for each year of service up to a maximum of 40.

(e) that, in the case of any employee who is a member of the scheme by virtue of two or more relevant associated employments, the amount payable by way of pension in respect of service in any one of them may not, when aggregated with any amount payable by way of pension in respect of service in the other or others, exceed the relevant amount;

(f) that, in the case of any employee who is a member of the scheme by virtue of two or more relevant associated employments, the amount payable by way of commuted pension in respect of service in any one of them may not, when aggregated with any amount payable by way of commuted pension in respect of service in the other or others, exceed the relevant amount;

(g) that, in the case of any employee in relation to whom the scheme is connected with another scheme which is (or other schemes each of which is) an approved scheme, the amount payable by way of pension under the scheme may not, when aggregated with any amount payable by way of pension under the other scheme or schemes, exceed the relevant amount;

(h) that, in the case of any employee in relation to whom the scheme is connected with another scheme which is (or other schemes each of which is) an approved scheme, the amount payable by way of commuted pension may not, when aggregated with any amount payable by way of commuted pension under the other scheme or schemes, exceed the relevant amount.

(4) The conditions set out in subsections (2) and (3) above are in this chapter referred to as 'the prescribed conditions'.

(4A) In subsection (3)(c) above 'benefits' does not include any benefits for whose payment the scheme makes provision in pursuance of any obligation imposed by legislation relating to social security.

(5), (6) . . .

(7) Subsections (8) to (10) below apply where the Board are considering whether a retirement benefits scheme satisfies or continues to satisfy the prescribed conditions.

(8) For the purpose of determining whether the scheme, so far as it relates to a particular class or description of employees, satisfies or continues to satisfy the prescribed conditions, that scheme shall be considered in conjunction with—

(a) any other retirement benefits scheme (or schemes) which relates (or relate) to employees of that class or description and which is (or are) approved for the purposes of this Chapter,
(b) any other retirement benefits scheme (or schemes) which relates (or relate) to employees of that class or description and which is (or are) at the same time before the Board in order for them to decide whether to give approval for the purposes of this Chapter,
(c) any section 608 scheme or schemes relating to employees of that class or description, and
(d) any relevant statutory scheme or schemes relating to employees of that class or description.

(9) If those conditions are satisfied in the case of both or all of those schemes taken together, they shall be taken to be satisfied in the case of the scheme mentioned in subsection (7) above (as well as the other or others).

(10) If those conditions are not satisfied in the case of both or all of those schemes taken together, they shall not be taken to

be satisfied in the case of the scheme mentioned in subsection (7) above.

(11) The reference in subsection (8)(c) above to a section 608 scheme is a reference to a fund to which section 608 applies.

590A   Section 590: supplementary provisions

(1) For the purposes of section 590(3)(e) and (f) two or more employments are relevant associated employments if they are employments in the case of which—

(a) there is a period during which the employee has held both or all of them,
(b) the period counts under the scheme in the case of both or all of them as a period in respect of which benefits are payable, and
(c) the period is one during which both or all of the employees in question are associated.

(2) For the purposes of section 590(3)(g) and (h) the scheme is connected with another scheme in relation to an employee if—

(a) there is a period during which he has been the employee of two persons who are associated employers,
(b) the period counts under both schemes as a period in respect of which benefits are payable, and
(c) the period counts under one scheme by virtue of service with one employer and under the other scheme by virtue of service with the other employer.

(3) For the purposes of subsections (1) and (2) above, the employers are associated if (directly or indirectly) one is controlled by the other or if both are controlled by a third person.

(4) In subsection (3) above the reference to control, in relation to a body corporate, shall be construed—

(a) where the body corporate is a close company, in accordance with section 416, and
(b) where it is not, in accordance with section 840.

590B Section 590: further supplementary provisions

(1) For the purposes of section 590(3)(e) the relevant amount, in relation to an employee, shall be found by applying the following formula—

$$\frac{A \times C}{60}$$

(2) For the purposes of section 590(3)(f) the relevant amount, in relation to an employee, shall be found by applying the following formula—

$$\frac{3 \times A \times C}{80}$$

(3) For the purposes of section 590(3)(g) the relevant amount, in relation to an employee, shall be found by applying the following formula—

$$\frac{B \times C}{60}$$

(4) For the purposes of section 590(3)(h) the relevant amount, in relation to an employee, shall be found by applying the following formula—

$$\frac{3 \times B \times C}{80}$$

(5) For the purposes of this section A is the aggregate number of years service (expressing parts of a year as a fraction), subject to a maximum of 40, which, in the case of the employee, count for the purposes of the scheme at the time the benefits in respect of service in the employment before payable.

(6) But where the same year (or part of a year) counts for the purposes of the scheme by virtue of more than one of the relevant associated employments it shall be counted only once in calculating the aggregate number of years service for the purposes of subsection (5) above.

(7) For the purposes of this section B is the aggregate number of years service (expressing parts of a year as a fraction), subject to a maximum of 40, which, in the case of the employee, count for the purposes of any of the following—

  (a) the scheme, and

(b) the other scheme or schemes with which the scheme is connected in relation to him

at the time the benefits become payable.

(8) But where the same year (or part of a year) counts for the purposes of more than one scheme it shall be counted only once in calculating the aggregate number of years service for the purpose of subsection (7) above.

(9) For the purposes of this section C is the permitted maximum in relation to the year of assessment in which the benefits in question become payable, that is, the figure found for that year by virtue of subsections (10) and (11) below.

(10) For the years 1988–89 and 1989–90 the figure is £60,000.

(11) For any subsequent year of assessment the figure is the figure found for that year, for the purposes of section 590C, by virtue of section 590C(4) and (5).

590C Earnings cap

(1) In arriving at an employee's final remuneration for the purposes of section 590(3)(a) or (d), any excess of what would be his final remuneration (apart from this section) over the permitted maximum for the year of assessment in which his participation in the scheme ceases shall be disregarded.

(2) In subsection (1) above 'the permitted maximum', in relation to a year of assessment, means the figure found for that year by virtue of subsections (3) and (4) below.

(3) For the years 1988–89 and 1989–90 the figure is £60,000.

(4) For any subsequent year of assessment the figure is also £60,000, subject to subsection (5) below.

(5) If the retail prices index for the month of December preceding a year of assessment falling within subsection (4) above is higher than it was for the previous December, the figure for that year shall be an amount arrived at by—

(a) increasing the figure for the previous year of assessment by the same percentage as the percentage increase in the retail prices index, and

(b) if the result is not a multiple of £600, rounding it up to the nearest amount which is such a multiple.

(6) The Treasury shall in the year of assessment 1989-90, and in each subsequent year of assessment, make an order specifying the figure which is by virtue of this section the figure for the following year of assessment.

591 Discretionary approval

(1) The Board may, if they think fit having regard to the facts of a particular case, and subject to such conditions, if any, as they think proper to attach to the approval, approve a retirement benefits scheme for the purposes of this Chapter notwithstanding that it does not satisfy one or more of the prescribed conditions; but this subsection has effect subject to subsection (5) below.

(2) The Board may in particular approve by virtue of this section a scheme—

- (a) which exceeds the limits imposed by the prescribed conditions as respects benefits for less than 40 years; or
- (b) which provides pensions for the widows of employees on death in service, or for the children or dependants of employees; or
- (c) which provides on death in service a lump sum of up to four times the employee's final remuneration (exclusive of any refunds of contributions); or
- (d) which allows benefits to be payable on retirement within ten years of the specified age, or on earlier incapacity; or
- (e) which provides for the return in certain contingencies of employees' contributions; or
- (f) which relates to a trade or undertaking carried on only partly in the United Kingdom and by a person not resident in the United Kingdom; or
- (g) which provides in certain contingencies for securing relevant benefits (but no other benefits) by means of an annuity contract approved by the Board and made with an insurance company of the employee's choice; or
- (h) to which the employer is not a contributor and which provides benefits additional to those provided by a scheme to which he is a contributor.

(3) In subsection (2)(g) above 'insurance company' means a company to which Part II of the Insurance Companies Act 1982 applies.

(4) In applying this section to a scheme which was in existence on 6th April 1980, the Board shall exercise their discretion, in such cases as appear to them to be appropriate, so as to preserve—

(a) benefits earned or rights arising out of service before 6th April 1980; and
(b) any rights to death-in-service benefits conferred by rules of the scheme in force on 26th February 1970.

(5) The Board shall not approve a scheme by virtue of this section if to do so would be inconsistent with regulations made by the Board for the purposes of this section.

(6) Regulations made by the Board for the purposes of this section may restrict the Board's discretion to approve a scheme by reference to the benefits provided by the scheme, the investments held for the purposes of the scheme, the manner in which the scheme is administered or any other circumstances whatever.

591A Effect on approved schemes of regulations under section 591

(1) Subsection (2) below applies where on or after 17th April 1991 regulations are made for the purposes of section 591 ('section 591 regulations') which contain provisions restricting the Board's discretion to approve a retirement benefits scheme by reference to any circumstances other than the benefits provided by the scheme ('relevant provisions').

(2) Any retirement benefits scheme approved by the Board by virtue of section 591 before the day on which the section 591 regulations come into force shall cease to be approved by virtue of that section at the end of the period of 36 months beginning with that day if at the end of that period the scheme—

(a) contains a provision of a prohibited description, or
(b) does not contain a provision of a required description,

unless the description of provision is specified in regulations made by the Board for the purposes of this subsection.

(3) For the purposes of this section, a provision contained in a scheme shall not be treated as being of a prohibited description by reason only of the fact that it authorises the retention of an investment held immediately before the day on which the section 591 regulations are made.

(4) In determining for the purposes of this section whether any provision contained in a scheme is of a required description, the fact that it is framed so as not to require the disposal of an investment held immediately before the day on which the section 591 regulations are made shall be disregarded.

(5) In this section—

(a) references to a provision of a prohibited description are to a provision of a description specified in the relevant provisions of the section 591 regulations as a description of provision which, if contained in a retirement benefits scheme, would prevent the Board from approving the scheme by virtue of section 591;
(b) references to a provision of a required description are to a provision of a description specified in the relevant provisions of the section 591 regulations as a description of provision which must be contained in a retirement benefits scheme before the Board may approve the scheme by virtue of section 591.

591B Cessation of approval: general provisions

(1) If in the opinion of the Board the facts concerning any approved scheme or its administration cease to warrant the continuance of their approval of the scheme, they may at any time, by notice to the administrator, withdraw their approval on such grounds, and from such date (which shall not be earlier than the date when those facts first ceased to warrant the continuance of their approval or 17th March 1987, whichever is the later), as may be specified in the notice.

(2) Where an alteration has been made in a retirement benefits scheme, no approval given by the Board as regards the scheme before the alteration shall apply after the date of the alteration unless—

(a) the alteration has been approved by the Board, or
(b) the scheme is of a class specified in regulations made by the Board for the purposes of this paragraph and the alteration is of a description so specified in relation to schemes of that class.

Tax reliefs

592 Exempt approved schemes

(1) This section has effect as respects—

(a) any approved scheme which is shown to the satisfaction of the Board to be established under irrevocable trusts; or
(b) any other approved scheme as respects which the Board, having regard to any special circumstances, direct that this section shall apply;

and any scheme which is for the time being within paragraph (a) or (b) above is in this Chapter referred to as an 'exempt approved scheme'.

(2) Exemption from income tax shall, on a claim being made in that behalf, be allowed in respect of income derived from investments or deposits if, or to such extent as the Board are satisfied that, it is income from investments or deposits held for the purposes of the scheme.

(3) Exemption from income tax shall, on a claim being made in that behalf, be allowed in respect of underwriting commissions if, or to such extent as the Board are satisfied that, the underwriting commissions are applied for the purposes of the schemes and would, but for this subsection, be chargeable to tax under Case VI of Schedule D.

(4) Any sum paid by an employer by way of contribution under the scheme shall, for the purposes of Case I or II of Schedule D and of sections 75 and 76, be allowed to be deducted as an expense, or expense of management, incurred in the chargeable period in which the sum is paid.

(5) The amount of an employer's contributions which may be deducted under subsection (4) above shall not exceed the amount contributed by him under the scheme in respect of employees in a trade or undertaking in respect of the profits of which the employer is assessable to tax (that is to say, to United Kingdom income tax or corporation tax).

(6) A sum not paid by way of ordinary annual contribution shall for the purposes of subsection (4) above be treated, as the Board may direct, either as an expense incurred in the chargeable period

in which the sum is paid, or as an expense to be spread over such period of years as the Board think proper.

(7) Any contribution paid under the scheme by an employee shall, in assessing tax under Schedule E, be allowed to be deducted as an expense incurred in the year of assessment in which the contribution is paid.

(8) Subject to subsection (8A) below, the amount allowed to be deducted by virtue of subsection (7) above in respect of contributions paid by an employee in a year of assessment (whether under a single scheme or under two or more schemes) shall not exceed 15%, or such higher percentage as the Board may in a particular case prescribe, of his remuneration for that year.

(8A) Where an employee's remuneration for a year of assessment includes remuneration in respect of more than one employment, the amount allowed to be deducted by virtue of subsection (7) above in respect of contributions paid by the employee in that year by virtue of any employment (whether under a single scheme or under two or more schemes) shall not exceed 15%, or such higher percentage as the Board may in a particular case prescribe, of his remuneration for the year in respect of that employment.

(8B) In arriving at an employee's remuneration for a year of assessment for the purposes of subsection (8) or (8A) above, any excess of what would be his remuneration (apart from this subsection) over the permitted maximum for that year shall be disregarded.

(8C) In subsection (8B) above 'permitted maximum', in relation to a year of assessment, means the figure found for that year by virtue of subsections (8D) and (8E) below.

(8D) For the year of assessment 1989-90 the figure is £60,000.

(8E) For any subsequent year of assessment the figure is the figure found for that year, for the purposes of section 590C, by virtue of section 590C(4) and (5).

(9) Relief shall not be given under sections 266 or 273 in respect of any payment in respect of which an allowance can be made under subsection (7) above.

(10) Subsection (2) of section 468 and subsection (3) of section 469 shall not apply to any authorised unit trust which is also an exempt approved scheme if the employer is not a contributor to the exempt approved scheme and that scheme provides benefits additional to those provided by another exempt approved scheme to which he is a contributor.

(11) Nothing in this section shall be construed as affording relief in respect of any sums to be brought into account under section 438.

(12) This section has effect only as respects income arising or contributions paid at a time when the scheme is an exempt approved scheme.

593 Relief by way of deductions from contributions

(1) Relief under section 592(7) shall be given in accordance with subsections (2) and (3) below in such cases and subject to such conditions as the Board may prescribe by regulations under section 612(3) in respect of schemes—

- (a) to which employees, but not their employers, are contributors; and
- (b) which provide benefits additional to benefits provided by schemes to which their employers are contributors.

(2) An employee who is entitled to relief under section 592(7) in respect of a contribution may deduct from the contribution when he pays it, and may retain, an amount equal to income tax at the basic rate on the contribution.

(3) The administrator of the scheme—

- (a) shall accept the amount paid after the deduction in discharge of the employee's liability to the same extent as if the deduction had not been made; and
- (b) may recover an amount equal to the deduction from the Board.

(4) Regulations under subsection (3) of section 612 may, without prejudice to the generality of that subsection—

- (a) provide for the manner in which claims for the recovery of a sum under subsection (3)(b) above may be made;

(b) provide for the giving of such information, in such form, as may be prescribed by or under the regulations;
(c) provide for the inspection by persons authorised by the Board of books, documents and other records.

594 Exempt statutory schemes

(1) Any contribution paid by an officer or employee under a statutory scheme established under a public general Act shall, in assessing tax under Schedule E, be allowed to be deducted as an expense incurred in the year of assessment in which the contribution is paid; and relief shall not be given under sections 266 or 273 in respect of any contribution allowable as a deduction under this section.

(2) Subject to subsection (3) below, the amount allowed to be deducted by virtue of subsection (1) above in respect of contributions paid by a person in a year of assessment (whether under a single scheme or under two or more schemes) shall not exceed 15%, or such higher percentage as the Board may in a particular case prescribe, of his remuneration for that year.

(3) Where a person's remuneration for a year of assessment includes remuneration in respect of more than one office or employment, the amount allowed to be deducted by virtue of subsection (1) above in respect of contributions paid by the person in that year by virtue of any office or employment (whether under a single scheme or under two or more schemes) shall not exceed 15%, or such higher percentage as the Board may in a particular case prescribe, of his remuneration for the year in respect of that office or employment.

(4) In arriving at a person's remuneration for a year of assessment for the purposes of subsections (2) or (3) above, any excess of what would be his remuneration (apart from this subsection) over the permitted maximum for that year shall be disregarded.

(5) In subsection (4) above 'permitted maximum', in relation to a year of assessment, means the figure found for that year by virtue of subsections (6) and (7) below.

(6) For the year 1989–90 the figure is £60,000.

(7) For any subsequent year of assessment the figure is the figure found for that year, for the purposes of section 590C, by virtue of section 590C(4) and (5).

Charge to tax in certain cases

595 Charge to tax in respect of certain sums paid by employer etc

(1) Subject to the provisions of this Chapter, where, pursuant to a retirement benefits scheme, the employer in any year of assessment pays a sum with a view to the provision of any relevant benefits for any employee of that employer, then (whether or not the accrual of the benefits is dependent on any contingency)—

  (a) the sum paid, if not otherwise chargeable to income tax as income of the employee, shall be deemed for all purposes of the Income Tax Acts to be income of that employee for that year of assessment and assessable to tax under Schedule E; and

  (b) where the payment is made under such an insurance or contract as is mentioned in section 266, relief, if not otherwise allowable, shall be given to that employee under that section in respect of the payment to the extent, if any, to which such relief would have been allowable to him if the payment had been made by him and the insurance or contract under which the payment is made had been made with him.

(4) Where the employer pays any sum as mentioned in subsection (1) above in relation to more than one employee, the sum so paid shall, for the purpose of that subsection, be apportioned among those employees by reference to the separate sums which would have had to be paid to secure the separate benefits to be provided for them respectively, and the part of the sum apportioned to each of them shall be deemed for that purpose to have been paid separately in relation to that one of them.

(5) Any reference in this section to the provision for an employee of relevant benefits includes a reference to the provision of benefits payable to that employee's wife or widow, children, dependants or personal representatives.

596 Exceptions from section 595

(1) Section 595(1) shall not apply where the retirement benefits scheme in question is—

  (a) an approved scheme, or
  (b) a relevant statutory scheme, or
  (c) a scheme set up by a government outside the United Kingdom for the benefit, or primarily for the benefit of, its employees.

(2) Section 595(1) shall not apply for any year of assessment—

(a) where the employee performs the duties of his employment in such circumstances that no tax is chargeable under Case I or II of Schedule E in respect of the emoluments of his employment (or would be so chargeable were there such emoluments), or
(b) where the emoluments from the employment are foreign emoluments within the meaning of section 192 and the Board are satisfied, on a claim made by the employee, that the retirement benefits scheme in question corresponds to such a scheme as is mentioned in paragraph (a), (b) or (c) of subsection (1) above.

(3) Where, in respect of the provision for an employee of any relevant benefits—

(a) a sum has been deemed to be income of his by virtue of subsection (1) of section 595, and
(b) subsequently, the employee proves to the satisfaction of the Board that—
  (i) no payment in respect of, or in substitution for, the benefits has been made, and
  (ii) some event has occurred by reason of which no such payment will be made
and makes application for relief under this subsection within six years from the time when that event occurred,

the Board shall give relief in respect of tax on that sum by repayment or otherwise as may be appropriate; and if the employee satisfies the Board as mentioned above in relation to some particular part, but not the whole, of the benefits, the Board may give such relief as may seem to them just and reasonable.

596A Charge to tax: benefits under non-approved schemes

(1) Where in any year of assessment a person receives a benefit provided under a retirement benefits scheme which is not of a description mentioned in section 596(1)(a), (b) or (c), tax shall be charged in accordance with the provisions of this section.

(2) Where the benefit is received by an individual, he shall be charged to tax under Schedule E for that year.

(3) Where the benefit is received by a person other than an individual, the administrator of the scheme shall be charged to tax under Case VI of Schedule D for that year.

(4) The amount to be charged to tax is—

(a) in the case of a cash benefit, the amount received, and
(b) in the case of a benefit in kind, an amount equal to whatever is the cash equivalent of the benefit.

(5) In the case of the charge under Case VI of Schedule D, the rate of tax is 40% or such other rate (whether higher or lower) as may for the time being be specified by the Treasury by order.

(6) Tax shall not be charged under this section in the case of a benefit which is chargeable to tax under Schedule E by virtue of section 19(1)1.

(7) But where the amount chargeable to tax by virtue of section 19(1)1 is less than the amount which would be chargeable to tax under this section—

(a) subsection (6) above shall not apply, and
(b) the amount chargeable to tax under this section shall be reduced by the amount chargeable to tax by virtue of section 19(1)1.

(8) Tax shall not be charged under this section to the extent that the benefit received is attributable to the payment of a sum—

(a) which is deemed to be the income of a person by virtue of section 595(1), and
(b) in respect of which that person has been assessed to tax.

(9) For the purpose of subsection (8) above the provision of a benefit shall be presumed not to be attributable to the payment of such a sum as is mentioned in that subsection unless the contrary is shown.

596B Section 596A: supplementary provisions

(1) For the purposes of section 596A the cash equivalent of a benefit in kind is—

(a) in the case of a benefit other than living accommodation, the amount which would be the cash equivalent of the benefit under Chapter II of Part V if it were chargeable under the appropriate provision of that Chapter (treating any sum made good by the recipient as made good by the employee), and

(b) in the case of living accommodation, an amount equal to the value of the accommodation to the recipient determined in accordance with the following provisions of this section less so much of any sum made good by him to those at whose cost the accommodation is provided as is properly attributable to the provision of the accommodation.

(2) Where the cost of providing the accommodation does not exceed £75,000, the value of the accommodation to the recipient in any period is the rent which would have been payable for the period if the premises had been let to him at an annual rent equal to their annual value as ascertained under section 837.

(3) But for a period in which those at whose cost the accommodation is provided pay rent at an annual rate greater than the annual value as so ascertained, the value of the accommodation to the recipient is an amount equal to the rent payable by them for the period.

(4) Where the cost of providing the accommodation does exceed £75,000, the value of the accommodation to the recipient shall be taken to be the aggregate of the value of the accommodation to him determined in accordance with subsections (2) and (3) above and the additional value of the accommodation to him determined in accordance with subsections (5) and (6) below.

(5) The additional value of the accommodation to the recipient in any period is the rent which would have been payable for that period if the premises had been let to him at an annual rent equal to the appropriate percentage of the amount by which the cost of providing the accommodation exceeds £75,000.

(6) Where throughout the period of six years ending with the date when the recipient first occupied the property any estate or interest in the property was held by a relevant person (whether or not it was the same estate, interest or person throughout), the additional value shall be calculated as if in subsection (7) below—

(a) the amount referred to in paragraph (a) were the market value of that property as at that date, and
(b) the amount referred to in paragraph (b) did not include expenditure on improvements made before that date.

(7) For the purposes of this section, the cost of providing any living accommodation shall be taken to be the aggregate of—

(a) the amount of any expenditure incurred in acquiring the estate or interest in the property held by a relevant person, and
(b) the amount of any expenditure incurred by a relevant person before the year of assessment in question on improvements to the property.

(8) The aggregate amount mentioned in subsection (7) above shall be reduced by the amount of any payment made by the recipient to a relevant person, so far as that amount represents a reimbursement of any such expenditure as is mentioned in paragraph (a) or (b) of that subsection or represents consideration for the grant to the recipient of a tenancy of the property.

(9) For the purposes of this section, any of the following persons is a relevant person—

(a) the person providing the accommodation,
(b) any person, other than the recipient, who is connected with a person falling within paragraph (a) above.

(10) In this section—
'the appropriate percentage' means the rate applicable for the purposes of section 160 as at the beginning of the year of assessment in question;
'market value', in relation to any property, means the price which that property might reasonably be expected to fetch on a sale in the open market with vacant possession, no reduction being made, in estimating the market value, on account of any option in respect of the property held by the recipient, or a person connected with him, or by any of the persons mentioned in subsection (9) above;
'property', in relation to any living accommodation, means the property consisting of that living accommodation;
'tenancy' includes a sub-tenancy;
and section 839 shall apply for the purposes of this section.

597 Charge to tax: pensions

(1) Subject to subsection (2) below, all pensions paid under any scheme which is approved or is being considered for approval under this Chapter shall be charged to tax under Schedule E, and section 203 shall apply accordingly.

(2) As respects any scheme which is approved or is being considered for approval under this Chapter, the Board may direct that, until such date as the Board may specify, pensions under the scheme shall be charged to tax as annual payments under Case III of Schedule D, and tax shall be deductible under sections 348 and 349 accordingly.

598 Charge to tax: repayment of employee's contributions

(1) Subject to the provisions of this section, tax shall be charged under this section on any repayment to an employee during his lifetime of any contributions (including interest on contributions, if any) if the payment is made under—

(a) a scheme which is or has at any time been an exempt approved scheme, or
(b) a relevant statutory scheme established under a public general Act.

(2) Where any payment is chargeable to tax under this section, the administrator of the scheme shall be charged to income tax under Case VI of Schedule D and, subject to subsection (3) below, the rate of tax shall be 20%.

(3) The Treasury may by order from time to time increase or decrease the rate of tax under subsection (2) above.

(4) The tax shall be charged on the amount paid or, if the rules permit the administrator to deduct the tax before payment, on the amount before deduction of tax, and the amount so charged to tax shall not be treated as income for any other purpose of the Tax Acts.

(5) Subsection (1)(a) above shall not apply in relation to a contribution made after the scheme ceases to be an exempt approved scheme (unless it again becomes an exempt approved scheme).

(6) This section shall not apply where the employee's employment was carried on outside the United Kingdom.

(7) In relation to a statutory scheme, 'employee' in this section includes any officer.

599 Charge to tax: commutation of entire pension in special circumstances

(1) Where a scheme to which this section applies contains a rule allowing, in special circumstances, a payment in commutation of an employee's entire pension, and any pension is commuted, whether wholly or not, under the rule, tax shall be charged on the amount by which the sum receivable exceeds—

 (a) the largest sum which would have been receivable in commutation of any part of the pension if the scheme had secured that the aggregate value of the relevant benefits payable to an employee on or after retirement, excluding any pension which was not commutable, could not exceed three-eightieths of his final remuneration (disregarding any excess of that remuneration over the permitted maximum) for each year of service up to a maximum of 40; or
 (b) the largest sum which would have been receivable in commutation of any part of the pension under any rule of the scheme authorising the commutation of part (but not the whole of the pension, or which would have been so receivable but for those special circumstances;

whichever gives the lesser amount chargeable to tax.

(2) This section applies to—

 (a) a scheme which is or has at any time been an approved scheme, or
 (b) a relevant statutory scheme established under a public general Act.

(3) Where any amount is chargeable to tax under this section the administrator of the scheme shall be charged to income tax under Case VI of Schedule D on that amount, and section 598(2), (3) and (4) shall apply as they apply to tax chargeable under that section.

(4) This section shall not apply where the employee's employment was carried on outside the United Kingdom.

(5) In relation to a statutory scheme, 'employee' in this section includes any officer.

(6) In applying paragraph (a) or (b) of subsection (1) above—

(a) the same considerations shall be taken into account, including the provisions of any other relevant scheme, as would have been taken into account by the Board in applying section 590; and
(b) where the scheme has ceased to be an approved scheme, account shall only be taken of the rules in force when the scheme was last an approved scheme.

(7) Where the pension has been secured by means of an annuity contract with an insurance company and the sum receivable is payable under that contract by the insurance company, the references to the administrator of the scheme in subsection (3) above and in section 598(2) and (4) as applied by that subsection are to be read as references to the insurance company.

(8) In subsection (7) above 'insurance company' means—

(a) a person authorised under section 3 or 4 of the Insurance Companies Act 1982 to carry on long term business and acting through a branch or agency in the United Kingdom; or
(b) a society registered as a friendly society under the Friendly Societies Act 1974 or the Friendly Societies Act (Northern Ireland) 1970.

(9) In relation to payments made under schemes approved or established before 17th March 1987 to employees who became members before that date, subsection (1)(a) above shall have effect with the omission of the words '(disregarding any excess of that remuneration over the permitted maximum)'.

(10) In subsection (1)(a) above 'the permitted maximum' means, as regards a charge to tax arising under this section in a particular year of assessment, the figure found for that year by virtue of subsections (11) and (12) below.

(11) For the years 1988-89 and 1989-90 the figure is £60,000.

(12) For any subsequent year of assessment the figure is the figure found for that year, for the purposes of section 590C, by virtue of section 590C(4) and (5).

599A Charge to tax: payments out of surplus funds

(1) This subsection applies to any payment which is made to or for the benefit of an employee or to his personal representatives out of funds which are or have been held for the purposes of—

   (a) a scheme which is or has at any time been an exempt approved scheme, or
   (b) a relevant statutory scheme established under a public general Act,

and which is made in pursuance of duty to return surplus funds.

(2) On the making of a payment to which subsection (1) above applies, the administrator of the scheme shall be charged to income tax under Case VI of Schedule D at the relevant rate on such amount as, after deduction of tax at that rate, would equal the amount of the payment.

(3) Subject to subsection (4) below, the relevant rate shall be 35 per cent.

(4) The Treasury may by order from time to time increase or decrease the relevant rate.

(5) Where a payment made to or for the benefit of an employee is one to which subsection (1) applies, it shall be treated in computing the total income of the employee for the year in which it is made as income for that year which is—

   (a) received by him after deduction of income tax at the basic rate from a corresponding gross amount, and
   (b) chargeable to income tax under Case VI of Schedule D.

(6) But, subject to subsection (7) below, no assessment to income tax shall be made on, and no repayment of income tax shall be made to, the employee.

(7) Subsection (6) above shall not prevent an assessment in respect of income tax at a rate other than the basic rate.

(8) Subsection (5) above applies whether or not the employee is the recipient of the payment.

(9) Any payment chargeable to tax under this section shall not be chargeable to tax under section 598, 599 or 600 or under the

Regulations mentioned in paragraph 8 of Schedule 3 to the Finance Act 1971.

(10) In this section—
'employee', in relation to a relevant statutory scheme, includes any officer;
references to any payment include references to any transfer of assets or other transfer of money's worth.

600 Charge to tax: unauthorised payments to or for employees

(1) This section applies to any payment to or for the benefit of an employee, otherwise than in course of payment of a pension, being a payment made out of funds which are held for the purposes of a scheme which is approved for the purposes of—

(a) this Chapter;
(b) Chapter II of Part II of the Finance Act 1970; or
(c) section 208 or Chapter II of Part IX of the 1970 Act.

(2) If the payment is not expressly authorised by the rules of the scheme or by virtue of paragraph 33 of Schedule 6 to the Finance Act 1989 the employee (whether or not he is the recipient of the payment) shall be chargeable to tax on the amount of the payment under Schedule E for the year of assessment in which the payment is made.

(3) Any payment chargeable to tax under this section shall not be chargeable to tax under section 598 or 599 or under the Regulations mentioned in paragraph 8 of Schedule 3 to the Finance Act 1971.

(4) References in this section to any payment include references to any transfer of assets or other transfer of money's worth.

601 Charge to tax: payments to employers

(1) Subsection (2) below applies where a payment is made to an employer out of funds which are or have been held for the purposes of a scheme which is or has at any time been an exempt approved scheme and whether or not the payment is made in pursuance of Schedule 22.

(2) An amount equal to 40% of the payment shall be recoverable by the Board from the employer.

(3) Subsection (2) above does not apply to any payment—

(a) to the extent that, if this section had not been enacted, the employer would have been exempt, or entitled to claim exemption, from income tax or corporation tax in respect of the payment; or
(b) made before the scheme became an exempt approved scheme; or
(c) of any prescribed description; or
(d) made in pursuance of the winding-up of the scheme where the winding-up commenced on or before 18th March 1986; or
(e) made in pursuance of an application which—
   (i) was made to the Board on or before that date and was not withdrawn before the making of the payment, and
   (ii) sought the Board's assurance that the payment would not lead to a withdrawal of approval under section 19(3) of the Finance Act 1970;

(4) Subsection (2) above does not apply where the employer is a charity (within the meaning of section 506).

(5) Where any payment is made or becomes due to an employer out of funds which are or have been held for the purposes of a scheme which is or has at any time been an exempt approved scheme then—

(a) if the scheme relates to a trade, profession or vocation carried on by the employer, the payment shall be treated for the purposes of the Tax Acts as a receipt of that trade, profession or vocation receivable when the payment falls due or on the last day on which the trade, profession or vocation is carried on by the employer, whichever is the earlier;
(b) if the scheme does not relate to such a trade, profession or vocation, the employer shall be charged to tax on the amount of the payment under Case VI of Schedule D.

This subsection shall not apply to a payment which fell due before the scheme became an exempt approved scheme or to a payment to which subsection (2) above applies or would apply but for subsection (3)(a) or (4) above.

(6) In this section—

(a) references to any payment include references to any transfer of assets or other transfer of money's worth; and

(b) 'prescribed' means prescribed by regulations made by the Treasury.

602 Regulations relation to pension fund surpluses

(1) In relation to an amount recoverable as mentioned in section 601(2), the Treasury may by regulations make any of the provisions mentioned in subsection (2) below; and for this purpose the amount shall be treated as if it were—

(a) an amount of income tax chargeable on the employer under Case VI of Schedule D for the year of assessment in which the payment is made; or
(b) where the employer is a company, an amount of corporation tax chargeable on the company for the accounting period in which the payment is made.

(2) The provisions are—

(a) provision requiring the administrator of the scheme or the employer (or both) to furnish to the Board, in respect of the amount recoverable and of the payment concerned, information of a prescribed kind;
(b) provision enabling the Board to serve a notice or notices requiring the administrator or employer (or both) to furnish to the Board, in respect of the amount and payment, particulars of a prescribed kind;
(c) provision requiring the administrator to deduct out of the payment the amount recoverable and to account to the Board for it;
(d) provision as to circumstances in which the employer may be assessed in respect of the amount recoverable;
(e) provision that, in a case where the employer has been assessed in respect of an amount recoverable but has not paid it (or part of it) within a prescribed period, the administrator may be assessed and charged (in the employer's name) in respect of the amount (or part unpaid);
(f) provision that, in a case where the amount recoverable (or part of it) has been recovered from the administrator by virtue of an assessment in the employer's name, the administrator is entitled to recover from the employer a sum equal to the amount (or part);
(g) provision enabling the employer or administrator (as the case may be) to appeal against an assessment made on him in respect of the amount recoverable;

(h) provision as to when any sum in respect of the amount recoverable is payable to the Board by the administrator or employer and provision requiring interest to be paid on any sum so payable;

(j) provision that an amount paid to the Board by the administrator shall be treated as paid on account of the employer's liability under section 601(2).

(3) For the purpose of giving effect to any provision mentioned in subsection (2)(c) to (j) above, regulations under this section may include provision applying (with or without modifications) provisions of the enactments relating to income tax and corporation tax.

(4) Subject to any provision of regulations under this section—

(a) a payment to which section 601(2) applies shall not be treated as a profit or gain brought into charge to income tax or corporation tax and shall not be treated as part of the employer's income for any purpose of this Act; and

(b) the amount recoverable shall not be subject to any exemption or reduction (by way of relief, set-off or otherwise) or be available for set-off against other tax.

(5) If the employer is a company and a payment to which section 601(1) and (2) applies is made at a time not otherwise within an accounting period of the company, an accounting period of the company shall for the purposes of subsection (1)(b) above be treated as beginning immediately before the payment is made.

603 Reduction of surpluses

Schedule 22 (which provides for the reduction of certain pension fund surpluses) shall have effect.

Supplementary provisions

604 Application for approval of a scheme

(1) An application for the approval for the purposes of this Chapter of any retirement benefits scheme shall be made in writing by the administrator of the scheme to the Board before the end of the first year of assessment for which approval is required, and shall be accompanied by—

(a) two copies of the instrument or other document constituting the scheme; and
(b) two copies of the rules of the scheme and, except where the application is being sought on the setting up of the scheme, two copies of the accounts of the scheme for the last year for which such accounts have been made up; and
(c) such other information and particulars (including copies of any actuarial report or advice given to the administrator or employer in connection with the setting up of the scheme) as the Board may consider relevant.

(2) The form in which an application for approval is to be made, or in which any information is to be given, in pursuance of this section may be prescribed by the Board.

605 Information

(1) In the case of every approved scheme, the administrator of the scheme, and every employer who pays contributions under the scheme, shall, within 30 days from the date of a notice from the inspector requiring them so to do—

(a) furnish to the inspector a return containing such particulars of contributions paid under the scheme as the notice may require;
(b) prepare and deliver to the inspector a return containing particulars of all payments under the scheme, being—
 (i) payments by way of return of contributions (including interest on contributions, if any);
 (ii) payments by way of commutation of, or in lieu of, pensions, or other lump sum payments;
 (iii) other payments made to an employer;
(c) furnish to the inspector a copy of the accounts of the scheme up to the last date previous to the notice to which such accounts have been made up together with such other information and particulars (including copies of any actuarial report or advice given to the administrator or employer in connection with the conduct of the scheme during the period to which the accounts relate) as the inspector considers relevant.

(2) Where benefits provided for an employee under an approved scheme or a relevant statutory scheme have been secured by means of an annuity contract with an insurance company (within the meaning given by section 599(8)), the insurance company shall,

within 30 days from the date of a notice from the inspector requiring it to do so, prepare and deliver to the inspector a return containing particulars of—

(a) any payments under the contract by way of commutation of, or in lieu of, a pension, or any other lump sum payments under the contract; and
(b) any payments made under the contract to the employer.

(3) It shall be the duty of every employer—

(a) if there subsists in relation to any of his employees a retirement benefits scheme to which he contributes and which is neither an approved scheme nor a relevant statutory scheme, to deliver particulars of that scheme to the Board within three months beginning with the date on which the scheme first comes into operation in relation to any of his employees, and
(b) when required to do so by notice given by the Board, to furnish within the time limited by the notice such particulars as the Board may require with regard to—
   (i) any retirement benefits scheme relating to the employer which is neither an approved scheme nor a statutory scheme; and
   (ii) the employees of his to whom any such scheme relates.

(4) It shall be the duty of the administrator of a retirement benefits scheme which is neither an approved scheme nor a statutory scheme, when required to do so by notice given by the Board, to furnish within the time limited by the notice such particulars as the Board may require with regard to the scheme.

606 Responsibilities of administrator of scheme, and employer

(1) If the administrator of a retirement benefits scheme defaults or cannot be traced or dies, the employer shall be responsible in his place for the discharge of all duties imposed on the administrator under this Chapter and shall be liable for any tax due from him in his capacity as administrator.

This subsection does not apply if the employer is not a contributor to the scheme.

(2) No liability incurred under this Chapter by the administrator of a scheme, or by an employer, shall be affected by the termination

of the scheme or by it ceasing to be an approved scheme, or to be an exempt approved scheme.

(3) References in this section to the employer include, where the employer is resident outside the United Kingdom, references to any branch or agent of the employer in the United Kingdom, and in this subsection 'branch or agent' has the meaning given by section 118(1) of the Management Act.

(4) This section does not apply for the purposes of sections 602 and 603 and Schedule 22.

607 Pilots' benefit fund

(1) The Board may, if they think fit, and subject to such conditions as they think proper to attach to the approval, approve a pilots' benefit fund for the purposes of this Chapter as if it were a retirement benefits scheme and notwithstanding that it does not satisfy one or more of the conditions set out in section 590(2) and (3).

(2) If a fund is approved by virtue of this section—

(a) sections 592, 597 to 600 and 604 to 606 shall have effect in relation to the fund with the modifications specified in subsection (3) below;
(b) pensions paid out of the fund and any sums chargeable to tax in connection with the fund under section 600 shall be treated for the purposes of the Income Tax Acts as earned income; and
(c) Chapter III of this Part shall have effect as if a member of the fund were the holder of a pensionable office or employment and his earnings as a pilot (estimated in accordance with the provisions of Case II of Schedule D) were remuneration from such an office or employment.

(3) The modifications referred to in subsection (2)(a) above are as follows—

(a) in section 592, for the references in subsection (7) to an employee and Schedule E there shall be substituted respectively references to a member of the fund and Schedule D, and subsections (4) to (6), and in subsection (7) the words from 'incurred' onwards, shall be omitted;
(b) in sections 597 to 606 (except sections 601 to 603)—
   (i) for references to an employee there shall be substituted references to a member or former member of the fund;

(ii) in section 599(1)(a) for the reference to a year of service there shall be substituted a reference to a year as a pilot licensed by a pilotage authority or authorised by a competent harbour authority;
(iii) section 606(1) and (3) and so much of any other provision as applies to an employer shall be omitted; and
(iv) in section 600, for references to Schedule E there shall be substituted references to Case VI of Schedule D.

(4) In this section 'pilots' benefit fund' means a fund established under section 15(1)(i) of the Pilotage Act 1983 or any scheme supplementing or replacing any such fund.

608 Superannuation funds approved before 6th April 1980

(1) This section applies to any fund which immediately before 6th April 1980 was an approved superannuation fund for the purposes of section 208 of the 1970 Act if—

(a) it has not been approved under this Chapter (or under Chapter II of Part II of the Finance Act 1970); and
(b) no sum has been paid to it by way of contribution since 5th April 1980.

(2) Subject to subsection (3) below, exemption from income tax shall, on a claim being made in that behalf, be allowed to a fund to which this section applies in respect of—

(a) income derived from investments or deposits of the fund;
(b) any underwriting commissions which apart from this subsection would be chargeable to tax under Case VI of Schedule D; and
(c) any profits or gains which (apart from this subsection) would be chargeable to tax under Case VI of Schedule D by virtue of section 56(1)(a) and (2);

if, or to such extent as the Board are satisfied that, the income, commissions, profits or gains are applied for the purposes of the fund.

(3) No claim under subsection (2) above shall be allowed unless the Board are satisfied that the terms on which benefits are payable from the fund have not been altered since 5th April 1980.

(4) An annuity paid out of a fund to which this section applies shall be charged to tax under Schedule E and section 203 shall apply accordingly.

609 Schemes approved before 23rd July 1987

Schedule 23 to this Act, which makes provision with respect to retirement benefit schemes approved before 23rd July 1987, shall have effect.

610 Amendments of schemes

(1) This section applies to any amendment of a retirement benefits scheme proposed in connection with an application for the Board's approval for the purposes of this Chapter which is needed in order to ensure that approval is so given, or designed to enhance the benefits under the scheme up to the limits suitable in a scheme for which approval is sought.

(2) A provision, however expressed, designed to preclude any amendment of a scheme which would have prejudiced its approval under section 208 or 222 of the 1970 Act shall not prevent any amendment to which this section applies.

(3) In the case of a scheme which contains no powers of amendment, the administrator of the scheme may, with the consent of all the members of the scheme, and of the employer (or of each of the employers), make any amendment to which this section applies.

611 Definition of 'retirement benefits scheme'

(1) In this Chapter 'retirement benefits scheme' means, subject to the provisions of this section, a scheme for the provision of benefits consisting of or including relevant benefits, but does not include any national scheme providing such benefits.

(2) References in this Chapter to a scheme include references to a deed, agreement, series of agreements, or other arrangements providing for relevant benefits notwithstanding that it relates or they relate only to—

(a) a small number of employees, or to a single employee, or
(b) the payment of a pension starting immediately on the making of the arrangements.

(3) The Board may, if they think fit, treat a retirement benefits scheme relating to employees of two or more different classes or descriptions as being for the purposes of this Chapter two or more separate retirement benefits schemes relating respectively to such one or more of those classes or descriptions of those employees as the Board think fit.

(4) For the purposes of this section, and of any other provision of this Chapter—

(a) employees may be regarded as belonging to different classes or descriptions if they are employed by different employers; and
(b) a particular class or description of employee may consist of a single employee, or any number of employees, however small.

(5) Without prejudice to subsections (3) and (4) above, the Board may continue to treat as two different schemes, for the purposes of this Chapter, any retirement benefits scheme which, in pursuance of paragraph 5 of Schedule 3 to the Finance Act 1971 (schemes in existence before 5th April 1973), they treated, immediately before the coming into force of this Chapter, as two separate schemes for the purposes of Chapter II of Part II of the Finance Act 1970.

611A Definition of relevant statutory scheme

(1) In this Chapter any reference to a relevant statutory scheme is a reference to a statutory scheme—

(a) established before 14th March 1989, or
(b) established on or after that date and entered in the register maintained by the Board for the purposes of this section.

(2) The Board shall maintain a register for the purposes of this section and shall enter in it the relevant particulars of any statutory scheme established on or after 14th March 1989 which is reported to the Board by the authority responsible for establishing it as a scheme the provisions of which correspond with those of an approved scheme.

(3) The reference in subsection (2) above to the relevant particulars, in relation to a scheme, is a reference to—

(a) the identity of the scheme,

(b) the date on which it was established,
(c) the authority responsible for establishing it, and
(d) the date on which that authority reported the scheme to the Board.

(4) Where the Board enter the relevant particulars of a scheme in the register maintained by them for the purposes of this section, they shall inform the authority responsible for establishing the scheme of the date of the entry.

612 Other interpretative provisions and regulations for purposes of this Chapter

(1) In this Chapter, except where the context otherwise requires—

'administrator', in relation to a retirement benefits scheme, means the person or persons having the management of the scheme;

'approved scheme' means a retirement benefits scheme for the time being approved by the Board for the purposes of this Chapter;

'director' in relation to a company includes—

(a) in the case of a company the affairs of which are managed by a board of directors or similar body, a member of that board or body,
(b) in the case of a company the affairs of which are managed by a single director or similar person, that director or person,
(c) in the case of a company the affairs of which are managed by the members themselves, a member of that company;

and includes a person who is to be or has been a director;

'employee'—

(a) in relation to a company, includes any officer of the company, any director of the company and any other person taking part in the management of the affairs of the company, and
(b) in relation to any employer, includes a person who is to be or has been an employee;

and 'employer' and other cognate expressions shall be construed accordingly;

'exempt approved scheme' has the meaning given by section 592(1);

'final remuneration' means the average annual remuneration of the last three years' service;

'pension' includes annuity;

'the permitted maximum' has the meaning given by section 590(3);

'relevant benefits' means any pension, lump sum, gratuity or other like benefit given or to be given on retirement or on death, or in anticipation of retirement, or, in connection with past service, after retirement or death, or to be given on or in anticipation of or in connection with any change in the nature of the service of the employee in question, except that it does not include any benefit which is to be afforded solely by reason of the disablement by accident of a person occurring during his service or of his death by accident so occurring and for no other reason;

'remuneration' does not include—

(a) anything in respect of which tax is chargeable under Schedule E and which arises from the acquisition or disposal of shares or an interest in shares or from a right to acquire shares; or
(b) anything in respect of which tax is chargeable by virtue of section 148;

'service' means service as an employee of the employer in question and other expressions, including 'retirement', shall be construed accordingly; and

'statutory scheme' means a retirement benefits scheme established by or under any enactment—

(a) the particulars of which are set out in any enactment, or in any regulations made under any enactment, or
(b) which has been approved as an appropriate scheme by a Minister or government department (including the head of a Northern Ireland department or a Northern Ireland department).

(2) Any reference in this Chapter to the provision of relevant benefits, or of a pension, for employees of an employer includes a reference to the provision of relevant benefits or a pension by means of a contract between the administrator or the employer or the employee and a third person; and any reference to pensions or contributions paid, or payments made, under a scheme includes a reference to pensions or contributions paid, or payments made, under such a contract entered into for the purposes of the scheme.

(3) The Board may make regulations generally for the purpose of carrying the preceding provisions of this Chapter into effect.

Chapter III

Retirement annuities

618 Termination of relief under this Chapter, and transitional provisions

(1) Nothing in this Chapter shall apply in relation to—

   (a) a contract made or trust scheme established on or after 1st July 1988; or
   (b) a person by whom contributions are first paid on or after that date under a trust scheme established before that date.

(2) Subject to subsection (4) below, the terms of a contract made, or the rules of a trust scheme established, on or after 17th March 1987 and before 1st July 1988 and approved by the Board under section 620 shall have effect (notwithstanding anything in them to the contrary) as if they did not allow the payment to the individual by whom the contract is made, or an individual paying contributions under the scheme, of a lump sum exceeding £150,000 or such other sum as may for the time being be specified in an order under section 635(4).

(3) Subject to subsection (5) below, the rules of a trust scheme established before 17th March 1987 and approved by the Board under section 620 shall have effect (notwithstanding anything in them to the contrary) as if they did not allow the payment to any person first paying contributions under the scheme on or after 17th March 1987 of a lump sum such as is mentioned in subsection (2) above.

(4) Subsection (2) above shall not apply—

   (a) to a contract if, before the end of January 1988, the persons by and to whom premiums are payable under it jointly give notice to the Board that subsection (2) is not to apply; or
   (b) to a scheme if, before the end of January 1988, the trustees or other persons having the management of the scheme give notice to the Board that subsection (2) is not to apply;

and where notice is given to the Board under this subsection, the contract or scheme shall, with effect from the date with effect from which it was approved, cease to be approved.

(5) Subsection (3) above shall not apply in the case of any person paying contributions under a scheme if, before the end of January 1988, he and the trustees or other persons having the management of the scheme jointly give notice to the Board that subsection (3) is not to apply; and where notice is given to the Board, the scheme shall cease to be approved in relation to the contributor with effect from the date on which he first paid a contribution under it or (if later) the date with effect from which it was approved.

619 Exemption from tax in respect of qualifying premiums

(1) Where in any year of assessment an individual is (or would but for an insufficiency of profits or gains be) chargeable to income tax in respect of relevant earnings from any trade, profession, vocation, office or employment carried on or held by him, and pays a qualifying premium then—

(a) relief from income tax shall be given under this section in respect of that qualifying premium, but only on a claim made for the purpose, and where relief is to be so given, the amount of that premium shall, subject to the provisions of this section, be deducted from or set off against his relevant earnings for the year of assessment in which the premium is paid; and

(b) any annuity payable to the same or another individual shall be treated as earned income of the annuitant to the extent to which it is payable in return for any amount on which relief is so given.

Paragraph (b) above applies only in relation to the annuitant to whom the annuity is made payable by the terms of the annuity contract under which it is paid.

(2) Subject to the provisions of this section and section 626, the amount which may be deducted or set off in any year of assessment (whether in respect of one or more qualifying premiums, and whether or not including premiums in respect of a contract approved under section 621) shall be more than $17\frac{1}{2}\%$ of the individual's net relevant earnings for that year.

(3) Subject to the provisions of this section, the amount which

may be deducted or set off in any year of assessment in respect of qualifying premiums paid under a contract approved under section 621 (whether in respect of one or more such premiums) shall not be more than 5% of the individual's net relevant earnings for that year.

(4) An individual who pays a qualifying premium in a year of assessment (whether or not a year for which he has relevant earnings) may before the end of that year elect that the premium shall be treated as paid—

(a) in the last preceding year of assessment; or
(b) if he had no net relevant earnings in the year referred to in paragraph (a) above, in the last preceding year of assessment but one;

and where an election is made under this subsection in respect of a premium the other provisions of this chapter shall have effect as if the premium had been paid in the year specified in the election and not in the year in which it was actually paid.

(5) Where relief under this section for any year of assessment is claimed and allowed (whether or not relief then falls to be given for that year), and afterwards there is made any assessment, alteration of an assessment, or other adjustment of the claimant's liability to tax, there shall be made also such adjustments, if any, as are consequential thereon in the relief allowed or given under this section for that or any subsequent year of assessment.

(6) Where relief under this section is claimed and allowed for any year of assessment in respect of any payment, relief shall not be given in respect of it under any other provision of the Income Tax Acts for the same or a later year of assessment nor (in the case of a payment under an annuity contract) in respect of any other premium or consideration for an annuity under the same contract; and references in the Income Tax Acts to relief in respect of life assurance premiums shall not be taken to include relief under this section.

(7) If any person, for the purpose of obtaining for himself or any other person any relief from or repayment of tax under this section, knowingly makes any false statement or false representation, he shall be liable to a penalty not exceeding £3000.

620 Qualifying premiums

(1) In this Chapter 'qualifying premium' means, subject to subsection (5) below, a premium or other consideration paid by an individual—

   (a) under an annuity contract for the time being approved by the Board under this section as having for its main object the provision for the individual of a life annuity on old age, or
   (b) under a contract for the time being approved under section 621.

(2) Subject to subsections (3) and (4) below, the Board shall not approve a contract under this section unless it appears to them to satisfy the conditions that it is made by the individual with a person lawfully carrying on in the United Kingdom the business of granting annuities on human life, and that it does not—

   (a) provide for the payment by that person during the life of the individual of any sum except sums payable by way of annuity to the individual; or
   (b) provide for the annuity payable to the individual to commence before he attains the age of 60 or after he attains the age of 75; or
   (c) provide for the payment by that person of any other sums except sums payable by way of annuity to the individual's widow or widower and any sums which, in the event of no annuity becoming payable either to the individual or to a widow or widower, are payable by way of return of premiums, by way of reasonable interest on premiums or by way of bonuses out of profits; or
   (d) provide for the annuity, if any, payable to a widow or widower of the individual to be of greater annual amount than that paid or payable to the individual; or
   (e) provide for the payment of any annuity otherwise than for the life of the annuitant;

and that it does include provision securing that no annuity payable under it shall be capable in whole or in part of surrender, commutation or assignment.

(3) A contract shall not be treated as not satisfying the requirements of subsection (2) above by reason only that it—

(a) gives the individual the right to receive, by way of commutation of part of the annuity payable to him, a lump sum not exceeding three times the annual amount of the remaining part of the annuity, taking, where the annual amount is or may be different in different years, the initial annual amount, and
(b) makes any such right depend on the exercise by the individual of an election at or before the time when the annuity first becomes payable to him.

(4) The Board may, if they think fit, and subject to any conditions they think proper to impose, approve, under this section, a contract otherwise satisfying the preceding conditions, notwithstanding that the contract provides for one or more of the following matters—

(a) for the payment after the individual's death of an annuity to a dependant not the widow or widower of the individual;
(b) for the payment to the individual of an annuity commencing before he attains the age of 60, if the annuity is payable on his becoming incapable through infirmity of body or mind of carrying on his own occupation or any occupation of a similar nature for which he is trained or fitted;
(c) if the individual's occupation is one in which persons customarily retire before attaining the age of 60, for the annuity to commence before he attains that age;
(d) for the annuity payable to any person to continue for a term certain (not exceeding ten years), notwithstanding his death within that term, or for the annuity payable to any person to terminate, or be suspended, on marriage (or re-marriage) or in other circumstances;
(e) in the case of an annuity which is to continue for a term certain, for the annuity to be assignable by will, and in the event of any person dying entitled to it, for it to be assignable by his personal representatives in the distribution of the estate so as to give effect to a testamentary disposition, or to the rights of those entitled on intestacy, or to an appropriation of it to a legacy or to a share or interest in the estate.

(5) Subject to section 621(5), section 619 and subsections (1) to (4) above shall apply in relation to a contribution under a trust scheme approved by the Board as they apply in relation to a premium under an annuity contract so approved, with the modification that, for the condition as to the person with whom the contract is made, there shall be substituted a condition that the scheme—

(a) is established under the law of any part of, and administered in, the United Kingdom; and
(b) is established for the benefit of individuals engaged in or connected with a particular occupation (or one or other of a group of occupations), and for the purpose of providing retirement annuities for them, with or without subsidiary benefits for their families or dependants; and
(c) is so established under irrevocable trusts by a body of persons comprising or representing a substantial proportion of the individuals so engaged in the United Kingdom, or of those so engaged in England, Wales, Scotland or Northern Ireland;

and with the necessary adaptations of other references to the contract or the person with whom it is made.

(6) Exemption from income tax shall be allowed in respect of income derived from investments or deposits of any fund maintained for the purpose mentioned in subsection (5)(b) above under a scheme for the time being approved under that subsection.

(7) The Board may at any time, by notice given to the persons by and to whom premiums are payable under any contract for the time being approved under this section, or to the trustees or other persons having the management of any scheme so approved, withdraw that approval on such grounds and from such date as may be specified in the notice.

(8) Nothing in sections 4 and 6 of the Policies of Assurance Act 1867 (obligations of assurance companies in respect of notices of assignment of policies of life assurance) shall be taken to apply to any contract approved under this section.

(9) For the purposes of any provision applying this subsection 'approved annuities' means—

(a) annuities under contracts approved by the Board under this section, being annuities payable wholly in return for premiums or other consideration paid by a person who (when the premiums or other consideration are or is payable) is, or would but for an insufficiency of profits or gains be, chargeable to tax in respect of relevant earnings from a trade, profession, vocation, office or employment carried on or held by him; and
(b) annuities or lump sums under approved personal pension arrangements within the meaning of Chapter IV of this Part.

621 Other approved contracts

(1) The Board may approve under this section—

(a) a contract the main object of which is the provision of an annuity for the wife or husband of the individual, or for any one or more dependants of the individual,
(b) a contract the sole object of which is the provision of a lump sum on the death of the individual before he attains the age of 75.

(2) The Board shall not approve the contract unless it appears to them that it is made by the individual with a person lawfully carrying on in the United Kingdom the business of granting annuities on human life.

(3) The Board shall not approve a contract under subsection (1)(a) above unless it appears to them to satisfy all the following conditions, that is to say—

(a) that any annuity payable to the wife or husband or dependant of the individual commences on the death of the individual;
(b) that any annuity payable to the individual commences at a time after the individual attains the age of 60, and, unless the individual's annuity is one to commence on the death of a person to whom an annuity would be payable under the contract if that person survived the individual, cannot commence after the time when the individual attains the age of 75;
(c) that the contract does not provide for the payment by the person contracting with the individual of any sum, other than any annuity payable to the individual's wife or husband or dependant, or to the individual, except, in the event of no annuity becoming payable under the contract, any sums payable by way of return of premiums, by way of reasonable interest on premiums or by way of bonuses out of profits;
(d) that the contract does not provide for the payment of any annuity otherwise than for the life of the annuitant;
(e) that the contract does include provision securing that no annuity payable under it shall be capable in whole or in part of surrender, cummutation or assignment.

(4) The Board may, if they think fit, and subject to any conditions that they think proper to impose, approve a contract under subsection (1)(a) above notwithstanding that, in one or more respects,

they are not satisfied that the contract complies with the provisions of paragraphs (a) to (e) of subsection (3) above.

(5) The main purpose of a trust scheme, or part of a trust scheme, within section 620(5) may be to provide annuities for the wives, husbands and dependants of the individuals, or lump sums payable on death and in that case—

(a) approval of the trust scheme shall be subject to subsections (1) to (4) above with any necessary modifications, and not subject to section 620(2) to (4);
(b) the provisions of this Chapter shall apply to the scheme or part of the scheme when duly approved as they apply to a contract approved under this section; and
(c) section 620(6) shall apply to an duly approved trust scheme, or part of a trust scheme.

(6) Except as otherwise provided in this Chapter (and in particular except in section 620), any reference in the Tax Acts to a contract or scheme approved under that section shall include a reference to a contract or scheme approved under this section.

622 Substituted retirement annuity contracts

(1) The Board may, if they think fit, and subject to any conditions they think proper to impose, approve an annuity contract under section 620 notwithstanding that the contract provides that the individual by whom it is made—

(a) may agree with the person with whom it is made that a sum representing the value of the individual's accrued rights under it should be applied as the premium or other consideration either under another annuity contract made between them and approved by the Board under section 620, or under personal pension arrangements made between them and approved by the Board under Chapter IV of this Part; or
(b) may require the person with whom it is made to pay such a sum to such other person as the individual may specify, to be applied by that other person as the premium or other consideration either under an annuity contract made between the individual and him and approved by the Board under section 620, or under personal pension arrangements made between the individual and him and approved by the Board under Chapter IV of this Part.

(2) References in subsection (1) above to the individual by whom the contract is made include references to any widow, widower or dependant having accrued rights under the contract.

(3) Where in pursuance of any such provision as is mentioned in subsection (1) above of an annuity contract approved under section 620, or of a corresponding provision of a contract approved under section 621(1)(a), a sum representing the value of accrued rights under one contract ('the original contract') is paid by way of premium or other consideration under another contract ('the substituted contract'), any annuity payable under the substituted contract shall be treated as earned income of the annuitant to the same extent that an annuity payable under the original contract would have been so treated.

623 Relevant earnings

(2) 'Relevant earnings', in relation to any individual, means, for the purposes of this Chapter, any income of his chargeable to tax for the year of assessment in question, being either—

(a) income arising in respect of remuneration from an office or employment held by him other than a pensionable office or employment; or
(b) income from any property which is attached to or forms part of the emoluments of any such office or employment held by him; or
(c) income which is chargeable under Schedule D and is immediately derived by him from the carrying on or exercise by him of his trade, profession or vocation either as an individual or, in the case of a partnership, as a partner personally acting therein; or
(d) income treated as earned income by virtue of section 529;

but does not include any remuneration as director of a company whose income consists wholly or mainly of investment income (that is to say, income which, if the company were an individual, would not be earned income), being a company of which he is a controlling director.

(3) For the purposes of this Chapter, an office or employment is a pensionable office or employment if, and only if, service in it is service to which a sponsored superannuation scheme relates (not being a scheme under which the benefits provided in respect of that service are limited to a lump sum payable on the termination

of the service through death or disability before the age of 75 or some lower age); but references to a pensionable office or employment apply whether or not the duties are performed wholly or partly in the United Kingdom or the holder is chargeable to tax in respect of it.

(4) Service in an office or employment shall not for the purposes of subsection (3) above be treated as service to which a sponsored superannuation scheme relates by reason only of the fact that the holder of the office or employment might (though he does not) participate in the scheme by exercising or refraining from exercising an option open to him by virtue of that service.

(5) For the purposes of relief under section 619, an individual's relevant earnings are those earnings before giving effect to any capital allowances, other than deductions allowable in computing profits or gains, but after taking into account the amounts on which charges fall to be made under any of the Capital Allowances Acts; and references to income in the following provisions of this section (other than references to total income) shall be construed similarly.

(6) Subject to the following provisions of this section 'net relevant earnings' means, in relation to an individual, the amount of his relevant earnings for the year of assessment in question, less the amount of any deductions falling to be made from the relevant earnings in computing for the purposes of income tax his total income for that year, being—

  (a) deductions which but for section 74(m), (p) or (q) could be made in computing his profits or gains; or
  (b) deductions in respect of relief under Schedule 9 of the Finance Act 1981 (stock relief); or
  (c) deductions in respect of losses or capital allowances arising from activities profits or gains of which would be included in computing relevant earnings of the individual.

(7) Where in any year of assessment for which an individual claims and is allowed relief under section 619—

  (a) there falls to be made in computing the total income of the individual a deduction in respect of any such loss or allowance of the individual as is mentioned in subsection (6)(c) above; and
  (b) the deduction or part of it falls to be so made from income other than relevant earnings,

the amount of the deduction made from that other income shall be treated as reducing the individual's net relevant earnings for subsequent years of assessment (being deducted as far as may be from those of the immediately following year, whether or not he claims or is entitled to claim relief under this section for that year, and so far as it cannot be so deducted, then from those of the next year, and so on).

(8) An individual's net relevant earnings for any year of assessment are to be computed without regard to any relief which falls to be given for that year under section 619 to that individual.

(9) An individual's relevant earnings, in the case of partnership profits, shall be taken to be his share of the partnership income, estimated in accordance with the Income Tax Acts, but the amount to be included in respect of those earnings in arriving at his net relevant earnings shall be his share of that income after making there from all such deductions (if any) in respect of payments made by the partnership or of relief given to the partnership under Schedule 9 of the Finance Act 1981 (stock relief) or in respect of capital allowances falling to be made to the partnership as would be made in computing the tax payable in respect of that income.

624 Sponsored superannuation schemes and controlling directors

(1) In section 623 'a sponsored superannuation scheme' means a scheme or arrangement—

- (a) relating to service in particular offices or employments, and
- (b) having for its object or one of its objects to make provision in respect of persons serving in those offices or employments against future retirement or partial retirement, against future termination of service through death or disability, or against similar matters,

being a scheme or arrangement under which any part of the cost of the provision so made is or has been borne otherwise than by those persons by reason of their service (whether it is the cost or part of the cost of the benefits provided, or of paying premiums or other sums in order to provide those benefits, or of administering or instituting the scheme or arrangement).

(2) For the purposes of subsection (1) above a person shall be treated as bearing by reason of his service the cost of any payment made or agreed to be made in respect of his service, if that payment

or the agreement to make it is treated under the Income Tax Acts as increasing his income, or would be so treated if he were chargeable to tax under Case I of Schedule E in respect of his emoluments from that service.

(3) In section 623 'controlling director' means a director of a company, the directors of which have a controlling interest in the company, who is the beneficial owner of, or able either directly or through the medium of other companies or by any other indirect means to control, more than 5 per cent of the ordinary share capital of the company; and for the purposes of this definition—
'company' means one within the Companies Act 1985 or the Companies (Northern Ireland) Order 1986; and
'director' means—

(a) in relation to a body corporate the affairs of which are managed by a board of directors or similar body, a member of that board or similar body;
(b) in relation to a body corporate the affairs of which are managed by a single director or similar person, that director or person;
(c) in relation to a body corporate the affairs of which are managed by the members themselves, a member of the body corporate;

and includes any person who is to be or has been a director.

625 Carry-forward of unused relief under section 619

(1) Where—

(a) in any year of assessment an individual is (or would but for an insufficiency of profits or gains be) chargeable to income tax in respect of relevant earnings from any trade, profession, vocation, office or employment carried on or held by him, but
(b) there is unused relief for that year, that is to say, an amount which could have been deducted from or set off against the individual's relevant earnings for that year under subsection (1) of section 619 if—
  (i) he had paid a qualifying premium in that year; or
  (ii) the qualifying premium or premiums paid by him in that year had been greater;

then, subject to section 655(1)(b), relief may be given under that section, up to the amount of the unused relief, in respect of so much of any qualifying premium or premiums paid by the individual in any of the next six years of assessment as exceeds the maximum applying for that year under subsection (2) of that section.

(2) Relief by virtue of this section shall be given for an earlier year rather than a later year, the unused relief taken into account in giving relief for any year being deducted from that available for giving relief in subsequent years and unused relief derived from an earlier year being exhausted before unused relief derived from a later year.

(3) Where a relevant assessment to tax in respect of a year of assessment becomes final and conclusive more than six years after the end of that year and there is an amount of unused relief for that year which results from the making of the assessment—

(a) that amount shall not be available for giving relief by virtue of this section for any of the six years following that year, but
(b) the individual may, within the period of six months beginning with the date on which the assessment becomes final and conclusive, elect that relief shall be given under section 619, up to that amount, in respect of so much of any qualifying premium or premiums paid by him within that period as exceeds the maximum applying under subsection (2) of that section for the year of assessment in which they were paid;

and to the extent to which relief in respect of any premium or premiums is given by virtue of this subsection it shall not be given by virtue of subsection (1) above.

(4) In this section 'a relevant assessment to tax' means an assessment on the individual's relevant earnings or on the profits or gains of a partnership from which the individual derives relevant earnings.

626 Modification of section 619 in relation to persons over 50

In the case of an individual whose age at the beginning of a year of assessment is within a range specified in the first column of the Table set out below, section 619(2) shall have effect for that year with the substitution for the reference to $17\frac{1}{2}$ per cent of a reference to the relevant percentage specified in the second column of the Table.

TABLE

Age range	Percentage
51 to 55	20
56 to 60	22½
61 or more	27½

627 Lloyd's underwriters

(1) Where for any year of assessment an individual—

   (a) is chargeable to income tax in respect of relevant earnings derived from Lloyd's underwriting activities; and
   (b) there is an amount of unused relief attributable to those earnings,

the individual may, subject to subsection (2) below, elect that there shall be treated as paid in that year any qualifying premium paid by him in the next year of assessment but two.

(2) An election under this section shall not have effect in relation to so much of any qualifying premium as exceeds the amount of unused relief referred to in subsection (1)(b) above.

(3) Any election under this section shall be made before the end of the year of assessment in which the premium is paid.

(4) Where an election is made under this section the provisions of this Chapter, other than section 619(4), shall have effect as if the premium or, as the case may be, the part of the premium in question had been paid in the year specified in the election and not in the year in which it was actually paid.

(5) In this section—
'unused relief' has the same meaning as in section 625; and
'relevant earnings derived from Lloyd's underwriting activities' means relevant earnings as an underwriting member of Lloyd's or by way of commission calculated by reference to the profits of Lloyd's underwriting business.

628 Partnership retirement annuities

(1) Where a person ('the former partner') has ceased to be a member of a partnership on retirement, because of age or ill-health or on death and, under—

(a) the partnership agreement; or
(b) an agreement replacing the partnership agreement or supplementing it or supplementing an agreement replacing it; or
(c) an agreement made with an individual who acquires the whole or part of the business carried on by the partnership;

annual payments are made for the benefit of the former partner or a widow, widower or dependant of the former partner and are for the purposes of income tax income of the person for whose benefit they are made, the payments shall be treated as earned income of that person, except to the extent that they exceed the limit specified in subsection (2) below.

(2) The limit mentioned in subsection (1) above is 50 per cent of the average of the amounts which, in the best three of the relevant years of assessment, were the former partner's shares of the relevant profits or gains; and for this purpose—

(a) the former partner's share in any year of the relevant profits or gains is, subject to subsection (3) below, so much of the relevant profits or gains as fell to be included in a return of his income for that year; and
(b) the relevant profits or gains are the profits or gains of any trade, profession or vocation on which the partnership or any other partnership of which the former partner was a member was assessed to income tax; and
(c) the relevant years of assessment are the last seven years of assessment in which he was required to devote substantially the whole of his time to acting as a partner in the partnership or those partnerships; and
(d) the best three of the relevant years of assessment are those three of them in which the amounts of his shares of the relevant profits were highest;

but where, in any of the relevant years, the circumstances were such that any of the profits or gains of a partnership were not assessable to income tax, paragraphs (a), (b) and (d) above shall apply as they would apply had those profits or gains been so assessable.

(3) If the retail prices index for the month of December in the last of the seven years referred to in paragraph (c) of subsection (2) above is higher than it was for the month of December in any of the other years referred to in that paragraph, the amount which, for that other year, was the former partner's share of the relevant profits or gains shall be treated for the purposes of that

subsection as increased by the same percentage as the percentage increase in that index.

(4) If the retail prices index for the month of December preceding a year of assessment after that in which the former partner ceased to be a member of the partnership is higher than it was for the month of December in the year of assessment in which he ceased to be such a member, the amount which under subsection (2) above is the limit for the first-mentioned year of assessment shall be treated as increased by the same percentage as the percentage increase in that index.

(5) Where the former partner ceased to be a member of the partnership before the year 1974-75, subsection (4) above shall have effect as if he had ceased to be a member in that year.

629 Annuity premiums of Ministers and other officers

(1) For the purposes of this Chapter so much of any salary which—

   (a) is payable to the holder of a qualifying office who is also a Member of the House of Commons, and
   (b) is payable for a period in respect of which the holder is not a participant in relation to that office in arrangements contained in the Parliamentary pension scheme but is a participant in relation to his membership of the House of Commons in any such arrangements, or for any part of such a period,

as is equal to the difference between a Member's pensionable salary and the salary which (in accordance with any such resolution as is mentioned in subsection (3)(a) below) is payable to him as a Member holding that qualifying office shall be treated as remuneration from the office of Member and not from the qualifying office.

(2) In this section—

'Member's pensionable salary' means a Member's ordinary salary under any resolution of the House of Commons which, being framed otherwise than as an expression of opinion, is for the time being in force relating to the remuneration of Members or, if the resolution provides for a Member's ordinary salary thereunder to be treated for pension purposes as being at a higher rate, a notional yearly salary at that higher rate;

'qualifying office' means an office mentioned in section 2(2)(b), (c) or (d) of the Parliamentary and other Pensions Act 1987;

'the Parliamentary pension scheme' has the same meaning as in that Act;

and without prejudice to the power conferred by virtue of paragraph 13 of Schedule 1 to that Act, regulations under section 2 of that Act may make provision specifying the circumstances in which a person is to be regarded for the purposes of this section as being or not being a participant in relation to his Membership of the House of Commons, or in relation to any office, in arrangements contained in the Parliamentary pension scheme.

(3) In subsection (2) above 'a Member's ordinary salary', in relation to any resolution of the House of Commons, means—

(a) if the resolution provides for salary to be paid to Members at different rates according to whether or not they are holders of particular offices, or are in receipt of salaries or pensions as the holders or former holders of particular offices, a Member's yearly salary at the higher or highest rate; and
(b) in any other case, a Member's yearly salary at the rate specified in or determined under the resolution.

Chapter IV

Personal pension schemes

Preliminary

630 Interpretation

In this Chapter—

'approved'—

(a) in relation to a scheme, means approved by the Board under this Chapter; and
(b) in relation to arrangements, means made in accordance with a scheme which is for the time being, and was when the arrangements were made, an approved scheme;

but does not refer to cases in which approval has been withdrawn;

'authorised insurance company' means either—

(a) a person authorised under section 3 or 4 of the Insurance Companies Act 1982 to carry on long term business and acting through a branch or office in the United Kingdom; or

(b) a society registered as a friendly society under the Friendly Societies Act 1974 or the Friendly Societies Act (Northern Ireland) 1970;

'member', in relation to a personal pension scheme, means an individual who makes arrangements in accordance with the scheme;

'personal pension arrangements' means arrangements made by an individual in accordance with a personal pension scheme;

'personal pension scheme' means a scheme whose sole purpose is the provision of annuities or lump sums under arrangements made by individuals in accordance with the scheme;

'scheme administrator' means the person referred to in section 638(1);

and references to an employee or to an employer include references to the holder of an office or to the person under whom the office is held.

631 Approval of schemes

(1) An application to the Board for their approval of a personal pension scheme shall be in such form, shall contain such information, and shall be accompanied by such documents, in such form, as the Board may prescribe.

(2) The Board may at their discretion grant or refuse an application for approval of a personal pension scheme, but their discretion shall be subject to the restrictions set out in sections 632 to 638.

(3) The Board shall give notice to the applicant of the grant or refusal of an application; and in the case of a refusal the notice shall state the grounds for the refusal.

(4) If an amendment is made to an approved scheme without being approved by the Board, their approval of the scheme shall cease to have effect.

Restrictions on approval
632 Establishment of schemes

(1) The Board shall not approve a personal pension scheme established by any person other than—

- (a) a person who is authorised under Chapter III of Part I of the Financial Services Act 1986 to carry on investment business and who carries on business of a kind mentioned in subsection (2) below;
- (b) a building society within the meaning of the Building Societies Act 1986;
- (bb) a pension company within the meaning of the Building Societies (Designation of Pension Companies) Order 1987 which is an associate of a building society within the meaning of section 18(17) of the Building Societies Act 1986;
- (c) an institution authorised under the Banking Act 1987;
- (cc) a body corporate which is a subsidiary or holding company of an institution authorised under the Banking Act 1987, or is a subsidiary of the holding company of such an institution;
- (d) a recognised bank or licensed institution within the meaning of the Banking Act 1979.

(2) The kinds of business referred to in subsection (1)(a) above are—

- (a) issuing insurance policies or annuity contracts;
- (b) managing unit trust schemes authorised under section 78(1) of the Financial Services Act 1986.

(2A) In subsection 1(cc) above 'holding company' and 'subsidiary' are to be construed in accordance with section 736 of the Companies Act 1985 or Article 4 of the Companies (Northern Ireland) Order 1986.

(3) Subsection (1) above shall not apply in relation to a scheme approved by the Board by virtue of section 620(5) if it was established before 1st July 1988.

(4) The Treasury may by order amend this section as it has effect for the time being.

633 Scope of benefits

(1) The Board shall not approve a personal pension scheme which makes provision for any benefit other than—

(a) the payment of an annuity satisfying the conditions in section 634;
(b) the payment to a member of a lump sum satisfying the conditions in section 635;
(c) the payment after the death of a member of an annuity satisfying the conditions in section 636;
(d) the payment on the death of a member of a lump sum satisfying either the conditions in section 637(1) or those in section 637(2).

(2) Subsection (1) above shall not prevent the approval of a scheme which makes provision for insurance against a risk relating to the non-payment of contributions.

634 Annuity to member

(1) The annuity must be payable by an authorised insurance company which may be chosen by the member.

(2) Subject to subsection (3) below, the annuity must not commence before the member attains the age of 50 or after he attains the age of 75.

(3) The annuity may commence before the member attains the age of 50 if—

(a) it is payable on his becoming incapable through infirmity of body or mind of carrying on his own occupation or any occupation of a similar nature for which he is trained or fitted; or
(b) the Board are satisfied that his occupation is one in which persons customarily retire before that age.

(4) Subject to subsection (5) below, the annuity must be payable to the member for his life.

(5) The annuity may continue for a term certain not exceeding ten years, notwithstanding the member's death within that term; and for this purpose an annuity shall be regarded as payable for a term certain notwithstanding that it may terminate, after the

death of the member and before expiry of that term, on the happening of any of the following—

(a) the marriage of the annuitant;
(b) his attaining the age of 18;
(c) the later of his attaining that age and ceasing to be in full-time education.

(6) The annuity must not be capable of assignment or surrender, except that an annuity for a term certain may be assigned by will or by the annuitant's personal representatives in the distribution of his estate so as to give effect to a testamentary disposition, or to the rights of those entitled on an intestacy, or to an appropriation of it to a legacy or to a share or interest in the estate.

635 Lump sum to member

(1) The lump sum must be payable only if the member so elects on or before the date on which an annuity satisfying the conditions in section 634 is first payable to him under the arrangements made in accordance with the scheme.

(2) The lump sum must be payable when that annuity is first payable.

(3) The lump sum must not exceed one quarter of the difference between

(a) the total value, at the time when the lump sum is paid, of the benefits provided for by the arrangements made by the member in accordance with the scheme, and
(b) the value, at that time, of such of the member's rights under the scheme as are protected rights for the purposes of the Social Security Act 1986 or the Social Security (Northern Ireland) Order 1986.

(5) The right to payment of the lump sum must not be capable of assignment or surrender.

636 Annuity after death of member

(1) The annuity must be payable by an authorised insurance company which may be chosen by the member or by the annuitant.

(2) The annuity must be payable to the surviving spouse of the

member, or to a person who was at the member's death a dependant of his.

(3) The aggregate annual amount (or, if that amount varies, the aggregate of the initial annual amounts) of all annuities to which this section applies and which are payable under the same personal pension arrangements shall not exceed—

(a) where before his death the member was in receipt of an annuity under the arrangements, the annual amount (or, if it varied, the highest annual amount) of that annuity; or
(b) where paragraph (a) does not apply, the highest annual amount of the annuity that would have been payable under the arrangements to the member (ignoring any entitlement of his to commute part of it for a lump sum) if it had vested on the day before his death.

(4) Subject to subsections (5) to (9) below, the annuity must be payable for the life of the annuitant.

(5) Where the annuity is payable to the surviving spouse of the member and at the time of the member's death the surviving spouse is under the age of 60, the annuity may be deferred to a time not later than—

(a) the time when the surviving spouse attains that age; or
(b) where the member's annuity is payable to the surviving spouse for a term certain as mentioned in section 634(5) and the surviving spouse attains the age of 60 before the time when the member's annuity terminates, that time.

(6) The annuity may cease to be payable on the marriage of the annuitant.

(7) Where the annuity is payable to the surviving spouse of the member, it may cease before the death of the surviving spouse if—

(a) the member was survived by one or more dependants under the age of 18 and at the time of the member's death the surviving spouse was under the age of 45; and
(b) at some time before the surviving spouse attains that age no such dependant remains under the age of 18.

(8) Where the annuity is payable to a person who is under the age of 18 when it is first payable, it must cease to be payable either—

(a) on his attaining that age; or
(b) on the later of his attaining that age and ceasing to be in full-time education,

unless he was a dependant of the member otherwise than by reason only that he was under the age of 18. .

(9) The annuity may continue for a term certain not exceeding ten years, notwithstanding the original annuitant's death within that term; and for this purpose an annuity shall be regarded as payable for a term certain notwithstanding that it may terminate, after the death of the original annuitant and before the expiry of that term, on the happening of any of the following—

(a) the marriage of the annuitant to whom it is payable;
(b) his attaining the age of 18;
(c) the later of his attaining that age and ceasing to be in full-time education.

(10) The annuity must not be capable of assignment or surrender, except that an annuity for a term certain may be assigned by will or by the annuitant's personal representatives in the distribution of his estate so as to give effect to a testamentary disposition, or to the rights of those entitled on an intestacy, or to an appropriation of it to a legacy or to a share or interest in the estate.

637 Lump sum on death of member

(1) The lump sum—

(a) must be payable by an authorised insurance company; and
(b) must be payable on the death of the member before he attains the age of 75.

(2) The lump sum—

(a) must be payable only if no annuity satisfying the conditions in either section 634 or section 636 has become payable; and
(b) subject to subsection (3) below, must represent no more than the return of contributions together with reasonable interest on contributions or bonuses out of profits.

(3) To the extent that contributions are invested in units under a unit trust scheme, the lump sum referred to in subsection (2) above may represent the sale or redemption price of the units.

638 Other restrictions on approval

(1) The Board shall not approve a personal pension scheme unless they are satisfied that there is a person resident in the United Kingdom who will be responsible for the management of the scheme.

(2) The Board shall not approve a personal pension scheme unless it makes such provision for the making, acceptance and application of transfer payments as satisfies any requirements imposed by or under regulations made by the Board.

(3) The Board shall not approve a personal pension scheme unless it makes provision, in relation to arrangements made in accordance with the scheme, for ensuring that—

   (a) the aggregate amount of the contributions that may be made in a year of assessment by the member and an employer of his under the arrangements, together with the aggregate amounts of such contributions under other approved personal pension arrangements made by that member, does not exceed the permitted maximum for that year; and
   (b) any excess is repaid to the member to the extent of his contributions and otherwise to his employer.

(4) In subsection (3) above 'the permitted maximum' for a year of assessment means an amount equal to the aggregate of—

   (a) the relevant percentage of the member's net relevant earnings for the year; and
   (b) so much of any relief given under section 639(1) for that year as is given by virtue of section 642;

and references in subsection (3) to contributions by the member do not include references to contributions treated by virtue of section 649(3) as paid by him.

(5) In subsection (4) above 'the relevant percentage' means 17.5% or, in a case where section 640(2) applies, the relevant percentage there specified.

(6) The Board shall not approve a personal pension scheme which permits the acceptance of contributions other than—

(a) contributions by members;
(b) contributions by employers of members;
(c) minimum contributions paid by the Secretary of State under Part I of the Social Security Act 1986 or by the Department of Health and Social Services for Northern Ireland under Part II of the Social Security (Northern Ireland) Order 1986.

(7) The Board shall not approve a personal pension scheme which permits the acceptance of minimum contributions paid as mentioned in subsection (6)(c) above in respect of an individual's service as director of a company, if his emoluments as such are within section 644(5).

(8) A personal pension scheme which permits the acceptance of minimum contributions paid as mentioned in subsection (6)(c) above in respect of an individual's service in an office or employment to which section 645 applies may be approved by the Board only if—

(a) the scheme does not permit the acceptance of contributions from the individual or from the person who is his employer in relation to that office or employment; or
(b) at the time when the minimum contributions are paid the individual is not serving in an office or employment to which section 645 applies.

Tax reliefs
639 Member's contributions

(1) A contribution paid by an individual under approved personal pension arrangements made by him shall, subject to the provisions of this Chapter, be deducted from or set off against any relevant earnings of his for the year of assessment in which the payment is made.

Except where subsections (2) to (4) below apply, relief under this subsection in respect of a contribution shall be given only on a claim made for the purpose.

(2) In such cases and subject to such conditions as the Board may prescribe in regulations, relief under subsection (1) above shall be given in accordance with subsections (3) and (4) below.

(3) An individual who is entitled to such relief in respect of a contribution may deduct from the contribution when he pays it, and may retain, an amount equal to income tax at the basic rate on the contribution.

(4) The scheme administrator—

(a) shall accept the amount paid after the deduction in discharge of the individual's liability to the same extent as if the deduction had not been made; and
(b) may recover an amount equal to the deduction from the Board.

(5) Regulations under this section may make provision for carrying subsections (3) and (4) above into effect and, without prejudice to the generality of that, may provide

(a) for the manner in which claims for the recovery of a sum under subsection (4)(b) may be made;
(b) for the giving of such information, in such form, as may be prescribed by or under the regulations;
(c) for the inspection by persons authorised by the Board of books, documents and other records.

(6) Where relief under this section for any year of assessment is claimed and allowed (whether or not it then falls to be given for that year), and afterwards an assessment, alteration of an assessment, or other adjustment of the claimant's liability to tax is made, there shall also be made such consequential adjustments in the relief allowed or given under this section for that or any subsequent year as are appropriate.

(7) Where relief under this section is claimed and allowed for any year of assessment in respect of a contribution, relief shall not be given in respect of it under any other provision of the Income Tax Acts for the same or any subsequent year, nor (in the case of a contribution under an annuity contract) in respect of any other premium or consideration for an annuity under the same contract.

(8) References in the Income Tax Acts to relief in respect of life assurance premiums shall not be taken to include relief under this section.

640 Maximum amount of deductions

(1) The maximum amount that may be deducted or set off in any year of assessment by virtue of section 639(1) shall be 17.5% of the individual's net relevant earnings for that year.

(2) In the case of an individual whose age at the beginning of the year of assessment is within a range specified in the first column of the following table, subsection (1) above shall have effect with the substitution for 17.5% of the relevant percentage specified in the second column.

TABLE

Age range	Percentage
36 to 45	20
46 to 50	25
51 to 55	30
56 to 60	35
61 or more	40

(3) Without prejudice to subsection (1) above, the maximum amount that may be deducted or set off in any year of assessment in respect of contributions paid by an individual to secure benefits satisfying the conditions in section 637(1) shall be 5% of the individual's net relevant earnings for that year.

(4) Where personal pension arrangements are made by an employee whose employer makes contributions under the arrangements, the maximum amount that may be deducted or set off in any year of assessment shall be reduced by the amount of the employer's contributions in the year.

(5) Any minimum contributions treated by virtue of section 649(3) as paid by the individual in respect of whom they are paid shall be disregarded for the purposes of this section.

640A Earnings cap

(1) In arriving at an individual's net relevant earnings for a year of assessment for the purposes of section 640 above, any excess of what would be his net relevant earnings for the year (apart from this subsection) over the allowable maximum for the year shall be disregarded.

(2) In subsection (1) above 'the allowable maximum' means, as

regards a particular year of assessment, the figure found for that year by virtue of subsections (3) and (4) below.

(3) For the year of assessment 1989–90 the figure is £60,000.

(4) For the year of assessment 1990–91 and any subsequent year of assessment the figure is the figure found for that year, for the purposes of section 590C, by virtue of section 590C(4) and (5).

641 Carry-back of contributions

(1) An individual who pays a contribution under approved personal pension arrangements in a year of assessment (whether or not a year for which he has relevant earnings) may elect that the contribution, or part of it, shall be treated as paid—

(a) in the year of assessment preceding that year; or
(b) if he had no net relevant earnings in that preceding year of assessment, in the year of assessment before that.

(2) Where for any year of assessment an individual—

(a) has relevant earnings as an underwriting member of Lloyd's or by way of commission calculated by reference to the profits of Lloyd's underwriting business; and
(b) there is an amount of unused relief attributable to those earnings,

the individual may elect that there shall be treated as paid in that year so much of any contributions paid by him under approved personal pension arrangements in the next year of assessment but two as does not exceed the amount of the unused relief.

(3) Subject to section 655(2), references in subsection (2) above to an amount of unused relief attributable to the earnings mentioned in subsection (2)(a) are to an amount which could have been deducted from or set off against those earnings under section 639(1) if—

(a) the individual had paid contributions under approved personal pension arrangements in the year of assessment for which he has the earnings; or
(b) any such contributions paid by him in that year had been greater.

(4) An election under this section must be made not later than three months after the end of the year of assessment in which the contributions treated as paid in another year are actually paid.

(5) Where an election is made under this section in respect of a contribution or part of a contribution, the other provisions of this Chapter shall have effect as if the contribution or part had been paid in the year specified in the election and not in the year in which it was actually paid.

642 Carry-forward of relief

(1) Where—

  (a) for any year of assessment an individual has relevant earnings from any trade, profession, vocation, office or employment carried on or held by him, and
  (b) there is an amount of unused relief for that year,

relief may be given under section 639(1), up to the amount of the unused relief, in respect of so much of any contributions paid by him under approved personal pension arrangements in any of the next six years of assessment as exceeds the maximum applying for that year under section 640.

(2) In this section, references to an amount of unused relief for any year are to an amount which could have been deducted from or set off against the individual's relevant earnings for that year under section 639(1) if—

  (a) the individual had paid contributions under approved personal pension arrangements in that year; or
  (b) any such contributions paid by him in that year had been greater.

(3) Relief by virtue of this section shall be given for an earlier year rather than a later year, the unused relief taken into account in giving relief for any year being deducted from that available for giving relief in subsequent years and unused relief derived from an earlier year being exhausted before unused relief derived from a later year.

(4) Where a relevant assessment to tax in respect of a year of assessment becomes final and conclusive more than six years after

the end of that year and there is an amount of unused relief for that year which results from the making of the assessment—

   (a) that amount shall not be available for giving relief by virtue of this section for any of the six years following that year; but
   (b) the individual may, within the period of six months beginning with the date on which the assessment becomes final and conclusive, elect that relief shall be given under section 639(1), up to that amount, in respect of so much of any contributions paid by him under approved personal pension arrangements within that period as exceeds the maximum applying under section 640 for the year of assessment in which they are paid;

and to the extent to which relief in respect of any contributions is given by virtue of this subsection it shall not be given by virtue of subsection (1) above.

(5) In this section 'a relevant assessment to tax' means an assessment on the individual's relevant earnings or on the profits or gains of a partnership from which the individual derives relevant earnings.

643 Employer's contributions and personal pension income etc

(1) Where contributions are paid by an employer under approved personal pension arrangements made by his employee, those contributions shall not be regarded as emoluments of the employment chargeable to tax under Schedule E.

(2) Income derived by a person from investments or deposits held by him for the purposes of an approved personal pension scheme shall be exempt from income tax.

(3) An annuity payable under approved personal pension arrangements shall be treated as earned income of the annuitant.

(4) Subsection (3) above applies only in relation to the annuitant to whom the annuity is made payable by the terms of the arrangements.

644 Meaning of 'relevant earnings'

(1) In this Chapter, 'relevant earnings', in relation to an individual, means any income of his which is chargeable to tax for the year of assessment in question and is within subsection (2) below.

(2) Subject to subsections (3) to (6F) below, income is within this subsection if it is—

  (a) emoluments chargeable under Schedule E from an office or employment held by the individual;
  (b) income from any property which is attached to or forms part of the emoluments of an office or employment held by him;
  (c) income which is chargeable under Schedule D and is immediately derived by him from the carrying on or exercise by him of his trade, profession or vocation (either as an individual or as a partner acting personally in a partnership);
  (d) income treated as earned income by virtue of section 529.

(3) Where section 645 applies to an office or employment held by the individual, neither emoluments from the office or employment nor income from any property which is attached to it or forms part of its emoluments are within subsection (2) above.

(4) The following are not income within subsection (2) above—

  (a) anything in respect of which tax is chargeable under Schedule E and which arises from the acquisition or disposal of shares or an interest in shares or from a right to acquire shares;
  (b) anything in respect of which tax is chargeable by virtue of section 148.

(5) Emoluments of an individual as director of a company are not income within subsection (2) above if—

  (a) the income of the company consists wholly or mainly of investment income; and
  (b) the individual, either alone or together with any other persons who are or have been at any time directors of the company, controls the company;

and section 840 shall apply for the purposes of this subsection.

(6) For the purposes of subsection (5) above—

'director' includes any person occupying the position of director by whatever name called; and
'investment income' means income which, if the company were an individual, would not be earned income.

(6A) Emoluments of an individual as an employee of a company are not income within subsection (2) above if—

(a) he is a controlling director of the company at any time in the year of assessment in question or has been a controlling director of the company at any time in the ten years immediately preceding that year of assessment, and
(b) any of subsections (6B) to (6E) below applies in his case.

(6B) This subsection applies in the case of the individual if—

(a) at any time in the year of assessment in question he is in receipt of benefits under a relevant superannuation scheme, and
(b) the benefits are payable in respect of past service with the company.

(6C) This subsection applies in the case of the individual if—

(a) at any time in the year of assessment in question he is in receipt of benefits under a personal pension scheme,
(b) the scheme has received a transfer payment relating to him from a relevant superannuation scheme, and
(c) the transfer payment is in respect of past service with the company.

(6D) This subsection applies in the case of the individual if—

(a) at any time in the year of assessment in question he is in receipt of benefits under a relevant superannuation scheme,
(b) the benefits are payable in respect of past service with another company,
(c) the emoluments are for a period during which the company mentioned in subsection (6A)) above has carried on a trade or business previously carried on by the other company, and
(d) the other company carried on the trade or business at any time during the period of service in respect of which the benefits are payable.

(6E) This subsection applies in the case of the individual if—

(a) at any time in the year of assessment in question he is in receipt of benefits under a personal pension scheme,
(b) the scheme has received a transfer payment relating to him from a relevant superannuation scheme,
(c) the transfer payment is in respect of past service with another company,
(d) the emoluments are for a period during which the company mentioned in subsection (6A) above has carried on a trade or business previously carried on by the other company, and
(e) the other company carried on the trade or business at any time during the period of service in respect of which the transfer payment was made.

(6F) For the purposes of subsections (6A) to (6E) above—

(a) a person is a controlling director of a company if he is a director (as defined by section 612(1)), and he is within paragraph (b) of section 417(5), in relation to the company;
(b) 'relevant superannuation scheme' has the same meaning as in section 645(1);
(c) references to benefits payable in respect of past service with a company include references to benefits payable partly in respect of past service with the company; and
(d) references to a transfer payment in respect of past service with a company include references to a transfer payment partly in respect of past service with the company.

645 Earnings from pensionable employment

(1) This section applies to an office or employment held by an individual if—

(a) service in it is service to which a relevant superannuation scheme relates; and
(b) the individual is a participant in the scheme; and
(c) subsection (4) below does not apply to his participation in the scheme.

(2) This section applies whether or not the duties of the office or employment are performed wholly or partly in the United Kingdom or the individual is chargeable to tax in respect of it.

(3) In subsection (1) above 'a relevant superannuation scheme' means a scheme or arrangement—

(a) the object or one of the objects of which is the provision, in respect of persons serving in particular offices or employments, of relevant benefits within the meaning of section 612;
(b) which is established by a person other than the individual, and
(c) which is of a description mentioned in sections 596(1)(a)(b) or (c).

(4) This subsection applies to an individual's participation in a scheme if the scheme provides no benefits in relation to him other than—

(a) an annuity payable to his surviving spouse or a dependant of his;
(b) a lump sum payable on his death in service.

(4A) Where the emoluments from an office or employment held by an individual are foreign emoluments within the meaning of section 192, this section shall have effect with the substitution of the following for paragraph (c) of subsection (3) above—

'(c) which corresponds to a scheme of a description mentioned in section 596(1)(a), (b) or (c).'

646 Meaning of 'net relevant earnings'

(1) Subject to subsections (3) to (7) below and section 646A, in this Chapter 'net relevant earnings', in relation to an individual, means the amount of his relevant earnings for the year of assessment in question, less the amount of any deductions within subsection (2) below which fall to be made from the relevant earnings in computing for the purposes of income tax his total income for that year.

(2) Deductions are within this subsection if they are—

(a) deductions which but for section 74(m), (p) or (q) could be made in computing the profits or gains of the individual;
(b) deductions made by virtue of section 198, 201 or 332(3);
(c) deductions in respect of relief under Schedule 9 to the Finance Act 1981 (stock relief);

(d) deductions in respect of losses or capital allowances, being losses or capital allowances arising from activities profits or gains of which would be included in computing relevant earnings of the individual.

(3) For the purposes of this section, an individual's relevant earnings shall be taken to be those earnings before giving effect to any capital allowances, other than deductions allowable in computing profits or gains, but after taking into account the amounts on which charges fall to be made under the 1990 Act (including enactments which under this Act are to be treated as contained in the 1990 Act); and in subsections (4) and (5) below, references to income (other than references to total income) shall be construed similarly.

(4) In the case of an individual's partnership profits, the amount to be included in arriving at his net relevant earnings shall be his share of the partnership income (estimated in accordance with the Income Tax Acts) after making from it any such deductions in respect of—

(a) payments made by the partnership;
(b) relief given to the partnership under Schedule 9 to the Finance Act 1981; or
(c) capital allowances falling to be made to the partnership,

as would be made in computing the tax payable in respect of that income.

(5) Where, in a year of assessment for which an amount is deducted or set off under section 639(1) against the net relevant earnings of an individual—

(a) a deduction in respect of such a loss or allowance of the individual as is mentioned in subsection (2)(d) above falls to be made in computing the total income of the individual; and
(b) the deduction or part of it falls to be so made from income other than relevant earnings;

the amount of the deduction made from that other income shall be treated as reducing the individual's net relevant earnings for subsequent years of assessment in accordance with subsection (6) below.

(6) The deduction shall be made so far as possible from the individual's net relevant earnings for the first of the subsequent years of assessment (whether or not he is entitled to relief under section 639(1) for that year), and than, so far as it cannot be so made, from those of the next year, and so on.

(7) An individual's net relevant earnings for any year of assessment shall be computed without regard to any deduction or set off under section 639(1) which falls to be made for that year in respect of the individual.

646A Earnings from association employments

(1) This section applies where in the year of assessment in question—

(a) an individual holds two or more offices or employments which are associated in that year,
(b) one or more of them is an office or employment to which section 645 applies ('pensionable job'), and
(c) one or more of them is an office or employment to which that section does not apply ('non-pensionable job').

(2) Where the emoluments for that year from the pensionable job (or jobs) are equal to or exceed the allowable maximum for that year, section 646(1) shall have effect in the case of the individual as if the references to relevant earnings were references to relevant earnings not attributable to the non-pensionable job (or jobs).

(3) Where the allowable maximum for that year exceeds the emoluments for that year from the pensionable job (or jobs), the individual's net relevant earnings, so far as attributable to the non-pensionable job (or jobs), shall not be greater than the amount of the excess.

(4) For the purposes of this section two or more offices or employments held by an individual in a year of assessment are associated in that year if the employers in question are associated at any time during it.

(5) For the purposes of subsection (4) above, employers are associated if (directly or indirectly) one is controlled by the other or if both are controlled by a third person.

(6) In subsection (5) above the reference to control, in relation to a body corporate, shall be construed—

(a) where the body corporate is a close company, in accordance with section 416, and
(b) where it is not, in accordance with section 840.

(7) In this section 'the allowable maximum' has the same meaning as in section 640A(1).

Charge to tax

647 Unauthorised payments

(1) This section applies to any payment within subsection (2) below which is made—

(a) out of funds which are or have been held for the purposes of a personal pension scheme which is or has at any time been approved; and
(b) to or for the benefit of an individual who has made personal pension arrangements in accordance with the scheme.

(2) A payment is within this subsection if—

(a) it is not expressly authorised by the rules of the scheme; or
(b) it is made at a time when the scheme or the arrangements are not approved and it would not have been expressly authorised by the rules of the scheme or by the arrangements when the scheme, or as the case may be the arrangements, were last so approved.

(3) The individual referred to in subsection (1)(b) above, whether or not he is the recipient of the payment, shall be chargeable to tax under Schedule E on the amount of the payment for the year of assessment in which the payment is made.

(4) This section applies to a transfer of assets or other transfer of money's worth as it applies to a payment, and in relation to such a transfer the reference in subsection (3) above to the amount of the payment shall be read as a reference to the value of the transfer.

648 Contributions under unapproved arrangements

Where contributions are paid by an employer under personal pension arrangements made by his employee then, if those arrangements are not approved arrangements and the contributions are not otherwise chargeable to income tax as income of the employee, the contributions shall be regarded for all the purposes of the Income Tax Acts as emoluments of the employment chargeable to tax under Schedule E.

Miscellaneous

649 Minimum contributions under Social Security Act 1986

(1) Where under Part I of the Social Security Act 1986 the Secretary of State pays minimum contributions for the purposes of approved personal pension arrangements, the amount of the employee's share of those contributions shall, instead of being the amount provided for in that part, be the grossed-up equivalent of the amount so provided for.

(2) For the purposes of this section—
'the employee's share' of minimum contributions is so much of the contributions as is attributable to the percentage mentioned in paragraph (a) of the definition of 'rebate percentage' in section 3(3) of the Social Security Act 1986;
'the grossed-up equivalent' of an amount is such sum as, after deduction of income tax at the basic rate in force for the year of assessment for which the contributions are paid, is equal to that amount.

(3) The employee's share of minimum contributions paid for a year of assessment by the Secretary of State for the purposes of approved personal pension arrangements shall be treated for the purposes of income tax—

(a) as the income for that year of the individual in respect of whom it is paid; and
(b) as contributions paid in that year by that individual under those arrangements.

(4) The Board may make regulations—

(a) providing for the recovery by the Secretary of State from the Board, in such circumstances as may be prescribed by the regulations, of any increase attributable to this section in the sums paid by the Secretary of State out of the National Insurance Fund;

(b) requiring the Secretary of State to give the Board such information as may be so prescribed about minimum contributions paid by the Secretary of State;
(c) prescribing circumstances in which this section or any provision of it shall not apply;
(d) making such provision as appears to the Board to be necessary or expedient for the purposes of supplementing the provisions of this section.

(5) Any payment received by the Secretary of State by virtue of this section shall be paid into the National Insurance Fund.

(6) In relation to Northern Ireland, this section shall have effect as if—

(a) references to the Secretary of State were references to the Department of Health and Social Services for Northern Ireland;
(b) references to Part I and section 3(3) of the Social Security Act 1986 were references to Part II and Article 5(3) of the Social Security (Northern Ireland) Order 1986; and
(c) references to the National Insurance Fund were references to the Northern Ireland National Insurance Fund.

650 Withdrawal of approval

(1) If in the opinion of the Board the facts concerning an approved personal pension scheme or its administration or arrangements made in accordance with it do not warrant the continuance of their approval of the scheme, they may at any time by notice given to the scheme administrator withdraw their approval of the scheme.

(2) If in the opinion of the Board the facts concerning any approved personal pension arrangements do not warrant the continuance of their approval in relation to the arrangements, they may at any time by notice given to the individual who made them and to the scheme administrator withdraw their approval in relation to the arrangements.

(3) Without prejudice to the generality of subsection (2) above, the Board may withdraw their approval in relation to any personal pension arrangements if they are of the opinion that securing the provision of benefits under the arrangements was not the sole purpose of the individual in making them.

(4) A notice under subsection (1) or (2) above shall state the grounds on which, and the date from which, approval is withdrawn.

(5) The Board may not withdraw their approval from a date earlier than the date when the facts were first such that they did not warrant the continuance of their approval (so, however, that in a case within subsection (3) above their approval may be withdrawn from the day the arrangements in question were made).

651 Appeals

(1) Where the Board—

   (a) refuse an application by notice under section 631; or
   (b) withdraw an approval by notice under section 650;
   the person to whom the notice is given may appeal to the Special Commissioners against the refusal or, as the case may be, the withdrawal.

(2) An appeal under this section shall be made by notice stating the grounds for the appeal and given to the Board before the end of the period of 30 days beginning with the day on which the notice of refusal or withdrawal was given to the appellant.

(3) On an appeal under this section against the withdrawal of an approval, the Special Commissioners may, instead of allowing or dismissing the appeal, order that the withdrawal shall have effect from a date other than that determined by the Board.

(4) The bringing of an appeal under this section shall not affect the validity of the decision appealed against pending the determination of the proceedings.

652 Information about payments

(1) An inspector may give a notice to a scheme administrator requiring him to provide the inspector with—

   (a) such particulars as the notice may require relating to contributions paid under approved personal pension arrangements made in accordance with the scheme;
   (b) such particulars as the notice may require relating to payments by way of return of contributions;
   (c) copies of such accounts as the notice may require.

(2) A person to whom a notice is given under this section shall comply with the notice within the period of 30 days beginning with the day on which it is given.

653 Information: penalties

A person who knowingly makes a false statement or false representation on making an application under section 631 or for the purpose of obtaining for himself or any other person any relief from or repayment of tax under this Chapter shall be liable to a penalty not exceeding £3,000.

654 Remuneration of Ministers and other officers

(1) This section applies to any salary—

(a) payable to the holder of a qualifying office who is also a Member of the House of Commons; and
(b) payable for a period in respect of which the holder is not a participant in relation to that office in arrangements contained in the Parliamentary pension scheme but is a participant in relation to his membership of the House of Commons in any such arrangements, or for any part of such a period.

(2) So much of any salary to which this section applies as is equal to the difference between a Member's pensionable salary and the salary which (in accordance with any such resolution as is mentioned in subsection (4)(a) below) is payable to him as a Member holding that qualifying office, shall be treated for the purposes of this Chapter as remuneration from the office of Member and not from the qualifying office.

(3) In this section—
'Member's pensionable salary' means a Member's ordinary salary under any resolution of the House of Commons which, being framed otherwise than as an expression of opinion, is for the time being in force relating to the remuneration of Members or, if the resolution provides for a Member's ordinary salary thereunder to be treated for pension purposes as being at a higher rate, a notional yearly salary at that higher rate;
'qualifying office' means an office mentioned in paragraph (b), (c) or (d) of subsection (2) of section 2 of the Parliamentary and other Pensions Act 1987;

'the Parliamentary pension scheme' has the same meaning as in that Act;

and, without prejudice to the power conferred by virtue of paragraph 13 of Schedule 1 to that Act, regulations under section 2 of that Act may make provision specifying the circumstances in which a person is to be regarded for the purposes of this section as being or not being a participant in relation to his membership of the House of Commons, or in relation to any office, in arrangements contained in the Parliamentary pension scheme.

(4) In subsection (3) above 'a Member's ordinary salary', in relation to any resolution of the House of Commons, means—

(a) if the resolution provides for salary to be paid to Members at different rates according to whether or not they are holders of particular offices or are in receipt of salaries or pensions as the holders or former holders of particular offices, a Member's yearly salary at the higher or highest rate; and
(b) in any other case, a Member's yearly salary at the rate specified in or determined under the resolution.

655 Transitional provisions

(1) Where approved personal pension arrangements are made by an individual who pays qualifying premiums within the meaning of section 620(1)—

(a) the amount that may be deducted or set off by virtue of section 639(1) in any year of assessment shall be reduced by the amount of any qualifying premiums which are paid in the year by the individual and in respect of which relief is given for the year under section 619(1)(a); and
(b) the relief which, by virtue of section 625, may be given under section 619 by reference to the individual's unused relief for any year shall be reduced by the amount of any contributions paid by him in that year under the approved personal pension arrangements.

(2) Where an individual elects under section 641 that a contribution or part of a contribution shall be treated as paid in the year of assessment 1985-86, 1986-87 or 1987-88, the payment shall be treated as the payment of a qualifying premium for the purposes of Chapter III of this Part; and in such a case references in section

641 to an amount of unused relief shall be construed in accordance with section 625.

(3) The references in section 642 to unused relief for any year are, for years of assessment before 1988–89, references to unused relief within the meaning of section 625.

(4) The Board shall not grant any application under section 631 so as to approve a scheme with effect from a date earlier than 1st July 1988.

(5) The Board may by regulations make provision for applications for approval of personal pension schemes to be granted provisionally notwithstanding that the Board have not satisfied themselves that the schemes comply with the requirements of sections 632 to 638; and such regulations may, in particular, provide—

(a) for the contents and form of certificates or other documents which the Board may require the applicant to give them before they grant an application provisionally;
(b) for the making of such amendments of the rules of the scheme after the provisional grant of an application as are necessary to enable the scheme to comply with the requirements of sections 632 to 638, and for those amendments to have effect as from the date of approval of the scheme;
(c) for the withdrawal of approval of the scheme as from that date if it does not comply with the requirements of sections 632 to 638 and such amendments as are mentioned in paragraph (b) above are not made;

and may make such supplementary provision as appears to the Board to be necessary or expedient.

SCHEDULE 23

OCCUPATIONAL PENSION SCHEMES

SCHEMES APPROVED BEFORE 23RD JULY 1987

Preliminary

1. This Schedule shall be deemed to have come into force on 17th March 1987 and, subject to sub-paragraphs (2) and (3) below, applies in relation to any retirement benefits scheme approved by

the Board before the passing of the Finance (No 2) Act 1987 (23rd July 1987).

(2) The Board may by regulations provide that, in circumstances prescribed in the regulations, this Schedule or any provision of it shall not apply or shall apply with such modifications as may be so prescribed.

(2A) Regulations under sub-paragraph (2) above—

(a) may include provision authorising the Board to direct that this Schedule or any provision of it shall not apply in any particular case where in the opinion of the Board the facts are such that its application would not be appropriate;
(b) may take effect (and may authorise any direction given under them to take effect) as from 17th March 1987 or any later date;
(c) may make such supplementary provision as appears to the Board to be necessary or expedient.

(3) This Schedule shall not apply to a retirement benefits scheme if, before the end of 1987, the administrator of the scheme gave notice to the Board that it is not to apply.

(4) Where a notice is given to the Board under sub-paragraph (3) above, the scheme shall, with effect from 17th March 1987 or (if later) the date with effect from which it was approved, cease to be approved.

Accelerated accrual

2.—(1) This paragraph applies where an employee becomes a member of the scheme on or after 17th March 1987.

(2) Notwithstanding anything to the contrary in the rules of the scheme, they shall have effect as if they did not allow the provision for the employee of a pension exceeding one-thirtieth of his relevant annual remuneration for each year of service up to a maximum of 20.

3.—(1) This paragraph applies where an employee becomes a member of the scheme on or after 17th March 1987 and the scheme allows him to commute his pension or part of it for a lump sum or sums.

(2) If the employee's full pension (that is, the pension before any commutation) is equal to or less than a basic rate commutable pension, the rules of the scheme shall have effect (notwithstanding anything in them to the contrary) as if they did not allow him to obtain by way of commutation a lump sum or sums exceeding in all a basic rate lump sum.

(3) If the employee's full pension is greater than a basic rate commutable pension but less than a maximum rate commutable pension, the rules of the scheme shall have effect (notwithstanding anything in them to the contrary) as if they did not allow him to obtain by way of commutation a lump sum or sums exceeding in all the aggregate of

   (a) a basic rate lump sum, and
   (b) an amount equal to the relevant percentage of the difference between a basic rate lump sum and a maximum rate lump sum.

(4) In this paragraph, as it applies in relation to an employee—

   (a) a 'basic rate commutable pension' means a pension of one-sixtieth of his relevant annual remuneration for each year of service up to a maximum of 40;
   (b) a 'maximum rate commutable pension' means a pension of one-thirtieth of his relevant annual remuneration for each year of service up to a maximum of 20;
   (c) a 'basic rate lump sum' means a lump sum of three-eighths of his relevant annual remuneration for each year of service up to a maximum of 40;
   (d) a 'maximum rate lump sum' means a lump sum of such amount as may be determined by or under regulations made by the Board for the purposes of this paragraph and paragraph 4 below;
   (e) 'the relevant percentage' means the difference between a basic rate commutable pension and the employee's full pension expressed as a percentage of the difference between a basic rate commutable pension and a maximum rate commutable pension.

4.—(1) This paragraph applies where an employee becomes a member of the scheme on or after 17th March 1987 and the scheme provides a lump sum or sums for him otherwise than by commutation of his pension or part of it.

(2) If the employee's pension is equal to or less than a basic rate non-commutable pension, the rules of the scheme shall have effect (notwithstanding anything in them to the contrary) as if they did not allow the payment to him, otherwise than by way of commutation, of a lump sum or sums exceeding in all a basic rate lump sum.

(3) If the employee's pension is greater than a basic rate non-commutable pension but less than a maximum rate non-commutable pension the rules of the scheme shall have effect (notwithstanding anything in them to the contrary) as if they did not allow the payment to him, otherwise than by way of commutation, of a lump sum or sums exceeding in all the aggregate of—

(a) a basic rate lump sum, and
(b) an amount equal to the relevant percentage of the difference between a basic rate lump sum and a maximum rate lump sum.

(4) In this paragraph, as it applies in relation to an employee—

(a) a 'basic rate non-commutable pension' means a pension of one-fortieth of his relevant annual remuneration for each year of service up to a maximum of 20,
(b) a 'maximum rate non-commutable pension' means a pension of one-fortieth of his relevant annual remuneration for each year of service up to a maximum of 20,
(c) 'basic rate lump sum' and 'maximum rate lump sum' have the same meanings as in paragraph 3 above, and
(d) 'the relevant percentage' means the difference between a basic rate non-commutable pension and the employee's actual pension expressed as a percentage of the difference between a basic rate non-commutable pension and a maximum rate non-commutable pension.

Final remuneration

5.—(1) This paragraph applies where an employee who is a member of the scheme retires on or after 17th March 1987.

(2) The rules of the scheme shall have effect as if they provided that in determining the employee's relevant annual remuneration for the purpose of calculating benefits, no account should be taken of anything excluded from the definition of 'remuneration' in section 612(1).

(3) In the case of an employee—

(a) whose employer is a company and who at any time in the last ten years of his service is a controlling director of the company, or
(b) whose relevant annual remuneration for the purpose of calculating benefits, so far as the remuneration is ascertained by reference to years beginning on or after 6th April 1987, would (apart from this Schedule) exceed the permitted maximum,

the rules of the scheme shall have effect as if they provided that his relevant annual remuneration must not exceed his highest average annual remuneration for any period of three or more years ending within the period of ten years which ends with the date on which his service ends.

(4) In the case of an employee within paragraph (b) of sub-paragraph (3) above who retires before 6th April 1991, the rules of the scheme shall have effect as if they provided that his relevant annual remuneration must not exceed the higher of—

(a) the average annual remuneration referred to in that sub-paragraph, and
(b) his remuneration (within the meaning given by section 612(1)) assessable to income tax under Schedule E for the year of assessment 1986-87.

(5) For the purposes of this paragraph a person is a controlling director of a company if—

(a) he is a director (as defined in section 612), and
(b) he is within paragraph (b) of section 417(5),

in relation to the company.

Lump sums

6.—(1) This paragraph applies where an employee becomes a member of the scheme on or after 17th March 1987.

(2) If the rules of the scheme allow the employee to obtain, (by commutation of his pension or otherwise), a lump sum or sums calculated by reference to his relevant annual remuneration, they shall have effect as if they included a rule that in calculating a

lump sum any excess of that remuneration over the permitted maximum should be disregarded.

Additional voluntary contributions

7.—(1) This paragraph applies where—

   (a) the rules of the scheme make provision for the payment by employees of voluntary contributions, and
   (b) on or after 8th April 1987 an employee enters into arrangements to pay such contributions.

(2) Notwithstanding anything in the rules of the scheme, they shall have effect as if they did not allow the payment to the employee of a lump sum in commutation of a pension if or to the extent that the pension is secured by the voluntary contributions.

8.—(1) This paragraph applies where an employee who is a member of the scheme ('the main scheme') is also a member of an approved scheme ('the voluntary scheme') which provides additional benefits to supplement those provided by the main scheme and to which no contributions are made by any employer of his.

(2) Any rules of the main scheme imposing a limit on the amount of a benefit provided for the employee shall have effect (notwithstanding anything in them to the contrary) as if they provided for the limit to be reduced by the amount of any like benefit provided for the employee by the voluntary scheme.

(This paragraph repealed by FA 1989, Sch 6, paras 17, 18(10) and Sch 17, Pt IV in relation to benefit provided after 26 July 1989.)

Supplementary

9. In this Schedule 'relevant annual remuneration' means final remuneration or, if the scheme provides for benefits to be calculated by reference to some other annual remuneration, that other annual remuneration.

Index

Accounts—
  insurance based hybrid scheme, 121
  small self-administered scheme, 114
  unfunded scheme, 73
Accrued rights premium, 275
Actuarial—
  certificate, 275
  report, 113, 114, 121
  valuation, 275
Additional voluntary contributions—
  meaning, 276
  doctor or dentist, 215
  free-standing, 126, 127, 133-6, 279
  scheme, 126, 127, 133
  tax relief, 74, 400
Administrator of scheme—
  meaning, 276
  appointment of, 23
  role of, 23, 346
Advertising executive, 259
Age—
  early retirement, 208-11, 259-60
  normal retirement, 29-30, 78
  pensionable, employment beyond, 142-3
  State pension, 137, 240, 272, 285
Airline pilots, 209, 259
Annuity—
  compulsory purchase, 86
  deferred, 235, 239
  Hancock, 7, 24, 249-50, 280
  personal pension scheme, member of, 372-3
  purchased life, 86, 266-8, 283
  rates, 85-6
  retired partner's, 218-19, 366-8
  retirement annuity, see Retirement annuity
  section 32 annuity, 236, 239-40, 276
Approval, see Inland Revenue approval

Approved pension scheme—
  meaning, 351
  before 6 April 1980, 348-9
  before 23 July 1987, 349
  directors' membership of, 77
  earnings cap, 61, 77
  exempt approved, see Exempt approved scheme
  information as to, 345-6
  maximum permitted benefits, see Maximum permitted benefits
  personal pension scheme and, 181, 369-77
  Practice Notes, 18, 28, 282, 303
  section 591 regulations, 326-7
Associate: meaning, 79
Associated company, 292, 298
Associated employments, 57-9, 186-7, 322, 388
Athletes, 209
Attendance allowance, 145

Back to back loans, 209
Bonus, sacrifice of, 132
Boxers, 209
Brass instrumentalists, 209
Brokers, 209
Business Expansion Schemes, 188
Buy-out plans, 236, 239-40, 276

Capital—
  allowances, 188
  funding for, 85-7
Captive pension scheme, see Small self-administered scheme
Certificate—
  cash sum, 241
  contracting-out, 15, 277
  controlling director's/high earner's, 241
Charges, insurance company, 97-100

Circus animal trainers, 209
Civil Service Superannuation Scheme, 7
Close company, golden handshake, 248-9
Commerical property, investment in, 110-11, 116-21, 223
Commission, sacrifice of, 132
Company—
  associated, 292, 298
  close, 248-9
  director, see Director
  investment company, 257-8
  loan, 107, 109-110, 115
  own shares, investment in, 107, 108-9, 111-12
  service company, 258
Compensation schemes, 273
Connected persons, 108
Connected schemes, 58, 60
Contracting-out—
  meaning, 277
  certificate, issue of, 15, 277
  cessation of, 165, 276
  generally, 19, 152-4
  guaranteed minimum pension—
    meaning, 153
    deferred, 156
    increases during payment, 157
    original basis, 153, 155
    revised basis, 155
    widow, 156-7
  major changes in law, 153, 157-8
  methods of, 153-4
  occupational pension scheme—
    defined benefit/final salary, 20, 137, 153, 158, 162, 246
    effect of changes in law, 163-5
    money purchase, 20, 137, 153, 158, 162-3, 246
  personal pension scheme—
    changes in law, 138, 153, 158, 163-5
    mechanics of contracting-out, 158-60
  requisite benefit test, abolition of, 154-5
  2% incentive, 160-1
  who should contract-out, 161-2
Contributions—
  additional voluntary, see Additional voluntary contributions executive pension plan, 2-5, 169-70
  funding and, see Funding

Contributions—*contd*
  personal pension scheme, see Personal pension scheme
  refund of, 244, 337
  retirement annuity, see Retirement annuity
  State scheme, 138-41
  unapproved pension scheme, see Unapproved pension scheme
Contributions equivalent premium, 277
Controlling director, see Director
Cricketers, 209
Croupiers, 209
Cyclists, professional, 209

Dancers, 209
Death—
  after retirement, approved scheme, 46-8
  benefits—
    personal pension scheme, 199-200
    retirement annuity, 199-200
  inheritance tax, see Inheritance tax
  service, in, benefits—
    after normal retirement date, 50
    approved scheme, 48-50
    controlling director, 78
    escalation of benefit, 49
    executive pension plan, 93
    small self-administered scheme, 113
    unapproved scheme, 72-3, 75
Declaration of trust, 22, 202
Decreasing term assurance 94
Deferment—
  annuity, 235, 239
  guaranteed minimum pension, 156
  pension, 235-8, 246
  retirement, of, 50, 52, 168
  State pension, 145-6
  tax relief, of, 73
Deferred SSAS, 121
Defined benefit scheme, 20, 137, 153, 158, 162, 246
Defined contribution scheme, 20, 272
Dentist—
  added years, 215
  carry back provisions, 216
  retired, 215
  Schedule D, 212-214
  Schedule E, 212
Dependant—
  meaning, 47
  benefits for, 46-50, 92

Deposit administration, 95, 100–101
Director—
　associate of, 79
　controlling—
　　meaning, 78–9, 364
　　benefits for, 77–8, 80
　　cash lump sum, 44
　　continuous service, 81
　　final salary, 34
　　generally, 77
　　New Code scheme, 8, 10
　　retirement age, 30, 78
　　serious ill-health, 80–1
　　transfer of benefits, 241
　employee, within meaning of, 27, 80
　executive pension plan, see Executive pension plan
　generally, 27
　lifetime service agreement, 10–11
　New Code pension scheme, 8, 10
　pensionable service, 80, 81
　personal pension scheme, use of, 163
　serious ill-health, 80–1
　SERPS, contracting-out of, 162–3
　top hat scheme, 9–10
　20% director—
　　meaning, 278
　　inheritance tax, 170
Disability benefits, 64, 146, 203–5
Discretionary trust, 201, 202
Divers, 209, 211
Dividends—
　foreign, 264
　waiver, 131
Divorce, pension benefits and, 274
Doctor—
　added years, 215
　carry back provisions, 216
　retired, 215
　Schedule D, 212–14
　Schedule E, 212
Documentation—
　Inland Revenue approval, application for, 24–5, 344–345
　small self-adminstered scheme, 114, 295, 309
Domestic servants, 27
Domicile, 260
Double taxation, 280, 262, 264
Dynamised final remuneration, 35–6, 49, 128, 278

Early leavers—
　frozen pension, 238–9

Early leavers—*contd*
　generally, see Leaving service benefits
　improvement of benefits for, 13, 20, 21
　preservation of benefits, 235–6
　problems of, 238–9
Early retirement—
　generally, 50
　ill health—
　　not through, 51–2
　　through, 52
　personal pension scheme, 208–11
　retirement annuity, 208–11
Earnings—
　cap, approved scheme, 61, 77, 278, 324
　limit for National Insurance purposes, 141–2
　overseas, 206–7
　personal pension scheme purposes, see Personal pension scheme
　retirement annuity, see Retirement annuity
Emoluments
　fluctuating, 34
　foreign, 207–8, 260, 262
Employee—
　meaning, 27
　information for, 19
　insolvent employer, of, 273
　maximum permitted benefits, see Maximum permitted benefits
　overseas resident, 263
　self-employed person, comparison with, 1–5
　unauthorised payment to or for, 341
Employer—
　contributions—
　　regular, 89–90
　　single, 89, 90–1
　overseas, 261–2
　payments to, charge to tax, 341–3
　responsibilities of, 346
　trust, 22, 23
Employment—
　associated, 57–9
　multiple, 59–60
　pensionable age, beyond, 142–3
Employment-related benefit scheme, scope of, 21
European Community—
　equal treatment of men and women, 13, 21, 243, 271–2
　transfer to pension scheme of staff of, 264

404 Index

Executive pension plan—
  meaning, 279
  assignment of policy under, 242
  contributions, 2–5, 169–70
  funding, 89–94
  generally, 1, 97
  group scheme, topping up, 128–9
  history of, 10, 11–12
  inheritance tax planning, 167–72
  insurance based hybrid scheme, 121–3
  international aspects, 260–3
  investment company, 257–8
  loans, 256
  personal pension scheme, comparison with, 2–5
  planning hints, 167–72, 225–31
  retirement dates, 259–60
  service company, 258
  use of, 151–2, 163
Exempt approved scheme—
  meaning, 279, 351
  conditions for, 16, 22
  tax relief, 65, 328–31
Exempt statutory scheme, 331

Final salary, 33–5, 279
Financial services legislation, 271, 273
Firemen, 209
Fluctuating emoluments, 34
Footballers, professional, 209, 259–60
Foreign aspects, *see* Overseas aspects
Free-standing addtional voluntary contributions, 126, 127, 133–6, 279
Friendly societies, 224
Frozen pension, 235, 238–9
Funding—
  annuity rates, 85–6
  capital, for, 85–7
  contributions—
    personal, 92
    regular, 89–90
    single, 89, 90–1
  death in service benefits, 93
  decreasing term assurance, 94
  dependant's death in retirement benefits, 92
  group scheme, 82–3
  individual arrangements, 82, 83–7
  overfunding, 21, 92–3, 192
  premiums—
    annual, 94
    single, 94
  salary increases, 86–7

Funding—*contd*
  small self-administered scheme, 304, 306–7
  yield assumption, 87–9

Glossary of terms, 275–86
Golden handshakes, 16, 247–9
Golfers, 209
Group personal pension plans, 21
Group scheme—
  funding, 82–3
  generally, 125–6
  tax planning vehicle, as, 172
  topping up—
    additional voluntary contributions, *see* Additional voluntary contributions
    bonus sacrifice, 132
    commission sacrifice, 132
    dividend waiver, 131
    executive pension plan, through, 128–9
    National Insurance contributions, effect on, 132–3
    salary sacrifice, 130–1
    scheme, under, 127
Guaranteed minimum pension—
  meaning, 280
  contracted-out scheme, *see* Contracting-out

Hancock annuity, 7, 24, 249–50, 280
Health visitors, 209
History—
  early schemes, 7
  executive pension plan, 10, 11–12
  legislation, 7
  lifetime service agreements, 10–11
  New Code, 8–9
  Old Code, 8–9
  recent changes, 13
  small self-administered scheme, 12
  State benefits, 12–13
  top hat scheme, 9–10
House of Commons, member of, 368–9, 393–4
House of Commons Social Security Select Committee Report, 272
Hybrid scheme, insurance based, 121–3

Ill health—
  company director, 80–1
  early retirement through, 52

Index

Information—
  approved scheme, 345–6, 392–3
  disclosure of, 20, 271, 274
  personal pension scheme, 391–3
  small self-administered scheme, 109, 113–14, 295, 301
Inheritance tax—
  executive pension plan, 167–72
  personal pension scheme, 167, 200–3
  retirement annuity, 167, 200–3
  unapproved pension scheme, 62, 69–70, 75
Inland Revenue approval—
  appeal as to, 392
  application for, 23–5, 344
  before 23 July 1987, 395–400
  case law, 7, 19
  conditions for, 16–19, 319–25
  discretionary, 28, 287–88, 294, 299, 303–17, 325–6
  history of, 7
  legislation—
    main, 16–19, 319 *et seq*
    other, 19–22
  maximum permitted benefits, *see* Maximum permitted benefits
  memorandum as to, 18, 287–301
  New Code, 8–9
  notification of, 25
  offshore plan, 262–3
  Old Code, 8–9
  personal pension scheme, 370–7, 391–2
  pilots' benefit fund, 347–8
  Practice Notes, 18, 28, 282, 303–17
  purpose of, 15–16
  simplified scheme, 26
  small self-administered scheme, 106, 287–8, 294, 299, 303–17
  trust, 16, 19, 22–3, 304–6
  withdrawal of, 18, 327, 391
Insurance based hybrid scheme, 121–3
Insurance bonds, 269
Insurance Ombudsman Bureau, 273
Insured pension arrangements—
  categories of, 95
  charging structures, 97–100
  deposit administration, 95, 100–101
  investment funds, types of, 100
  small self-administered scheme, comparison with, 106
  unit-linked policy, *see* Unit linked policy

Insured pension arrangements—*contd*
  with-profits policy—
    conventional, 95–7, 101
    unitised, 95, 101
Insured pension schemes, 273–4
Interest—
  loan on, 188, 254, 255
  unpaid tax, 198
Interest in possession trust, 201–2
International aspects, *see* Overseas aspects
Investigation settlements, 198–9
Investment—
  cash lump sum, 268
  company, 28, 257–8
  income—
    current, 268–9
    future, 270
  investor protection, 272–3
  retirement, options on 265
  small self-administered scheme, *see* Small self-administered scheme

Jockeys, 209

Late assessments to tax, 198
Late retirement, benefits on, 52–3
LAUTRO, 99, 274, 280
Leaving service benefits—
  deferred pension, 235, 236–7
  frozen pension, 238–9
  golden handshake, 247–9
  Hancock annuity, 249–50
  improvement of, 13, 20, 245
  personal pension plans, 240–4
  preservation of benefits, 235–6
  refund of members' contributions, 244
  section 32 annuity, 236, 239–40
  Social Security Act 1990, effect of, 245–6
Legislation—
  financial services, 271, 273
  future, 13, 271–4
  history of, 7–13
Life assurance—
  insured pension arrangements, *see* Insured pension arrangements
  personal pension scheme, 180–1
  retirement annuity, 181
Life office small self-administered arrangement, 121
Lifetime service agreement, 10–11
Limited revaluation premium, 281

Lloyd's underwriter, 211, 366
Loan—
  back to back, 293–4
  costs, comparison of, 252–3
  executive pension plan, 256
  insurance based hybrid scheme, 121–2
  interest, 188, 254, 255
  lifetime, 254
  pension-related, 251–6
  personal, 256
  small self-administered scheme, 107–9, 113, 292, 298
  tax relief, 251–5
  usecured, 255
Lump sum payments—
  approved retirement benefits scheme, *see* Maximum permitted benefits
  investment, 268
  personal pension scheme, 176–8, 372, 373, 375
  unapproved pension scheme, 68–9, 75

Martial arts instructors, 209
Maximum permitted benefits—
  accelerated scale, 32–3, 41
  combination of schemes, 54
  death—
    retirement, after, 46–8
    service, in, 48–50
  dynamised final remuneration, 35–6, 49, 128, 278
  early retirement, 50–2
  escalation of pension in payment, 39, 49
  final salary, 33–5
  Finance Act 1989 changes, 28, 54, 56–7
  Finance (No 2) Act 1987 changes, 28, 54–6
  generally, 30
  late retirement, 52–3
  lump sums—
    cash, 39–44
    death in service, 48–9
    pension values of, 45–6
    retained benefits, 44–5
  membership categories, 28–9
  multiple employments, 59–60
  opting for 1989 benefits, 57
  options on retirement, 53–4
  recent changes, 28–9
  retained benefits, 37–8, 44–5

Maximum permitted benefits—*contd*
  retirement ages, 29–30, 78
  simplification of calculation of, 28
  straight 60ths scale, 31–2
  trivial benefits, 54
  uplifted 60ths scale, 31–2
  who can qualify for, 27
  who cannot qualify for, 27–8
Maxwell affair, 272–3
Men and women, equal treatment of, 13, 20, 21, 243, 271–2
Midwives, 209
Ministers, remuneration of, 368–9, 393–4
Moneybroker dealers, 209, 259
Money purchase scheme, 20, 52, 137, 153, 158, 162–3, 246, 281
Mortgage interest relief, 194
Motor cycle riders, 209
Motor racing drivers, 209
Multi-national corporations, 262–3

National health payments, 138
National Insurance contributions—
  effect of income sacrifice on, 132–3
  State pensions, 138–41
  unapproved scheme, 70–1
Newscasters (ITV), 209
Nurses, 209

Occupational pension scheme—
  meaning, 71
  Annual Survey, 165
  approval, *see* Inland Revenue approval
  approved—
    generally, *see* Approved pension scheme
    maximum permitted benefits, *see* Maximum permitted benefits
  contracting-out, *see* Contracting-out
  disclosure of information, 271
  early leavers, *see* Early leavers
  equal treatment of men and women, 13, 20, 21, 243, 271–2
  future legislation 271–3
  history of legislation, 19–22
  register, 246
  Social Security Act 1990, 245–6
  unapproved, *see* Unapproved pension scheme
Occupational Pensions Advisory Service, 246

Occupational Pension Board, functions of, 15, 273
Offshore plans, 262–3
Offshore trusts, 74
Offshore riggers, 209
Overseas aspects—
  earnings overseas, 206–7
  executive pension plan, 260–3
  foreign emoluments, 207–8, 260, 262
  offshore plans, 262–3
  offshore trusts, 74
  overseas employer with UK resident employee, 27, 261–2
  overseas transfers, 264
  pensioner resident abroad, 206, 208, 263–4
  UK resident employer with overseas resident employee, 263

Partnership—
  retired partner's annuity, 218–19, 366–8
  salaried partners, 27
  self-managed scheme for partner, 219–24
  tax planning, 188
Pension Schemes Office, functions of, 15, 282
Pensioneer trustee—
  meaning, 282
  insurance based hybrid scheme, 121
  small self-administered scheme, 108, 112, 289, 304
Pensioner's rights premium, 282
Pensions Ombudsman, 22, 274
Pensions Tracing Registry, 22
Personal Equity Plans, 269
Personal pension scheme—
  meaning, 173
  added years, 215, 276
  administrative requirements, 196–8
  annuity to member, 372–3
  appropriate: meaning, 160–1
  approval, *see* Inland Revenue approval
  associated employments, 186–7, 388
  background, 173
  benefit age, 175, 176, 208–11
  benefit levels, 216–18
  benefits available, 176–8, 181–2
  consultant, 28
  contributions—
    carry back provisions, 195–6, 380–1

Personal pension scheme—*contd*
  contributions—*contd*
    carry forward of unused tax relief, 194–5, 281–2
    deductions, 379
    employer's, 383
    excess, 192
    generally, 2–5, 164, 377–8
    inheritance tax, 200
    maximum, 189–92, 216–18
    minimum, 390–1
    retirement annuity, to, 189–92
    unapproved arrangements, under, 389–90
  death before taking benefit, 180
  death benefits, 199
  deferring benefits, 203
  dentist, 211–16
  disability benefits, 203–5
  discretionary trusts, 201–2
  doctor, 211–16
  early retirement age, 208–11
  earnings—
    associated employments, 388–9
    cap, 379–90
    net relevant, 185–90, 386–8
    overseas, 206–7
    pensionable employment, from, 385–6
    relevant: meaning, 182–3, 383–5
  eligibility for, 1, 182–5
  equal treatment of men and women, 13, 20, 21, 243, 271–2
  establishment of, 371
  executive pension plan, comparison with, 2–5
  flexible trust, 199–200
  forerunner of, 1
  future developments, 274
  information—
    false statements, 393
    payments, as to, 392
  inheritance tax, 167, 200–3
  interest in possesion trust, 201–2
  life assurance, 180–2
  Lloyd's underwriter, 211
  lump sum payments, 176, 372, 373, 375
  overfunding, 192
  overseas aspects, 206–8
  partner, *see* Partnership
  pension-related loan, 251–5
  personal pension income, 382
  protected rights, 137, 202, 283
  purpose of, 176

408 Index

Personal pension scheme—*contd*
  putting existing policy in trust, 202–3
  register, 246
  retirement annuity—
    comparison with, 158, 173–6
    concurrent with, 173
  retirement benefit scheme,
    comparison with, 181
  self-employed person, 27
  specialised occupations, 208–16
  tax assessments, 198–9
  tax, charge to, 389–90
  tax planning, 216–18, 231–3
  tax reliefs, 192–6, 198, 377–89
  tax treatment of pensions, 21, 205–6
  transfer of benefits, 240–4
  type of pension available, 179, 265
  unauthorised payments, 389
  use of, 137, 138
  working of, 174
Physiotherapists, 209
Pilots' benefit fund, 347–8
Planning, *see* Tax planning
Practice Notes, 17–18, 28, 282, 296, 303–17
Preservation of benefits, 19, 235–6
Property—
  commercial, investment in, 110–11, 116–21, 223
  residential, investment in, 108, 116–21, 222–3
Protected rights, 137, 162, 202, 283
Psychiatrists, 209
Public sector scheme, added years of service, 117
Purchased life annuity, 86, 266–8, 283

Redundancy payments, 19, 138, 247
Refund of contributions, 244, 337
Relevant statutory scheme: meaning, 350–1
Residence—
  abroad, *see* Overseas aspects
  tax purposes, for, 260
Residential property, investment in, 108, 116–21, 223
Retirement—
  age, *see* Age
  annuity, *see* Retirement annuity
  dates, 259–60
  deferment of, 50, 52, 168
  early, *see* Early retirement
  investment contributions, *see* Investment

Retirement—*contd*
  late, 52–3
  options on, 170–1, 265–70
Retirement annuity—
  meaning, 173
  benefit age, 175, 176, 208–11
  benefit levels, 216–18
  benefits available, 182
  consultant, 28
  contributions—
    excess, 192
    generally, 2
    inheritance tax, 200
    personal pension scheme, 189–92
  deferring benefits, 203
  dentist, 211–16
  disability benefits, 203–5
  discretionary trust, 201
  doctor, 211–16
  earnings—
    net relevant, 185–90
    overseas, 206–7
    relevant, 183, 184, 361–3
  eligibility for, 184–5
  existing, legislation as to, 182, 353–369
  generally, 1
  inheritance tax, 167, 200–3
  interest in possession trust, 201–2
  life assurance, 181
  Lloyd's underwriter, 211
  open market option, 178–9
  partners, *see* Partnership
  pension-related loan, 251–6
  personal pension scheme—
    comparison with, 158, 173–6
    concurrent with, 173
  putting existing policy in trust, 202–6
  self-employed person, 27
  specialised occupations, 208–16
  substituted, 360–1
  tax planning, 216–18, 231–3
  tax relief, 192–6, 353–60
  tax treatment of pensions, 205–6
  working of, 174
Retirement benefits scheme—
  meaning, 62–64, 349–50
  approval, *see* Inland Revenue approval
  approved, *see* Approved pension scheme
  inheritance tax, 167
  unapproved, *see* Unapproved pension scheme

Revaluation of pensions, 20
Royal Marine Reservists, 209
Rugby League players and referees, 209

Salary—
  final, 30–8
  increases, 86–7
  sacrifice, 9, 130, 284
Section 32 annuity, 236, 239–40, 276
Section 218 plan, 263
Section 614 plan, 263
Self-administered scheme—
  meaning, 285
  small, see Small self-administered scheme
Self-employed person—
  approved retirement benefits scheme, 27
  employed, comparison with, 1–5
  personal pension scheme, see Personal pension scheme
  retirement annuity, see Retirement annuity
  State pension, 137, 151
  tax planning, 225
SERPS—
  adequacy of, 151–2
  amount of pension, 143
  annual rate—
    pre-April 1988 calculation, 143–5
    post April 1988 calculation, 144–5
  contracting back into, 165
  contracting-out, see Contracting-out
  deferred pension, 145–6
  DSS leaflets, 152
  earnings limit—
    lower, 141
    upper, 142
  employment beyond pensionable age, 142–3
  increases during payment, 145
  objective of, 137–8
  qualifying conditions, 142
  summary of, 149–51
  widow's benefits, 146–7
  widower's benefits, 148
Service company, 258
Sex discrimination, 13, 20, 21, 243, 271–2
Shares, small self-administered scheme, 108–9, 111–112, 291, 299, 307
Sick pay, 64, 138

Simplified defined contribution scheme, 26
Singers, 209
Small-self administered scheme—
  meaning, 105, 288, 303
  accounts, 114
  actuarial reports, 113, 114
  advantages, 115
  approval, 106, 113, 287–8, 294, 299, 303–17, 325–6
  borrowing, 109, 113, 290, 300, 307, 313
  company shares, 108–9, 111–112, 114, 291
  cost of setting up, 114–15
  death in service benefits, 113
  disadvantages, 115–16
  documentation, 114, 295, 309
  funding, 304, 306–7
  generally, 12
  history, 12
  information, provision of, 109, 113–14, 295–301, 309
  insurance-based hybrid scheme, 121–3
  insured scheme, comparison with, 105
  investment—
    restrictions on, 106–11, 290–1, 307–11
    strategy, 113
  leasing, 315
  loans, 107, 109, 113, 292–4, 298
  notification of transactions, 108, 314
  pensioneer trustee, see Pensioneer trustee
  pensions, purchase of, 113
  Practice Notes, 28, 296, 303–11
  property, investment in, 107–8, 110–11, 116–21, 291, 297, 315
  records, 114
  rules, 295, 306
  self-investment—
    generally, 106
    restrictions on, 106–11, 290–1, 307–11
  SFO Memorandum, 107, 287–301
  transactions wth scheme, 292
  works of art etc, investment in, 109, 291
Speedway riders, 210
Sponsored superannuation scheme, 363–4

Spouse—
  pension for, 46–50
  self-employed person, of, 27
Squash players, 210
State benefits—
  adequacy of, 151–2
  basic old age pension, 137
  earnings related additional pension, *see* SERPS
  history of, 12–13, 137
  State pension age, 137, 240, 272, 285
  summary of, 149
State earnings related pension scheme, *see* SERPS
State pensionable age, 137, 240, 272, 285
Superannuation Funds Office, 15
Surpluses, 21, 92–3, 192, 340–3

Table tennis players, 210
Tax—
  approval by Inland Revenue, *see* Inland Revenue approval
  charge to, statutory provisions, 332–44
  inheritance tax, *see* Inheritance tax
  investigation settlements, 198–9
  late assessment, 198
  personal pension scheme, *see* Personal pension scheme
  planning, *see* Tax planning
  relief, *see* Tax relief
  retirement annuity *see* Retirement annuity
  unapproved scheme, *see* Unapproved scheme
Tax planning—
  executive pension plan 167–72, 225–31
  group scheme, 172
  loans, 251–6
  partners, 188
  personal pension scheme, 231–3
  retirement annuity, 215–18, 231–3
Tax relief—
  additional voluntary contributions, 74, 400
  carry back provisions, 195–6, 380–1
  carry forward of unused relief, 194–5, 364–5, 381–2
  deferment of, 73
  exempt approved scheme, 65, 328–31
  exempt statutory scheme, 331
  loan, 251–5

Tax relief—*contd*
  personal pension scheme, 192–6, 198, 377–89
  retirement annuity, 192–6, 353–60
Temporary employees, 27
Tennis players, professional, 210, 259
Term assurance, 94, 171
Territorial Army members, 210
Top hat scheme, 9–10, 285
Toping up group scheme, *see* Group scheme
Tracing service, establishment of, 22
Transfer values, 20, 242–5
Trapeze artists, 210
Trawlermen, 259
Trivial benefits, 54
Trust—
  Board resolution, 23
  declaration of, 22, 202
  discretionary, 201, 202
  employer, 22, 23
  flexible, use of, 199–200
  formal deed, 22
  Inland Revenue approval, 22
  interest in possession, 201–2
  setting up, 22–3
Trustee, pensioneer, *see* Pensioneer

Unapproved pension scheme—
  accounting for costs, 73
  alternatives, 74
  changes in law, summary of, 61–2
  contributions, taxation of—
    employee's position, 66–8, 75
    employer's position, 65–6, 75
  death in service benefits, 72–3
  establishment of, 61, 62
  fund, taxation of, 68
  funded scheme: meaning, 67
  future trends, 73–4
  generally, 18
  inheritance tax, 62, 69–70, 75
  lump sum benefits, taxation of, 68, 75
  national insurance contributions, 70–1
  pensions, taxation of, 69, 74–5
  relevant benefits: meaning, 63–4
  retirement benefits scheme: meaning, 61, 62–4
  scheme: meaning, 63
  social security legislation, 71
  summary of tax position, 75, 333
  uses of, 13, 26, 71–2
Underwriters, 211, 366

Unit-linked policy—
  bid/offer prices, 99
  charging structures, 97–100
  comparison of unit-linked funds, 101–4
  management charges, 99
  policy charges, 99–100
  units—
    allocation to, 97–8
    type of, 98
  use of, 97
United Kingdom: meaning, 260
Unitised with-profits policy, 95, 101
Unsecured loan, 255

Widow—
  death in retirement benefits, 92

Widow—*contd*
  guaranteed minimum pension, 155–7
  SERPS benefits, availability of, 146–8
Widowed mother's allowance, 146
Widower—
  death in retirement benefits, 92
  SERPS benefits, availability of, 148, 152
With-profits policy—
  conventional, 95–7, 101
  unitised, 95, 101
Women, equal treatment of, 13, 20, 21, 243, 271–2
Works of art, investment in, 109, 291
Wrestlers, 210

Other titles in the Allied Dunbar Library

Allied Dunbar Tax Guides

- Allied Dunbar Business Tax and Law Guide — WI Sinclair & John McMullen

- Allied Dunbar Capital Taxes and Estate Planning Guide — WI Sinclair & PD Silke

- Allied Dunbar Expatriate Tax and Investment Guide — Nigel Eastaway and Jonathan Miller

- Allied Dunbar Investment and Savings Guide 1990–91 — General Editor. Harry Littlefair

- Allied Dunbar Pensions Guide — AM Reardon

- Allied Dunbar Tax Guide — WI Sinclair

All of these titles in the Allied Dunbar Library are available from leading bookshops

For more information please contact: Longman Law, Tax and Finance, 21–27 Lamb's Conduit St, London WC1N 3NJ
Tel: **(071) 242 2548**

Other titles in the Allied Dunbar Library

Allied Dunbar Money Guides

- Buying and Selling Your Home — Richard Newell
- Buying and Selling Your Home in France — Henry Dyson
- Buying and Selling Your Home in Spain — Per Svensson
- Financial Care for your Elderly Relatives — Beverley Chandler
- Financial Planning for the Over 50s — Robert Leach
- Insurance: Are you Covered? — Mihir Bose
- Investing in Shares — Hugh Pym & Nick Kochan
- Leaving Your Money Wisely — Tony Foreman
- Making Your Job Work — David Williams
- Managing Your Finances — Helen Pridham
- Planning School and College Fees — Danby Block & Amanda Pardoe
- Planning Your Pension — Tony Reardon
- Running Your Own Business — David Williams
- Tax and Finance for Women — Helen Pridham
- Tax for the Self-Employed — David Williams
- Your Home in Italy — Flavia Maxwell
- Your Home in Portugal — Rosemary de Rougemont

All of these titles in the Allied Dunbar Library are available from leading bookshops

**For more information please contact: Longman Law, Tax and Finance, 21–27 Lamb's Conduit St, London WC1N 3NJ
Tel: (071) 242 2548**